Writing
in Action

Andrea A. Lunsford
Stanford University

Advice for multilingual writers by

Paul Kei Matsuda
Arizona State University

Christine M. Tardy
University of Arizona

Bedford/St. Martin's
Boston ◆ New York

For Bedford/St. Martin's

Publisher for Composition: Leasa Burton
Executive Editor: Carolyn Lengel
Senior Developmental Editor: Adam Whitehurst
Senior Production Editor: Ryan Sullivan
Senior Production Supervisor: Dennis J. Conroy
Marketing Manager: Scott Berzon
Editorial Assistant: Leah Rang
Copy Editor: Wendy Polhemus-Annibell
Indexer: Ellen Kuhl Repetto
Photo Researcher: Connie Gardner
Art Director: Lucy Krikorian
Text Design: Claire Seng-Niemoeller
Cover Design: Donna Dennison
Composition: Graphic World, Inc.
Printing and Binding: RR Donnelley and Sons

President, Bedford/St. Martin's: Denise B. Wydra
Editorial Director, English and Music: Karen S. Henry
Director of Marketing: Karen R. Soeltz
Production Director: Susan W. Brown
Director of Rights and Permissions: Hilary Newman

Printed in China.

8   7   6
f   e   d   c   b

For information, write: Bedford/St. Martin's, 75 Arlington Street,
Boston, MA 02116   (617-399-4000)

ISBN 978-1-4576-6503-5 (Student Edition)
ISBN 978-1-4576-6563-9 (Instructor's Edition)

Acknowledgments

Preface

As I visit with teachers and students around the country—and increasingly in other countries as well—I can see the effects of what I've called the greatest literacy revolution we've seen in more than two thousand years. Students today are, by definition, readers and writers who are connected to a vast network of others through the Internet, and especially through social media. I hear over and over from students that they understand and appreciate the opportunities for instant communication that are now available to them—but that they often feel overwhelmed by the sheer mass of information coming at them from all sides and by the time it takes just to keep up. So students today are feeling rushed, even harried, and they are constantly having to try to do more with less. They are exquisitely aware, for example, of the draconian cuts to higher education that have accompanied the great recession; they know that tuitions are rising faster than they and their families can afford; they know that they often must work, sometimes full time, to help foot those bills. But they also know that the struggle is worth it, that earning a college degree is still one of the best investments students can make in their future.

In times like these, students want and need to squeeze as much value as they possibly can from their courses—and from their textbooks. And a major goal of *Writing in Action* is to help them do just that by providing a handbook that speaks to tight times. Thus, we have crafted this book very carefully, making sure that every single thing in it is valuable and necessary for student writers. That means, of course, introducing students to rhetorical principles that can help them make wise choices. It also means privileging coverage of writing that students are asked to do in most of their classes and focusing particularly on argument and on how writers can develop and support compelling arguments, whether print, oral, or online. And it means streamlining our coverage of grammar, mechanics, and punctuation; providing clear and easy-to-understand guidelines for dealing with sentence-level features of writing; and guiding students in how to identify, evaluate, integrate, and document sources in their writing—with an emphasis on how to document the kinds of contemporary sources that may not fit with the "models" textbooks usually provide. *Writing in Action* includes access to the book's integrated media, which expands on the coverage in the print book by offering more help with student models (including multimodal student writing they can work with in context), more practice with grammar and mechanics, and more opportunities to think about and reflect on their own writing processes. Finally, we've included plenty of exercises to help students put the advice offered in this book to good use, all in a user-friendly, easy-on-the-eyes, efficient design.

In short, *Writing in Action* recognizes that student writers today are pretty much "in action" all the time. Indeed, they are extraordinarily busy juggling college, work, and life. This text aims to be a no-nonsense, get-up-and-go kind of book, one that can provide just the right backup at just the right time.

Features

ATTENTION TO GOOD WRITING, NOT JUST SURFACE CORRECTNESS. *Writing in Action* helps students understand that effective texts follow conventions that depend on their audience, situation, and purpose. Integrated exercises throughout the text help students consider their writing processes and practice writing strategies.

INFORMED BY THE LITERACY REVOLUTION. Students today are writing more than ever to communicate with friends and reach a wider public. The Literacy Revolution has brought with it opportunities for student writers to make their voices heard by audiences never before accessible to them; to create texts that include images, sound, and video as well as words; and to present these texts across a range of genres, from brochures and posters to blogs and Web-based reports.

A FOCUS ON BRIDGING SOCIAL AND ACADEMIC WRITING. *Writing in Action* shows students how to use the rhetorical strategies that they employ in their extracurricular writing—including an intuitive understanding of audience and purpose—to create more effective academic writing. Examples throughout show student writers using social media effectively, and advice in several chapters helps students consider the differences between social and academic writing.

AN AWARENESS THAT TODAY'S ACADEMIC WRITING GOES BEYOND PRINT. Rhetorical advice in *Writing in Action* never assumes that students are producing only traditional print products. In addition to new coverage that specifically addresses the rhetorical considerations of tasks such as planning an online text and turning a print text into a presentation, advice throughout the book aims to help students create rhetorically effective texts for any situation.

A FOCUS ON THE "WHY" AS WELL AS THE "HOW" OF DOCUMENTING SOURCES. Coverage of the basics of various documentation styles helps students understand why academic work calls for more specific citation than popular writing, how to tell the difference between a work from a database and a work online, why medium matters, and more. And visual help with documentation models makes it easy to see what information writers should include in citations. Up-to-date advice on research and documentation provides information on using both library and Internet sources effectively, tips for avoiding plagiarism, and guidelines for documentation in MLA, APA, *Chicago*, and CSE styles.

COMPREHENSIVE COVERAGE OF CRITICAL THINKING AND ARGUMENT. Because first-year writing assignments increasingly call for argument, *Writing in Action* provides all of the information student writers need to respond effectively to their writing assignments, including practical advice on critical reading and analysis of all kinds of texts, instruction on composing arguments, and a complete model student essay.

UNIQUE COVERAGE OF LANGUAGE AND STYLE. Unique chapters on language help students think about language in context and about the consequences that language choices have on writers and readers. Boxed tips throughout the book help students communicate effectively across cultures—and use varieties of language both wisely and well.

AN EFFICIENT DESIGN. *Writing in Action* makes information easy to find and appealing to read.

A USER-FRIENDLY, ALL-IN-ONE INDEX. Combined with a glossary of terms, the index includes both everyday words (such as *that* or *which*) and grammatical terms (such as *pronoun*, which is defined in the index), so students can find what they're looking for quickly and easily.

BEDFORD INTEGRATED MEDIA, TO TAKE ADVANTAGE OF WHAT THE WEB CAN DO. LearningCurve, Bedford's new online adaptive quizzing, is integrated into the text, and helps students focus on the grammar and writing topics that they need the most help with. Videos of real student writers help students reflect on their own writing processes, while additional student writing, analysis activities, and exercises offer models and practice with the strategies discussed in the book. To access the integrated media site for *Writing in Action*, visit **bedfordstmartins.com/wia**.

Acknowledgments

To Adam Whitehurst, my editor extraordinaire, I am grateful for assistance at every stage of this book. His unerring eye for detail; his efficiency, persistence, and imagination; and his knowledge of what writing teachers and students today value most have enriched this book in too many ways to count. I am also indebted, as always, to the incomparable Carolyn Lengel, my editor for this and three other handbooks as well: her patience, fortitude, and sheer hard work, her astute judgment, her wellspring of good ideas, her meticulous attention to detail, and most of all her great wit and sense of humor are gifts that just keep on giving. I am also thankful to Karrin Varucene for her work on the teaching material of the Instructor's Edition and for keeping the blog and Facebook pages on track; to Leah Rang for editorial assistance; to Claire Seng-Niemoeller for her brilliant design; to Donna Dennison for cover art; to Wendy Polhemus-Annibell for her meticulous copy-editing; and to Ryan Sullivan, our diligent project editor.

Many thanks, also, to the unfailingly generous and supportive members of the Bedford/St. Martin's team: Joan Feinberg, Denise Wydra, Karen Henry, Erica Appel, Nancy Perry, Jimmy Fleming, Karen Soeltz, Scott Berzon, Sue Brown, Elise Kaiser, Shuli Traub, Nick Carbone, and Dennis Conroy.

I am also indebted to Paul Kei Matsuda and Christine Tardy for their extraordinarily helpful additions to the multilingual writer sections of this book; to Lisa Ede for her ongoing support and advice; and to Lisa Dresdner at Norwalk Community College for her fine work on *Teaching with Lunsford Handbooks*, as well as Michael Moore at DePaul University for his new sections on creating multimodal texts and teaching with e-books. I have also benefited greatly from the excellent advice of some very special colleagues: Colin Gifford Brooke, Syracuse University; Patrick Clauss, Butler University; Danielle Nicole DeVoss, Michigan State University; Barbara Fister, Gustavus Adolphus College; Beverly Moss, Ohio State University; Arnold Zwicky, Stanford University; and Marilyn Moller.

I owe special thanks to the group of student writers whose work appears in and has enriched this and previous editions, both in print and in integrated media: Michelle Abbott, Carina Abernathy, Milena Ateyea, Julie Baird, Jennifer Bernal, Valerie Bredin, Taurean Brown, Deborah Jane Burke, Jamie Burke, Tessa Cabello, Ben Canning, Leah Clendening, David Craig, Kelly Darr, Allyson Goldberg, Tara Gupta, Joanna Hays, Dana Hornbeak, Ajani Husbands, Bory Kea, James Kung, Emily Lesk, Nastassia Lopez, Heather Mackintosh-Sims, Merlla McLaughlin, Benjy Mercer-Golden, Alicia Michalski, Laura Montgomery, Elva Negrete, Thanh Nguyen, Katie Paarlberg, Shannan Palma, Stephanie Parker, Teal Pfeifer, Amrit K. Rao, Tawnya Redding, Heather Ricker, Amanda Rinder, Dawn Rodney, Rudy Rubio, Melissa Schraeder, Bonnie Sillay, Shuqiao Song, Jessica Thrower, Dennis Tyler, and Caroline Warner.

You get more choices for *Writing in Action*

Bedford/St. Martin's offers resources and format choices that help you and your students get even more out of the book and your course. To learn more about or order any of the following products, contact your Bedford/St. Martin's sales representative, e-mail sales support (sales_support@bfwpub.com), or visit the Web site at **bedfordstmartins.com/wia/catalog**.

Choose from alternative formats of *Writing in Action*

Bedford/St. Martin's offers a range of affordable formats, allowing students to choose the one that works for them. For details, visit **bedfordstmartins.com/wia/formats**.

- **Spiral-bound**
- **Bedford e-Book to Go**   A portable, downloadable e-book at about half the price of the print book
- **Other popular e-book formats**   For details, visit **bedfordstmartins .com/ebooks**

Upgrade your composition space with *LaunchPad for Writing in Action*

LaunchPad takes advantage of everything that Bedford/St. Martin's knows about composition. *LaunchPad* offers robust writing tools that help you start conversations around content, build regular writing practice into every assignment, and create peer review groups as your students work toward larger projects. Diagnostics and LearningCurve, our adaptive quizzing engine, offer remediation and practice as students build skills in reading, writing, and grammar. *LaunchPad for Writing in Action* can be purchased separately or packaged with the print book at a significant discount. An activation code is required. To order *LaunchPad for Writing in Action* with the print book, use **ISBN 978-1-4576-9073-0**.

Choose the flexible *Bedford e-Portfolio*

Students can collect, select, and reflect on their coursework and personalize and share their e-portfolio for any audience—instructors, peers, potential employers, or family and friends. Instructors can provide as much or as little structure as they see fit. Rubrics and learning outcomes can be aligned to student work, so instructors and programs can gather reliable and useful assessment data. Every *Bedford e-Portfolio* comes pre-loaded with *Portfolio Keeping* and *Portfolio Teaching*, by Nedra Reynolds and Elizabeth Davis. *Bedford e-Portfolio* can be purchased separately or packaged with the print book at a significant discount. An activation code is required. To order *Bedford e-Portfolio* with the print book, use **ISBN 978-1-4576-8776-1**. Visit **bedfordstmartins.com/eportfolio**.

Watch peer review work

Eli Review lets instructors scaffold their assignments in a clearer, more effective way for students—making peer review more visible and teachable. Because teachers get real-time analytics about how well students have met criteria in a writing task *and* about how helpful peer comments have been, they can intervene in real time to teach how to give good feedback and how to shape writing to meet criteria. When students can instantly see which comments are endorsed by their teacher and how their feedback has been rated by their peers, they're motivated to give the best reviews, get the best ratings, think like writers, and revise with a plan. *Eli Review* can be purchased separately or packaged with the print book at a significant discount. An activation code is required. To order *Eli Review* with the print book, use **ISBN 978-1-4576-8781-5**. Visit **bedfordstmartins.com/eli**.

Select value packages

Add value to your text by packaging one of the following resources with *Writing in Action*. To learn more about package options for any of the following products, contact your Bedford/St. Martin's sales representative or visit **bedfordstmartins.com/wia/catalog**.

VIDEOCENTRAL is a growing collection of videos for the writing class that captures real-world, academic, and student writers talking about how and why they write. Writer and teacher Peter Berkow interviewed hundreds of people—from Michael Moore to Cynthia Selfe—to produce over 140 brief videos about topics such as revising and getting feedback. VideoCentral can be packaged with *Writing in Action* at a significant discount. An activation code is required. To order VideoCentral packaged with the print book, use **ISBN 978-1-4576-9148-5**.

I-SERIES. This popular series presents multimedia tutorials in a flexible format—because there are things you can't do in a book.

- *ix visualizing composition 2.0* helps students put into practice key rhetorical and visual concepts. To order *ix visualizing composition* packaged with the print book, use **ISBN 978-1-4576-9146-1**.

- *i·claim: visualizing argument* offers a new way to see argument—with six multimedia tutorials, an illustrated glossary, and a wide array of multimedia arguments. To order *i·claim: visualizing argument* packaged with the print book, use **ISBN 978-1-4576-9145-4**.

PORTFOLIO KEEPING, **THIRD EDITION, BY NEDRA REYNOLDS AND ELIZABETH DAVIS** provides all the information students need to use the portfolio method successfully in a writing course. *Portfolio Teaching*, a companion guide for instructors, provides the practical information instructors and writing program administrators need to use the portfolio method successfully in a writing course. To order *Portfolio Keeping* packaged with the print book, use **ISBN 978-1-4576-9144-7**.

Instructor resources: bedfordstmartins.com/wia/catalog

You have a lot to do in your course. Bedford/St. Martin's wants to make it easy for you to find the support you need—and to get it quickly.

TEACHING WITH LUNSFORD HANDBOOKS, **2014 UPDATE**, is available in print or as a PDF that can be downloaded from the Bedford/ St. Martin's online catalog. *Teaching with Lunsford Handbooks* is packed with advice for integrating the handbook into your teaching, including course planning materials, sample syllabi, and exercises and activities that put the handbook into action in your course. The 2014 update includes new material on teaching with an e-book, assigning multimodal projects, and using digital portfolios, as well as help using Bedford Integrated Media to broaden your teaching and take advantage of what the Web can do.

TEACHINGCENTRAL offers the entire list of Bedford/St. Martin's print and online professional resources in one place. You'll find landmark reference works, sourcebooks on pedagogical issues, award-winning collections, and practical advice for the classroom — all free for instructors.

TEACHER TO TEACHER, Andrea Lunsford's channel on the award-winning *Bedford Bits* **blog**. *Bits* collects creative ideas for teaching a range of composition topics in an easily searchable blog format. A community of teachers — leading scholars, editors, and authors, including Andrea Lunsford — discuss revision, research, grammar and style, technology, peer review, and much more. Take, use, adapt, and pass the ideas around. Then, come back to the site to comment or share your own suggestions.

How to Use This Book

Chances are that you're called on to write and do research often, maybe even every day. Whenever you have questions about writing and research, *Writing in Action* offers quick and reliable answers.

▶ Online tutorials

bedfordstmartins.com/wia

Video Tutorial > What's in a handbook?
Video Tutorial > How to find what you need in your handbook
Video Tutorial > How to use the handbook documentation guidelines

Finding help in the print book

BRIEF CONTENTS. The first thing you see when you open the book is a brief table of contents inside the front cover, which lists general contents. If you're looking for advice on a broad topic, just flip to the chapter. The tabs at the top of each page tell you where you are.

CONTENTS. If you're looking for specific information, the detailed table of contents inside the back cover lists chapter titles, major headings, and media content.

THE TOP TWENTY. On page 2 is advice on the twenty most common problems teachers are likely to identify in academic writing by first-year students. The Top Twenty provides examples and brief explanations to guide you toward recognizing, understanding, and editing these common errors. Cross-references point to other places in the book where you'll find more detailed information.

INTEGRATED MEDIA REFERENCES. Look at the card in the front of your book for information on all the integrated media—online videos of student writers, exercises, adaptive quizzing, student writing models, and more. Cross-references at the bottom of a page direct you to **bedfordstmartins.com/wia** for media content related to that section of the book.

DOCUMENTATION NAVIGATION. Each documentation section has its own color-tabbed pages; look for directories within each section to find models for citing your sources. Source maps walk you through the process of citing sources.

GLOSSARY/INDEX. The index lists everything that's covered in the book. You can find information by looking up a topic, or, if you're not sure what your topic is called, by looking up the word you need help with. The index doubles as a glossary that defines important terms.

REVISION SYMBOLS. The list of symbols on p. 587 can help you learn more about any markings an instructor or a reviewer may make on your draft.

GLOSSARY OF USAGE. This glossary, located in Chapter 21, gives help with commonly confused words.

Page navigation help

The descriptions below correspond to the numbered elements on the sample pages on the next page.

❶ **Guides at the top of every page.** Headers tell you what **chapter** or **section** you're in, the **chapter number** and **section letter**, and the **page number**.

❷ **Hand-edited examples.** **Example sentences** are hand-edited in green, allowing you to see an error or nonstandard usage and its revision at a glance. Green pointers and boldface type make examples easy to spot on the page.

❸ **Cross-references to integrated media.** Cross-references at the bottom of a page point you to video, quizzing, student writing models, and more.

❹ **Boxed tips.** Many chapters include quick-reference **Checklist** boxes with an overview of important information. **For Multilingual Writers** boxes appear throughout the book, and additional advice can be found in Chapters 45–48. **Considering Disabilities** boxes highlight issues of accessibility for all readers. A directory listing all of these boxes, as well as student writing, appears on p. 585.

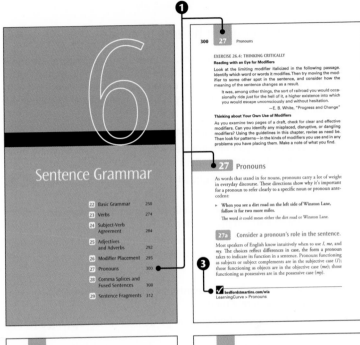

6

Sentence Grammar

EXERCISE 26.4: THINKING CRITICALLY
Reading with an Eye for Modifiers
Look at the limiting modifier italicized in the following passage. Identify which word or words it modifies. Then try moving the modifier to some other spot in the sentence, and consider how the meaning of the sentence changes as a result.

It was, among other things, the sort of railroad you would occasionally ride *just* for the hell of it, a higher existence into which you would escape unconsciously and without hesitation.
—E. B. White, "Progress and Change"

Thinking about Your Own Use of Modifiers
As you examine two pages of a draft, check for clear and effective modifiers. Can you identify any misplaced, disruptive, or dangling modifiers? Using the guidelines in this chapter, revise as need be. Then look for patterns—in the kinds of modifiers you use and in any problems you have placing them. Make a note of what you find.

27 Pronouns

As words that stand in for nouns, pronouns carry a lot of weight in everyday discourse. These directions show why it's important for a pronoun to refer clearly to a specific noun or pronoun antecedent:

▶ **When you see a dirt road on the left side of Winston Lane, follow it for two more miles.**

The word *it* could mean either the dirt road or Winston Lane.

27a   Consider a pronoun's role in the sentence.

Most speakers of English know intuitively when to use *I*, *me*, and *my*. The choices reflect differences in case, the form a pronoun takes to indicate its function in a sentence. Pronouns functioning as subjects or subject complements are in the subjective case (*I*); those functioning as objects are in the objective case (*me*); those functioning as possessives are in the possessive case (*my*).

☑ bedfordstmartins.com/wia
LearningCurve > Pronouns

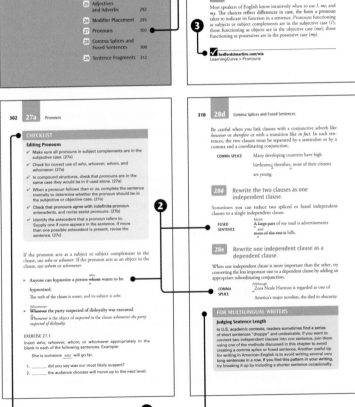

CHECKLIST

Editing Pronouns
✓ Make sure all pronouns in subject complements are in the subjective case. (27a)
✓ Check for correct use of *who*, *whoever*, *whom*, and *whomever*. (27a)
✓ In compound structures, check that pronouns are in the same case they would be in if used alone. (27a)
✓ When a pronoun follows *than* or *as*, complete the sentence mentally to determine whether the pronoun should be in the subjective or objective case. (27a)
✓ Check that pronouns agree with indefinite-pronoun antecedents, and revise sexist pronouns. (27b)
✓ Identify the antecedent that a pronoun refers to. Supply one if none appears in the sentence. If more than one possible antecedent is present, revise the sentence. (27c)

If the pronoun acts as a subject or subject complement in the clause, use *who* or *whoever*. If the pronoun acts as an object in the clause, use *whom* or *whomever*.

                                   who
▶ Anyone can hypnotize a person ~~whom~~ wants to be

hypnotize.
The verb of the clause is *wants*, and its subject is *who*.

  Whomever
▶ ~~Whoever~~ the party suspected of disloyalty was executed.
Whomever is the object of *suspected* in the clause *whomever the party suspected of disloyalty.*

EXERCISE 27.1
Insert *who*, *whoever*, *whom*, or *whomever* appropriately in the blank in each of the following sentences. Example:

She is someone _who_ will go far.

1. _____ did you say was our most likely suspect?
2. _____ the audience chooses will move up to the next level.

Be careful when you link clauses with a conjunctive adverb like *however* or *therefore* or with a transition like *in fact*. In such sentences, the two clauses must be separated by a semicolon or by a comma and a coordinating conjunction.

COMMA SPLICE   Many developing countries have high
                               ;
                birthrates,̭ therefore, most of their citizens
                are young.

28d   Rewrite the two clauses as one
independent clause.

Sometimes you can reduce two spliced or fused independent clauses to a single independent clause.

                    Most
FUSED   A ~~large part~~ of my mail is advertisements
SENTENCE   *and*
               ~~most of the rest is~~ bills.

28e   Rewrite one independent clause as a
dependent clause.

When one independent clause is more important than the other, try converting the less important one to a dependent clause by adding an appropriate subordinating conjunction.

                    Although
COMMA   ~~Zora Neale Hurston is regarded as one of~~
SPLICE
               America's major novelists, she died in obscurity.

FOR MULTILINGUAL WRITERS

Judging Sentence Length
In U.S. academic contexts, readers sometimes find a series of short sentences "choppy" and undesirable. If you want to connect two independent clauses into one sentence, join them using one of the methods discussed in this chapter to avoid creating a comma splice or fused sentence. Another useful tip for writing in American English is to avoid writing several very long sentences in a row. If you find this pattern in your writing, try breaking it up by including a shorter sentence occasionally.

A tutorial on using *Writing in Action*

For this book to serve you well, you need to get to know it—to know what's inside (and in the integrated media) and how to find it. The following tutorial is designed to help you familiarize yourself with *Writing in Action*; the answers appear on the pages following the tutorial.

Getting Started with *Writing in Action*

1. Where will you find advice on identifying the top twenty most common errors in student writing?

2. Where can you find out what a comma splice is and how to fix one?

3. Where will you find guidelines on including quotations in your project without plagiarizing?

4. If you are a multilingual writer, where will you find advice on using appropriate prepositions?

Planning and Drafting

5. Where in *Writing in Action* can you find advice on brainstorming to explore a topic?

6. Where can you find general guidelines for developing effective paragraphs?

7. Your instructor wants you to adapt your print essay into a multimedia presentation. Where would you find an example of this kind of presentation?

Doing Research

8. You have a topic for your research project, but your instructor asks you to narrow it down. What section can you use to help you move from a broad topic to a hypothesis?

9. What information can you find in *Writing in Action* for keeping track of your research?

10. Your instructor has reviewed your bibliography and has asked you to replace some popular sources with scholarly sources, but you're not sure how to identify the differences. Where can you find help in distinguishing them?

11. You are unsure whether you need to cite a paraphrase from a magazine article that you integrated into one of the body paragraphs of your essay. Where can you find the answer in *Writing in Action*?

12. Your instructor has asked you to use MLA style. Where can you find guidelines for documenting information from an article on a Web site?

Editing

13. A peer reviewer thinks there is a sentence fragment in the following passage: *Because the actor had a reputation for delivering Oscar-worthy performances. He received the best roles.* How and where do you find out if this is a sentence fragment, and what should you do if it is?

14. You grew up speaking a language other than English at home, and you have trouble with the articles *a*, *an*, and *the*. Where can you find help?

15. Your instructor has written *wrdy* next to this sentence: *The person who wrote the article is a scientist who makes the argument that it seems as though the scientific phenomenon of global warming is becoming a bigger issue at this point in time.* Where do you look in your handbook for help responding to your instructor's comment?

16. You have finished your essay and now decide to use an unusual font to make your essay more visually appealing. Is it a good idea to use this font? What information does *Writing in Action* provide?

Meeting Your Instructor's Expectations

17. Your instructor asks the students in your writing class to review each other's drafts. How can *Writing in Action* help you find out what questions you need to ask your reviewers?

18. You are required to turn in a portfolio of writing samples at the end of the semester, but you're not sure what to include. What advice can your handbook give you about building a portfolio?

19. Your instructor returns a draft to you and says that your paper contains mostly summary, and you need to do more critical thinking and analysis. Where can you look for information on how to read and write critically?

20. You've learned a lot by looking at the samples of good writing that your instructor has shared with the class. Where in *Writing in Action* can you find more sample student work?

21. Your professor has created a blog with a discussion forum, and you are required to comment on the week's discussion topic. You're not sure how to write online as part of a class requirement. Where in *Writing in Action* can you look for help?

Writing in Any Discipline

22. You need to write a paper for your sociology class, but you've never written a sociology paper before, and you're unsure what citation style to use. Where can you look for help in *Writing in Action*?

23. For a chemistry course, you're writing a lab report, and your instructor wants you to include a table to detail the results of your experiment. Where can you look in your handbook for help incorporating this visual?

24. You're used to writing online for social media sites, but you aren't sure what "normal" academic writing should look like. Where can you look in your handbook to help you figure out how to write for an academic audience?

Using Integrated Media

25. Your tutor at your school's writing center suggested that you work on summarizing your sources. Where can you find integrated media that will help you work on this research skill?

26. Your instructor has assigned a research project, but you can't decide on a topic. Where can you find a video that might help you figure out what topic would work for you?

27. Before you write a research essay, you want to see how another student has incorporated sources. Where can you find an integrated media activity that will help you analyze how a student uses evidence?

Answers to the Tutorial

1. "The Top Twenty" on pp. 2–11. (Searching for *common errors* in the index also points students toward "The Top Twenty.")

2. Chapter 28, "Comma Splices and Fused Sentences." (*Comma splice* in the index takes you to pp. 308–12.) Or look at the "Top Twenty" section—"comma splice" is item 16.

3. Chapter 15, on integrating sources and avoiding plagiarism.

4. Chapter 48, on prepositions and prepositional phrases.

5. Looking up *brainstorming* in the index leads you to Chapter 5, on exploring, planning, and drafting (specifically section 5a, pp. 39–41, on exploring and narrowing a topic).

6. Looking up *paragraphs* in the index leads you to Chapter 5, on exploring, planning, and drafting (specifically section 5e, pp. 45–47, on developing paragraphs).

7. Looking in the Directory of Student Writing on p. 585 points you toward the excerpts from a student presentation in section 6b, pp. 56–67. You can also find *multimedia presentations* in the index.

8. Searching for *hypothesis* in the index will lead you to section 12b, p. 152, on formulating a research question and hypothesis.

9. Skimming the table of contents under the header "Research" leads you to Chapter 14 and specifically 14f, "Take notes and annotate sources."

10. Consulting the index under *sources* and then *scholarly and popular* leads you to section 13a, "Understand different kinds of sources," where there are columns of text and images that compare the two types.

11. Looking in the index for *paraphrases* will lead you to section 15b, pp. 188–91, where there is information about integrating material from sources appropriately.

12. The table of contents leads you to Chapter 49, the dark green color-coded pages, which provide a full discussion of MLA documentation conventions. The directory to MLA style for a list of works cited, on pp. 411–12, points you to the models for documenting Web site sources on a works cited page. The source map on pp. 434–35 provides a visual guide to locating the information you need.

13. The table of contents can lead you to Chapter 29, "Sentence Fragments," where you will find examples of sentence fragments and several options for revising them.

14. Under the section "Multilingual Writers" in the table of contents, you will see "Use articles" in section 46c, part of a chapter on nouns and noun phrases.

15. A list of revision symbols appears at the back of *Writing in Action* on p. 587. Consulting this list tells you that *wrdy* refers to "wordy" and that this subject is discussed in Chapter 32, on conciseness.

16. Looking up *fonts* or *formatting* in the index will take you to an entry on choosing appropriate formats in Chapter 8, on making design decisions. The information under "Type" in section 8b, p. 92, points out that most college writing requires a standard 11- to 12-point serif font.

17. Looking up *reviewing* in the index will take you to section 5f, pp. 47–48, which offers a list of suggested questions to ask someone to use when responding to your draft.

18. Searching for *portfolios* in the index will lead you to section 5i, on pp. 50–52, which includes guidelines for creating portfolios and including a portfolio cover letter.

19. Skimming the table of contents under the section "Critical Thinking and Argument" will lead you to Chapters 9 and 10, which contain information on reading and analyzing texts and arguments.

20. On p. 585 of *Writing in Action*, you will find a Directory of Student Writing that lists all of the model essays and essay excerpts from students in both the print book and the integrated media. You can choose which topic or documentation style would be most helpful to you for your project.

21. Skimming the table of contents will lead you to Chapter 6, on multimodal assignments, where section 6a discusses planning online assignments. Searching in the index under *blogs* or *digital writing* will also lead you to section 6a.

22. Chapter 7 covers writing in the disciplines, and 7j provides more information on writing in the social sciences. Searching for *social sciences* in the index will also lead you to this section.

23. Chapter 8 covers making design decisions, and 8d provides more information on selecting and integrating visuals effectively. The index entry for *tables* will also bring you to this section. Under *visuals and multimedia*, you will find specific entries for documenting visuals according to which citation style your instructor requires.

24. Searching the table of contents under "Writing for College and Beyond" will lead you to Chapter 2, on expectations for college writing. The information in sections 2a and 2b will prepare you for academic writing.

25. Looking in the table of contents under "Research," you'll find Chapter 15, on integrating sources and avoiding plagiarism. The 🄴 icons next to sections 15b and 15g direct you to the integrated media for that chapter. Section 14f also contains helpful information. A cross-reference at the bottom of p. 184 will direct you to an online exercise titled "Research: Summarizing Sources."

26. Searching the integrated media directory at **bedfordstmartins .com/wia** under the section "Videos" will lead you to several useful videos of student writers, including "Pay attention to what you're interested in" and "Research something exciting."

27. If you search the integrated media directory at **bedfordstmartins .com/wia**, you'll find an analysis activity that allows you to evaluate Benjy Mercer-Golden's use of sources.

Writing
in Action

1

Writing for College and Beyond

1 The Top Twenty: A Quick Guide to Troubleshooting Your Writing

Surface errors—grammar, punctuation, word choice, and other small-scale matters—don't always disturb readers. Whether your instructor marks an error in any particular assignment will depend on personal judgments about how serious and distracting it is and about what you should be focusing on in the draft. In addition, not all surface errors are consistently viewed as errors: some of the patterns identified in the research for this book are considered errors by some instructors but as stylistic options by others. Such differing opinions don't mean that there is no such thing as correctness in writing—only that *correctness always depends on some context*, on whether the choices a writer makes seem appropriate to readers.

Research for this book reveals a number of changes that have occurred in student writing over the past twenty-plus years. First, writing assignments in first-year composition classes now focus less on personal narrative and much more on research essays and argument. As a result, students are now writing longer essays than they did twenty years ago and working much more often with sources, both print and digital. Thus it's no surprise that students today are struggling with the conventions for using and citing sources, a problem that did not show up in most earlier studies of student writing.

What else has changed? For starters, wrong-word errors are *by far the most common* errors among first-year student writers today. Twenty years ago, spelling errors were most common by a factor of more than three to one. The use of spell checkers has reduced the number of spelling errors in student writing—but spell checkers' suggestions may also be responsible for some (or many) of the wrong words students are using.

All writers want to be considered competent and careful. You know that your readers judge you by your control of the conventions you have agreed to use, even if the conventions change from time to time. To help you in producing writing that is conventionally correct, you should become familiar with the twenty most common error patterns among U.S. college students today, listed here in order of frequency. A brief explanation and examples of each error are provided in the following sections, and each error pattern is cross-referenced to other places in this book where you can find more detailed information and additional examples.

CHECKLIST

The Top Twenty

1. Wrong word
2. Missing comma after an introductory element
3. Incomplete or missing documentation
4. Vague pronoun reference
5. Spelling (including homonyms)
6. Mechanical error with a quotation
7. Unnecessary comma
8. Unnecessary or missing capitalization
9. Missing word
10. Faulty sentence structure
11. Missing comma with a nonrestrictive element
12. Unnecessary shift in verb tense
13. Missing comma in a compound sentence
14. Unnecessary or missing apostrophe (including *its/it's*)
15. Fused (run-on) sentence
16. Comma splice
17. Lack of pronoun-antecedent agreement
18. Poorly integrated quotation
19. Unnecessary or missing hyphen
20. Sentence fragment

---

1   Wrong word

▶ Religious texts, for them, take ~~prescience~~ precedence over other kinds of

sources.

Prescience means "foresight," and *precedence* means "priority."

▶ The child suffered from a severe ~~allegory~~ allergy to peanuts.

Allegory is a spell checker's replacement for a misspelling of *allergy*.

▶ The panel discussed the ethical implications ~~on~~ *of* the situation.

Wrong-word errors can involve using a word with the wrong shade of meaning, using a word with a completely wrong meaning, or using a wrong preposition or another wrong word in an idiom. Selecting a word from a thesaurus without knowing its meaning, or allowing a spell checker to correct spelling automatically, can lead to wrong-word errors, so use these tools with care. If you have trouble with prepositions and idioms, memorize the standard usage. (See Chapter 20 on word choice and spelling and Chapter 48 on prepositions and idioms.)

2 Missing comma after an introductory element

▶ Determined to get the job done, we worked all weekend.

▶ Although the study was flawed, the results may still be useful.

Readers frequently need a small pause—signaled by a comma—between an introductory word, phrase, or clause and the main part of the sentence. Use a comma after every introductory element. When the introductory element is very short, you don't always need a comma, but including it is never wrong. (See 35a.)

3 Incomplete or missing documentation

▶ Satrapi says, "When we're afraid, we lose all sense of analysis and reflection/" (263).

This quotation comes from a print source, so a page number is needed.

▶ Some experts agree that James Joyce wrote two of the five best novels of all time/ ("100 Best Novels").

The source of this information should be identified (this online source has no page numbers).

Cite each source you refer to in the text, following the guidelines of the documentation style you are using. (The preceding examples follow MLA style—see Chapter 49; for other styles, see Chapters 50–52.) Omitting documentation can result in charges of plagiarism (see Chapter 15).

4   Vague pronoun reference

POSSIBLE REFERENCE TO MORE THAN ONE WORD

▶ Transmitting radio signals by satellite is a way of overcoming

the problem of scarce airwaves and limiting how ~~they~~ are used.
   the airwaves

In the original sentence, *they* could refer to the signals or to the airwaves.

REFERENCE IMPLIED BUT NOT STATED

▶ The company prohibited smoking, ~~which~~ many employees
   a policy

resented.

What does *which* refer to? The editing clarifies what employees resented.

A pronoun should refer clearly to the word or words it replaces (called the *antecedent*) elsewhere in the sentence or in a previous sentence. If more than one word could be the antecedent, or if no specific antecedent is present, edit to make the meaning clear. (See Chapter 27.)

5   Spelling (including homonyms)

▶ Ronald ~~Regan~~ won the election in a landslide.
   Reagan

▶ ~~Every where~~ we went, we saw crowds of tourists.
   Everywhere

The most common misspellings seen today are those that spell checkers cannot identify. The categories that spell checkers are most likely to miss include homonyms, compound words incorrectly spelled as separate words, and proper nouns, particularly names. After you run the spell checker, you should proofread carefully for errors such as these—and be sure to run the spell checker to catch other kinds of spelling mistakes. (See 20e.)

6   Mechanical error with a quotation

▸ "I grew up the victim of a disconcerting confusion,"/ Rodriguez
   ^

says (249).

The comma should be placed *inside* the quotation mark.

Follow conventions when using quotation marks with commas (35h), colons (40d), and other punctuation (39c). Always use quotation marks in pairs, and follow the guidelines of your documentation style for block quotations (39a). Use quotation marks for titles of short works (39b), but use italics for titles of long works (43a).

7   Unnecessary comma

BEFORE CONJUNCTIONS IN COMPOUND CONSTRUCTIONS THAT ARE NOT COMPOUND SENTENCES

▸ This conclusion applies to the United States/ and to the rest of

the world.

No comma is needed before *and* because it is joining two phrases that modify the same verb, *applies.*

WITH RESTRICTIVE ELEMENTS

▸ Many parents/ of gifted children/ do not want them to skip a

grade.

No comma is needed to set off the restrictive phrase *of gifted children,* which is necessary to indicate which parents the sentence is talking about.

Do not use commas to set off restrictive elements that are necessary to the meaning of the words they modify. Do not use a comma before a coordinating conjunction (*and, but, for, nor, or, so, yet*) when the conjunction does not join parts of a compound sentence. Do not use a comma before the first or after the last item in a series, between a subject and verb, between a verb and its object or complement, or between a preposition and its object. (See 35i.)

8 Unnecessary or missing capitalization

> Some ~~Traditional~~ traditional Chinese ~~Medicines~~ medicines containing ~~Ephedra~~ ephedra

remain legal.

Capitalize proper nouns and proper adjectives, the first words of sentences, and important words in titles, along with certain words indicating directions and family relationships. Do not capitalize most other words. When in doubt, check a dictionary. (See Chapter 41.)

9 Missing word

> The site foreman discriminated against women and promoted men

with less experience.

Proofread carefully for omitted words, including prepositions (48a), parts of two-part verbs (48b), and correlative conjunctions (22h). Be particularly careful not to omit words from quotations.

10 Faulty sentence structure

> ~~The information which~~ High school athletes are presented with ~~mainly includes~~ information on what credits they needed to graduate, ~~and thinking about the college~~ which ~~athletes are trying~~ colleges to try to play for, and apply how to.

A sentence that starts out with one kind of structure and then changes to another kind can confuse readers. Make sure that each sentence contains a subject and a verb (22a), that subjects and predicates make sense together (30b), and that comparisons have clear meanings (30d). When you join elements (such as subjects or verb phrases) with a coordinating conjunction, make sure that the elements have parallel structures (see Chapter 33).

11   Missing comma with a nonrestrictive element

▶ **Marina, who was the president of the club, was first to speak.**

   The clause *who was the president of the club* does not affect the basic meaning of the sentence: Marina was first to speak.

A nonrestrictive element gives information not essential to the basic meaning of the sentence. Use commas to set off a nonrestrictive element (35c).

12   Unnecessary shift in verb tense

▶ **Priya was watching the great blue heron. Then she** ~~slips~~ slipped **and** ~~falls~~ fell **into the swamp.**

Verbs that shift from one tense to another with no clear reason can confuse readers (34a).

13   Missing comma in a compound sentence

▶ **Meredith waited for Samir, and her sister grew impatient.**

   Without the comma, a reader may think at first that Meredith waited for both Samir and her sister.

A compound sentence consists of two or more parts that could each stand alone as a sentence. When the parts are joined by a coordinating conjunction, use a comma before the conjunction to indicate a pause between the two thoughts (35b).

14   Unnecessary or missing apostrophe (including *its/it's*)

▶ **Overambitious parents can be very harmful to a** ~~childs~~ child's **well-being.**

▶ **The car is lying on** ~~it's~~ its **side in the ditch.** ~~Its~~ It's **a white 2004 Passat.**

To make a noun possessive, add either an apostrophe and an *-s* (*Ed's book*) or an apostrophe alone (*the boys' gym*). Do not use an apostrophe in the possessive pronouns *ours*, *yours*, and *hers*. Use *its* to mean *belonging to it*; use *it's* only when you mean *it is* or *it has*. (See Chapter 38.)

15 Fused (run-on) sentence

▶ Klee's paintings seem simple, ^but^ they are very sophisticated.

▶ ~~She~~ ^Although she^ doubted the value of meditation, she decided to try it once.

A fused sentence (also called a *run-on*) joins clauses that could each stand alone as a sentence with no punctuation or words to link them. Fused sentences must either be divided into separate sentences or joined by adding words or punctuation. (See Chapter 28.)

16 Comma splice

▶ I was strongly attracted to her, ^for^ she was beautiful and funny.

▶ We hated the meat loaf ^that^ the cafeteria served ~~it~~ every Friday.

A comma splice occurs when only a comma separates clauses that could each stand alone as a sentence. To correct a comma splice, you can insert a semicolon or period, connect the clauses with a word such as *and* or *because*, or restructure the sentence. (See Chapter 28.)

17 Lack of pronoun-antecedent agreement

▶ ~~Every student~~ ^All students^ must provide their own ~~uniform.~~ ^uniforms.^

▶ Each of the puppies thrived in ~~their~~ ^its^ new home.

Pronouns must agree with their antecedents in gender (male or female) and in number (singular or plural). Many indefinite pronouns, such as *everyone* and *each*, are always singular. When a singular antecedent can refer to a man or a woman, either rewrite the sentence to make the antecedent plural or to eliminate the pronoun, or use *his or her, he or she,* and so on. When antecedents are joined by *or* or *nor,* the pronoun must agree with the closer antecedent. A collective noun such as *team* can be either singular or plural, depending on whether the members are seen as a group or as individuals. (See 27b.)

18   Poorly integrated quotation

▶ Schlosser cites a 1970s study that ^{showed how color affects taste:} "Once it became apparent ^ that the steak was actually blue and the fries were green, some people became ill" (565).

CHECKLIST

Taking a Writing Inventory

One way to learn from your mistakes is to take a writing inventory. It can help you think critically and analytically about how to improve your writing skills.

1. Collect two or three pieces of your writing to which either your instructor or other students have responded.

2. Read through these writings, adding your own comments about their strengths and weaknesses. How do your comments compare with those of others?

3. Group all the comments into three categories — *broad content issues* (use of evidence and sources, attention to purpose and audience, and overall impression), *organization and presentation* (overall and paragraph-level organization, sentence structure and style, and formatting), and *surface errors* (problems with spelling, grammar, punctuation, and mechanics).

4. Make an inventory of your own strengths in each category.

5. Study your errors. Mark every instructor and peer comment that suggests or calls for an improvement, and put all these comments in a list. Consult the relevant part of this book or speak with your instructor if you don't understand a comment.

6. Make a list of the top problem areas you need to work on. How can you make improvements? Then note at least two strengths that you can build on in your writing. Record your findings in a writing log that you can add to as the class proceeds.

▶ According to Lars Eighner,
"Dumpster diving has serious drawbacks as a way of life"
^
(~~Eighner~~ 383). Finding edible food is especially tricky.

Quotations should always fit smoothly into the surrounding sentence structure. They should be linked clearly to the writing around them (usually with a signal phrase) rather than dropped abruptly into the writing. (See 15b.)

19   Unnecessary or missing hyphen

▶ This paper looks at fictional and real life examples.
A compound adjective modifying a noun that follows it requires a hyphen.

▶ The buyers want to fix/up the house and resell it.
A two-word verb should not be hyphenated.

A compound adjective that appears before a noun needs a hyphen. However, be careful not to hypenate two-word verbs or word groups that serve as subject complements. (See Chapter 44.)

20   Sentence fragment

NO SUBJECT

▶ Marie Antoinette spent huge sums of money on herself and her
   Her extravagance
favorites. ~~And~~ helped bring on the French Revolution.
         ^

NO COMPLETE VERB
                        was
▶ The old aluminum boat sitting on its trailer.
                       ^

BEGINNING WITH A SUBORDINATING WORD
                                  where
▶ We returned to the drugstore/, ~~Where~~ we waited for our buddies.
                                ^

A sentence fragment is part of a sentence that is written as if it were a complete sentence. Reading your draft out loud, backwards, sentence by sentence, will help you spot sentence fragments. (See Chapter 29.)

bedfordstmartins.com/wia
Top Twenty Editing Practice

2   Expectations for College Writing

Your college instructors—and your future colleagues and supervisors—will expect you to demonstrate your ability to think critically, to consider ethical issues, to find as well as solve problems, to do effective research, to work productively with people of widely different backgrounds, and to present the knowledge you construct in a variety of ways and in a variety of genres and media. Your success will depend on communicating clearly and on making choices that are appropriate for each context.

2a   Move between social and academic writing.

Social connections today involve so much writing—text messages, tweets, Facebook posts, blogs, YouTube videos, and the like—that you probably do more writing out of class than in class. In fact, Web 2.0 and social networking have opened doors for writers like never before. Writing on social networking sites allows writers to get almost instant feedback, and anticipating responses from an audience often has the effect of making online writers very savvy: they know the importance of analyzing the audience and of using an appropriate style, level of formality, and tone to suit the online occasion.

As you know, writers on Twitter tell followers what's going on in short bursts of no more than 140 characters. Here are two representative tweets from the Twitter feed of Stephanie Parker, a college student whose interests include technology and Korean pop culture.

sparker2

Rain's over, going to Trader Joe's to buy some healthy stuff to fight this cold. . suggestions?

Watching Queen Seon Duk/선덕여왕 on @dramafever, love it so far! http://www.dramafever.com/drama /56/ #nowplaying

In these tweets, Stephanie shows a keen awareness both of her audiences on Twitter and of two very common purposes for this kind of informal writing—to seek information (in the first tweet, about foods to fight off a cold) and to share information (in the second tweet, about her view of a Korean drama, with a link so readers can check it out for themselves).

 Alicia Michalski Long, long day ahead of me. And the toughest won't even be my classes.
Yesterday at 8:14am • Comment • Like

 Ryan Sundheimer http://www.youtube.com/watch?v=rCvtIdLxu1Y
Tell me that doesn't inspire you!
Yesterday at 8:23am

 Alicia Michalski If I had you at work yelling that to me, then yes, it'd be pretty inspiring! I'll just loop it on the speakers there!!
Yesterday at 8:26am

Facebook and similar sites allow for fast-paced conversation between writers. This status update from Alicia Michalski got a response in the form of a link to a YouTube video (of a man exercising to a song called "You Can Do It"), to which Alicia then replied—all in the space of twelve minutes.

Like Stephanie and Alicia, many writers today are adept at informal social writing across a range of genres and media. You may not think very hard about the audience you'll reach in a tweet or Facebook post, or about your purpose for writing in such spaces, but you are probably more skilled than you give yourself credit for when it comes to making appropriate choices for your informal writing.

Of course, informal writing is not the only writing a student needs to master. You'll also need to move back and forth between informal social writing and formal academic writing, and to write across a whole range of genres and media. Look closely at your informal writing: What are you assuming about your audience?

 bedfordstmartins.com/wia
Video > Lessons from informal writing

What is your purpose? How do you achieve a particular tone? In short, why do you write the way you do in these situations? Analyzing the choices you make in a given writing context will help you develop the ability to make good choices in other contexts as well—an ability that will allow you to move between social and academic writing.

2b Position yourself as an academic writer.

If you're like most students, you probably have less familiarity with academic writing contexts than you do with informal contexts. You may not have written anything much longer than five pages of formal academic writing before coming to college, and you may have done only minimal formal research. The contexts for your college writing will require you to face new challenges; you may be asked, for example, to create a persuasive Web site or to research, write, and deliver a multimedia presentation. You can begin the process of learning by figuring out what your instructors expect from you. Of course, expectations about academic writing vary considerably in different courses and different disciplines (see Chapter 7), but becoming familiar with widespread conventions will prepare you well for most academic situations.

Establishing authority.   In the United States, most college instructors expect student writers to begin to establish their own authority—to become constructive critics who can analyze and interpret the work of others. But what does establishing authority mean in practice?

- Assume that your opinions count (as long as they are informed rather than tossed out with little thought) and that your audience expects you to present them in a well-reasoned manner.
- Show your familiarity with the ideas and works of others, both from the assigned course reading and from good points your instructor and classmates have made.

Being direct and clear.   Your instructors will most often expect you to get to the point quickly and to be direct throughout an essay or other project. Research for this book confirms that readers depend on writers to both organize and present their material — using sections, paragraphs, sentences, arguments, details, and source citations — in ways that aid understanding. Good academic writing prepares readers for what is coming next, provides definitions, and includes topic sentences. (See 17c for a description of the organization that instructors often prefer in student essays.) To achieve directness in your writing, try the following strategies:

- State your main point early and clearly.

- Avoid overqualifying your statements. Instead of writing *I think the facts reveal*, come right out and say *The facts reveal.*

- Avoid digressions. If you use an anecdote or example from personal experience, be sure it relates directly to the point you are making.

- Use appropriate evidence, such as examples and concrete details, to support each point.

- Make transitions from point to point obvious and clear. The first sentence of a new paragraph should reach back to the paragraph before and then look forward to what is to come (see 5e).

- Follow logical organizational patterns (see Chapter 5).

- Design and format the project appropriately for the audience and purpose you have in mind (see Chapter 8).

- If your project is lengthy, you may also want to use brief summary statements between sections, but avoid unnecessary repetition.

EXERCISE 2.1

Choose a sample of your own informal writing from a social networking site: a blog, posting, text message, or instant message, for example. Why did you write the post? What did you assume about your readers, and why? Why did you choose the words, images, links, or other parts of the text, and how do these choices contribute to the way the writing comes across to an audience? Does the writing do what you want it to do? Why, or why not?

CHECKLIST

U.S. Academic Style

✔ Consider your purpose and audience carefully, making sure that your topic is appropriate to both. (Chapter 4)

✔ State your claim or thesis explicitly, and support it with examples, statistics, anecdotes, and authorities of various kinds. (Chapter 5)

✔ Carefully document all of your sources. (Chapters 49–52)

✔ Make explicit links between ideas. (Chapter 5)

✔ Consistently use the appropriate level of formality. (Chapter 19)

✔ Use conventional formats for academic genres. (Chapters 3, 6, and 7)

✔ Use conventional grammar, spelling, punctuation, and mechanics. (Chapters 22–29 and 35–44)

✔ Use an easy-to-read type size and typeface, conventional margins, and double spacing. (Chapter 8)

2c　Join class discussions.

Your instructors will expect you to be an active participant in class. So make sure your contributions to class discussions—whether live or online—are effective by following these guidelines:

- Be prepared.
- Follow the flow of conversation. Taking notes can help you listen purposefully in a classroom.
- Make sure your comments are relevant. Ask a key question, take the conversation in a new direction, or summarize or analyze what others have said.
- Be specific in your comments: *The passage in the middle of page 42 backs up what you're saying* is more useful than *I agree.*

2d　Read actively.

Your instructors expect you to be an active reader—to offer informed opinions on what readings say. Stating your opinion doesn't require

FOR MULTILINGUAL WRITERS

Speaking Up in Class

Speaking up in class is viewed as inappropriate or even rude in some cultures. In the United States, however, doing so is expected and encouraged. Some instructors even assign credit for such class participation.

you to be negative or combative, just engaged with the class and the text. The following strategies will help you read actively:

- Note the name of the author and the date and place of publication; these items can give you clues to the writer's purpose and intended audience.
- Understand the overall content of a piece well enough to summarize it (9c).
- Formulate critical questions about the text, and bring these questions up in class.
- Understand each sentence, and make direct connections between sentences and paragraphs. Keep track of repeated themes or images, and figure out how they contribute to the entire piece.
- Note the author's attitude toward and assumptions about the topic. Then you can speculate on how the attitude and assumptions may have affected the author's thinking.
- Note the writer's sources: what evidence does the writer rely on, and why?
- Distinguish between the author's stance and the author's reporting on the stances of others. Watch for key phrases an author uses to signal an opposing argument: *while some have argued that*, *in the past*, and so on.
- Go beyond content to notice organizational patterns, use of sources, and choice of words.
- Consider annotating your readings, especially if they are very important (9b). Make notes in the margins that record your questions, challenges, or counter-examples to the text.
- If the readings are interactive—that is, if they allow you to post a comment—take advantage of this opportunity to get your voice into the conversation.

2e   Plan research.

Much of the work you do in college may turn an informal curiosity into various kinds of more formal research: you might start by wondering how many students on your campus are vegetarians, for example, and end up with a research project for a sociology class that then becomes part of a multimedia presentation for a campus organization. Many of your writing assignments will require extensive formal research with a wide range of sources from various media as well as information drawn from observations, interviews, or surveys.

Research can help you find important information that you didn't know, even if you know a topic very well. And no matter what you discover, college research is an important tool for establishing credibility with your audience members and thus gaining their confidence. Often, what you write will be only as good as the research on which it is based. (For more on research, see Chapters 12–16.)

2f   Use media to communicate effectively.

Your instructors will probably expect you to communicate both in and out of class using a variety of media. You may be asked to post to course management systems, lists, blogs, and wikis, and you may respond to the work of others on such sites. In addition, you will probably contact your instructor and classmates using email and text messages. Because electronic communication is so common, it's easy to fall into the habit of writing very informally. If you forget to adjust style and voice for different occasions and readers, you may undermine your own intentions.

Best practices for formal messages and posts.   Email was once seen as highly informal, but you will probably use it today mainly for more formal purposes, particularly to communicate for work and for school. When writing most academic and professional messages, then, or when posting to a public list that may be read by people you don't know well, follow the conventions of standard academic English (2b), and be careful not to offend or irritate your audience—remember that jokes may be read as insults and that ALL CAPS may look like shouting. Finally, proofread to make sure your message is clear and free of errors, and that it is addressed to your intended audience, before you hit SEND.

EMAIL

- Use a subject line that states your purpose clearly.
- Use a formal greeting and closing (*Dear Ms. Aulie* rather than *Hey*).
- Keep messages as concise as possible.
- Conclude your message with your name and email address.
- Ask for permission before forwarding a sensitive message from someone else.
- Consider your email messages permanent and always findable, even if you delete them. Many people have been embarrassed (or worse, prosecuted) because of email trails.
- Make sure that the username on the email account you use for formal messages does not present a poor impression. If your username is *Party2Nite*, consider changing it, or use your school account for academic and professional communication.

DISCUSSION LISTS AND FORUMS

- Avoid unnecessary criticism of others' spelling or language. If a message is unclear, ask politely for a clarification. If you disagree with an assertion, offer what you believe to be the correct information, but don't insult the writer.
- If you think you've been insulted, give the writer the benefit of the doubt. Replying with patience establishes your credibility and helps you appear mature and fair.
- For email discussion lists, decide whether to reply off-list to the sender of a message or to the whole group, and be careful to use REPLY or REPLY ALL accordingly to avoid potential embarrassment.
- Keep in mind that because many forums and email lists are archived, more people than you think may read your messages.

Best practices for informal situations. Sometimes audiences expect informality. When you write in certain situations—Twitter posts, for example, and most text messages—you can play with (or ignore) the conventions you would probably follow in formal writing. Most people receiving text messages expect shorthand such as *u* for "you," but be cautious about using such shortcuts with an employer or instructor. You may want to stick to a more formal method of contact if your employer or instructor has not explicitly invited you to send text messages—or texted you first.

Even when you think the situation calls for an informal tone, be attuned to your audience's needs and your purpose for writing. And when writing for any online writing space that allows users to say almost anything about themselves or to comment freely on the postings of others, bear in mind that anonymity sometimes makes online writers feel less inhibited than they would be in a face-to-face discussion. Don't say anything you want to remain private, and even if you disagree with another writer, avoid personal attacks.

EXERCISE 2.2: THINKING CRITICALLY

How do you define good college writing? Make a list of the characteristics you come up with. Then make a list of what you think your instructors' expectations are for good college writing, and note how they may differ from yours. (Research suggests that many students today define good writing as "writing that makes something happen in the world." Would that match your definition or that of your instructors?) What might account for the differences — and the similarities — in the definitions and lists? Do you need to alter your ideas about good college writing to meet your instructors' expectations? Why, or why not?

3 Writing to Make Something Happen in the World

A large group of college students participating in a research study were asked, "What is good writing?" The researchers expected fairly straightforward answers like "writing that gets its message across," but the students kept coming back to one central idea: good writing "makes something happen in the world." They felt particular pride in the writing they did for family, friends, and community groups—and for many extracurricular activities that were meaningful to them. Furthermore, once these students graduated from college, they continued to create—and to value—these kinds of public writing.

At some point during your college years or soon after, you are highly likely to create writing that is not just something that you turn in for a grade but writing that you do because you want to

> ### CHECKLIST
>
> #### Characteristics of Writing That Makes Something Happen
>
> ✔ Public writing has a very clear *purpose* (to promote a local cause or event, to inform or explain an issue or a problem, to persuade others to act, sometimes even to entertain).
>
> ✔ It is intended for a specific *audience* and addresses those people directly.
>
> ✔ It uses the *genre* most suited to its purpose and audience (a poster to alert people to an upcoming fund drive, a newsletter to inform members of a group, a brochure to describe the activities of a group, a letter to the editor to argue for a candidate or an issue), and it appears in a *medium* (print, online, or both) where the intended audience will see it.
>
> ✔ It generally uses straightforward, everyday *language*.

make a difference. The writing that matters most to many students and citizens, then, is writing that has an effect in the world: writing that gets up off the page or screen, puts on its working boots, and marches out to get something done!

3a   Decide what should happen.

When you decide to write to make something happen, you'll generally have some idea of what effect you want that writing to have. Clarify what actions you want your readers to take in response to your writing, and then think about what people you most want to reach—audiences today can be as close as your immediate neighbors or as dispersed as global netizens. Who will be interested in the topic you are writing about? For example, if you are trying to encourage your elementary school to plant a garden, you might try to interest parents, teachers, and PTA members; if you are planning a voter registration drive, you might start with eighteen-year-olds on your campus.

bedfordstmartins.com/wia
Video > Writing for the real world

3b   Connect with your audience.

Once you have a target audience in mind, you'll need to think carefully about where and how you are likely to find them, how you can get their attention so they will read what you write, and what you can say to get them to achieve your purpose.

If you want to convince your neighbors to pool time, effort, and resources to build a local playground, then you have a head start: you know something about what they value and about what appeals would get their attention and convince them to join in this project. If you want to create a flash mob to publicize ineffective security at chemical plants near your city, on the other hand, you will need to reach as many people as possible, most of whom you will not know.

Genre and medium.   Even if you know the members of your audience, you still need to think about the genre and medium that will be most likely to reach them. To get neighbors involved in the playground project mentioned above, you might decide that a colorful print flyer delivered door to door and posted at neighborhood gathering places would work best. For a flash mob, however, an easily forwarded message—text, Twitter, or email—will probably work best.

Appropriate language.   For all public writing, think carefully about the audience you want to reach—as well as *unintended* audiences your message might reach. Doing so can help you craft writing that will be persuasive without being offensive.

Timing.   Making sure your text will appear in a timely manner is crucial to the success of your project. If you want people to plan to attend an event, present your text to them at least two weeks ahead of time. If you are issuing a newsletter or blog, make sure that you create posts or issues often enough to keep people interested (but not so often that readers can't or won't keep up). If you are reporting information based on something that has already happened, make it available as soon as possible so that your audience won't consider your report "old news."

3c   Sample writing that makes something happen in the world

On the following pages are some examples of the forms public writing can take.

This poster, created by student Amrit Rao, has a very clear purpose: to attract participants to a walk aimed at raising money in support of AIDS research. In this case, Rao wanted to reach college students in the DC area; students, he felt, would be particularly aware of the need for such research and likely to respond by showing up for the walk. To reach as many students as possible, he decided to distribute the poster in both print and digital forms. He called on friends in the area to help place the poster in key locations on a dozen college campuses, and he emailed PDF versions of the poster to student body presidents on each campus, asking them to help spread the word.

Poster

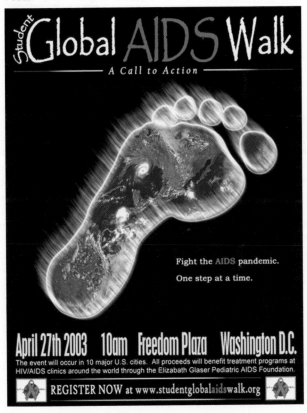

Flyer

Student Anna Mumford created and posted copies of this flyer advocating for pay raises for campus workers. Again, her purpose is clear: she wants to raise awareness on her campus of what she views as highly inequitable salaries and working conditions for temporary workers. Her audience in this case is a local one that includes the temporary workers as well as the students, faculty, and administrators on her campus. Mumford did not have an easy way to distribute the information electronically to temporary workers, nor was she certain that all of them had access to computers, so she chose to produce a print flyer that would be easy to distribute across campus. She wrote in Spanish (on an English-speaking campus), the home language of most of the temporary workers, to reach her target audience more effectively.

e **bedfordstmartins.com/wia**
Student Writing > Reflective blog post, Thanh Nguyen
Student Writing > Pitch package, Deborah Jane and Jamie Burke

Newsletter

As with the writers of the poster and flyer, yoga teacher Joelle Hann has a clear purpose in mind for her e-newsletter: to provide information to her audience—students and others interested in her yoga classes and developments in the yoga community. Emailing the newsletter to her subscribers allows Hann to reach an interested audience quickly and to provide links to more of the content she's discussing, and it also means that she can include photos, illustrations, and color to enhance her document's design impact.

Event Invitation on Social Networking Site

+ Select Guests to Invite

Pure Hell / The Bad Luck Charms / TV Tramps
• Share • Public Event

Time:	Saturday, October 16 · 6:00pm - 9:30pm
Location:	Europa
Created By:	Scenic Nyc, Bryan Swirsky
More Info:	All Ages (16+ with government issued ID, under 16 w/ parent, guardian) $8 adv, $10 day of. !!! Early show.

Pure Hell, one of the earliest all-black American punk-rock bands, formed in Philadelphia, Pennsylvania, in 1974, as punk rock was taking off and developing a following in nearby New York City. Discovered by Johnny Thunders during the heyday of the New York Dolls, the band moved to New York. In 1978, they toured Europe and released their only single ("These Boots are Made for Walking" b/w "No Rules"). Live performances by Pure Hell have been compared to the MC5, Sex Pistols, Dead Boys, Germs, and fellow Afropunks the Bad Brains, who identified Pure Hell as an influence. Their album (Noise Addiction), recorded in the late 1970s, was finally released this year. Pure Hell also has an unreleased album (The Black Box) produced in the mid 1990's by former members of L.A. Guns, Nine Inch Nails, and Lemmy Kilmister of Motorhead. Recent performances by Pure Hell in NYC showed that they still have what it takes!

Band promoter Bryan Swirsky used Facebook, where he has many friends who share his interest in punk rock, to reach an audience interested in seeing a reunion show by an all-black punk band that had a cult following in the 1970s. Those invited by Bryan could also invite their own interested friends, allowing news of the event to spread virally.

Online Report

Less Trash, More Compost!
A report on a community partnership to reduce trash and promote composting and recycling at a summer camp

Funded in part by the New England Grassroots Environmental Fund

...When campers have something in their hand, they are very likely to ask where is the compost, where is the recycling... and that is exciting...
                                   Counselor, Athol Area YMCA Day Camp

Deb Habib and Kaitlin Doherty
Seeds of Solidarity
November, 2007

Project Background and Goals

"Gross, but fun!" exclaims an eight-year old compost enthusiast, one of over 200 campers, plus counselors and staff at the Athol Area YMCA day camp in Orange, Massachusetts who worked together to successfully divert over one ton of their breakfast and lunch waste from the landfill to compost. And they won't mind telling you that they had fun doing it.

Seeds of Solidarity, a non-profit organization based in Orange, partnered with the summer food service director, the Athol Area YMCA, and a local hauler to implement a composting and recycling initiative, diverting the waste from approximately 3,600 meals at two sites over an eight-week period in the summer of 2007. This pilot project was inspired by success using biodegradable and compostable utensils and plates at the annual North Quabbin Garlic and Arts Festival, also sponsored by Seeds of Solidarity, which results in only two bags of trash for 10,000 people.

Athol and Orange are located in the North Quabbin region, where 20% of the children live below the federal poverty line. Food service director Sherry Fiske runs a state and federally funded summer food service program at 11 sites in Orange and Athol, providing free breakfast and lunch to children and families during the summer months. The YMCA camps based both at the Y site in Athol and Lake Selah in North Orange are among these summer food service sites. While school year lunch programs in the area utilize washable dishes and utensils, the summer food service program is held at temporary sites, resulting in heaping dumpsters of paper, plastic and polystyrene waste.

This report, created by Deb Habib and Kaitlin Doherty of the nonprofit group Seeds of Solidarity, provides information about a successful experimental recycling and composting program at a Massachusetts camp. (Only the first page of the twenty-six-page PDF is shown.) Other sections include "Project Description," "Voices of Campers," "Successes and Challenges," "Summary of Key Considerations," and an appendix with additional documents (interviews with campers, letters to campers' parents before the program began, and graphs quantifying the outcomes). The report appears on the organization's Web site, which notes that Seeds of Solidarity "provid[es] people of all ages with the inspiration and practical tools to use renewable energy and grow food in their communities." While the report offers information about an experiment that has already taken place, the document also serves to encourage and inform others who might want to create a similar program.

EXERCISE 3.1: THINKING CRITICALLY

You have probably done quite a bit of writing to make something happen in the world, though you might not have thought of it as official "writing." Yet as this chapter shows, such writing is important to those who do it — and to those affected by it. Think about the groups you belong to — informal or formal, home- or community- or school-based — and choose a piece of writing you have done for the group, whether on your own or with others. Then take a careful look at it: looking at it with a critical eye, is its purpose clear? What audience does it address, and how well does it connect to that audience? Are the genre (newsletter, poster, flyer, brochure, report, etc.) and the medium (print, electronic) appropriate to achieving the purpose and reaching the audience? How might you revise this text to make it even more effective?

2

Writing

4   A Writer's Choices

What do a documented essay on global warming research, a Facebook message objecting to the latest change to the site's privacy policy, a tweet to other students in your psychology class, a comment on a blog post, a letter to the editor of your local newspaper, and a Web site devoted to sustainability all have in common? To communicate effectively, the writers of these texts must analyze their particular situation and then respond to it in appropriate ways.

4a   Write to connect.

If it is true that "no man [or woman!] is an island," then it is equally true that no piece of writing is an island, isolated and alone. Instead, writing is connected to a broad web of other writings as a writer extends, responds to, or challenges what others say. This has always been the case, but today it's especially important to remember that all writing exists within a rich and broad context and that all writers listen and respond to what others have said, even as they shape messages about particular topics and for particular purposes that help them connect to their audiences.

4b   Make good choices for your rhetorical situation.

A *rhetorical situation* is the full set of circumstances surrounding any communication. When you communicate, whether you're posting on a social networking site, creating a video, or writing an essay for your psychology class, you need to consider and make careful choices about all the elements of your situation.

The rhetorical situation is often depicted as a triangle to present the idea that three important elements are closely connected—your *text*, including your topic and the message you want to convey (4c); your role as the *communicator*, including your purpose and your stance, or attitude toward the text (4d); and your *audience* (4e). If all the pieces making up the larger triangle don't work together, the communication will not be effective. But as important as these elements are, they are connected to a *context* that shapes all the angles of the triangle. Considering context fully requires you to consider many other questions about the rhetorical situation, such as what kind of text you should cre-

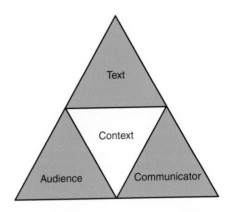

ate and what conventions you should follow to meet audience expectations for creating and delivering the text (4f).

Informal and formal rhetorical situations.   Most people are accustomed to writing in some rhetorical situations without analyzing them closely. When you post something on a friend's social networking page, for example, you probably spend little time pondering what your friend values or finds funny, how to phrase your words, which links or photos would best emphasize your point, or why you're taking the time to post. However, academic and other formal rhetorical situations may seem less familiar than the social writing you share with friends. Until you understand clearly what such situations demand of you, allow extra time to analyze the overall context, the topic and message, the purpose and stance, the audience, and other elements carefully.

4c   Plan your text's topic and message.

An instructor or employer may tell you what topic to write about, but sometimes the choice will be yours. When the topic is left open, you may be tempted to put off getting started because you can't decide what to do. Experienced writers say that the best way to choose a topic is literally to let it choose you. Look to the topics that compel, puzzle, confuse, or pose a problem for you: these are likely to engage your interest and hence produce some of your best writing.

Deciding on a broad topic is an essential step before beginning to write, but you need to go further than that to decide what you want to say about your topic and how you will shape what you want to say into a clear, powerful message.

EXERCISE 4.1

The following assignment was given to an introductory business class: "Discuss in an essay the contributions of the Apple and Microsoft companies to the personal computing industry." What would you need to know about the assignment in order to respond successfully? Using the questions on pp. 32–33, analyze this assignment.

4d   Consider your purpose and stance as a communicator.

Whether you choose to communicate for purposes of your own or have that purpose set for you by an instructor or employer, you should consider the purpose for any communication carefully. For the writing you do that is not connected to a class or work assignment, your purpose may be very clear to you: you may want to convince neighbors to support a community garden, get others in your office to help keep the kitchen clean, or tell blog readers what you like or hate about your new phone. Even so, analyzing exactly what you want to accomplish and why can make you a more effective communicator.

Purposes for academic assignments.   An academic assignment may clearly explain why, for whom, and about what you are supposed to write. But sometimes college assignments seem to come out of the blue, with no specific purpose, audience, or topic. Because comprehending the assignment fully and accurately is crucial to your success in responding to it, make every effort to understand what your instructor expects.

- What is the primary purpose of the piece of writing—to explain? to persuade? to entertain? some other purpose?

- What purpose did the person who gave you the assignment want to achieve—to make sure you have understood something? to evaluate your thinking and writing abilities? to test your ability to think outside the box?

- What are your own purposes in this piece of writing — to respond to a question? to learn about a topic? to communicate your ideas? to express feelings? How can you achieve these goals?

- What, exactly, does the assignment ask you to do? Look for such words as *analyze*, *classify*, *compare*, *define*, *describe*, *explain*, *prove*, and *survey*. Remember that these words may differ in meaning from discipline to discipline.

Stances for academic assignments. Thinking about your own position as a communicator and your attitude toward your text — your rhetorical stance — is just as important as making sure you communicate effectively.

- Where are you coming from on this topic? What is your overall attitude toward your topic? How strong are your opinions?

- What social, political, religious, personal, or other influences account for your attitude? Will you need to explain any of these influences?

- What is most interesting to you about the topic? Why do you care?

- What conclusions do you think you'll reach as you complete your text?

- How will you establish your credibility? How will you show you are knowledgeable and trustworthy?

- How will you convey your stance? Should you use words alone, combine words and images, include sound, or do something else?

EXERCISE 4.2

Consider a writing project that you are currently working on for a course. What are the purposes of the project in terms of the instructor, the assignment, and you, the writer?

4e   Analyze your audience.

Every communicator can benefit from thinking carefully about who the audience is, what the audience already knows or thinks, and what the audience needs and expects to find out. One of the

> ### FOR MULTILINGUAL WRITERS
>
> #### Bringing In Other Languages
>
> Even when you write in English, you may want or need to include words, phrases, or whole passages in another language. If so, consider whether your readers will understand that language and whether you need to provide a translation. See 19d for more on bringing other languages into your writing.

characteristics of an effective communicator is the ability to write for a variety of audiences, using the language, style, and evidence appropriate to particular readers, listeners, or viewers. Even if your text can theoretically reach people all over the world, focus your analysis on those you most want or need to reach and those who are most likely to take an interest.

Informal and formal audiences.   For some informal writing, you know exactly who your audience is, and communicating appropriately may be a simple matter. It's still worth remembering that when you post in a public space, you may not be aware of how large and varied your online audience can be. Can your friend's parents, or her prospective employer, see your posts on her Facebook page? (The answer depends partly on her privacy settings.) Who's reading the blogs you comment on?

Even if you write with intuitive ease in tweets and texts to friends, you may struggle when asked to write for an instructor or for a "general audience." You may wonder, for example, what a general audience might know about your topic, what they value, or what evidence they will find persuasive. When you are new to academic writing, making assumptions about such questions can be tricky. If you can identify samples of writing that appeal to a similar audience, look for clues about what that audience expects; if still in doubt, check with your instructor or drop by your campus writing center.

Appropriate language for an audience

- Is the language of your text as clear as it needs to be for your audience? If your readers can't understand what you mean, they're not likely to accept your points.

CONSIDERING DISABILITIES

Your Whole Audience

Remember that considering your whole audience means thinking about members with varying abilities and special needs. Approximately one in five Americans was living with a disability in the year 2010. All writers need to think carefully about how their words reach out and connect with such very diverse audiences.

- For academic writing, should you use any specialized varieties of English along with standard academic English? any occupational, professional, regional, or ethnic varieties? any words from a language other than English? any dialogue? (See Chapter 19.) How will these choices help you connect to your audience?

As you think about your audience, consider how you want them to respond to both the words and the images you use. And remember that images can evoke very strong responses in your audience and can affect the tone of your writing (4f), so choose them with special care.

EXERCISE 4.3

Describe one of your courses to three audiences: your best friend, your parents, and a group of high school students attending an open house at your college. Then describe the differences in content, organization, and wording that the differences in audience led you to make.

EXERCISE 4.4: THINKING VISUALLY

Consider your own writing process for an assignment you are currently working on. What specific decisions have you made about your topic, purpose and stance, and intended audience for the project? Sketch an image that suggests how your topic, stance, and audience will fit together. Will your decisions about this rhetorical situation help you create a unified piece of writing that accomplishes your goals?

 bedfordstmartins.com/wia
Video > Developing a sense of audience

4f Consider other elements of the writing context.

After you have chosen a topic, shaped a message, and analyzed your purpose, stance, and audience in relation to your message, you still have other important decisions to make about the text you are developing.

Time and length

- How much time do you have to complete the text? Do you need to schedule research? Do you need to find or create images or media content? Be sure to allow time for revision and editing.

- How long is the finished draft of the writing supposed to be? If you are writing a presentation, what time limits do you face for delivering it? If you are creating a work for the public, how much time can you expect the audience to devote to your work?

Genre, medium, and format. You may be assigned—or able to choose—to work in genres other than straightforward essays or in a medium other than print.

- What genre does your text call for—report? review? argument essay? research project? letter? blog posting? instructions for completing a task? promotional brochure? If you aren't familiar with the conventions of the genre, study examples created by others.

- What format or method of organization is expected for this genre? (See Chapter 5.) Should you conform to traditional formats, or will you gain from going in an unexpected direction?

- In what medium will the text appear—on the Internet? on a password-protected Web site? in a print essay submitted to your instructor? in a spoken presentation? Will your text use images, video, or audio? How will the media you use affect other choices you make?

- What design considerations should you keep in mind? (See Chapter 8.)

Tone and style

- What tone do you want to achieve—humorous? serious? impassioned? ironic? sincere? deeply knowledgeable?

- What words, sentence structures, and images or media will help you achieve this tone?
- Is the tone of the writing appropriate to your audience, purpose, and message? Do the words, images, or sounds you choose have the connotations you intend?

Remember that visual and audio elements can influence the tone of your writing as much as the words you choose. Such elements create associations in viewers' minds: one audience may react more positively than another to an element such as a rap or heavy metal soundtrack, for example—and a presentation with a heavy metal accompaniment will make a far different impression than the same presentation with an easy-listening soundtrack. Writers can influence the way their work is perceived by carefully analyzing their audience and choosing audio and visual elements that set a mood appropriate to the point they want to make.

EXERCISE 4.5

Consider some of the genres that you have encountered as a student, jotting down answers to the following questions and bringing them to class for discussion.

1. What are some genres that you read but don't usually write?
2. What are some genres that you write for teachers?
3. What are some genres that you write to or with other students?
4. What are some genres that you will likely encounter in your major or in your career?
5. How are some of the genres you listed different from those you encountered in high school?

EXERCISE 4.6

Consider a writing assignment you are currently working on. What is its genre? What medium or media does it use? How would you describe the style and tone? Finally, what visuals are you going to include and how well do they work to create the appropriate style and tone?

4g   A sample writing situation

Let's take an example of how one writer analyzes a rhetorical situation. Emily Lesk, a student in a first-year English course, gets an assignment that asks her to "explore the ways in which one or more media have affected an aspect of American identity." (More examples of Emily's work appear in the Student Writing section of this book's integrated media site.) Because Emily is interested in advertising, she plans first to investigate how advertising might help shape American identity. Deciding that such a broad topic is not manageable in the time she has available, however, she shifts her focus to advertising for one company that seems particularly "American," Coca-Cola.

Since Emily's primary audience includes her instructor and her classmates, she needs to find ways to connect with them on an emotional as well as a logical level. She will do so, she decides, first by telling a story about being drawn into buying Coca-Cola products (even though she didn't really like the soft drink) because of the power of the advertising. She thinks that others in her audience may have had similar experiences. Here is a portion of her story and the visual she chose to illustrate it:

STUDENT WRITING

Even before setting foot in the Promised Land three years ago, I knew exactly where I could find the Coke T-shirt. The shop in the central block of Jerusalem's Ben Yehuda Street did offer other shirt designs, but the one with the bright white "Drink Coca-Cola Classic" written in Hebrew cursive across the chest was what drew in most of the dollar-carrying tourists. While waiting almost twenty minutes for my shirt (depicted in Fig. 1), I watched nearly everyone ahead of me say "the Coke shirt, *todah rabah* [thank you very much]."

At the time, I never thought it strange that I wanted one, too. Yet, I *had* absorbed sixteen years of Coca-Cola propaganda.

Fig. 1. Hebrew Coca-Cola T-shirt. Personal photograph.

Thinking about how she relates to her audience brings Emily to reflect more deeply on herself as the writer: Why has she chosen this topic? What does it say about her beliefs and values? What is her attitude toward her topic and toward her audience? What does she need to do to establish her credentials to write on this topic and to this audience?

Finally, Emily knows she will need to pay careful attention to the context in which she is writing: the assignment is due in two weeks, so she needs to work fast; the assignment calls for an essay written in academic English, though she plans to include some dialogue and a number of visuals to keep it lively; and since she knows she tends to sound like a know-it-all, she determines to work carefully on her tone and style.

EXERCISE 4.7: THINKING CRITICALLY

Reading with an Eye for Purpose, Audience, and Context

Advertisements provide good examples of writing that is tailored carefully for specific audiences. Find two ads for the same product in contexts that suggest that the ads aim to appeal to different audiences — for example, men and women. What differences do you see in the messages and photography? What conclusions can you draw about ways of appealing to specific audiences?

5   Exploring, Planning, and Drafting

One student defines drafting as the time in a writing project "when the rubber meets the road." As you explore your topic, decide on a thesis, organize materials to support that central idea, and sketch out a plan for your writing, you have already begun the drafting process.

5a   Explore and narrow a topic.

Among the most important parts of the writing process are choosing a topic (see 4c), exploring what you know about it, and determining what you need to find out. These strategies can help you explore your topic:

• Brainstorm. Try out ideas, alone or with another person. Jot down key words and phrases about the topic, and see what they prompt you to think about next.

---

 bedfordstmartins.com/wia
Video > Brain mapping
Video > Writing processes

FOR MULTILINGUAL WRITERS

Stating a Thesis

In some cultures, it is considered rude to state an opinion outright. In the United States, however, academic and business practices require writers to make key positions explicitly clear.

- Freewrite without stopping for ten minutes or so to see what insights or ideas you come up with.
- Draw or make word pictures about your topic.
- Try clustering—writing your topic on a sheet of paper, then writing related thoughts near the topic idea. Circle each idea or phrase, and draw lines to show how ideas are connected.
- Ask questions about the topic: *What is it? What caused it? What is it like or unlike? What larger system is the topic a part of? What do people say about it?* Or choose the journalist's questions: *Who? What? When? Where? Why? How?*
- Browse sources to find out what others say about the topic.

After exploring ideas, you may have found a topic that interests you and that you think would also be interesting to your readers. The topic, however, may be too large to be manageable. If that is the case, narrow your topic using any exploring technique that works for you.

Emily Lesk planned to discuss how advertising affects American identity, but she knew that such a topic was far too broad. After thinking about products that are pitched as particularly "American" in their advertising, she posted a Facebook status update asking friends to "name products that seem super-American." She quickly got seventeen responses ranging from Hummers and Winchester rifles to "soft toilet paper," Spam, Wheaties, and apple pie. One friend identified Coca-Cola and Pepsi-Cola, two products that Emily associated with many memorable and well-documented advertising campaigns.

EXERCISE 5.1

Choose a topic that interests you, and explore it by using two of the strategies described in 5a. When you have generated some material, you might try comparing your results with those of other members of the class to see how effective or helpful each strategy was. If you have trouble choosing a topic, use one of the preliminary working theses in Exercise 5.2.

5b Develop a working thesis.

Academic and professional writing in the United States often contains an explicit thesis statement. You should establish a working thesis early in your writing process. Your final thesis may be very different from the working thesis you begin with. Even so, a working thesis focuses your thinking and research, and helps keep you on track.

A working thesis should have two parts: a topic, which indicates the subject matter the writing is about, and a comment, which makes an important point about the topic.

▶ In the graphic novel *Fun Home*, illustrations and words combine to make meanings that are more subtle than either words alone or images alone could convey.

A successful working thesis has three characteristics:

1. It is potentially *interesting* to the intended audience.
2. It is as *specific* as possible.
3. It limits the topic enough to make it *manageable*.

You can evaluate a working thesis by checking it against each of these characteristics, as in the following examples:

▶ Graphic novels combine words and images.

INTERESTING? The topic of graphic novels could be interesting, but this draft of a working thesis has no real comment attached to it—instead, it states a bare fact, and the only place to go from here is to more bare facts.

▶ In graphic novels, words and images convey interesting meanings.

SPECIFIC? This thesis is not specific. What are "interesting meanings," exactly? How are they conveyed?

▶ **Graphic novels have evolved in recent decades to become an important literary genre.**

> MANAGEABLE?   This thesis would not be manageable for a short-term project because it would require research on several decades of history and on hundreds of texts from all over the world.

EXERCISE 5.2

Choose one of the following working theses, and after specifying an audience, evaluate the thesis in terms of its interest, specificity, and manageability. Revise the working thesis as necessary to meet these criteria.

1. The benefits of standardized testing are questionable.
2. Vaccinations are dangerous.
3. Too many American parents try to micromanage their children's college education.
4. Many people are afraid to fly in a plane, although riding in a car is statistically more dangerous.
5. An educated public is the key to a successful democracy.

EXERCISE 5.3

Using the topic you chose in Exercise 5.1, write a working thesis. Evaluate the thesis in terms of its interest, specificity, and manageability. Revise it as necessary to create a satisfactory working thesis.

5c   Gather evidence and do research.

What kinds of evidence will be most persuasive to your audience and most effective in the field you are working in—historical precedents? expert testimony? statistical data? experimental results? personal anecdotes? Knowing what kinds of evidence count most in a particular field or with particular audiences will help you make appropriate choices.

If the evidence you need calls for research, determine what research you need to do:

- Make a list of what you already know about your topic.
- Keep track of where information comes from so you can return to your sources later.

- What else do you need to know, and where are you likely to find good sources of information? Consider library resources, authoritative online sources, field research, and so on.

(For more on research, see Chapters 12–16.)

5d **Plan and create a draft.**

Sketch out a rough plan for organizing your writing. You can simply begin with your thesis; review your notes, research materials, and media; and list all the evidence you have to support the thesis. An informal way to organize your ideas is to figure out what belongs in your introduction, body paragraphs, and conclusion. You may also want—or be required—to make a formal outline, which can help you see exactly how the parts of your writing fit together.

Thesis statement
I. First main idea
  A. First subordinate idea
    1. First supporting detail or point
    2. Second supporting detail
    3. Third supporting detail
  B. Second subordinate idea
    1. First supporting detail
    2. Second supporting detail
II. Second main idea
  A. First subordinate idea
    1. First supporting detail
    2. Second supporting detail
  B. Second subordinate idea
    1. First supporting detail
    2. Second supporting detail
      a. First supporting detail
      b. Second supporting detail

The technique of storyboarding—working out a narrative or argument in visual form—can also be a good way to come up with an organizational plan. You can create your own storyboard by using note cards or sticky notes, taking advantage of different colors to keep track of threads of argument, subtopics, and so on. Move the cards and notes around, trying out different arrangements, until you find an organization that works well for your writing situation.

CHECKLIST

Drafting

✔ **Set up a computer folder or file for your essay.** Give the file a clear and relevant name, and save to it often. Number your drafts. If you decide to try a new direction, save the file as a new draft — you can always pick up with a previous one if the new version doesn't work out.

✔ **Have all your information close at hand and arranged according to your organizational plan.** Stopping to search for a piece of information can break your concentration or distract you.

✔ **Try to write in stretches of at least thirty minutes.** Writing can provide momentum, and once you get going, the task becomes easier.

✔ **Don't let small questions bog you down.** Just make a note of them in brackets — or in all caps — or make a tentative decision and move on.

✔ **Remember that first drafts aren't perfect.** Concentrate on getting all your ideas down, and don't worry about anything else.

✔ **Stop writing at a place where you know exactly what will come next.** Doing so will help you start easily when you return to the draft.

No matter how good your planning, investigating, and organizing have been, chances are you will need to do more work as you draft. The first principle of successful drafting is to be flexible. If you see that your plan is not working, don't hesitate to alter it. If some information now seems irrelevant, leave it out. You may learn that you need to do more research, that your whole thesis must be reshaped, or that your topic is still too broad and should be narrowed further. Very often you will continue planning, investigating, and organizing throughout the writing process.

EXERCISE 5.4

Write out a plan for a piece of writing supporting the working thesis you developed for Exercise 5.3.

EXERCISE 5.5

Write a draft from the plan you produced for Exercise 5.4.

5e   Develop paragraphs.

Three qualities essential to most academic paragraphs are unity, development, and coherence.

Unity.   An effective paragraph focuses on one main idea. You can achieve unity by stating the main idea clearly in one sentence—the topic sentence—and relating all other sentences in the paragraph to that idea. Like a thesis (see 5b), the topic sentence includes a topic and a comment on that topic. A topic sentence often begins a paragraph, but it may come at the end—or be implied rather than stated directly.

Development.   In addition to being unified, a paragraph should hold readers' interest and explore its topic fully, using whatever details, evidence, and examples are necessary. Without such development, a paragraph may seem lifeless and abstract.

Most good academic writing backs up general ideas with specifics. Shifting between the general and the specific is especially important at the paragraph level. If a paragraph contains nothing but specific details, its meaning may not be clear—but if a paragraph makes only general statements, it may seem boring or unconvincing.

Coherence.   A paragraph has coherence—or flows—if all its details fit together in a way that readers can easily follow. The following methods can help you achieve paragraph coherence:

- A general-to-specific or specific-to-general *organization* helps readers move from one point to another.
- *Repetition* of key words or phrases links sentences and suggests that the words or phrases are important.
- *Parallel structures* help make writing more coherent (see Chapter 33).
- *Transitions* such as *for example* and *however* help readers follow the progression of one idea to the next.

The same methods you use to create coherent paragraphs can be used to link paragraphs so that a whole piece of writing flows more smoothly. You can create links to previous paragraphs by

 bedfordstmartins.com/wia
Video > It's hard to delete things
Video > You just have to start

CHECKLIST

Strong Paragraphs

Most readers of English have certain expectations about paragraphs:

✔ Paragraphs begin and end with important information.

✔ The opening sentence is often the topic sentence that tells what the paragraph is about.

✔ The middle of the paragraph develops the idea.

✔ The end may sum up the paragraph's contents, closing the discussion of an idea and anticipating the paragraph that follows.

✔ A paragraph makes sense as a whole; the words and sentences are clearly related.

✔ A paragraph relates to other paragraphs around it.

---

repeating or paraphrasing key words and phrases and by using parallelism and transitions.

This sample paragraph from David Craig's research project (49e), which identifies a topic and a comment on the topic and then offers detailed evidence in support of the point, achieves coherence with a general-to-specific organization, repetition of key content related to digital communication and teenagers, and transitions that relate this paragraph to the preceding one and relate sentences to one another.

Transition from preceding paragraph

Topic sentence

STUDENT WRITING

Supporting evidence

Based on the preceding statistics, parents and educators appear to be right about the decline in youth literacy. And this trend coincides with another phenomenon: digital communication is rising among the young. According to the Pew Internet & American Life Project, 85 percent of those aged 12–17 at least occasionally write text messages, instant messages, or comments on social networking sites (Lenhart, Arafeh, Smith, and Macgill). In 2001, the most conservative estimate based on Pew numbers showed that American youths spent, at a minimum, nearly three million hours per day on messaging services (Lenhart and Lewis 20). These numbers are now exploding thanks to texting, which was "the dominant daily mode of communication" for teens in 2012 (Lenhart), and messaging on popular social networking sites such as Facebook and Tumblr.

Sentence-to-sentence transition

EXERCISE 5.6

Choose one of the following topic sentences, and spend some time exploring the topic. Then write a paragraph that includes the topic sentence. Make sure that each of the other sentences relates to it. Assume that the paragraph will be part of a letter you are writing to an acquaintance.

1. I found out quickly that college life was not quite what I had expected.
2. Being part of the "in crowd" used to be essential to me.
3. My work experience has taught me several important lessons.
4. Until recently, I never appreciated my parents fully.
5. One of my high school teachers helped prepare me for life as an adult.

EXERCISE 5.7

Choose an essay you have written recently, and examine the second, third, and fourth paragraphs. Does each have a topic sentence or strongly imply one? Do all the other sentences in the paragraph focus on its main idea? Would you now revise any of these paragraphs — and, if so, how?

EXERCISE 5.8

Look at the essay you drafted for Exercise 5.5, and identify the ways your paragraphs are linked together. Identify each use of repetition, parallel structures, and transitional expressions, and then evaluate how effectively you have joined the paragraphs.

5f Review.

Ask classmates or your instructor to respond to your draft, answering questions like these:

- What do you see as the major point, claim, or thesis?

- How convincing is the evidence? What can I do to support my thesis more fully?

- What points are unclear? How can I clarify them?

- How easy is it to follow my organization? How can I improve it?

- What can I do to make my draft more interesting?

EXERCISE 5.9

Take twenty to thirty minutes to look critically at the draft you pre-pared for Exercise 5.5. Reread it carefully, check to see how well the purpose is accomplished, and consider how appropriate the draft is for the audience. Then write a paragraph about how you would go about revising the draft.

5g   Revise.

Revising means using others' comments along with your own analysis of the draft make sure it is as complete, clear, and effective as possible. These questions can help you revise:

- How does the draft accomplish its purpose?

- Does the title tell what the draft is about?

- Is the thesis clearly stated, and does it contain a topic and a comment?

- How does the introduction catch readers' attention?

- Will the draft interest and appeal to its audience?

- How does the draft indicate your stance on the topic?

- What are the main points that illustrate or support the thesis? Are they clear? Do you need to add material to the points or add new points?

- Are the ideas presented in an order that will make sense to readers?

---

bedfordstmartins.com/wia
Video > Lessons from being a peer reviewer
Video > Lessons from peer review
Analysis Activity > Practice peer review with Emily Lesk's draft

- Are the points clearly linked by logical transitions?
- Have you documented your research appropriately?
- How are visuals, media, and research sources (if any) integrated into your draft? Have you commented on their significance?
- How does the draft conclude? Is the conclusion memorable?

EXERCISE 5.10

After rereading the draft you wrote for Exercise 5.5, evaluate the revised working thesis you produced for Exercise 5.3. Then evaluate its support in the draft. Identify points that need further support, and list those things you must do to provide that support.

EXERCISE 5.11

Revise the draft you wrote for Exercise 5.5.

EXERCISE 5.12: THINKING CRITICALLY

Answer the following questions about your reviewing and revising process.

1. How did you begin reviewing your draft?
2. What kinds of comments on or responses to your draft did you get? How helpful were they, and why?
3. How long did the revising process take? How many drafts did you produce?
4. What kinds of changes did you tend to make? in organization, paragraphs, sentence structure, wording, adding or deleting information? in the use of visuals?
5. What gave you the most trouble as you were revising?
6. What pleased you most? What is your very favorite sentence or passage in the draft, and why?
7. What would you most like to change about your process of revising, and how do you plan to go about doing so?

bedfordstmartins.com/wia
Student Writing > Early draft, Emily Lesk
Video > Revision happens

5h Edit.

Once you are satisfied with your revised draft's big picture, edit your writing to make sure that every detail is as correct as you can make it.

- Read your draft aloud to make sure it flows smoothly and to find typos or other mistakes.
- Are your sentences varied in length and in pattern or type?
- Have you used active verbs and effective language?
- Are all sentences complete and correct?
- Have you used the spell checker—and double-checked its recommendations?
- Have you chosen an effective design and used white space, headings, and color appropriately?
- Have you proofread one last time, going word for word?

(For more on troubleshooting your writing, see Chapter 1, "The Top Twenty.")

EXERCISE 5.13

Find a paragraph in your own writing that lacks variety in sentence length, sentence openings, or sentence structure. Then write a revised version.

EXERCISE 5.14

Using several essays you have written, establish your own editing checklist.

EXERCISE 5.15

Edit and proofread the draft you wrote for Exercise 5.5.

5i Reflect.

Thinking back on what you've learned helps make that learning stick. Whether or not your instructor requires you to write a formal reflection on a writing course or piece of writing, make time to think about what you have learned from the experience.

Your development as a writer. The following questions can help you think about your writing:

- What lessons have you learned from the writing? How will they help you with future writing projects?
- What aspects of your writing give you most confidence? What needs additional work, and what can you do to improve?
- What confused you during this writing? How did you resolve your questions?
- How has this piece of writing helped you clarify your thinking or extend your understanding?
- Identify a favorite passage of your writing. What pleases you about it? Can you apply what you learn from this analysis to other writing situations?
- How would you describe your development as a writer?

Portfolios. You may want (or be required) to select samples of writing for inclusion in a portfolio.

- Consider your purpose and audience to make good choices about what to include and about whether the portfolio should be print or electronic.
- Choose pieces that show your strengths as a writer, and decide how many to include.
- Consider organization. What arrangement will make most sense to readers?
- Think about what layout and design will present your work most effectively.
- Edit and proofread each piece, and get responses from peers or an instructor.

A student's portfolio cover letter. The following is the first paragraph of a reflective statement written by student James Kung to accompany the portfolio for his first-year college composition course.

e **bedfordstmartins.com/wia**
Student Writing > Reflective cover letter, James Kung
Analysis Activity > Analyze formal reflection, James Kung
Analysis Activity > Analyze informal reflection, Thanh Nguyen

"Writing is difficult and takes a long time." This simple yet powerful statement has been uttered so many times in our class that it has become our motto. In just ten weeks, my persuasive writing skills have improved dramatically, thanks to many hours spent writing, revising, polishing, and (when I wasn't writing) thinking about my topic. These improvements are clearly illustrated by the drafts, revisions, and other materials included in my course portfolio.

James Kung's letter goes on to analyze his revisions and the benefits of his writing process. He concludes with information about his future plans and a signature.

6   Multimodal Assignments

As Clive Thompson noted in *Wired* magazine in 2009, "Before the Internet came along, most Americans never wrote anything, ever, that wasn't a school assignment." Times have indeed changed. More and more Americans are reading and writing for social purposes and for their jobs and communities, not just for school. Your "life writing" is increasingly likely to include blogs, online videos, PowerPoint presentations, and other texts incorporating not just words but images, sound, and video. And college writing classes are increasingly likely to require you to shift gears in similar ways—from writing posts on class forums and creating Web texts to making oral presentations with multimedia support. As one student explains, the multimodal realities of today's academic work require you to become "ambidextrous in the digital age."

6a   Plan online assignments.

Writing assignments that your audiences will encounter online may repurpose your print-based work, or they may be entirely new, online-only texts that take advantage of the technology to include material that print texts can't offer, such as sound and video. Whether you are starting with work on a printed page or tackling an online assignment from scratch, you will need to think just as carefully about your online context as you would about any other writing situation.

CHECKLIST

Guidelines for Creating an Online Text

✔ Consider purpose, audience, and message. How can your text appeal to the right readers? How will it accomplish its purpose? (Chapter 4)

✔ Be realistic about the time available for the project, and plan accordingly.

✔ Think about the various types of online texts you can create, and determine which suits your needs based on what you want or need to do and what your audience expects: text, images, audio, video, or a combination? the latest updates first, or an index page? the ability to collaborate or comment? Make appropriate choices for your project and skills.

✔ Create an appealing design, or choose a template that follows basic design principles. (Chapter 8)

✔ Pay attention to user feedback, and make appropriate adjustments.

Rhetorical considerations of online texts. Early on, consider time and technical constraints carefully to make sure that your plan for an online text is manageable. But also remember to think about rhetorical concerns, such as your purpose for creating the text, the needs of your audience, and the main point or message you want to get across.

- Why are you creating this text (4d)? How do you want readers to use it? Considering purpose helps you determine what features your online text will need to incorporate.

- What potential audience (4e) can you identify? Considering audience will help you make good choices about tone, word choice, graphic style and design, level of detail, and many other factors. If your intended audience is limited to people you know (such as a wiki available only to members of your literature class), you may be able to make assumptions about their background, knowledge, and likely responses to your text. If you are covering a particular topic, you may have ideas about the type of audience you think you'll attract. Plan your text to appeal to the readers you expect—but remember that an online text may reach other, unanticipated audiences.

- What will you talk about? Your topic will also affect the content and design of your project. For example, if you want to write about the latest Hong Kong film releases, you might create a blog; if you want to explore the works of 1940s detective writers, you might produce a Web site. If you prefer to talk about or show information on your topic, you might consider creating an infographic or a video or audio text that you can post to an existing site.

- How do you relate to your subject matter? Your rhetorical stance (4d) determines how your audience will see you. Will you present yourself as an expert, a fan, or a novice seeking input from others? What information will make you seem credible and persuasive to your audience?

Types of online texts.   Among the most common types of texts online are Web sites, blogs, wikis, and audio or video texts.

- Web sites and blogs are similar in appearance, and both usually include links to other parts of the site or to other sites. Both are relatively easy to update. Web sites are often organized as a cluster of associations. Readers expect blog content to be refreshed frequently (more often than the contents of a Web page), so blog posts are commonly time-stamped, and the newest content appears first. Blogs usually invite readers to comment publicly on each post, while Web sites often have a single contact link allowing readers to email the site's creator(s) directly.

- Wikis—collaborative online texts—create communities where all content is peer reviewed and evaluated by other members. They are powerful tools for sharing a lot of information because they draw on the collective knowledge of many contributors.

- Audio and video content can vary as widely as the content found in written-word media—audiobooks, video diaries, pop-culture mashups, radio shows, short documentaries, fiction films, and so on. Writers who create podcasts (which can be downloaded for playback) and streaming media (which can be played without downloading) may produce episodic content united by a common host or theme. Audio and video files can stand alone as online texts on sites such as YouTube, but they can also be embedded on a Web page or blog or included in a presentation to add dimension to still images and written words.

Features of online texts.   Choose the features that will enable your audience to get the most from your online text.

- Online readers generally prefer short, manageable chunks of verbal text. If you are writing a long piece, consider breaking it up with headings and visuals. Include enough text to help readers make sense of your content, captions for visuals, sound transcripts (if you include audio files), and so on.

- Links to external sites are one method of documenting sources online. You can link to content that helps to prove a point—complex explanations, supporting statistics, bibliographies, referenced Web sites, or additional readings, for example. Links also help readers navigate from one part of a text to another. Each link should have a clear rhetorical purpose and be in an appropriate location. If it's important for users to read the whole paragraph, for instance, you may want to move the link to the end of it.

- Online texts—from blogs and video channels to online newspaper articles—often incorporate interactive features, such as "like" buttons, comments or forums, and a link to contact the writer.

- Online writers who give credit where credit is due have greater authority. If you have not created a verbal text, graphic, or audio or video clip yourself, provide a caption or link identifying the source, and ask permission to use it in a text for an online audience (see Chapter 15).

CONSIDERING DISABILITIES

Accessible Web Texts

Much on the Web remains hard to access and read for persons with disabilities. The Web site for the Americans with Disabilities Act provides guidelines on designing accessible sites, which include offering textual descriptions of any visuals and captions for any sound files. For details, visit www.ada.gov.

Time management.   You already know that time management is crucial for your success in any writing situation. How well you can manage decisions will be affected both by your deadline and by how much time you can squeeze out of your other interests and responsibilities to meet that deadline. How much technical expertise do you have, and how much will you need to learn in order to create your text? Allow enough time for that learning to take place. Also consider how much research you will have to do and how much time you will need to find, prepare, and seek permission (if needed—see 15c) for any images, sound, or video files you want to use.

Design and organization of online texts.   Ultimately, the organization and look of your text depend on what you are trying to achieve. You should make decisions about page length, color, visuals, multimedia, and interactive elements based on rhetorical choices (your audience, purpose, and message) and on practical constraints (the time and tools available). For more on design, see Chapter 8.

Just as you might outline an essay or create a storyboard for a video, you should develop a clear structure for your Web text. Some types of texts are organized in standard ways; others allow you to make choices about how to arrange materials. (For more on organizing a text, see 5d.) Choose a structure that makes sense for your purpose, audience, and message. Arrange your text to allow readers to find what they are looking for as quickly and intuitively as possible. Asking others to try out your site and give you feedback is a good way to learn what works and what doesn't.

6b   Prepare for presentations.

More and more students report that multimodal presentations are becoming part of their work both in and out of class. Good preparation is as necessary for a successful presentation as for any other writing assignment.

Considering your assignment, purpose, and audience for presentations.   Begin preparing for a presentation as soon as you get the assignment. Think about how much time you have to prepare; how long the presentation is to be; whether you will use

CHECKLIST

Preparing for Presentations

✔ How can you ensure that your text meets the expectations of a live audience?

✔ How does your presentation fulfill your purpose, including the goals of the assignment?

✔ How do the introduction and conclusion hold the audience's attention?

✔ Is your organizational structure crystal clear? How do you guide listeners? Are your transitions and signpost language explicit? Do you effectively repeat key words or ideas?

✔ Have you marked the text you are using for pauses and emphasis?

✔ Have you prepared all necessary visuals, including presentation slides and other multimedia? Are they large enough to be seen? Would other visuals be helpful?

✔ Have you practiced your presentation and gotten responses to it?

written-out text or note cards; whether visual aids, handouts, or other materials are called for; and what equipment you will need. If you are making a group presentation, you will need time to divide duties and practice. Make sure that you understand the criteria for evaluation—how will the presentation be graded or assessed?

Consider the purpose of your presentation (4d). Are you to lead a discussion? teach a lesson? give a report? engage a group in an activity? Also consider the audience (4e). If your instructor is a member of the audience, what will he or she expect you to do—and do well? What do audience members know about your topic? What opinions do they already hold about it? What do they need to know to follow your presentation and perhaps accept your point of view?

Student Shuqiao Song got a two-part assignment for her writing class on graphic novels: she had to write an argument essay based on her research on a graphic novel, and then she had to turn that information into a script for a twelve-minute oral presentation with slides. After brainstorming and talking with her instructor, she chose Alison Bechdel's memoir *Fun Home: A Family Tragicomic* as her topic. She realized that although she wanted very much to earn a good grade, she also wanted to convince her classmates that Bechdel's book was complex and important—and she wanted to turn in a truly *impressive* performance in her presentation.

Making your introduction and conclusion memorable.   Listeners, like readers, tend to remember beginnings and endings most readily, so work extra hard to make these elements memorable. Consider, for example, using a startling statement, opinion, or question; a dramatic anecdote; a powerful quotation; or a vivid image. Shifting language, especially into a variety of language that your audience will identify with, is another effective way to catch their attention (see Chapter 19). Whenever you can link your subject to the experiences and interests of your audience, do so.

Shuqiao Song began her presentation this way:

**STUDENT
WRITING**

Welcome, everyone. I'm Shuqiao Song and I'm here today to talk about residents of a dys*FUN*ctional *HOME*. We meet these residents in a graphic memoir called *Fun Home*.

(Here, Shuqiao showed a video clip of author Alison Bechdel saying, "I love words, and I love pictures. But especially, I love them together—in a mystical way that I can't even explain.")

That was Alison Bechdel, author of *Fun Home*. In that clip, she conveniently introduces the topics of my presentation today: Words. Pictures. And the mystical way they work together.

Note that this presentation opened with a play on words ("dys-*FUN*ctional *HOME*") and with a short, vivid video clip that summed up the main topic of the presentation. Also note the use of short sentences and fragments, special effects that act like drumbeats to get and hold the attention of the audience.

---

e **bedfordstmartins.com/wia**
Student Writing > Multimedia presentation, Shuqiao Song
Analysis Activity > Analyze Shuqiao Song's genre choices

CONSIDERING DISABILITIES

Accessible Presentations

Do all you can to make your presentations accessible.

- Do not rely on color or visuals alone to get information across — some individuals may be unable to pick up such cues.

- If you use video, provide captions to explain any sounds that won't be audible to some audience members.

Using explicit structure and signpost language.   Organize your presentation clearly and carefully, and give an overview of the main points at the outset. (You may want to recall these points toward the end of the talk.) Then, throughout your presentation, call attention to a new point by pausing before it and by using signpost language as an explicit transition: *The second crisis point in the breakup of the Soviet Union occurred shortly after the first* is more explicit than *Another thing went wrong.* Repeated key words and ideas work as signposts, too.

At the end of Shuqiao's introduction, she set forth the structure of her presentation in a very clear, straightforward, and simple way to help her audience follow what came next:

So, let me outline the rest of my presentation. First, I'll show how **STUDENT WRITING** text is *insufficient*, but also why it is *necessary* in Bechdel's story.

Second, I'll show how images can't be trusted yet why they are still necessary for Bechdel's purpose.

Third and finally, I'll show how the interplay of text and image in *Fun Home* creates a more complex and comprehensive understanding of the story.

Choosing words and sentence structures.   Avoid long, complicated sentences, and use straightforward sentence structure (subject-verb-object) as much as possible. Listeners prefer action verbs and concrete nouns to abstractions. You may need to deal with abstract ideas, but try to provide concrete examples for them (20c).

Shuqiao Song's presentation script included the following example:

STUDENT
WRITING

Now, to argue my second point, I'll begin with an image. This is a René Magritte painting. The text means, "This is not a pipe." Is this some surrealist Jedi mind trick? Not really. Now listen to the title of the painting to grasp Magritte's point. The painting is called *The Treason of Images*. Here Magritte is showing us that "this is not a pipe" because it is an *image* of a pipe.

Her short, straightforward sentences and vivid word choice ("Jedi mind trick") help make this passage easy on listeners.

Turning writing into a script for presentation. Even though you will rely on some written material, you will need to adapt it for speech. Depending on the assignment, the audience, and your personal preferences, you may even speak from a full script. If so, double- or triple-space it, and use print that is large enough to read. Try to end each page with the end of a sentence so that you won't have to pause while you turn a page. In addition, you may decide to mark spots where you want to pause and to highlight words you want to emphasize.

Take a look at this paragraph from Shuqiao Song's formal written essay on *Fun Home*:

A PARAGRAPH FROM A WRITTEN ESSAY

Finally, we can see how image and text function together. On the one hand, image and text support each other in that each highlights the subtleties of the other; but on the other hand, the more interesting interaction comes when there is some degree of distance between what is written and what is depicted. In *Fun Home*, there is no one-to-one closure that mentally connects text and image. Rather, Bechdel pushes the boundaries of mental closure between image and text. If the words and pictures match exactly, making the same point, the story would read like a children's book, and that would be too simple for what Bechdel is trying to accomplish. However, text and image can't be so mismatched that meaning completely eludes the readers. Bechdel crafts her story deliberately, leaving just enough mental space for the reader to solve the rest of the puzzle and resolve the cognitive dissonance. The reader's mental closure, which brings coherence to the text and images and draws together loose ends, allows for a more complex and sophisticated understanding of the story.

Now look at how she revised that paragraph into a script for oral presentation:

A PARAGRAPH REVISED FOR A LISTENING AUDIENCE

Finally, image and text can work together. They support each other: each highlights the subtleties of the other. But they are even more interesting when there's a gap — some distance between the story the words tell and the story the pictures tell. In *Fun Home*, text and image are never perfectly correlated. After all, if the words and pictures matched up exactly, the story would read like a kids' book. That would be way too simple for Bechdel's purposes. But we wouldn't want a complete disconnect between words and images either, since we wouldn't be able to make sense of them.

Still, Bechdel certainly pushes the boundaries that would allow us to bring closure between image and text. So what's the take-home point here? That in Bechdel's *Fun Home*, image and text are not just supporting actors of each other. Instead, each offers a *version* of the story. It's for us—the readers. We take these paired versions and weave them into a really rich understanding of the story.

Note that the revised paragraph presents the same information, but this time it is written to be heard, using helpful signpost language, some repetition, simple syntax, and informal varieties of English.

Speaking from notes.   If you decide to speak from notes rather than from a full script, here are some tips for doing so effectively:

- In general, use one note card for each point in your presentation.
- Number the cards in case they get scrambled.
- On each card, start with the major point you want to make in large bold text. Include subpoints in a bulleted list below the main point, again printed large enough for you to see easily.
- Include signpost language on each note, and use it to guide your listeners.
- Practice your presentation using the notes at least twice.
- Use color or brackets to mark material in your notes that you can skip if you run out of time.

The following note card for Shuqiao Song's introduction reminds her to emphasize her title and her three points. Notice how she has highlighted her signpost language as well as the card's number.

NOTE CARD FOR AN ORAL PRESENTATION

[Card 3]

Overview of the rest of the presentation
- First, text is insufficient but necessary
- Second, images can't be trusted but are necessary
- Finally, interplay of text and image creates complex, comprehensive understanding

Using visuals. Visuals are often an integral part of an oral presentation, carrying a lot of the message that the speaker wants to convey. So think of your visuals not as add-ons but as a major means of getting your points across. Many speakers use presentation software (such as PowerPoint or Prezi) to help keep themselves on track and to guide the audience. In addition, posters, flip charts, chalkboards, or interactive whiteboards can also help you make strong visual statements.

SLIDES FROM A STUDENT POWERPOINT PRESENTATION. For her class presentation, "Words, Images, and the Mystical Way They Work Together in Alison Bechdel's *Fun Home*," Shuqiao Song developed a series of very simple slides aimed at underscoring her points and keeping her audience focused on them. After introducing Bechdel and her book, Shuqiao provided an overview of the presentation as she clicked through the following slides:

So let me tell you, quickly, what I'll be doing in the rest of this presentation:

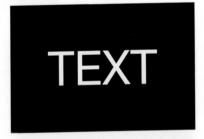

First, I'll show how text is *insufficient*, but also why it is *necessary* in Bechdel's story.

Second, I'll show how images can't be trusted yet why they are still necessary for Bechdel's purpose.

Each of these slides—with simple text and punctuation—serves to emphasize Shuqiao's point and keep the audience's attention on the relationship between word and image.

When you work with visuals for your own presentation, remember that they must be large enough to be easily seen and read. Be sure the information is simple, clear, and easy to understand. And remember *not* to read from your visuals or turn your back on your audience as you refer to them. Most important, make sure your visuals engage and help your listeners rather than distract them from your message. Try out each visual on your classmates, friends, or roommates: if they do not clearly grasp the meaning and purpose of the visual, scrap it and try again.

You may also want to prepare handouts for your audience: pertinent bibliographies, for example, or text too extensive to be presented otherwise. Unless the handouts include material you want your audience to use while you speak, distribute them at the end of the presentation.

TIPS FOR USING PRESENTATION MEDIA. Before you begin designing your presentation, make sure that the equipment you need will be available. As you design presentation slides, keep some simple principles in mind (for more on design, see Chapter 8):

- Audiences can't read and listen to you at the same time, so make the slides support what you are saying as clearly and visually as possible. Just one or two words — or a visual without words — may back up what you are saying more effectively than a list of bullets.
- Never simply read the text of your slides.
- Use your media wisely, and respect your audience's time. If you feel that you need to include more than three or four images or bullet points (or more than fifty words of text) on a slide, you may be trying to convey information in a slide show that would make more sense in a report. Rethink your presentation so that what you say and what you show work together to win over your audience.
- Use text on your slides to guide and interest your audience — not as a teleprompter.
- Make sure any text or visual you show is big and clear enough to be visible, and create a clear contrast between text or illustration and background. In general, light backgrounds work better in a darkened room, and dark backgrounds in a lighted one.
- Make sure that sound or video clips are audible and that they relate directly to your topic. If you use sound as background, make sure it does not distract from what you are trying to say.
- Take time to get peer reviews of your slides; others will see more clearly than you do whether the slides are clear and memorable.
- Give credit for any visuals or audio that you have not created yourself.

Practicing your presentation. Prepare a draft of your presentation far enough in advance to allow for several run-throughs. Some speakers record their rehearsals and then revise based on the taped performance. Others practice in front of a mirror or in front of colleagues or friends, who can comment on content and style.

Make sure you will be heard clearly. If you are soft-spoken, concentrate on projecting your voice; if your voice tends to rise when you're in the spotlight, practice lowering the pitch. If you speak rapidly, practice slowing down. It's usually best to avoid sarcasm in favor of a tone that conveys interest in your topic and listeners.

Timing your run-throughs will tell you whether you need to cut (or expand) material to make the presentation an appropriate length.

Making your presentation. To calm your nerves and get off to a good start, know your material thoroughly and use the following strategies to good advantage before, during, and after your presentation:

- Visualize your presentation with the aim of feeling comfortable during it.
- Consider doing some deep-breathing exercises before the presentation, and concentrate on relaxing; avoid too much caffeine.
- Be sure you can access everything you need. Assume that microphones are always live, and don't say anything you don't want the audience to hear.
- Pause before you begin, concentrating on your opening lines.
- If possible, stand up. Most speakers make a stronger impression standing rather than sitting.
- Face your audience at all times, and make eye contact as much as possible.
- Allow time for the audience to respond and ask questions.
- Thank your audience at the end of your presentation.

EXERCISE 6.1

Attend a lecture or presentation, and analyze its effectiveness. How does the speaker capture and hold your interest? What signpost language and other guides to listening can you detect? How well are visuals integrated into the presentation? How do the speaker's tone of voice, dress, and eye contact affect your understanding and appreciation (or lack of it)? What is most memorable about the presentation, and why? Bring your analysis to class, and report your findings.

EXERCISE 6.2: THINKING CRITICALLY

Study the text of an oral or multimedia presentation you've prepared or given. Using the advice in this chapter, see how well your presentation appeals to your audience. Look in particular at how well you catch and hold their attention. How effective is your use of signpost

 bedfordstmartins.com/wia
Video > Presentation is performance
Video > You want them to hear you

language or other structures that help guide your listeners? How helpful are the visuals (PowerPoint slides, posters) in conveying your message? What would you do to improve this presentation?

7   Writing in the Disciplines

A recent survey confirmed that good writing plays an important role in almost every profession. One MBA wrote, "Those who advance quickly in my company are those who write and speak well—it's as simple as that." But while writing is always a valuable skill, writing well means different things in different disciplines. As you prepare written assignments for various courses, then, you will need to become familiar with the expectations, vocabularies, styles, methods of proof, and conventional formats used in each field.

7a   Reading and writing for every discipline

Writing is central to learning regardless of the discipline. So whether you are explaining the results of a telephone survey you conducted for a psychology class, preparing a lab report for chemistry, conducting a case study for anthropology, or working on a proposal for material sciences and engineering, writing helps you get the job done.

One good way to learn to write well in a discipline is to read the texts others write. So read a lot, and pay attention to the texts you are reading. To get started, choose an article in an important journal in the field you plan to major in and then answer the following questions:

- How does a journal article in this discipline begin?
- How is the article organized? Does it have specific sections with subheads?
- What sources are cited, and how are they used—as backup support, as counter-examples, or as an argument to refute?
- How does the article conclude?
- What audience does the text seem to address? Is it aimed at a narrow technical or disciplinary audience, or a broader reading public? Is it addressed to readers of a specific journal? Is it published in print or online?

Finally, make sure you know whether the articles you are reading are from juried or nonjuried journals (13a). Juried journals use panels of expert readers to analyze proposed articles, so articles in juried journals have been recommended for publication by experts in the field. Nonjuried journals can also offer valuable information, but they may bear the stamp of the editor's biases more strongly than a juried journal would. To find out whether a journal is juried or nonjuried, check the submissions guidelines for information about whether submitted articles are sent to reviewers before publication.

For additional guidelines on reading critically, see Chapter 9.

CHECKLIST

Analyzing an Assignment

✔ **What is the purpose of the assignment?** Are you expected to join a discussion, demonstrate your mastery of the topic in writing, or something else?

✔ **Who is the audience?** The instructor will be one audience, but are there others? If so, who are they?

✔ **What does the assignment ask of you?** Look for key terms such as *summarize, explain, evaluate, interpret, illustrate,* and *define.*

✔ **Do you need clarification of any terms?** If so, ask your instructor.

✔ **What do you need to know or find out to complete the assignment?** You may need to do background reading, develop a procedure for analyzing or categorizing information, or carry out some other kind of preparation.

✔ **What does the instructor expect in a written response?** How will you use sources? What kinds of sources should you use? How should you organize and develop the assignment? What is the expected format and length?

✔ **Can you find a model of an effective response to a similar assignment?**

✔ **What do other students think the assignment requires?** Talking over an assignment with classmates is one good way to test your understanding.

7b   Academic assignments and expectations

When you receive an assignment, your first job is to be sure you understand what that assignment is asking you to do. Some assignments may be as vague as "Write a five-page essay on one aspect of the Civil War" or "Write an analysis of the group dynamics at play in your recent collaborative project for this course." Others may be fairly specific: "Collect, summarize, and interpret data drawn from a sample of letters to the editor published in two newspapers, one in a small rural community and one in an urban community, over a period of three months." Whatever the assignment, use the questions in the Checklist on p. 68 (and the information in Chapter 4) to analyze it.

EXERCISE 7.1

Analyze the following assignment from a communications course using the questions in the Checklist on p. 68.

> Assignment: Distribute a questionnaire to twenty people (ten male, ten female) asking these four questions: (1) What do you expect to say and do when you meet a stranger? (2) What don't you expect to say and do when you meet a stranger? (3) What do you expect to say and do when you meet a very close friend? (4) What don't you expect to say and do when you meet a very close friend?
>
> When you have collected your twenty questionnaires, read them over and answer the following questions:
>
> - What, if any, descriptions were common to all respondents' answers?
> - How do male and female responses compare?
> - What similarities and differences did you find between the responses to the stranger and to the very close friend?
> - What factors (environment, time, status, gender, and so on) do you think had an impact on these responses?
>
> Discuss your findings, using concepts and theories explained in your text.

 7c   Specialized vocabulary

Entering into an academic discipline or a profession is like going to a party where you don't know anyone. At first you feel like an outsider, and you may not understand much of what you hear or see. Before you enter the conversation, you have to listen and observe carefully. Eventually, however, you will be able to join in—and if you stay long enough, participating in the conversation becomes easy and natural.

To learn the routines, practices, and ways of knowing in a new field, you must also make an effort to enter into the conversation. A good way to get started is to study the vocabulary of the field you are most interested in.

Highlight the key terms in your reading or notes to learn how much specialized or technical vocabulary you will be expected to know. If you find only a small amount of specialized vocabulary, try to master the new terms quickly by reading your textbook carefully, looking up key words or phrases, and asking questions. If you find a great deal of specialized vocabulary, however, you may want to familiarize yourself with it methodically. Any of the following procedures may help:

- Keep a log of unfamiliar words used in context. Check definitions in your textbook's glossary or index, or consult a specialized dictionary.

- See if your textbook has a glossary of terms (see the index) or sets of definitions. Study pertinent sections to master the terms.

- Work with key concepts. Even if the concepts are not yet entirely clear to you, using them will help you understand them. For example, in a statistics class, try to work out (in words) how to do an analysis of *covariance*, step by step, even if you are not sure of the precise definition of the term. Or try to plot the narrative progression in a story even if you are still not entirely sure of the definition of *narrative progression*.

- Take special note of the ways technical language or disciplinary vocabulary is used in online information related to a particular field.

7d   Disciplinary style

Another important way to learn about a discipline is to identify its stylistic features. Study pieces of writing in the field with the following in mind:

- **Overall tone.** How would you describe it? (See 4f.)
- **Title.** Are titles generally descriptive ("Findings from a Double-Blind Study of the Effect of Antioxidants"), persuasive ("Antioxidants Proven Effective"), or something else? How does the title shape your expectations?
- **Stance.** To what extent do writers in the field strive for distance and objectivity? What strategies help them to achieve this stance? (See 4d.)
- **Sentence length.** Are sentences long and complex? Simple and direct?
- **Voice.** Are verbs generally active or passive? Why? (See 23e.)
- **Person.** Do writers use the first-person *I* or third-person terms such as *the investigator*? What is the effect of this choice?
- **Visuals.** Do writers typically use elements such as graphs, tables, maps, or photographs? How are visuals integrated into the text? What role, if any, do headings and other formatting elements play in the writing? (See Chapter 8.)
- **Documentation style.** Do writers use MLA, APA, *Chicago*, or CSE style? (See Chapters 49–52.)

Of course, writings within a single discipline may have different purposes and different styles. A chemist may write a grant proposal, a lab notebook, a literature review, a research report, and a lab report, each with a different purpose and style.

7e Use of evidence

As you grow familiar with an area of study, you will develop a sense of what it takes to prove a point in that field. You can speed up this process, however, by investigating and questioning. The following questions will help you think about the use of evidence in materials you read:

- How do writers in the field use precedent and authority? What or who counts as an authority in this field? How are the credentials of an authority established? (See 11e.)
- What kinds of quantitative data (countable or measurable items) are used, and for what purposes? How are the data gathered and presented?

- How are qualitative data (systematically observed items) used?
- How are statistics used and presented? Are tables, charts, graphs, or other visuals important, and why?
- How is logical reasoning used? How are definition, cause and effect, analogy, and example used?
- How does the field use primary materials—firsthand sources of information—and secondary sources reported by others? (See 13a.) How is each type of source presented?
- What kinds of textual evidence are cited?
- How are quotations and other references to sources used and integrated into the text? (See Chapter 15.)

EXERCISE 7.2

Read a few journals associated with your prospective major or a discipline of particular interest to you, using the preceding questions to study the use of evidence in that discipline. If you are keeping a writing log, make an entry summarizing all that you have learned.

7f   Conventional patterns and formats

To produce effective writing in a discipline, you need to know the field's generally accepted formats for organizing and presenting evidence. Although these formats can vary widely from discipline to discipline and even from instructor to instructor, common patterns do emerge. A typical laboratory report, for instance, follows a fairly standard organizational framework and usually has a certain look. A case study in sociology or education or anthropology likewise follows a typical organizational plan. Ask your instructor to recommend good examples of the kind of writing you will do in the course; then analyze these examples in terms of format, design, and organization. You might also look at major scholarly journals in the field to see what types of formats seem most common and how each is organized.

7g   Ethical issues

Writers in all disciplines face ethical questions. Those who plan and carry out research on living people, for example, must be careful to avoid harming their subjects. Researchers in all fields must be scrupulous in presenting data to make sure that others can replicate research and test claims. And although writers in any discipline should take into consideration their own interests, those of their collaborators, and those of their employers, they must also responsibly safeguard the interests of the general public.

Fortunately, a growing number of disciplines have now adopted guidelines for ethics. The American Psychological Association has been a pioneer in this area, and many other professional organizations and companies have their own codes or standards of ethics. These guidelines can help you make decisions about day-to-day writing. Even so, you will no doubt encounter situations where the right or ethical decision is murky at best. In such situations, consult your own conscience first and then talk your choices over with colleagues you respect before coming to a decision on how to proceed.

7h Collaboration and communication

In contemporary academic and business environments, working with others is a highly valued skill. Such collaboration happens when classmates divide research and writing duties to create a multimedia presentation, when peer reviewers share advice on a draft, or when colleagues in an office offer their views on appropriate revisions for a company-wide document.

Because people all over the world now have the ability to research, study, write, and work together, you must be able to communicate effectively within and across cultures. Conventions for academic writing (or for forms of online communication) can vary from culture to culture, from discipline to discipline, and from one form of English to another. What is considered polite in one culture may seem rude in another, so those who communicate globally must take care to avoid giving offense — or taking it where none was intended. (For more information on writing across cultures, see Chapter 17.)

EXERCISE 7.3: THINKING CRITICALLY

Thinking about Your Own Writing in a Discipline

Choose a piece of writing you have produced for a class in a particular discipline — a blog or other posting, a laboratory report, a review of the literature, or any other written assignment. Examine your writing closely for its use of that discipline's vocabulary, style, methods of proof, and conventional formats. How comfortable are

---

 bedfordstmartins.com/wia
Video > Working with other people

you writing a piece of this kind? In what ways are you using the conventions of the discipline easily and well? What conventions give you difficulty, and why? You might talk to an instructor in this field about the conventions and requirements for writing in the discipline. Make notes on how to be a better writer in the field.

7i   Writing for the humanities

Disciplines in the humanities are concerned with what it means to be human: historians reconstruct the past; literary critics analyze and interpret texts portraying the human condition; philosophers raise questions about truth, knowledge, beauty, and justice; scholars of languages learn to inhabit other cultures. In these and other ways, those in the humanities strive to explore, interpret, and reconstruct the human experience.

Reading texts in the humanities.   The interpretation of texts is central to the humanities disciplines. A reader in the humanities needs the tools to analyze a text — whether a primary or secondary source, ancient or modern, literary or historical, verbal or visual — and carefully consider the arguments it makes.

To read critically in the humanities (2d and Chapter 9), you will need to pose questions and construct hypotheses as you read. You may ask, for instance, why a writer makes some points or develops some examples but omits others. Rather than finding meaning only in the surface information that texts or artifacts convey, use your own questions and hypotheses to create fuller meanings — to construct the significance of what you read.

To successfully engage texts, you must recognize that you are not a neutral observer, not an empty cup into which meaning is poured. If such were the case, writing would have exactly the same meanings for all of us, and reading would be a fairly boring affair. If you have ever gone to a movie with a friend and each come away with a completely different response, you already understand that a text never has just one meaning. Most humanities courses will expect you to exercise your interpretive powers; the following guidelines will help you build your strengths as a close reader of humanities texts.

Writing texts in the humanities.   The strongest writers in the humanities use the findings from their close examination of a text or artifact to develop an argument or to construct an analysis.

CHECKLIST

Guidelines for Reading Texts in the Humanities

1. **Be clear about the purpose of the text.** The two most common purposes for works in the humanities are to provide information and to argue for a particular interpretation. Pay attention to whether the text presents opinions or facts, to what is included and omitted, and to how facts are presented to the audience. (14c)

2. **Get an overall impression.** What does the work make you think about — and why? What is most remarkable or memorable? What confuses you?

3. **Annotate the text.** Be prepared to "talk back," ask questions, note emerging patterns or themes, and point out anything out of place or ineffective. (See Chapter 9.)

4. **Look at the context.** Consider the time and place represented in the work as well as when and where the writer lived. You may also consider social, political, or personal forces that may have affected the writer.

5. **Think about the audience.** Who are the readers or viewers the writer seems to address? Do they include you?

6. **Pay attention to genre.** What category does the work fall into (graphic novel, diary, political cartoon, sermon, argumentative essay, Hollywood western)? What is noteworthy about the form? How does it conform to or subvert your expectations about the genre? (4f)

7. **Note the point of view.** Whose point of view is represented? How does it affect your response?

8. **Notice the major themes.** Are specific claims being advanced? How are these claims supported?

9. **Understand the difference between primary and secondary sources.** Primary sources provide firsthand knowledge, while secondary sources report on or analyze the research of others. (13a)

ASSIGNMENTS. Common assignments that make use of these skills of close reading, analysis, and argument include summaries, response pieces, position papers, critical analyses of primary and secondary sources, and research-based projects. A philosophy student, for example, might need to summarize an argument, critique a text's logic and effectiveness, or discuss a moral issue from a particular philosophical perspective. A literature assignment may ask a reader to look very closely at a particular text ("Examine the role of chocolate in Toni Morrison's *Tar Baby*") or to go well beyond a primary text ("Discuss the impact of agribusiness on modernist novels"). History students often write reviews of books or articles ("Write a critical review of Jane Addams's *Twenty Years at Hull-House*, paying special attention to the writer's purpose and goals and relating these to the larger settlement house movement in America") along with primary source analyses or research papers.

For papers in literature, modern languages, and philosophy, writers often use the documentation style of the Modern Language Association; see Chapter 49 for advice on using MLA style. For papers in history and other areas of the humanities, writers often use the documentation style of the University of Chicago Press; see Chapter 51 for advice on using *Chicago* style.

ANALYSIS AND CRITICAL STANCE. To analyze a text, you need to develop a critical stance—the approach you will take to the work—that can help you develop a thesis or major claim (see 4d and 5b). To evaluate the text and present a critical response to it, you should look closely at the text itself, including its style; at the context in which it was produced; and at the audience the text aims to reach, which may or may not include yourself.

A close look at the text itself includes considering its genre, form, point of view, and themes, and looking at the stylistic features, such as word choice, use of imagery, visuals, and design. Considering context means asking why the text was created—thinking about the original (and current) context and about how attitudes and ideas of its era may have influenced it. Considering audience means thinking about who the intended audience might be, and about how people outside this intended group might respond. Think about your personal response to the text as well. (See also Chapters 4, 9, and 10.)

Carrying out these steps should provide you with plenty of material to work with as you begin to shape a critical thesis and write your analysis. You can begin by grounding your analysis in one or more important questions you have about the work.

WRITING A LITERARY ANALYSIS. When you analyze or interpret a literary work, think of your thesis as answering a question about an aspect of the work. The guiding question you bring to the literary work will help you decide on a critical stance toward the work. For example, a student writing about Shakespeare's *Macbeth* might find her curiosity piqued by the many comic moments that appear in this tragedy. She could build on her curiosity by turning the question of why Shakespeare uses so much comedy in *Macbeth* into the following thesis statement, which proposes an answer to the question: "The many unexpected comic moments in *Macbeth* emphasize how disordered the world becomes for murderers like Macbeth and his wife."

EXERCISE 7.4: THINKING CRITICALLY

Choose at least two projects or assignments you have written for different disciplines in the humanities — say, history and film. Re-read these papers with an eye to their similarities. What features do they have in common? Do they use similar methods of analysis and value similar kinds of evidence, for instance? In what ways do they differ? Based on your analysis, what conclusions can you draw about these two disciplines?

7j Writing for the social sciences

When do most workers begin to save toward retirement? What role do television ads play in a voter's decision-making process? How do children learn to read? The social sciences — psychology, anthropology, political science, speech, communication, sociology, economics, and education — try to answer such questions. The social sciences share with the humanities an interest in what it means to be human, and they share with the natural and applied sciences the goal of engaging in systematic, observable study. All the social sciences aim to identify, understand, and explain patterns of human behavior.

Reading texts in the social sciences. Strong readers in the social sciences — as in any subject — ask questions, analyze, and interpret as they read, whether they are reading an academic paper that sets forth a theoretical premise or overall theory and defends it, a case study that describes a particular case and draws out inferences and implications from it, or a research report that presents the results of an investigation into an important question in the field. Most of what students read in the social sciences is trying to prove a point, and readers need to evaluate whether that point is supported.

The social sciences, like other disciplines, often use specialized vocabulary as shorthand for complex ideas that otherwise would take paragraphs to explain.

QUALITATIVE AND QUANTITATIVE STUDIES. Different texts in the social and natural sciences may call for different methods and strategies. Texts that report the results of *quantitative* studies collect data represented with numerical measurements drawn from surveys, polls, experiments, and tests. For example, a study of voting patterns in southern states might rely on quantitative data such as statistics. Texts that report the results of *qualitative* studies rely on non-numerical methods such as interviews and observations to reveal social patterns. A study of the way children in one kindergarten class develop rules of play, for instance, would draw on qualitative data — observations of social interaction, interviews with students and teachers, and so on. Of course, some work in the social and behavioral sciences combines quantitative and qualitative data and methods: an educational report might begin with statistical data related to a problem and then move to a qualitative case study to exemplify what the statistics reveal.

In the social sciences, both quantitative and qualitative researchers must determine what they are examining and measuring in order to get answers to research questions. A researcher who studies childhood aggression must first define and measure *aggression*. If the research is qualitative, a researcher may describe types of behavior that indicate aggression and then discuss observations of children and interviews with teachers and peers about those behaviors. A quantitative researcher, on the other hand, might design an experiment that notes how often children hit a punching bag or that asks children to rate their peers' aggression on a scale of one to ten.

It's important to recognize that both quantitative and qualitative studies have points of view, and that researchers' opinions influence everything from the hypothesis and the design of the research study to the interpretation of findings. Readers must consider whether the researchers' views are sensible and solidly supported by evidence, and they must pay close attention to the kind of data the writer is using and what those data can — and cannot — prove. For example, if researchers of childhood aggression define *aggression* in a way that readers find unpersuasive, or if they observe behaviors that readers consider playful rather than aggressive, then the readers will likely not accept their interpretation of the findings.

CONVENTIONAL FORMATS. Make use of conventional disciplinary formats to help guide your reading in the social sciences. Many such texts conform to the format and documentation style of the American Psychological Association (APA). In addition, articles often include standard features—an abstract that gives an overview of the findings, followed by the introduction, review of literature, methods, results, discussion, and references. Readers who become familiar with such a format can easily find the information they need. (For more on APA style, see Chapter 50.)

Writing texts in the social sciences. Perhaps because the social sciences share concerns with both the humanities and the sciences, the forms of writing within the social sciences are particularly varied, including summaries, abstracts, literature reviews, reaction pieces, position papers, radio scripts, briefing notes, book reviews, briefs, research proposals, research papers, quantitative research reports, case studies, ethnographic analyses, and meta-analyses. Such an array of writing assignments could seem overwhelming, but in fact these assignments can be organized under five main categories:

- **Writing that encourages student learning**—reaction pieces, position papers
- **Writing that demonstrates student learning**—summaries, abstracts, research papers
- **Writing that reflects common on-the-job communication tasks undertaken by members of a discipline**—radio scripts, briefing notes, informational reports
- **Writing that requires students to analyze and evaluate the writings of others**—literature reviews, book reviews, briefs
- **Writing that asks students to replicate the work of others or to engage in original research**—quantitative research reports, case studies, ethnographic analyses

Many forms of writing in the social sciences call either explicitly or implicitly for argument (see Chapter 10). If you write an essay reporting on the results of a survey you developed about attitudes toward physician-assisted suicide among students on your campus, you will make an explicit argument about the significance of your data. But even in other forms of writing, such as summaries and book reports, you will implicitly argue that your description and analysis provide a clear, thorough overview of the text(s) you have read.

THE LITERATURE REVIEW. Students of the social sciences carry out literature reviews to find out the most current thinking about a topic, to learn what research has already been carried out on that topic, to evaluate the work that has been done, and to set any research they will do in context. The following guidelines are designed to help you explore and question sources, looking for flaws or gaps. Such a critical review could then lead to a discussion of how your own research will avoid such flaws and advance knowledge.

- What is your topic of interest? What is the dependent variable (the item or characteristic being studied)?

- What is already known about this topic? What characteristics does the topic or dependent variable have? How have other researchers measured the item or characteristic being studied? What other factors are involved, and how are they related to each other and to your topic or variable? What theories are used to explain the way things are now?

- How has research been done so far? Who or what has been studied? How have measurements been taken?

- Has there been change over time? What has caused any changes?

- What problems do you identify in the current research? What questions have not been answered yet? What conclusions have researchers drawn that might not be warranted?

- What gaps will your research fill? What new information or ideas does it contribute? What problems do you want to correct?

EXERCISE 7.5

Identify a literature review in a social-science field you are interested in (ask your instructor or a reference librarian if you need help finding one), and read it carefully, noting how it addresses the questions above. Bring your notes to class for discussion.

EXERCISE 7.6: THINKING CRITICALLY

Reading with an Eye for Writing in the Social Sciences

Choose two readings from a social-science discipline, and read them with an eye toward issues of style. Does the use of disciplinary terms and concepts seem appropriate? In what ways do the

---

 bedfordstmartins.com/wia
Student Writing > Social sciences research essay, Merlla McLaughlin

texts attempt to engage readers? If the texts are not clear and understandable, how might they be improved?

Thinking about Your Own Writing in the Social Sciences

Choose a text you like that you have written for a social-science discipline. Then examine your style in this paper to see how well you have engaged your readers. Note variation in sentence length and type (do you, for example, use any questions?), number of active and passive verbs, use of concrete examples and everyday language, and so on. How would you rate your writing as a social scientist?

7k   Writing for the natural and applied sciences

Whether they are studying geological faults or developing a stronger support structure for suspension bridges, scientists and engineers in the natural and applied sciences want to understand how the physical and natural worlds work. Natural sciences such as biology, chemistry, and physics study the natural world and its phenomena; applied sciences such as nanotechnology and mechanical engineering apply knowledge from the natural sciences to practical problems. More than many other scholars, scientists and engineers are likely to leave the privacy of their office or lab for fieldwork and experimentation. Whether done in the lab or the field, however, writing—from the first grant proposal to the final report or scientific paper—plays a key role in the natural and applied sciences.

Reading texts in the natural and applied sciences.   Scientists and engineers work with evidence that can be observed, verified, and controlled. Though they cannot avoid interpretation, they strive for objectivity by using the scientific method—observing or studying phenomena, formulating a hypothesis about the phenomena, and testing that hypothesis through controlled experiments and observations. Scientists and engineers aim to generate precise, replicable data; they develop experiments to account for extraneous factors. In this careful, precise way, scientists and engineers identify, test, and write persuasively about theoretical and real-world problems.

IDENTIFYING THE ARGUMENT.   As you read in the sciences, try to become familiar with disciplinary terms, concepts, and formats as soon as possible, and practice reading—and listening—for detail.

If you are reading a first-year biology textbook, you can draw upon some general critical-reading strategies. In addition, charts, graphs, illustrations, models, and other visuals often play an important role in scientific writing, so your ability to read and comprehend these visual displays of knowledge is particularly important. (See Chapter 9.)

When you read a science or engineering textbook, you can assume that the information presented there is authoritative and as objective as possible. When you read specialized materials, however, recognize that although scholarly reports undergo significant peer review, they nevertheless represent arguments (see Chapter 10). The connection between facts and claims in the sciences, as in all subject areas, is created by the author rather than simply revealed by the data. So read both facts and claims with a questioning eye: Did the scientist choose the best method to test the hypothesis? Are there other reasonable interpretations of the experiment's results? Do other studies contradict the conclusions of this experiment? When you read specialized texts in the sciences with questions like these in mind, you are reading—and thinking—like a scientist. (For additional information on assessing a source's credibility, see 14c.)

CONVENTIONAL FORMATS. As you advance in your course work, you will need to develop reading strategies for increasingly specialized texts. Many scientific texts conform to the format and documentation style of the Council of Science Editors (CSE); for more on CSE style, see Chapter 52. (However, you should be prepared to follow an instructor's guidelines for citation and references if another style is used in your discipline or in a particular course.) In addition, articles often include standard features—an abstract that gives an overview of the findings, followed by an introduction, literature review, materials and methods, results, discussion, and references.

You might expect to read a journal article for a science or engineering course from start to finish, giving equal weight to each section. However, an experienced reader in sciences and engineering might skim an abstract to see if an article warrants further reading. If it does—and this judgment is based on the reader's own research interest—he or she might then read the introduction to understand the rationale for the experiment and then skip to the results. A reader with a specific interest in the methods will read that section with particular care.

EXERCISE 7.7

Choose a respected journal in a discipline in the natural or applied sciences that interests you. (Ask your instructor or a reference librarian if you need help identifying a journal.) Then read quickly through two articles, taking notes on the author's use of any headings and subheadings, specialized vocabulary, visuals, and evidence. Bring the results of your investigation to class for discussion.

Writing texts in the natural and applied sciences.

Students in the sciences and engineering must be able to respond to a diverse range of writing and speaking tasks. Often, they must maintain lab or engineering notebooks that include careful records of experiments. They also write memos, papers, project proposals and reports, literature reviews, and progress reports; in addition, they may develop print and Web-based presentations for both technical and lay audiences (see 6b). Particularly common writing assignments in the sciences are the literature review, research proposal, and research report.

Scientists undertake *literature reviews* to keep up with and evaluate developments in their field. Literature reviews are an essential first step in any research effort, for they enable scientists to discover what research has already been completed and how they might build on earlier efforts. Successful literature reviews demonstrate a student's ability to identify relevant research on a topic and to summarize and in some instances evaluate that research.

Most scientists spend a lot of time writing research or *grant proposals* aimed at securing funds to support their research. Undergraduate writers often have an opportunity to make similar proposals—to an office of undergraduate research or to a science-based firm that supports student research, for instance. Funding agencies often have guidelines for preparing a proposal. Proposals for research funding generally include the following sections: title page, introduction, purpose(s) and significance of the study, methods, timeline, budget, and references. You may also need to submit an abstract.

Research reports, another common writing form in the sciences, may include both literature reviews and discussions of primary research, most often experiments. Like journal articles, research reports generally follow this form: title, author(s), abstract, introduction, literature review, materials and methods, results, discussion, and references. Many instructors ask students to write lab reports, which are briefer versions of research reports and may not include a literature review.

Today, a great deal of scientific writing is collaborative. As students move from introductory to advanced courses and then to the workplace, they increasingly find themselves working as part of teams or groups. Indeed, in such areas as engineering, collaborative projects are often the norm.

STYLE IN THE NATURAL AND APPLIED SCIENCES. In general, use the present tense for most writing you do in the natural and applied sciences. Use the past tense, however, when you are describing research already carried out (by you or others) or published in the past (23c).

Writers in the sciences need to produce complex figures, tables, images, and models, and use software designed to analyze data or run computer simulations. In addition, they need to present data carefully. If you create a graph, you should provide headings for columns, label axes with numbers or units, and identify data points. Caption figures and tables with a number and descriptive title. And avoid orphan data — data that you present in a figure or table but don't comment on in your text.

Finally, make sure that any writing you do is as clear, concise, and grammatically correct as possible to ensure that readers see you as capable and credible.

EXERCISE 7.8: THINKING CRITICALLY

Reading with an Eye for Writing in the Sciences

Identify one or more features of scientific texts, and consider their usefulness. Why, for instance, does an abstract precede the actual article? How do scientific nomenclatures, classification systems, and other features of scientific writing aid the work of scientists? Try to identify the functions that textual elements such as these play in the ongoing work of science. Finally, research the scientific method to see how it is served by the features of scientific writing discussed in this chapter.

Thinking about Your Own Writing in the Sciences

Choose a piece of writing you did for a natural or applied science class — a lab report, a research report, a proposal — and read it carefully. Note the format and headings you used, how you presented visual data, what kinds of evidence you used, and what citation system you used. Compare your piece of writing with a similar piece of writing published in a journal in the field. How well does your writing compare? What differences are most noticeable between your writing and that of the published piece?

e bedfordstmartins.com/wia
Student Writing > Chemistry lab report, Allyson Goldberg

71   # Writing for business

Written communication is essential in identifying and solving the complex problems of today's companies. To succeed in business, you need to know how to manage many kinds of writing — from negotiating an ever-increasing number of email messages to communicating effectively with readers from Manhattan, Montgomery, Mexico City, and Mumbai.

Reading texts for business.   Readers in business face a dizzying array of demands. A team of businesspeople today has almost unlimited access to information and to people, such as economists and scientists, whose expertise can be of use in the business world. Somehow, the members of this team need to negotiate a huge stream of information and to evaluate that information.

To meet these demands, you can draw on general strategies for effective reading (see Chapter 9). One such strategy — keeping a clear purpose in mind when you read — is particularly important when you are engaged in work-related reading. Are you reading to solve a problem? to gather and synthesize information? to make a recommendation? Knowing why you are reading will increase your productivity. Time constraints and deadline pressures will also affect your decisions about what and how to read; the ability to identify important information quickly is a skill you will cultivate as a business reader.

Writing texts for business.   Writing assignments in business classes serve two related functions. While their immediate goal is to help you master the theory and practice of business, these assignments also prepare you for the kinds of writing you will face in the world of work. For this reason, students in *every* discipline need to know how to write effective business memos, emails, letters, résumés, and reports.

MEMO. Memos are a common form of print or electronic correspondence sent within and between organizations. Memos tend to be brief internal documents, often dealing with only one subject.

EMAIL. Business email can be formatted much like a print memo but is easier to create and store and faster to distribute. Remember, however, that email is essentially public and that employers have

e bedfordstmartins.com/wia
Student Writing > Memo, Michelle Abbott and Carina Abernathy

CHECKLIST

Guidelines for Writing Effective Memos

✔ Write the name of the recipient, your name, the subject, and the date on separate lines at the top.

✔ Begin with the most important information: depending on the memo's purpose, you may provide background information, define the task or problem, or clarify the memo's goal.

✔ Use your opening paragraph to focus on how the information you convey affects your readers.

✔ Focus each subsequent paragraph on one idea pertaining to the subject.

✔ Present information concisely and from the readers' perspective.

✔ Emphasize exactly what you want readers to do and when.

✔ Use attachments for detailed supporting information.

✔ For print memos, initial your memo next to your name.

✔ Adjust your style and tone to fit your audience.

✔ Attempt to build goodwill in your conclusion.

easy access to email written by employees. As always, it's best to use discretion and caution in email, especially on the job.

LETTER. Despite the popularity of email, letter writing remains an important skill. When you send a business or professional letter, you are writing either as an individual or as a representative of an organization. In either case, and regardless of your purpose, a business letter should follow certain conventions.

The letter of application or cover letter often accompanies a résumé. The purpose of a letter of application is to demonstrate how the experiences and skills you outline in your résumé have prepared you for a particular job; it is important to focus on how you can benefit the company, not how the company can help you. If you are responding to a particular advertisement, mention it in the opening paragraph. Finally, be sure to indicate how you can be reached for an interview.

e bedfordstmartins.com/wia
Student Writing > Application letter, Nastassia Lopez

CHECKLIST

Guidelines for Writing Effective Letters

✔ Use a conventional format.

✔ Whenever possible, write to a specific person (*Dear Tom Robinson* or *Dear Ms. Otuteye*) rather than to a general *Dear Sir or Madam*.

✔ Open cordially and be polite — even if you have a complaint.

✔ State the reason for your letter clearly. Include whatever details will help your reader see your point and respond.

✔ If appropriate, make clear what you hope your reader will do.

✔ Express appreciation for your reader's attention.

✔ Make it easy for your reader to respond by including contact information and, if appropriate, a self-addressed, stamped envelope.

RÉSUMÉ. While a letter of application usually emphasizes specific parts of the résumé, telling how your background is suited to a particular job, a résumé summarizes your experience and qualifications and provides support for your letter. An effective résumé is brief, usually one or two pages.

Research shows that employers generally spend less than a minute reading a résumé. Remember that they are interested not in what they can do for you but what you can do for them. They expect a résumé to be formatted neatly, and your aim is to use clear headings and adequate spacing that will make it easy to read. Although you may be tempted to use colored paper or unusual type styles, avoid such temptations. A well-written résumé with a standard format and typeface is the best way to distinguish yourself.

Your résumé may be arranged chronologically (from most to least recent) or functionally (based on skills or expertise). Include the following information:

1. **Name, address, phone numbers, and email address.**
2. **Career objective(s).** List immediate or short-term goals and specific jobs for which you realistically qualify.

---

e **bedfordstmartins.com/wia**
Student Writing > Résumé, Dennis Tyler Jr.

3. **Educational background.** Include degrees, diplomas, majors, and special programs or courses that pertain to your field of interest. List honors and scholarships and your grade-point average if it is high.

4. **Work experience.** Identify each job — whether a paying job, an internship, or military experience — with dates and names of organizations. Describe your duties by carefully selecting strong action verbs.

5. **Skills, personal interests, activities, awards, and honors.**

6. **References.** List two or three people who know your work well, first asking their permission. Give their titles, addresses, and phone or fax numbers. Or simply say that your references are available on request.

7. **Keywords** (for a scannable résumé). In general, nouns function as keywords for résumés that are scanned by search engines. Look for places where you can convert verbs (*performed laboratory tests*) to nouns (*laboratory technologist*). Place the most important keywords toward the beginning of the résumé.

Increasingly, job seekers are composing online résumés as hypertext screen documents, which make keywords more visible to search engines and thus tend to produce more hits. In addition, some businesses ask applicants to fill out résumé forms on company Web sites. In such cases, take special care to make sure that you have caught any error or typo before submitting the form.

EXERCISE 7.9: THINKING CRITICALLY

Reading with an Eye for Writing in Business

Monitor your mail and email for a few days, saving everything that tries to sell a product, provide a service, or solicit information or money. Then go through these pieces of business writing and advertising, and choose the one you find most effective. What about the writing appeals to you or gets and holds your attention? What might lead you to buy the product, choose the service, or make a contribution? What might make the piece of writing even more effective? Bring the results of your investigation to class for discussion.

Thinking about Your Own Business Writing

Chances are, you have written a letter of application for a job, completed a résumé, or sent some business-related letters or email messages. Choose a piece of business-related writing that is important to you or that represents your best work, and then analyze it carefully. How clear is the writing? How well do you represent yourself in the writing? Do you follow the conventions for business letters, résumés, memos, and so on? Make notes on what you could do to improve this piece of writing.

8 Making Design Decisions

Because visual and design elements such as headings, lists, fonts, images, and graphics can help you get and keep a reader's attention, they bring a whole new dimension to writing — what some call *visual rhetoric*.

8a Plan a visual structure.

Effective writers consider the visual structure of any text they create. Their design decisions guide readers by making texts easier on the eyes and easier to understand.

Print and electronic options.   One of your first design decisions will be choosing between print delivery and electronic delivery. In general, print documents are easily portable, easy to read without technical assistance, and relatively fast to produce. In addition, the tools for producing print texts are highly developed and stable. Electronic texts, on the other hand, can include sound, animation, and video; updates are easy to make; distribution is fast and efficient; and feedback can be swift. In many writing situations, the assignment will tell you whether to create a print document or an electronic text. Whether you are working to produce a text to be read in print or on a screen (or both), however, you should rely on some basic design principles.

Design principles.   Designer Robin Williams, in her *Non-Designer's Design Book*, points out several very simple principles for designing effective texts — contrast, alignment, repetition, and proximity.

CONTRAST.   Contrast attracts your eye to elements on a page and guides you around it, helping you follow an argument or find information. You may achieve contrast through the use of color, icons, boldface or large type size, headings, and so on. Begin with a focus point — the dominant point, image, or words where you want your reader's eye to go first — and structure the flow of your visual information from this point.

ALIGNMENT. Alignment refers to the way visuals and text on a page are lined up, both horizontally and vertically. The overall guideline is not to mix alignments arbitrarily. That is, if you begin with a left alignment, stick with it for the major parts of your page. The result will be a cleaner and more organized look. In this book, for example, headings always align with the left margin.

REPETITION. Readers are guided by the repetition of key words and elements. Use a consistent design throughout your document for such elements as color, typeface, and images.

PROXIMITY. Parts of a text that are closely related should appear together (*proximate* to one another). Your goal is to position related points, text, and visuals near one another and to use clear headings to identify these clusters.

CONSISTENT OVERALL IMPRESSION. Aim for a design that creates the appropriate overall impression or mood for your text. For an academic essay, you will probably make conservative choices that strike a serious scholarly note. In a newsletter for a campus group, you might choose attention-getting images.

8b Choose appropriate formats.

With so many options available, you should spend some time thinking about appropriate formatting elements for your text. Although the following guidelines often apply, remember that print documents, Web pages, slide shows, videos, and so on all have their own formatting conventions.

White space. Use white space, or negative space, to emphasize and direct readers to parts of the page. White space determines a page's density—the distance between information bits. You consider white space at the page level (margins), paragraph level (space between paragraphs), and sentence level (space between sentences). Within the page, you can also use white space around particular content, such as a graphic or list, to make it stand out.

Color. Decisions about color depend to a large extent not only on the kind of equipment you are using—and, for printing, who's paying for the color ink cartridges—but also on the purpose(s) of your document and its intended audience. As you design your documents, keep in mind that some colors can evoke powerful responses,

CONSIDERING DISABILITIES

Color for Contrast

Remember when you are using color that not everyone will see it as you do. Some individuals do not perceive color at all; others perceive color in a variety of ways, especially colors like blue and green, which are close together on the color spectrum. When putting colors next to one another, then, use those on opposite sides of the color spectrum, such as purple and gold, in order to achieve high contrast. Doing so will allow readers to see the contrast, if not the nuances, of color.

so take care that the colors you use match the message you are sending. Here are some other tips about the effective use of color:

- Use color to draw attention to elements you want to emphasize: headings, bullets, text boxes, or parts of charts or graphs.

- Be consistent in your use of color; use the same color for all subheads, for example.

- For most documents, keep the number of colors fairly small; too many colors can create a jumbled or confused look.

- Avoid colors that clash or that are hard on the eyes.

- Make sure all color visuals and text are legible in the format where they will be read. What appears readable on the screen — where colors can be sharper — may be less legible in a printed document.

Paper.   The quality of the paper affects the overall look and feel of print documents. Although inexpensive paper is fine for your earlier drafts, use 8½" × 11" good-quality white bond paper for your final presentation. For résumés, you may wish to use parchment or cream-colored bond. For brochures and posters, colored paper may be appropriate as long as your text is still readable. Use the best-quality printer that's available to you for your final product.

Pagination.   Your instructor may ask that you follow a particular pagination format for print texts (for MLA, APA, *Chicago,* and CSE styles, see Chapters 49–52); if not, beginning with the first page of text, place your last name and a number in the upper-right-hand corner of the page.

FOR MULTILINGUAL WRITERS

Reading Patterns

In documents written in English and other Western languages, information tends to flow from left to right and top to bottom — since that is the way English texts are written. In some languages, which may be written from right to left or vertically, documents may be arranged from top right to bottom left. Understanding the reading patterns of the language you are working in will help you design your documents most effectively.

Type. Computers allow writers to choose among a great variety of type sizes and typefaces, or fonts. For most college writing, the easy-to-read 11- or 12-point type size is best.

This is 12-point Times New Roman
This is 11-point Times New Roman

A serif font, as is used in the main text of this book, is generally easier to read in print than a **sans serif font**. Although unusual fonts might seem attractive at first glance, readers may find such styles distracting and hard to read over lengthy stretches of material.

Remember that typefaces help you create the tone of a document, so consider your audience and purpose when selecting type.

Different fonts convey different feelings.
Different fonts convey different feelings.
DIFFERENT FONTS CONVEY DIFFERENT FEELINGS.
Different fonts convey different feelings.

Most important, be consistent in the size and style of typeface you use, especially for the main part of your text. Unless you are striving for some special effect, shifting sizes and fonts within a document can give an appearance of disorderliness.

Spacing. Final drafts for most of your college writing should be double-spaced, with the first line of paragraphs indented one-half inch. Certain kinds of writing for particular disciplines may call for different spacing. Letters, memorandums, and online texts, for example, are usually single-spaced, with no paragraph indentation.

Some long print reports may be printed with one-and-a-half-line spacing to save paper. Other kinds of documents, such as flyers and newsletters, may call for multiple columns. If in doubt, consult your instructor.

In general, leave one space after all punctuation except in the following cases:

- Leave no space before or after a dash (*Please respond—right away—to this message*).
- Leave no space before or after a hyphen (*a red-letter day*).
- Leave no space between punctuation marks (*"on my way,"*).

Computers allow you to decide whether or not you want both side margins justified, or squared off—as they are on this page. Except in posters and other writing where you are trying to achieve a distinctive visual effect, you should always justify the left margin, though you may decide to indent lists and blocks of text that are set off. However, most readers—and many instructors—prefer the right margin to be "ragged," or unjustified.

8c Use headings appropriately.

For brief essays and reports, you may need no headings at all. For longer documents, however, these devices call attention to the organization of the text and thus aid comprehension. Some kinds of reports use set headings (such as *Abstract* and *Summary*), which readers expect and writers therefore must provide; see 50e for an example. When you use headings, you need to decide on type size and style, wording, and placement.

Type size and style. This book, which is a long and complex document, uses various levels of headings. These levels of headings are distinguished by type sizes and fonts as well as by color.

In a college paper, you will usually distinguish levels of headings using only type—for example, all capitals for the first-level headings, capitals and lowercase boldface for the second level, capitals and lowercase italics for the third level, and so on.

FIRST-LEVEL HEADING

Second-Level Heading

Third-Level Heading

Consistent headings.   Look for the most succinct and informative way to word headings. In general, state a topic in a single word, usually a noun (*Toxicity*); in a phrase, usually a noun phrase (*Levels of Toxicity*) or a gerund phrase (*Measuring Toxicity*); in a question that will be answered in the text (*How Can Toxicity Be Measured?*); or in an imperative that tells readers what steps to take (*Measure the Toxicity*). Whichever structure you choose, make sure you use it consistently for all headings of the same level.

Positioning.   Be sure to position each level of heading consistently throughout the text. And remember not to put a heading at the very bottom of a page, since readers would have to turn to the next page to find the text that the heading is announcing.

8d   Use visuals effectively.

Creating a visual design is more likely than ever before to be a part of your process of planning for a completed writing project. Visuals can help make a point more vividly and succinctly than words alone. In some cases, visuals may even be your primary text.

Selecting visuals.   Consider carefully what you want visuals to do for your writing before making your selections. What will your audience want or need you to show? Try to choose visuals that will enhance your credibility, allow you to make your point more emphatically, and clarify your overall text. (See the following series of figures for advice on which visuals are best for particular situations.)

Effective visuals can come from many sources—your own drawings or photographs, charts or graphs you create on a computer, or materials created by others. If you are using a visual from another source, be sure to give appropriate credit and to get permission before using any visual that will be posted online or otherwise available to the public.

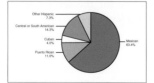

Use *pie charts* to compare parts to the whole.

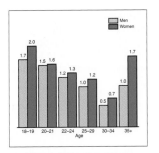

Use *bar graphs* and *line graphs* to compare one element with another, to compare elements over time, or to show correlations and frequency.

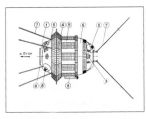

Use *tables* to draw attention to detailed numerical information.

Use *diagrams* to illustrate textual information or to point out details of objects or places described.

Use *maps* to show geographical locations and to emphasize spatial relationships.

Use *cartoons* to illustrate a point dramatically or comically.

Use *photographs* or *illustrations* to show particular people, places, objects, and situations described in the text or to help readers find or understand types of content.

Identifying visuals in your writing.   Position visuals alongside or after the text that refers to them. Number your visuals (number tables separately from other visuals), and give them informative titles. In some instances, you may need to provide captions to give readers additional data as source information.

Figure 1. College Enrollment for Men and Women by Age, 2007 (in millions)

Table 1. Word Choice by Race: *Seesaw* and *Teeter-totter*, Chicago, 1986

Analyzing and altering visuals.   Technical tools available to writers and designers today make it relatively easy to manipulate visuals. As you would with any source material, carefully assess any visuals you find for effectiveness, appropriateness, and validity. Here are tips for evaluating visuals:

- Check the context in which the visual appears. Is it part of an official government, school, or library site?
- If the visual is a photograph, are the date, time, place, and setting shown or explained? Is the information about the photo believable?
- If the visual is a chart, graph, or diagram, are the numbers and labels explained? Are the sources of the data given? Will the visual representation help readers make sense of the information, or could it mislead them? (See 15c.)
- Is biographical and contact information for the designer, artist, or photographer given?

At times, you may make certain changes to visuals that you use, such as cropping an image to show the most important detail or digitally brightening a dark image. Here, for example, are separate photos of a mountaintop cabin and a composite that digitally combines the originals into a single panoramic image to convey the setting more accurately. As long as the photograph is identified as a composite, the alteration is ethical.

Combining photos can sometimes be an appropriate choice.

This composite photo conveys the setting more effectively than the individual images.

To ensure that any alterations to images are ethical, follow these guidelines:

- Do not attempt to mislead readers. Show things as accurately as possible.
- Tell your audience what changes you have made.
- Include all relevant information about the visual, including the source.

CHECKLIST

Using Visuals Effectively

✔ Use visual elements for a specific purpose in your text — to illustrate something, to help prove a point, or to guide readers, for example.

✔ Tell the audience explicitly what the visual demonstrates, especially if it presents complex information. Do not assume readers will "read" the visual the way you do; your commentary on it is important.

✔ Number and title all visuals. Number and label tables and figures separately.

✔ Refer to each visual *before* it appears.

✔ Follow established conventions for documenting visual sources, and ask permission for use if your work will become available to the public. (15c and e)

✔ Get responses to your visuals in an early draft. If readers can't follow them or are distracted by them, revise accordingly.

✔ If you crop, brighten, or otherwise alter visuals to include them in your writing, be sure to do so ethically. (8d)

EXERCISE 8.1

Take an essay or other writing assignment you have done recently, one that makes little use of visuals or the other design elements discussed in this chapter. Reevaluate the effectiveness of your text, and make a note of all the places where visuals and other design elements (color, different type size, and so on) would help you get your ideas across more effectively.

3

Critical Thinking
and Argument

9 Reading Critically

Film critic Roger Ebert wrote in a notebook as he watched movies, tearing out the pages as he filled them, until he "looks as though he's sitting on top of a cloud of paper," as an *Esquire* profile observed. Reading critically means questioning and commenting thoughtfully on a text—whether an assignment for a psychology class, a graphic novel, a business email, or a YouTube video. Any method you use to keep track of your questions and make yourself concentrate on a text can help you become a better critical reader.

9a Preview the text.

Find out all you can about a text before beginning to look closely at it, considering its context, author, subject, genre, and design.

PREVIEWING THE CONTEXT

- Where have you encountered the work? Are you encountering it in its original context? For example, an essay in a collection of readings may have been previously published in a magazine; a speech you watch on YouTube may have been delivered to a live or televised audience; a painting on a museum wall may have been created for a wealthy patron in a distant country centuries earlier.
- What can you infer from the original or current context of the work about its intended audience and purpose?

LEARNING ABOUT THE AUTHOR OR CREATOR

- What information can you find about the author or creator of the text?
- What purpose, expertise, and possible agenda might you expect this person to have? Where do you think the author or creator is coming from in this text?

PREVIEWING THE SUBJECT

- What do you know about the subject of the text?
- What opinions do you have about the subject, and on what are your opinions based?

- What would you like to learn about the subject?
- What do you expect the main point to be? Why?

CONSIDERING THE TITLE, MEDIUM, GENRE, AND DESIGN

- What does the title (or caption or other heading) indicate?
- What do you know about the medium (or media) in which the work appears? Is it a text on the Web, a printed advertising brochure, a speech stored in iTunes, an animated cartoon on television, or some combination of media? What role does the medium play in achieving the purpose and connecting to the audience?
- What is the genre of the text—and what can it help illuminate about the intended audience or purpose? Why might the authors or creators have chosen this genre?
- How is the text presented? What do you notice about its formatting, use of color, visuals or illustrations, overall design, general appearance, and other design features?

Sample preview of an assigned text. A student in a first-year composition class who had been asked to read and analyze Abraham Lincoln's Gettysburg Address made preview notes, a few of which are excerpted here.

President Lincoln delivered the speech at a ceremony dedicating a national cemetery for Civil War soldiers. Crowds of people gathered in a field near Gettysburg, Pennsylvania, on November 19, 1863, to listen to him and other speakers. In July of that year, a Civil War battle that ended with 7,500 soldiers killed had taken place near where Lincoln spoke.

My textbook has the most famous version of the speech — but nobody knows for sure exactly what Lincoln said 150 years ago. There's obviously no audio recording of him giving the speech! Newspapers at the time reported what listeners heard, but he didn't write the speech out until later.

Lincoln gave this speech in the middle of the war, dedicating a national cemetery, so it must have been a pretty solemn occasion. He probably wanted his audience to think about why the war was worth

fighting. He probably also thought that some of the dead soldiers'
families might be there listening—as well as people who had seen
the battle or its aftermath. Did he think about the possibility that
future generations would read and think about this speech? As the
leader of the Union, he was probably very interested in showing why
the United States needed to stay together.

EXERCISE 9.1
Following the guidelines in 9a, preview a text that you have been
assigned to read.

9b   Read and annotate.

As you read a text for the first time, mark it up (if the medium
allows you to do so) or take notes. Consider the text's content,
author, intended audience, and genre and design.

READING FOR CONTENT

- What do you find confusing or unclear about the text? Where
  can you look for explanations or more information? Do you
  need background information in order to understand fully?

- What key terms and ideas—or key patterns—do you see?
  What key images stick in your mind?

- What sources or other works does this text cite, refer to, or
  allude to?

- How does the content fit with what you already know?

- Which points do you agree with? Which do you disagree
  with? Why?

READING FOR AUTHOR/CREATOR AND AUDIENCE

- Do the authors or creators present themselves as you
  anticipated in your preview?

- For what audience was this text created? Are you part of its
  intended audience?

- What underlying assumptions can you identify in the text?

- Are the medium and genre appropriate for the topic,
  audience, and purpose?

READING FOR DESIGN, COMPOSITION, AND STYLE

- Is the design appropriate for the subject and genre?
- Does the composition serve a purpose—for instance, does the layout help you see what is more and less important in the text?
- Do words, images, sound, and other media work together well?
- How would you describe the style of the text? What contributes to this impression—word choice? references to research or popular culture? formatting? color? something else?

Sample annotation of an assigned text.   After previewing the context, author, subject, and other aspects of the following article from the online magazine *Good*, a student assigned to write about the article annotated the text as shown.

Is the Internet Warping Our Brains? ❶
CORD JEFFERSON, SENIOR EDITOR, *GOOD*

New research from Columbia University psychologist Betsy Sparrow ❷ suggests that Google, your favorite search engine turned email host turned social network, might actually be making you less likely to absorb information. Sparrow's study, "Google Effects on Memory: Cognitive Consequences of Having Information at Our Fingertips," found that people who were confident they could use the internet to access some bit of information in the future were less likely to recall that information themselves. ❸ However, they were more likely to recall how to go about accessing the information if necessary. Sparrow calls it "<u>outsourcing data</u>," letting the internet take care of some stuff so we can save our brains for things that can't be Googled, like parents' birthdays and coworkers' names. ❹

Is this a bad thing? ❺ Not necessarily, says Sparrow. For instance, for years people in the educational community have known that rote learning—that is, <u>forcing children to memorize facts and dates</u>—is a poor way to educate. ❻ If that's the case, allowing computers to do some of the memorizing for us might be a way to focus more on the more philosophical aspects of learning. ❼

"Perhaps ❽ those who teach in any context, be they college professors, doctors or business leaders, will become increasingly focused on imparting greater understanding of ideas and ways of thinking, and less focused on memorization," Sparrow told *Time*.

Of course, while you might think that this research suggests people on the internet are using less of their brains than those not online, you'd be wrong. Back in 2008, the neuroscientist Gary Small discovered the difference in brain activity between a person reading a book and a person searching for information on Google. According to Small, the person searching the internet was using a lot more of their mind than the person simply reading a book. **9** Like Sparrow, Small says he's not willing to say if the difference is bad or good, just that our minds react entirely differently when stimulated by the internet as opposed to other forms of media. **10**

[Video: Gary Small discusses "Your Brain on Google" (2:43)] **11**

1 This sounds like a leading question to me — makes me think the author's answer must be "yes."

2 Look for more information on this psychologist and her research.

3 How did the research show this? What were the participants asked to do?

4 Haven't we done this in other ways already — like taking notes so we don't have to remember?

5 Interesting question! Not sure how I would answer.

6 Check out this link to see what the arguments are against "rote learning."

7 This sounds right. But are we really going to become more philosophical if we don't have to remember things? What if we just get more distracted by trivia?

8 Or perhaps not! This seems pretty optimistic.

9 Wow! *Seems* like it should be a good thing to use more of our brain. But what does it really mean?

10 So the researchers here aren't ready to draw conclusions about what the differences mean for us. (Not that people would stop Googling if it turned out to be a bad thing.)

11 Watch a little of this to see if it might have important information to add.

EXERCISE 9.2

Following is the full text of Abraham Lincoln's Gettysburg Address. Using the guidelines in 9b, read and annotate Lincoln's speech.

Four score and seven years ago our fathers brought forth on this continent a new nation, conceived in Liberty, and dedicated to the proposition that all men are created equal.

Now we are engaged in a great civil war, testing whether that nation, or any nation so conceived and so dedicated, can long endure. We are met on a great battle-field of that war. We have come to dedicate a portion of that field, as a final resting place for those who here gave their lives that that nation might live. It is altogether fitting and proper that we should do this.

But, in a larger sense, we can not dedicate — we can not consecrate — we can not hallow — this ground. The brave men, living and dead, who struggled here, have consecrated it, far above our poor power to add or detract. The world will little note, nor long remember what we say here, but it can never forget what they did here. It is for us the living, rather, to be dedicated here to the unfinished work which they who fought here have thus far so nobly advanced. It is rather for us to be here dedicated to the great task remaining before us — that from these honored dead we take increased devotion to that cause for which they gave the last full measure of devotion — that we here highly resolve that these dead shall not have died in vain — that this nation, under God, shall have a new birth of freedom — and that government of the people, by the people, for the people, shall not perish from the earth.   — Abraham Lincoln, Gettysburg Address

9c   Summarize the main ideas.

When you feel that you have read and thoroughly understood the text, try to summarize the contents in your own words. A summary *briefly* captures the main ideas of a text and omits information that is less important. Try to identify the key points in the text, find the essential evidence supporting those points, and explain the contents concisely and fairly, so that a reader unfamiliar with the original can make sense of it all. Deciding what to leave out can make summarizing a tricky task — but mastering this skill can serve you well in all the reading you do in your academic, professional, and civic life. To test your understanding — and to avoid unintentional plagiarism — it's wise to put the text aside while you write your summary. (For more information on writing a summary, see 14f.)

Sample summary of an assigned text. The following is a student summary of the article "Is the Internet Warping Our Brains?" (9b).

> The writer discusses two recent studies, one from 2011 and one from 2008, looking at how Internet use affects a person's mind. The 2011 study, by psychologist Betsy Sparrow, showed that if a person expects to be able to use Google to get information, then he or she is less likely to remember that information. Sparrow doesn't see this result as necessarily negative. She hopes that the widespread use of Google might lead educators to focus on "imparting greater understanding of ideas" rather than on "rote learning," which the writer says has been shown to be a bad way to teach students. (A link explains more about "rote learning.") The 2008 study, by neuroscientist Gary Small, shows that using the Internet actually activates more of a person's brain than reading a book. Like Sparrow, Small didn't draw conclusions about whether Internet use is therefore better or worse for a person's mind. It's just different.

9d   Analyze the text.

When you feel that you understand the meaning of the text, move on to your analysis. You may want to begin the process by asking additional questions about the text.

ANALYZING IDEAS AND EXAMPLES

- What are the main points in this text? Are they implied or explicitly stated?
- Which points do you agree with? Which do you disagree with? Why?
- Does anything in the text surprise you? Why, or why not?
- What kind of examples does the text use? What other kinds of evidence does the text offer to back up the main points? Can you think of other examples or evidence that should have been included?
- Are viewpoints other than those of the author or creator included and treated fairly?

- How trustworthy are the sources the text cites or refers to?
- What assumptions does the text make? Are those assumptions valid? Why, or why not?

ANALYZING FOR OVERALL IMPRESSION

- Do the authors or creators achieve their purpose? Why, or why not?
- What intrigues, puzzles, or irritates you about the text? Why?
- What else would you like to know?

Sample analysis of a text.   Following is a Pulitzer Prize–winning photograph (by Craig F. Walker of the *Denver Post*) and its caption. This image appeared as part of a series documenting the experiences of a Colorado teenager, Ian Fisher, who joined the U.S. Army to fight in Iraq.

During a weekend home from his first assignment at Fort Carson, Colorado, Ian walked through a Denver-area mall with his new girlfriend, Kayla Spitzlberger, on December 15, 2007, and asked whether she wanted to go ring shopping. She was excited, but working out the financing made him nervous. They picked out the engagement ring in about five minutes, but Ian wouldn't officially propose until Christmas Day in front of her family. The couple had met in freshman math class but never really dated until now. She wrote to him during basic training and decided to give Ian a chance. The engagement would end before Valentine's Day.

One student's analysis of this photograph made the following points:

> The couple are in the center of the photo—and at the center of our attention. But at this moment of choosing an engagement ring, they do not look "engaged" with each other. Kayla looks excited but uncertain, as if she knows that Ian feels doubts, but she hopes he will change his mind. She is looking right at him, with her body leaning toward him but her head leaning away: she looks very tentative. Ian is looking away from Kayla, and the expression on his face suggests that he's already having second thoughts about the expense of the ring (we see his wallet on the counter by his elbow) and perhaps even about asking Kayla to marry him. The accompanying caption helps us interpret the image, telling us about the couple's brief history together and noting that the engagement will last less than two months after this moment. But the message comes through pretty clearly without words.
>
> Ian and Kayla look as if they're trying on roles in this photograph. She looks ready to take the plunge, and he is resisting. These attitudes conform to stereotypical gender roles for a man and woman considering marriage (or going shopping, for that matter). The woman is expected to want the marriage and the ring; the man knows that he shouldn't show too much enthusiasm about weddings and shopping. It's hard for the reader to tell whether Ian and Kayla really feel that they are making good or careful choices for their situation at this moment or whether they're just doing what they think they're supposed to do under the circumstances.
>
> The reader also can't tell how the presence of the photographer, Craig F. Walker, affected the couple's actions. The photo is part of a series of images documenting Ian Fisher's life after joining the military, so Walker had probably spent a lot

of time with Ian before this photo was taken. Did Ian want to give a particular impression of himself on this day? Were he and Kayla trying on "adult" roles in this situation? Were they feeling pressure to produce a memorable moment for the camera? And what was Walker thinking when he accompanied them to the mall and took this photograph? Did he foresee the end of their engagement when he captured this revealing moment? What was his agenda?

EXERCISE 9.3
Write a two- to three-paragraph analysis of a text you have read or seen.

EXERCISE 9.4: THINKING VISUALLY
Think about the last film you watched for fun. What did you know about it before you watched it? What did you feel and learn as you watched? What have you told others about the film, both in terms of summarizing the story and of analyzing what the experience meant to you? Write a paragraph or create a brief slide show describing how you might use the techniques of previewing, reading, summarizing, and analyzing the next time you are asked to read a written-word text.

EXERCISE 9.5: THINKING CRITICALLY
Choose a text you have been assigned to read for a class. Read it over carefully, annotating the material, and then write a one- or two-paragraph summary of the contents. Then analyze your summary. Did your annotations help you summarize? Why, or why not? Does your summary interpret the material or aim for an objective stance? What does your summary omit from the original material, and how did you decide what to leave out?

e bedfordstmartins.com/wia
Student Writing > Critical analysis, Shuqiao Song

10 Analyzing Arguments

In one important sense, all language has an argumentative edge. When you greet friends, you probably wish to convince them that you're glad to see them; when advertisers pay for spots that appear alongside your social networking page, they want to persuade you to click and shop. Even apparently objective news reporting has strong argumentative overtones: when a news outlet highlights a particular story, for example, the editors are arguing that this subject is more important than others. Since argument is so pervasive, you need to be able to recognize and use it effectively — and to question your own arguments as well as those put forth by others.

10a Think critically about argument.

Critical thinking is a crucial component of argument, for it guides you in recognizing, formulating, and examining arguments. Here are some ways to think critically about argument:

- **Check understanding.** First, make sure you understand what is being argued and why. If you need to find out more about an unfamiliar subject to grasp the argument, do the research.

- **Ask where the writer is coming from and what his or her agenda is.** How can you tell?

- **Play the believing—and the doubting—game.** Begin by playing the *believing game*: put yourself in the position of the person creating the argument to see the topic from that person's point of view as much as possible. Once you have given the argument sympathetic attention, play the *doubting game*: look skeptically at each claim, and examine each piece of evidence to see how well (or poorly) it supports the claim. Eventually, this process of believing and doubting will become natural.

- **Ask pertinent questions.** Whether you are thinking about others' ideas or your own, you should question unstated purposes and assumptions, the writer's qualifications, the

CHECKLIST

Analyzing an Argument

Here are some questions that can help you judge the effectiveness of an argument:

✔ What conclusions about the argument can you reach by playing both the believing and the doubting game? (10a)

✔ What cultural contexts inform the argument, and what do they tell you about where the writer is coming from? (10b)

✔ What emotional, ethical, and logical appeals is the writer making in support of the argument? (10c)

✔ How has the writer established credibility to write about the topic? (10c)

✔ What is the claim (or arguable statement)? Is the claim qualified in any way? (10d)

✔ What reasons and assumptions support and underlie the claim? (10d)

✔ What additional evidence backs up the assumption and claim? How current and reliable are the sources? (10d)

✔ How does the writer use images, graphics, or other visuals to support the argument?

✔ What fallacies can you identify, and what effect do they have on the argument's persuasiveness? (10e)

✔ What is the overall impression you get from analyzing the argument? Are you convinced?

context, the goal of the argument, and the evidence presented. What objections might be made to the argument?

- **Interpret and assess information.** All information that comes to you has a perspective—a spin. Your job is to identify the perspective and assess it, examining its sources and finding out what you can about its context.

- **Assess your own arguments.** The ultimate goal of all critical thinking is to reach your own conclusions. These, too, you must question and assess.

10b Recognize cultural contexts.

To understand as fully as possible the arguments of others, pay attention to clues to cultural context and to where the writer or creator is coming from. Put yourself in the position of the person creating the argument before looking skeptically at every claim and examining every piece of evidence. Above all, watch out for your own assumptions as you analyze what you read or see. For example, just because you assume that the use of statistics as support for your argument holds more water than, say, precedent drawn from religious belief, you can't assume that all writers agree with you. Take a writer's cultural beliefs into account before you begin to analyze an argument. (See Chapter 17.)

10c Identify an argument's basic appeals.

Aristotle categorized argumentative appeals into three types: emotional appeals that speak to readers' hearts and values (known to the ancient Greeks as *pathos*), ethical appeals that support the writer's character (*ethos*), and logical appeals that use facts and evidence (*logos*).

Emotional appeals. Emotional appeals stir your emotions and remind you of deeply held values. When politicians argue that the country needs more tax relief, they almost always use examples of one or more families they have met, stressing the concrete ways in which a tax cut would improve the quality of their lives. Doing so creates a strong emotional appeal. Some have criticized the use of emotional appeals in argument, claiming that they are a form of manipulation intended to mislead an audience. But emotional appeals are an important part of almost every argument. Critical readers are perfectly capable of "talking back" to such appeals by analyzing them, deciding which are acceptable and which are not.

The photo on p. 113 shows protesters at an Occupy Wall Street demonstration outside police headquarters in New York City. The protesters' signs range from a simple logo for the United Auto Workers union to hand-painted cardboard slogans ("This is patriotic") to an American flag. To what emotions are the protesters appealing? Do you find this appeal effective, manipulative, or both? Would you accept this argument?

Ethical appeals.   Ethical appeals support the credibility, moral character, and goodwill of the argument's creator. These appeals are especially important for critical readers to recognize and evaluate. We may respect and admire an athlete, for example, but should we invest in the mutual funds the athlete promotes? To identify ethical appeals in arguments, ask yourself these questions: How does the creator of the argument show that he or she has really done the homework on the subject and is knowledgeable and credible about it? What sort of character does he or she build, and how? More important, is that character trustworthy? What does the creator of the argument do to show that he or she has the best interests of an audience in mind? Do those best interests match your own, and if not, how does that alter the effectiveness of the argument?

Logical appeals.   Logical appeals are viewed as especially trustworthy: "The facts don't lie," some say. Of course, facts are not the only type of logical appeals, which also include firsthand evidence drawn from observations, interviews, surveys and questionnaires, experiments, and personal experience; and secondhand evidence drawn from authorities, the testimony of others, statistics, and other print and online sources. Critical readers need to examine logical appeals just as carefully as emotional and ethical ones. What is the source of the logical appeal—and is that source trustworthy? Are all terms defined clearly? Has the logical evidence presented been taken out of context, and if so, does that change its meaning?

Analyzing appeals in a visual argument. The poster below, from TurnAround, an organization devoted to helping victims of domestic violence, is "intended to strike a chord with abusers as well as their victims." The dramatic combination of words and image builds on an analogy between a child and a target and makes strong emotional and ethical appeals.

The bull's-eye that draws your attention to the center of the poster is probably the first thing you notice when you look at the

A child is not a target.

Stop the cycle of domestic violence.

TurnAround, a non-profit agency serving victims of sexual assault and domestic violence, provides counseling, community outreach, emergency shelter and hospital accompaniment to more than 10,000 women, children and men each year.

TurnAround can help: (410) 377-8111
The cycle of violence ends here.

Baltimore & Carroll Counties' Sexual Assault/Domestic Violence 24-hour crisis hotline: (410) 828-6390

turn
around
the first place to turn

image. Then you may observe that the "target" is, in fact, a child's body; it also has arms, legs, and a head with wide, staring eyes. The heading at the upper left, "A child is not a target," reinforces the bull's-eye/child connection.

This poster's stark image and headline appeal to viewers' emotions, offering the uncomfortable reminder that children are often the victims of domestic violence. The design causes viewers to see a target first and only afterward recognize that the target is actually a child—an unsettling experience. But the poster also offers ethical appeals ("TurnAround can help") to show that the organization is credible and that it supports the worthwhile goal of ending "the cycle of domestic violence" by offering counseling and other support services. Finally, it uses the logical appeal of a statistic, noting that TurnAround has served "more than 10,000 women, children and men each year" and giving specific information about where to get help.

10d   Analyze the elements of argument.

According to philosopher Stephen Toulmin's framework for analyzing arguments, most arguments contain common features: a *claim* or *claims*, *reasons* for the claim, *assumptions* (whether stated or unstated) that underlie the argument, *evidence* (facts, authoritative

Elements of a Sample Toulmin Argument

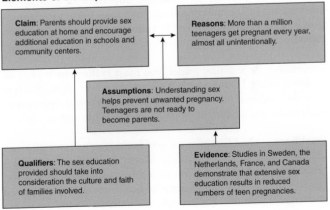

Claim: Parents should provide sex education at home and encourage additional education in schools and community centers.

Reasons: More than a million teenagers get pregnant every year, almost all unintentionally.

Assumptions: Understanding sex helps prevent unwanted pregnancy. Teenagers are not ready to become parents.

Qualifiers: The sex education provided should take into consideration the culture and faith of families involved.

Evidence: Studies in Sweden, the Netherlands, France, and Canada demonstrate that extensive sex education results in reduced numbers of teen pregnancies.

opinion, examples, statistics, and so on), and *qualifiers* that limit the claim in some way. In the following discussion, we will examine each of these elements in more detail. The figure on p. 115 shows how these elements might be applied to an argument about sex education.

Claims.　Claims (arguable statements) are statements of fact, opinion, or belief that form the backbone of arguments. Claims worthy of arguing are those that are debatable: to say "Ten degrees Fahrenheit is cold" is a claim, but it is probably not debatable — unless you are describing northern Alaska, where ten degrees might seem relatively balmy.

Reasons.　A claim is only as good as the reasons explaining why the claim should be accepted. As you analyze claims, look for reasons drawn from facts, from authorities, from personal experience, and from examples. Test each reason by asking how directly it supports the claim, how timely it is, and what counter-reasons you could offer to question it.

Assumptions.　Putting a claim and reasons together often results in what Aristotle called an *enthymeme*, an argument that rests on an assumption the writer expects the audience to hold. These assumptions (which Toulmin calls *warrants*) that connect claim and reasons are often the hardest to detect in an argument, partly because they are often unstated, sometimes masking a weak link. As a result, it's especially important to identify the assumptions in arguments you are analyzing. Once the assumption is identified, you can test it against evidence and your own experience before accepting it.

Evidence.　As a critical reader, you must evaluate each piece of evidence (what Toulmin calls *backing*) the writer offers. Analyze how the evidence relates to the claim, whether it is appropriate and timely, and whether it comes from a credible source.

Qualifiers.　Qualifiers offer a way of limiting or narrowing a claim so that it is as precise as possible. Words or phrases that signal a qualification include *few, often, in these circumstances, rarely, some, typically*, and so on. Claims having no qualifiers can sometimes lead to overgeneralizations. For example, the statement *Grading damages* *learning* is less precise than *Grading can damage learning in some circumstances.* Look carefully for qualifiers in the arguments you analyze, since they will affect the strength and reach of the claim.

Analyzing elements of a visual argument. Visual arguments, too, can be analyzed using Toulmin's methods. Look at the accompanying advertising parody: it contains few words, yet it makes a subtle argument. A group of students discussed this advertisement, observing that the image intends to evoke a 1960s-era detergent commercial. They came up with several possible claims that the ad might be making.

POSSIBLE CLAIM	Pharmaceutical companies want to convince consumers that taking drugs to cure depression is no more serious than trying a new detergent.
POSSIBLE CLAIM	Consumers should beware of drug advertisements that make hard-to-prove claims aimed at getting customers to ask for a prescription.
POSSIBLE CLAIM	Buying products will not lead to greater happiness.

All of these claims can be supported by the ad. If you were to choose the first claim, for instance, you might word a reason like this:

This parody of a Prozac ad looks like a detergent commercial from the 1960s, but the product is a chemical that promises to "wash your blues away." With some research into the actual dangers and benefits of antidepressants, you might find evidence that ads for such drugs sometimes minimize their downside and exaggerate their promise. You might also note that the ad's design takes viewers back to a decades-old picture of domestic happiness, suggesting that Prozac could return all of its users to some mythically perfect time in

the past—and you would be well on your way to an analysis of this visual argument.

10e Think critically about fallacies.

Fallacies have traditionally been viewed as serious flaws that damage the effectiveness of an argument. But arguments are ordinarily fairly complex in that they always occur in some specific rhetorical situation and in some particular place and time; thus what looks like a fallacy in one situation may appear quite different in another. The best advice is to learn to identify fallacies but to be cautious in jumping to quick conclusions about them. Rather than thinking of them as errors you can use to discredit an arguer, you might think of them as barriers to common ground and understanding, since they often shut off rather than engender debate.

Verbal fallacies

AD HOMINEM. Ad hominem charges make a personal attack rather than focusing on the issue at hand.

▶ **Who cares what that fat loudmouth says about the health care system?**

GUILT BY ASSOCIATION. Guilt by association involves attacking someone's credibility by linking that person with a person or activity the audience considers bad, suspicious, or untrustworthy.

▶ **She does not deserve reelection; her husband had extramarital affairs.**

FALSE AUTHORITY. False authority is often used by advertisers who show famous actors or athletes testifying to the greatness of a product about which they may know very little.

▶ **He's today's greatest NASCAR driver—and he banks at National Mutual!**

BANDWAGON APPEAL. A bandwagon appeal suggests that a great movement is underway and the reader will be a fool or a traitor not to join it.

▶ **This new phone is everyone's must-have item. Where's yours?**

FLATTERY. Flattery tries to persuade readers by suggesting that they are thoughtful, intelligent, or perceptive enough to agree with the writer.

▶ You have the taste to recognize the superlative artistry of Bling diamond jewelry.

IN-CROWD APPEAL. The in-crowd appeal, a special kind of flattery, invites readers to identify with an admired and select group.

▶ Want to know a secret that more and more of Middletown's successful young professionals are finding out about? It's Mountainbrook Manor condominiums.

VEILED THREAT. Veiled threats try to frighten readers into agreement by hinting that they will suffer adverse consequences if they don't agree.

▶ If Public Service Electric Company does not get an immediate 15 percent rate increase, its services may be seriously affected.

FALSE ANALOGY. False analogies make comparisons between two situations that are not alike in important respects.

▶ The volleyball team's sudden descent in the rankings resembled the sinking of the *Titanic*.

BEGGING THE QUESTION. Begging the question is a kind of circular argument that treats a debatable statement as if it had been proved true.

▶ Television news covered that story well; I learned all I know about it by watching TV.

POST HOC FALLACY. The post hoc fallacy (from the Latin *post hoc, ergo propter hoc*, which means "after this, therefore caused by this") assumes that just because B happened *after* A, it must have been *caused* by A.

▶ We should not rebuild the town docks because every time we do, a big hurricane comes along and damages them.

NON SEQUITUR. A non sequitur (Latin for "it does not follow") attempts to tie together two or more logically unrelated ideas as if they were related.

▶ If we can send a spaceship to Mars, then we can discover a cure for cancer.

EITHER-OR FALLACY. The either-or fallacy insists that a complex situation can have only two possible outcomes.

▸ If we do not build the new highway, businesses downtown will be forced to close.

HASTY GENERALIZATION. A hasty generalization bases a conclusion on too little evidence or on bad or misunderstood evidence.

▸ I couldn't understand the lecture today, so I'm sure this course will be impossible.

OVERSIMPLIFICATION. Oversimplification claims an overly direct relationship between a cause and an effect.

▸ If we prohibit the sale of alcohol, we will get rid of binge drinking.

STRAW MAN. A straw-man argument misrepresents the opposition by pretending that opponents agree with something that few reasonable people would support.

▸ My opponent believes that we should offer therapy to the terrorists. I disagree.

Visual fallacies.   Fallacies can also take the form of misleading images. The sheer power of images can make them especially difficult to analyze — people tend to believe what they see. Nevertheless, photographs and other visuals can be manipulated to present a false impression.

MISLEADING PHOTOGRAPHS. Faked or altered photos have existed since the invention of photography. On the following page, for example, is a photograph of Joseph Stalin, the Soviet Union's leader from 1929 to 1953, with his commissar Nikolai Yezhov. Stalin and the commissar had a political disagreement that resulted in Yezhov's execution in 1940. The second image shows the same photo after Stalin had it doctored to rewrite history.

Today's technology makes such photo alterations easier than ever. But photographs need not be altered to try to fool viewers. Think of all the photos that make a politician look misleadingly bad or good. In these cases, you should closely examine the motives of those responsible for publishing the images.

MISLEADING CHARTS AND GRAPHS. Facts and statistics, too, can be presented in ways that mislead readers. For example, the following bar graph purports to deliver an argument about how differently Democrats, on the one hand, and Republicans and Independents, on the other, felt about an issue.

Data Presented Misleadingly

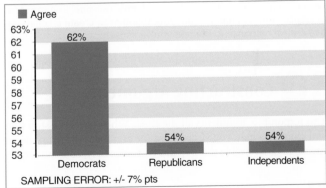

Look closely and you'll see a visual fallacy: the vertical axis starts not at zero but at 53 percent, so the apparently large difference between the groups is misleading. In fact, a majority of all respondents agree about the issue, and only eight percentage points separate Democrats from Republicans and Independents (in a poll with a margin of error of +/− seven percentage points). Here's how the graph would look if the vertical axis began at zero:

Data Presented More Accurately

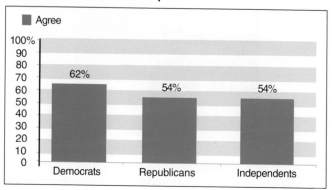

EXERCISE 10.1

Working with one or two classmates, analyze a brief argumentative text — an essay, an advertisement, or an editorial cartoon — by playing the believing and doubting game; identifying emotional, ethical, and logical appeals; and listing claims, reasons, assumptions, evidence, and qualifiers. Then work together to create a collaborative critical response to the text you've chosen.

11 Constructing Arguments

You respond to arguments all the time. When you see a stop sign and come to a halt, you've accepted the argument that stopping at such signs is a sensible thing to do. Unfortunately, constructing an

> ## CHECKLIST
>
> ### Reviewing Your Argument
>
> ✔ What is the purpose of your argument — to win? to convince others? to explore an issue? (11a)
>
> ✔ Is the point you want to make arguable? (11a)
>
> ✔ Does your thesis include a clear claim and good reasons? (11b)
>
> ✔ Have you considered your audience in shaping your appeals? (11d)
>
> ✔ How have you established your own credibility? (11e)
>
> ✔ Have you considered counterarguments fairly? (11e)
>
> ✔ How have you incorporated logical and emotional appeals into your argument? (11f and g)
>
> ✔ If you use sources, how effectively are they integrated into your argument? (11h)
>
> ✔ How is your argument organized? (11i)
>
> ✔ What design elements help you make your argument? (11j)

effective argument of your own is not as easy as putting up a stop sign. Creating a thorough and convincing argument requires careful reasoning and attention to your audience and purpose.

11a   Understand what counts as argument.

Although winning is an important purpose of argument, it is by no means the only purpose.

TO WIN. The most traditional purpose of academic argument, arguing to win, is common in campus debating societies, in political debates, in trials, and often in business. The writer or speaker aims to present a position that will prevail over some other position.

TO CONVINCE. Often, out-and-out defeat of another's position is not only unrealistic but undesirable. Instead, the goal might be to convince another person to change his or her mind. Doing so calls on a writer to provide *compelling reasons* for an audience to accept some or all of the writer's conclusions.

TO EXPLORE AN ISSUE. Argument to explore an issue or reach a decision seeks a sharing of information and perspectives in order to make informed choices.

Checking whether a statement can be argued. At school, at home, or on the job, you will often need to convince someone or decide something. To do so, start with an arguable statement, which should meet three criteria:

1. It attempts to convince readers of something, change their minds about something, or urge them to do something — or it explores a topic in order to make a wise decision.

2. It addresses a problem for which no easily acceptable solution exists or asks a question to which no absolute answer exists.

3. It presents a position that readers might realistically have varying perspectives on.

> **ARGUABLE STATEMENT**   Advertising in women's magazines contributes to the poor self-image that afflicts many young women.

This statement seeks to convince, addresses a problem — poor self-image among young women — that has no clear-cut solution, and takes a position many could disagree with.

> **UNARGUABLE STATEMENT**   Women's magazines earn millions of dollars every year from advertising.

This statement does not present a position; it states a fact that can easily be verified and thus offers a poor basis for argument.

EXERCISE 11.1

Using the three characteristics just listed, decide which of the following statements are arguable and which are not.

1. *The Dark Knight* was the best movie of the last decade.
2. The climate of the earth is gradually getting warmer.
3. The United States must further reduce social spending in order to balance the budget.
4. Shakespeare died in 1616.

5. President Roosevelt knew that the Japanese were planning to bomb Pearl Harbor in December 1941.

6. Water boils at 212 degrees Fahrenheit.

7. Van Gogh's paintings are the work of a madman.

8. The incidence of breast cancer has risen in the last ten years.

9. The Federal Emergency Management Agency's response to disasters must be radically improved.

10. A fifty-five-mile-per-hour speed limit lowers accident rates.

11b Make a claim and formulate a working thesis.

Once you have an arguable statement, you need to develop it into a working thesis (5b). One way to do so is to identify the main elements of an argument (10d): the claim or arguable statement, one or more reasons for the claim, and assumptions—sometimes unstated—that underlie the claim and reasons.

To turn a claim into a working thesis for an argument, include at least one good reason to support the arguable statement.

REASON	Pesticides endanger the lives of farmworkers.
WORKING THESIS (CLAIM WITH REASON ATTACHED)	Because they endanger the lives of farmworkers, pesticides should be banned.

EXERCISE 11.2

Using two arguable statements from Exercise 11.1 or two that you create, formulate two working theses, identifying the claim, reason(s), and assumption(s) for each.

11c Examine your assumptions.

Once you have a working thesis, examine your assumptions to help test your reasoning and strengthen your argument. Begin by identifying underlying assumptions that support the working thesis.

WORKING THESIS	Because they endanger the lives of farmworkers, pesticides should be banned.
ASSUMPTION 1	Workers have a right to a safe working environment.
ASSUMPTION 2	Substances that endanger the lives of workers deserve to be banned.

Once you have a working thesis, you may want to use qualifiers to make it more precise and thus less susceptible to criticism. The preceding thesis might be qualified in this way:

▶ Because they *often* endanger the lives of farmworkers, *most* pesticides should be banned.

EXERCISE 11.3

Formulate an arguable statement, and create a working thesis, for two of the following general topics.

1. the Palestinian-Israeli conflict
2. sex education in public schools
3. lowering college tuition
4. reinstatement of a U.S. military draft
5. music downloading

11d Shape your appeal to your audience.

Arguments and the claims they make are effective only if they appeal to the appropriate audience. For example, if you want to argue for increased lighting in parking garages on campus, you might appeal to students by citing examples drawn from their experiences of the safety problems in such dimly lit garages. If you are writing to university administrators, however, you might focus on the negative publicity associated with past attacks in campus garages and evoke the anger that such attacks cause in parents, alumni, and other influential groups.

EXERCISE 11.4

Working with two other members of your class, find two current advertisements you consider particularly eye-catching and persuasive. Then work out what central claim each ad is making, and identify reasons and assumptions in support of the claim. Finally, prepare a brief collaborative report of your findings for the class.

11e   Establish credibility through ethical appeals.

To make your argument convincing, you must first gain the respect and trust of your readers, or establish credibility with them. In general, writers can establish credibility by making ethical appeals (10c) in four ways.

Demonstrating knowledge.   A writer can establish credibility first by establishing credentials. To decide whether you know enough to argue an issue credibly, consider the following questions:

- Can you provide information about your topic from sources other than your own knowledge?
- How reliable are your sources?
- If sources contradict one another, can you account for or resolve the contradictions?
- Would a personal experience relating to the issue help support your claim?

These questions may well show that you must do more research, check sources, resolve contradictions, refocus your working thesis, or even change your topic.

Establishing common ground.   Many arguments between people or groups are doomed to end without resolution because the two sides seem to occupy no starting point of agreement. The following

FOR MULTILINGUAL WRITERS

Counting Your Own Experience

You may have been told that your personal experience doesn't count in making academic arguments. If so, reconsider this advice, for showing an audience that you have relevant personal experience with a topic can carry strong persuasive appeal with many English-speaking readers.

questions can help you find common ground in presenting an argument. (See also Chapter 18.)

- On this issue, how can you discover opinions that differ from your own?
- What are the differing perspectives on the issue?
- What aspects of the issue can all sides agree on?
- How can you express such common ground clearly to all sides? Can you use other languages or varieties of English to establish common ground with those you address? (See Chapter 19.)

Demonstrating fairness.   In arguing a position, writers must deal fairly with opposing arguments (also called counterarguments). Audiences are more inclined to listen to writers who seem to consider their opponents' views fairly than to those who ignore or distort such views. The following questions can help you discover ways of establishing yourself as open-minded and evenhanded:

- How can you show that you are taking into account all significant points of view?
- How can you demonstrate that you understand and sympathize with points of view other than your own?
- What can you do to show that you have considered evidence carefully, even when it does not support your position?

Some writers, instead of demonstrating fairness, may make unjustified attacks on an opponent's credibility. Avoid such attacks in your writing.

Visuals that make ethical appeals.   In arguments and other kinds of writing, visuals can combine with text to help present a writer or an organization as trustworthy and credible. As with businesses, many institutions and individuals are now using logos and other images to brand themselves as they wish the public to see them. This logo from the Sustainable Food Labora-

tory suggests that the organization is concerned about both food production and the environment.

Visuals that make ethical appeals add to your credibility and fairness as a writer. Just as you probably consider the impression your Facebook profile photo makes on your audience, you should think about what kind of case you're making for yourself when you choose images and design elements for your argument.

EXERCISE 11.5

List the ways in which the Sustainable Food Laboratory's logo demonstrates knowledge, establishes common ground, and shows fairness. Do you think the visuals are helpful in convincing you of the organization's credibility? Why, or why not?

EXERCISE 11.6

Using a working thesis you drafted for Exercise 11.2 or 11.3, write a paragraph or two describing how you would go about establishing your credibility in arguing that thesis.

11f Use effective logical appeals.

Credibility alone cannot and should not carry the full burden of convincing readers. Indeed, many are inclined to think that the logic of the argument—the reasoning behind it—is as important as its ethos.

Examples, precedents, and narratives. Just as a picture can sometimes be worth a thousand words, so can a well-conceived example be extremely valuable in arguing a point. Examples are used most often to support generalizations or to bring abstractions to life. In making the general statement that popular media send the message that a woman must be thin to be attractive, you might include these examples:

At the supermarket checkout, a tabloid publishes unflattering photographs of a young singer and comments on her apparent weight gain in shocked captions that ask, "What happened?!?" Another praises a star for quickly shedding "ugly pounds" after the recent birth of a child. The cover of *Cosmopolitan* features a glamorously made-up and airbrushed actress in an outfit that reveals her remarkably tiny waist and flat stomach. Every woman in every advertisement in the magazine is thin — and the context makes it clear that we're supposed to think that she is beautiful.

Precedents are examples taken from the past. If, as part of a proposal for increasing lighting in the library garage, you point out that the university has increased lighting in four other garages in the past year, you are arguing on the basis of precedent.

The following questions can help you check any use of example or precedent:

- How representative are the examples?
- Are they sufficient in strength or number to lead to a generalization?
- In what ways do they support your point?
- How closely does a precedent relate to the point you're trying to make? Are the situations really similar?
- How timely is the precedent? (What would have been applicable in 1920 is not necessarily applicable today.)

Because storytelling is universal, *narratives* can be very persuasive in helping readers understand and accept the logic of an argument. Narratives that use video and audio to capture the faces and voices of the people involved are often particularly compelling. In *As We Sow*, a documentary arguing against corporate pork production methods, the farmers shown here tell stories of their struggle to continue raising animals as their families have for generations.

Stories drawn from your own experience can appeal particularly to readers, for they not only help make your point in true-to-life, human terms but also help readers know you better and therefore identify with you more closely.

When you include stories in an argument, ask yourself the following questions:

- Does the narrative support your thesis?
- Will the story's significance to the argument be clear to your readers?
- Is the story one of several good reasons or pieces of evidence — or does it have to carry the main burden of the argument?

In research writing, you must identify your sources for any examples, precedents, or narratives that are not based on your own knowledge.

Authority and testimony.   Another way to support an argument logically is to cite an authority. The use of authority has figured prominently in the controversy over smoking. Since the U.S. surgeon general's 1964 announcement that smoking is hazardous to health, many Americans have stopped smoking, largely persuaded by the authority of the scientists offering the evidence.

Ask the following questions to be sure you are using authorities effectively:

- Is the authority *timely*? (The argument that the United States should pursue a policy that was supported by Thomas Jefferson will probably fail since Jefferson's time was so radically different from ours.)
- Is the authority *qualified* to judge the topic at hand? (To cite a movie star in an essay on linguistics may not help your argument.)
- Is the authority likely to be *known and respected* by readers? (To cite an unfamiliar authority without identification will reduce the impact of the evidence.)
- Are the authority's *credentials* clearly stated and verifiable? (Especially with Web-based sources, it is crucial to know whose authority guarantees the reliability of the information.)

Testimony—the evidence that an authority presents in support of a claim—is a feature of much contemporary argument. If testimony is timely, accurate, representative, and provided by a respected authority, then it, like authority itself, can add powerful support.

In research writing (see Chapters 12–16), you should cite your sources for authority and for testimony not based on your own knowledge.

Causes and effects.   Showing that one event is the cause or the effect of another can help support an argument. Suppose you are trying to explain, in a petition to change your grade in a course, why you were unable to take the final examination. You would probably trace the causes of your failure to appear—your illness or the theft of your car, perhaps—so that the committee reading the petition would reconsider the effect—your not taking the examination.

Tracing causes often lays the groundwork for an argument, particularly if the effect of the causes is one we would like to change. In an environmental science class, for example, a student may argue that a national law regulating smokestack emissions from utility plants is needed because (1) acid rain on the East Coast originates from emissions at utility plants located in the Midwest, (2) acid rain kills trees and other vegetation, (3) utility lobbyists have prevented midwestern states from passing strict laws controlling emissions from such plants, and (4) if such laws are not passed, acid rain will eventually destroy most eastern forests. In this case, the fourth point ties all of the previous points together to provide an overall argument from effect: if X, then Y.

Inductive and deductive reasoning.   Traditionally, logical arguments are classified as using either inductive or deductive reasoning; in practice, the two almost always work together. Inductive reasoning is the process of making a generalization based on a number of specific instances. If you find you are ill on ten occasions after eating seafood, for example, you will likely draw the inductive generalization that seafood makes you ill. It may not be an absolute certainty that seafood is to blame, but the probability lies in that direction.

Deductive reasoning, on the other hand, reaches a conclusion by assuming a general principle (known as a major premise) and then applying that principle to a specific case (the minor premise). In practice, this general principle is usually derived from induction. The inductive generalization *Seafood makes me ill*, for instance, could serve as the major premise for the deductive argument *Since all seafood makes me ill, the shrimp on this buffet is certain to make me ill.*

Deductive arguments have traditionally been analyzed as syllogisms, reasoning that contains a major premise, a minor premise, and a conclusion.

MAJOR PREMISE	All people die.
MINOR PREMISE	I am a person.
CONCLUSION	I will die.

Syllogisms, however, are too rigid and absolute to serve in arguments about questions that have no absolute answers, and they often lack any appeal to an audience. Aristotle's simpler alternative, the enthymeme, asks the audience to supply the implied major premise. Consider the following example:

Since violent video games can be addictive and cause psychological harm, players and their parents must carefully evaluate such games and monitor their use.

You can analyze this enthymeme by restating it in the form of two premises and a conclusion.

MAJOR PREMISE	Games that cause harm to players should be evaluated and monitored.
MINOR PREMISE	Violent video games can cause psychological harm to players.
CONCLUSION	These games should be evaluated and monitored.

Note that the major premise is one the writer can count on an audience agreeing with or supplying: safety and common sense demand that potentially harmful games be used with great care. By implicitly asking an audience to supply this premise to an argument, a writer engages the audience's participation.

Toulmin's system (10d) looks for claims, reasons, and assumptions instead of major and minor premises.

CLAIM	Parents should not allow children to play violent video games.
REASON	Exposure to violent video games may make children more indifferent to violence.

ASSUMPTION   Parents do not want their children to be indifferent to violence.

Whether it is expressed as a syllogism, an enthymeme, or a claim, a deductive conclusion is only as strong as the premise or reasons on which it is based.

EXERCISE 11.7

The following sentences contain deductive arguments based on implied major premises. Identify each of the implied premises.

1. The use of marijuana for medical purposes should be legal if it can improve a patient's condition and does not harm anyone.
2. Women soldiers should not serve in combat positions because doing so would expose them to a much higher risk of death.
3. Animals can't talk; therefore they can't feel pain as humans do.

Visuals that make logical appeals. Visuals that make logical appeals can be especially useful in arguments, since they present factual information that can be taken in at a glance. *Mother Jones* used the following simple chart to carry a big message about income distribution in the United States. Consider how long it would take to explain all the information in this chart with words alone.

A Visual That Makes a Logical Appeal

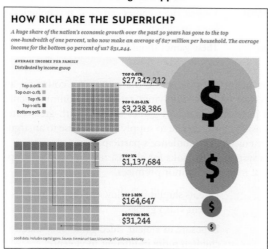

HOW RICH ARE THE SUPERRICH?

A huge share of the nation's economic growth over the past 30 years has gone to the top one-hundredth of one percent, who now make an average of $27 million per household. The average income for the bottom 90 percent of us? $31,244.

AVERAGE INCOME PER FAMILY
Distributed by income group

Top 0.01%
Top 0.01-0.1%
Top 1%
Top 1-10%
Bottom 90%

TOP 0.01%
$27,342,212

TOP 0.01-0.1%
$3,238,386

TOP 1%
$1,137,684

TOP 1-10%
$164,647

BOTTOM 90%
$31,244

2008 data, includes capital gains. Source: Emmanuel Saez, University of California–Berkeley

EXERCISE 11.8

Using a working thesis you drafted for Exercise 11.2 or 11.3, write a paragraph describing the logical appeals you would use to support the thesis.

11g   Use appropriate emotional appeals.

Most successful arguments appeal to our hearts as well as to our minds — as is vividly demonstrated by the campaign to curb the AIDS epidemic in Africa. Facts and figures (logical appeals) convince us that the problem is real and serious. What elicits an outpouring of support, however, is the arresting emotional power of stories and images of people living with the disease. But credible writers take particular care when they use emotional appeals; audiences can easily begin to feel manipulated when an argument tries too hard to appeal to their pity, anger, or fear.

Concrete descriptive details.   Like photographs, vivid words can bring a moving immediacy to any argument. A student may amass facts and figures, including diagrams and maps, to illustrate the problem of wheelchair access to the library. But only when the student asks a friend who uses a wheelchair to accompany her to the library does the student writer discover the concrete details necessary to move readers. The student can then write, "Marie inched her heavy wheelchair up the steep entrance ramp, her arms straining, her face pinched with the sheer effort."

Figurative language.   Figurative language, or figures of speech, can paint a detailed and vivid picture by making striking comparisons between something you are writing about and something else that helps a reader visualize, identify with, or understand it (20d).

Figures of speech include metaphors, similes, and analogies. Most simply, metaphors compare two things directly: *Richard the Lion-Hearted; old age is the evening of life.* Similes make comparisons using *like* or *as: Richard is as brave as a lion; old age is like the evening of life.* Analogies are extended metaphors or similes that compare an unfamiliar concept or process to a more familiar one.

Visuals can also create vivid comparisons. The panels on p. 136 come from a cartoon from Tom Tomorrow's comic strip, *This Modern World*, called "If Real Life Were More Like the Internet." Tomorrow, whose work appears regularly online, suggests in these panels that digital content has value, just as physical products and

A Visual That Creates a Vivid Comparison

services do — and that those who create such content should be able to earn a living from it. Tomorrow adds emotional weight to the comparison by making the cartoon characters who want free content seem selfish and blind to the needs of those who serve them.

Visuals that make emotional appeals.   Visuals that make emotional appeals can also add substance to your argument. To make sure that such visual appeals will enhance your argument, test them out with several potential readers to see how they interpret the appeal. Consider, for example, the photograph below, which shows a funeral arranged by an American Legion post in Florida to honor four U.S. military veterans who died homeless. Some readers might

A Visual That Makes an Emotional Appeal

see this image as an indictment of the government, which allowed soldiers who had fought for their country to end up without a place to live—but others might view it instead (or also) as confirmation that patriots come from every walk of life or that veterans honor their own even when others fail to do so.

EXERCISE 11.9

Make a list of common human emotions that might be attached to each of the following topics, and suggest appropriate ways to appeal to those emotions in a specific audience you choose to address.

1. banning drinking on campus
2. airport security
3. birth control
4. health care reform
5. steroid use among athletes

EXERCISE 11.10

Using a working thesis you formulated for Exercise 11.2 or 11.3, make a list of the emotional appeals most appropriate to your topic and audience. Then spend ten to fifteen minutes brainstorming, looking for descriptive and figurative language as well as images to carry out the appeals.

11h Consult sources.

In constructing an academic argument, it is often essential to use sources. The key to persuading people to accept your argument is providing good reasons; and even if your assignment doesn't specify that you must consult outside sources, they are often the most effective way of finding and establishing these reasons. Sources can help you to do the following:

- provide background information on your topic
- demonstrate your knowledge of the topic to readers
- cite authority and testimony in support of your thesis
- find opinions that differ from your own, which can help you sharpen your thinking, qualify your thesis if necessary, and demonstrate fairness to opposing arguments

For a thorough discussion of finding, gathering, and evaluating sources, see Chapters 12–16.

11i   Organize your argument.

Once you have assembled good reasons and evidence in support of an argumentative thesis, you must organize your material to present the argument convincingly. Although there is no universally favored, one-size-fits-all organizational framework, you may find it useful to try one of the following patterns.

The classical system.   The system of argument often followed by ancient Greek and Roman orators is now referred to as *classical*. You can adapt the ancient format to written arguments as follows:

1. Introduction
   - Gain readers' attention and interest.
   - Establish your qualifications to write about your topic.
   - Establish common ground with readers.
   - Demonstrate fairness.
   - State or imply your thesis.

2. Background
   - Present any necessary background information, including relevant personal narrative.

3. Lines of argument
   - Present good reasons (including logical and emotional appeals) in support of your thesis.
   - Present reasons in order of importance, with the most important ones generally saved for last.
   - Demonstrate ways your argument may be in readers' best interest.

4. Alternative arguments
   - Examine alternative points of view.
   - Note advantages and disadvantages of alternative views.
   - Explain why one view is better than other(s).

5. Conclusion
   - Summarize the argument if you choose.
   - Elaborate on the implication of your thesis.
   - Make clear what you want readers to think or do.
   - Reinforce your credibility.

The Toulmin system.   This simplified form of the Toulmin system (10d and 11f) can help you organize an argumentative essay:

1. Make your claim (arguable statement).

   ▶ **The federal government should ban smoking.**

2. Qualify your claim if necessary.

   ▶ **The ban would be limited to public places.**

3. Present good reasons to support your claim.

   ▶ **Smoking causes serious diseases in smokers.**
   ▶ **Nonsmokers are endangered by others' smoke.**

4. Explain the assumptions that underlie your claim and your reasons. Provide additional explanations for any controversial assumptions.

ASSUMPTION	The Constitution was established to "promote the general welfare."
ASSUMPTION	Citizens are entitled to protection from harmful actions by others.
ADDITIONAL EXPLANATION	The United States is based on a political system that is supposed to serve the basic needs of its people, including their health.

5. Provide additional evidence to support your claim (statistics, facts, testimony, and other logical, ethical, or emotional appeals).

STATISTICS	Cite the incidence of deaths attributed to secondhand smoke.
FACTS	Cite lawsuits won against large tobacco companies, including one that awarded billions of dollars to states in reparation for smoking-related health care costs.
FACTS	Cite bans on smoking already imposed on indoor public spaces in many cities.
AUTHORITY	Cite the surgeon general.

6. Acknowledge and respond to possible counterarguments.

> **COUNTER-**   Smokers have rights, too.
> **ARGUMENT**
>
> **RESPONSE**   The suggested ban applies only to public
>   places; smokers are free to smoke in private.

7. Finally, state your conclusion in the strongest way possible.

11j   Consider design issues.

Most writers today create arguments that are carefully designed
to make the best use of space, font style and type size, color,
visuals, and technology. Chapter 8 provides extensive information on design issues, and it would be wise to consult that
chapter as you design an argument. The following tips will get
you thinking about how to produce and design an argument
that will add to the ethical, logical, and emotional appeals you
are making:

- Spend some time deciding on a distinct visual style for your
  argument, one that will appeal to your intended readers, set
  a clear voice or tone for your argument, and guide readers
  through your text.

- Check out any conventions that may be expected in the
  kind of argument you are writing. Look for examples of
  similar arguments, or ask your instructor for information
  about such conventions (4f).

- Consider the use of white space, titles, and headings and how
  each page will look. Choose titles, headings, and subheadings
  that will guide readers from point to point (8c). You may
  want to set off an especially important part of your argument
  (such as a list of essential evidence) in a box, carefully
  labeled.

- Make sure that your visual design is consistent. If you choose a
  particular color, font, or type style for a particular purpose, such
  as a second-level heading, make sure that you use the same color,
  font, or type style for that purpose throughout your paper.

- Be sure to choose readable fonts and font sizes (8b and c).

- Choose colors carefully, and make sure that you use color
  appropriately for the genre and medium.

- Place images close to the text they illustrate, and label each one clearly (8d). Make sure that audio and video files appear in appropriate places and are identified for users.
- After you have a rough draft of your design, test it out on friends and classmates, asking them to describe how readable it is, how easy it is to follow, and what you need to change in order to make it more effective. Decide what adjustments you need to make—in format, spacing, alignment, use of color and fonts, and so on.

EXERCISE 11.11

Using the guidelines in this chapter, draft an argument in support of one of the working theses you formulated in Exercise 11.2 or 11.3.

EXERCISE 11.12: THINKING CRITICALLY

Using the checklist on p. 123, analyze an argument you've recently written or the draft you wrote for Exercise 11.11. Decide what you need to do to revise your argument, and write out a brief plan for revision.

11k   A student's argument essay

The following essay by Benjy Mercer-Golden argues that sustainability and capitalism can and must work together for an effective response to environmental degradation.

e **bedfordstmartins.com/wia**
Student Writing > Argument project, Benjy Mercer-Golden
Analysis Activity > Analyze evidence, Benjy Mercer-Golden

Mercer-Golden 1

Benjy Mercer-Golden
Dr. Andrea Lunsford
English 87N
28 Nov. 2012

Title clearly
announces
topic

Emotional
appeals and
statement of
problem

Thesis
statement
outlines
three-step
plan

Explanation
of first step of
thesis

Opposing
argument

Rebuttal of
opposing
argument

Reasons in
support of
claim

Lessons from Tree-Huggers and Corporate Mercenaries:
A New Model of Sustainable Capitalism

Televised images of environmental degradation — seagulls
with oil coating their feathers, smokestacks belching gray
fumes — often seem designed to shock, but these images also
represent very real issues: climate change, dwindling energy
resources like coal and oil, a scarcity of clean drinking water.
In response, businesspeople around the world are thinking
about how they can make their companies greener or more
socially beneficial to ensure a brighter future for humanity. But
progress in the private sector has been slow and inconsistent.
Accelerating the move to sustainability requires both businesses
and investors to make changes: for-profit businesses must
operate more sustainably, "social good" businesses should run
more efficiently and profitably, and investors need to support
companies with long-term, revolutionary visions for improving
the world.

To start with, for-profit corporations could reshape their
strategies to operate sustainably and to be evaluated for their
performance with long-term measurements and incentives. The
conventional argument against for-profit companies deeply
embedding environmental and social goals into their corporate
strategies is that caring about the world does not go hand
in hand with lining pockets. This morally toxic case is also
problematic from a business standpoint. A 2012 study of 180
high-profile companies by Harvard Business School professors
Robert G. Eccles and George Serafeim and London Business
School professor Ioannis Ioannou shows that "high sustainability
companies," as defined by environmental and social variables,
"significantly outperform their counterparts over the long term,

both in terms of stock market and accounting performance." The study argues that the better financial returns of these companies are especially evident in sectors where "companies' products significantly depend upon extracting large amounts of natural resources" (Eccles, Ioannou, and Serafeim).

   Such empirical financial evidence to support a shift toward, say, using energy from renewable sources to run manufacturing plants argues that executives should think more sustainably, but other underlying incentives need to evolve in order to bring about tangible change. David Blood and Al Gore of Generation Investment Management, an investment firm focused on "sustainable investing for the long term" ("About Us"), wrote a groundbreaking white paper that outlined the perverse incentives company managers face. For public companies, the default practice is to issue earnings guidances — announcements of projected future earnings — every quarter. This practice encourages executives to manage for the short term instead of adding long-term value to their company and the earth (Gore and Blood). Only the most uncompromisingly green CEOs would still advocate for stricter carbon emissions standards at the company's factories if a few mediocre quarters left investors demanding that they be fired. Gore and Blood make a powerful case against requiring companies to be subjected to this "What have you done for me lately?" philosophy, arguing that quarterly earnings guidances should be abolished in favor of companies releasing information when they consider it appropriate. And to further persuade managers to think sustainably, companies need to change the way the managers get paid. Currently, the CEO of ExxonMobil is rewarded for a highly profitable year but is not held accountable for depleting nonrenewable oil reserves. A new model should incentivize thinking for the long run. Multiyear milestones for performance evaluation, as Gore and Blood suggest, are essential to pushing executives to manage sustainably.

Logical appeal explains underlying problem

Ethical appeal shows need for change

Logical appeals and examples in support of claim

Mercer-Golden 3

Explanation of
second step of
thesis

But it's not just for-profit companies that need to rethink strategies. Social good–oriented leaders also stand to learn from the people often vilified in environmental circles: corporate CEOs. To survive in today's economy, companies building sustainable products must operate under the same strict business standards as profit-driven companies. Two social enterprises, Nika Water and Belu, provide perfect examples. Both sell bottled water in the developed world with the mission of providing clean water to impoverished communities through their profits. Both have visionary leaders that define the lesson that all environmental and social entrepreneurs need to

Writer's claim

understand: financial pragmatism will add far more value to the world than idealistic dreams. Nika Water founder Jeff Church explained this in a speech at Stanford University:

Evidence in
support of
claim

Social entrepreneurs look at their businesses as nine parts cause, one part business. In the beginning, it needs to be nine parts business, one part cause, because if the business doesn't stay around long enough because it can't make it, you can't do anything about the cause.

When U.K.-based Belu lost £600,000 ($940,000) in 2007, it could only give around £30,000 ($47,000) to charity. Karen Lynch took over as CEO, cutting costs, outsourcing significant parts of the company's operations, and redesigning the entire business model; the company now donates four times as much

Alternative
argument
related to
claim

to charity (Hurley). The conventional portrayal of do-gooders is that they tend to be terrible businesspeople, an argument often grounded in reality. It is easy to criticize the Walmarts of the world for caring little about sustainability or social good, but the idealists with big visions who do not follow through on their promises because their businesses cannot survive are no more praiseworthy. Walmart should learn from nonprofits and social enterprises on advancing a positive environmental and social agenda, but idealist entrepreneurs

Mercer-Golden 4

should also learn from corporations about building successful businesses.

The final piece of the sustainable business ecosystem is the investors who help get potentially world-changing companies off the ground. Industries that require a large amount of money to build complex products with expensive materials, such as solar power companies, rely heavily on investors — often venture capitalists based in California's Silicon Valley (Knight). The problem is that venture capitalists are not doing enough to fund truly groundbreaking companies. In an oft-cited blog post entitled "Why Facebook Is Killing Silicon Valley," entrepreneur Steve Blank argues that the financial returns on social media companies have been so quick and so outsized that the companies with the *really* big ideas — like providing efficient, cheap, scalable solar power — are not being backed: "In the past, if you were a great [venture capitalist], you could make $100 million on an investment in 5–7 years. Today, social media startups can return hundreds of millions or even billions in less than 3 years." The point Blank makes is that what is earning investors lots of money right now is not what is best for the United States or the world.

There are, however, signs of hope. Paypal founder Peter Thiel runs his venture capital firm, the Founders Fund, on the philosophy that investors should support "flying cars" instead of new social media ventures (Packer). While the next company with the mission of making photo-sharing cooler or communicating with friends easier might be both profitable and valuable, Thiel and a select few others fund technology that has the potential to solve the huge problems essential to human survival.

The world's need for sustainable companies that can build products from renewable energy or make nonpolluting cars will inevitably create opportunities for smart companies to make money. In fact, significant opportunities already exist for

Explanation of third step of thesis

Logical appeal explains problem

Emotional appeal

Emotional appeal

venture capitalists willing to step away from what is easy today and shift their investment strategies toward what will help us continue to live on this planet tomorrow — even if seeing strong returns may take a few more years. Visionaries like Blank and Thiel need more allies (and dollars) in their fight to help produce more pioneering, sustainable companies. And global warming won't abate before investors wise up. It is vital that this shift happen now.

Thesis revisited

When we think about organizations today, we think about nonprofits, which have long-term social missions, and corporations, which we judge by their immediate financial returns, like quarterly earnings. That is a treacherous dichotomy. Instead, we need to see the three major players in the business ecosystem — corporations, social enterprises, and investors — moving toward a *single* model of long-term, sustainable capitalism. We need visionary companies that not only set out to solve humankind's biggest problems but also have the business intelligence to accomplish these goals, and we need investors willing to fund these companies. Gore and Blood argue that "the imperative for change has never been greater." We will see this change when the world realizes that sustainable capitalism shares the same goals as creating a sustainable environment. Let us hope that this realization comes soon.

Concluding
emotional
appeal

STUDENT
WRITING

Works Cited

"About Us." *Generation*. Generation Investment Management
    LLC, 2012. Web. 26 Nov. 2012.

Blank, Steve. "Why Facebook Is Killing Silicon Valley."
    Steveblank.com. N.p., 21 May 2012. Web. 23 Nov. 2012.

Church, Jeff. "The Wave of Social Entrepreneurship."
    Entrepreneurial Thought Leaders Seminar. NVIDA
    Auditorium, Stanford University, Stanford, CA. 11 Apr.
    2012. Guest lecture.

Eccles, Robert G., Ioannis Ioannou, and George Serafeim.
    "The Impact of a Corporate Culture of Sustainability on
    Corporate Behavior and Performance." *Harvard Business
    School Working Matters*. May 2012. Web. 24 Nov. 2012.

Gore, Al, and David Blood. "A Manifesto for Sustainable
    Capitalism." *Generation*. Generation Investment
    Management LLC, 14 Dec. 2011. PDF file.

Hurley, James. "Belu Boss Shows Bottle for a Turnaround." *Daily
    Telegraph*. Telegraph Media Group, 28 Feb. 2012. Web. 26
    Nov. 2012.

Knight, Eric R. W. "The Economic Geography of Clean
    Tech Venture Capital." *School of Geography and the
    Environment*. U of Oxford, June 2010. PDF file.

Packer, George. "No Death, No Taxes: The Libertarian Futurism
    of a Silicon Valley Billionaire." *New Yorker*. New Yorker, 28
    Nov. 2011. Web. 24 Nov. 2012.

Research

12 Preparing for a Research Project

Your employer asks you to recommend the best software for a particular project. You want to plan an alternative spring break trip to work with Habitat for Humanity. Your instructor assigns a term paper about a jazz musician. Each of these situations calls for research, for examining various kinds of sources. Preparing to begin your research means taking a long look at what you already know, the best way to proceed, and the amount of time you have to find out what you need to know. For success in college and beyond, you need to understand how to start the process of academic research.

12a Analyze the research assignment.

In an introductory writing course, you might receive an assignment like this one:

> Choose a subject of interest to you, and use it as the basis for a research essay of approximately two thousand words that makes and substantiates a claim. You should use a minimum of five credible, authoritative sources.

Topic. If your assignment doesn't specify a topic, consider the following questions (see also 4c):

- What subjects do you already know something about? Which of them would you like to explore more fully?
- What subjects do you care about? What might you like to become an expert on?
- What subjects evoke a strong reaction from you, whether positive or negative?

Be sure to get responses about your possible topic from your instructor, classmates, and friends. Ask them whether they would be interested in reading about the topic, whether it seems manageable, and whether they know of any good sources for information on the topic.

Situation. Be sure to consider the rhetorical situation (see Chapter 4) of any research project. Here are detailed questions to think about:

AUDIENCE

- Who will be the audience for your research project (4e)?
- Who will be interested in the information you gather, and why? What will they want to know? What will they already know?
- What do you know about their backgrounds? What assumptions might they hold about the topic?
- What response do you want from them?
- What kinds of evidence will you need to convince them?
- What will your instructor expect?

PURPOSE

- If you can choose the purpose, what would you like to accomplish (4d)?
- If you have been assigned a specific research project, keep in mind the key words in that assignment. Does the assignment ask that you *describe, survey, analyze, persuade, explain, classify, compare,* or *contrast*? What do such words mean in this field?

YOUR POSITION ON THE TOPIC (STANCE)

- What is your attitude toward your topic? Are you curious about it? critical of it? Do you like it? dislike it? find it confusing?
- What influences have shaped your position (4d)?

SCOPE

- How long is the project supposed to be? Base your research and writing schedule on the scale of the finished project (a short versus a long paper or presentation, a brief oral report or a longer multimedia presentation, a simple versus a complex Web site) and the amount of time you have to complete it.
- How many and what kind(s) of sources should you use (13a)? What kind(s) of visuals—charts, maps, photographs, and so on—will you need? Will you need to do any field research—interviewing, surveying, or observing (13e)?

EXERCISE 12.1

Come up with at least two topics you would like to research. Then write a brief response to some key questions about each topic: How much information do you think is available on this topic? What sources on this topic do you know about or have access to? Who would know about this topic — historians? doctors? filmmakers? psychologists? others?

12b Formulate a research question and hypothesis.

Once you have analyzed your task, chosen your topic, and narrowed the topic to make it manageable (see 4c and 5a), formulate a research question that you can tentatively answer with a hypothesis. The hypothesis, a statement of what you anticipate your research will show, needs to be manageable, interesting, and specific (see 5b). In addition, it must be a debatable proposition that you can prove or disprove with a reasonable amount of research evidence.

David Craig, the student whose research paper appears in 49e, made the following move from general topic to a narrowed topic and then to a research question and hypothesis:

TOPIC	Electronic messaging
NARROWED TOPIC	The language of messaging
ISSUE	The effect of messaging on youth literacy
RESEARCH QUESTION	How has the popularity of messaging affected literacy among today's youth?
HYPOTHESIS	Messaging seems to have a negative influence on the writing skills of young people.

EXERCISE 12.2

Using the tips provided in 12a, write down as much as you can about one of the topics you identified in Exercise 12.1. Then take some time to reread your notes, and jot down the questions you still need to answer as well as the sources you need to find.

12c Plan your research.

Once you have formulated a hypothesis, determine what you already know about your topic. Tap your memory for sources by listing everything that you can remember about *where* you learned about your topic: the Internet, text messages, books, magazines, courses, conversations, television. What you know comes from somewhere, and that somewhere can serve as a starting point for your research. (See 5a for more strategies for exploring ideas and getting your initial thoughts about a topic down on paper.)

Next, develop your research plan by answering the following questions:

- What kinds of sources (books, journal articles, databases, Web sites, government documents, reference works, and so on) will you need to consult (13a)? How many sources should you use?

- How current do your sources need to be? For topical issues, especially those related to science, current sources are usually most important. For historical subjects, older sources may offer the best information.

- How can you determine the location and availability of the kinds of sources you need?

One goal of your research plan is to build a strong working bibliography (14b). Carrying out systematic research and keeping careful notes on your sources will make developing your works-cited list or bibliography easier.

12d Set up a research log.

Keeping a research log will make the job of writing and documenting your sources more efficient and accurate. Use your research log to jot down ideas about possible sources and to keep track of materials. When you record an online source in your log, include the URL or other information that will help you find the source again.

Here are a few guidelines for setting up a research log:

1. Create a folder, and label it with a name that will be easy to identify, such as *Research Log for Project on Messaging*.
2. Within this folder, create subfolders that will help you manage your project. These subfolders might include *Notes on Hypothesis and Thesis, Background Information, Visuals, Draft 1, Working Bibliography*, and so on.

You might prefer to begin a blog for your research project. You can use it to record your thoughts on the reading you are doing and, especially, add links from there to Web sites, documents, and articles you have found online.

Whatever form your research log takes, you must clearly distinguish the notes and comments you make from quoted passages you record (see Chapter 14).

12e Move from hypothesis to working thesis.

As you gather information, search catalogs and databases, and read and evaluate sources, you will probably refine your research question and change your hypothesis significantly. Only after you have explored your hypothesis, tested it, and sharpened it by reading, writing, and talking with others does it become a working thesis.

David Craig, the student whose hypothesis appears in 12b, did quite a bit of research on messaging language, youth literacy, and the possible connection between the two. The more he read, the more he felt that the hypothesis suggested by his discussion with instructors—that messaging had contributed to a decline in youth literacy—did not hold up. Thus, he shifted his attention to the positive effects of messaging on communication skills and developed the following working thesis: "Although some educators criticize messaging, it may aid literacy by encouraging young people to use words and to write—even if messaging requires a different kind of writing."

In doing your own research, you may find that your interest shifts, that a whole line of inquiry is unproductive, or that your hypothesis is simply wrong. The process of research pushes you to learn more about your hypothesis and to make it more precise.

EXERCISE 12.3: THINKING CRITICALLY

If you have done a research project before, go back and evaluate the work you did as a researcher and as a writer in light of the principles developed in this chapter. What was the purpose of the research? Who was your audience? How did you narrow and focus your topic? What kinds of sources did you use? Did you use a research log? What about your research and your essay pleased you most? What pleased you least? What would you do differently if you were to revise the essay now?

13 Doing Research

How would you find out where to get the best coffee in town, or how to find sources for a Web project on a 1930s film star? Whether you are researching pizza or Picasso, you need to be familiar with the kinds of sources you are likely to use, the searches you can perform, and the types of research you will do most often: library, Internet, and field research.

13a Understand different kinds of sources.

Research sources can include data from interviews and surveys, books and articles both in print and online, Web sites, film, video, images, and more. Consider these important differences among sources.

Primary and secondary sources.   Primary sources provide firsthand knowledge, while secondary sources report on or analyze the research of others. Primary sources are basic sources of raw information, including your own field research; films, works of art, or other objects you examine; literary works you read; and eyewitness accounts, photographs, news reports, and historical documents (such as letters and speeches). Secondary sources are descriptions or interpretations of primary sources, such as researchers' reports, reviews, biographies, and encyclopedia articles. Often what constitutes a primary or secondary source depends on the purpose of your research. A critic's evaluation of a film, for instance, serves as a secondary source if you are writing about the film but as a primary source if you are studying the critic's writing.

Scholarly and popular sources.   While nonacademic sources like magazines can help you get started on a research project, you will usually want to depend more heavily on authorities in a field, whose work generally appears in scholarly journals in print or online. The following list will help you distinguish scholarly and popular sources:

Scholarly

Popular

Scholarly	Popular
Title often contains the word *Journal*	*Journal* usually does not appear in title
Source available mainly through libraries and library databases	Source generally available outside of libraries (at newsstands or from a home Internet connection)
Few commercial advertisements	Many advertisements
Authors identified with academic credentials	Authors are usually journalists or reporters hired by the publication rather than academics or experts
Summary or abstract appears on first page of article; articles are fairly long	No summary or abstract; articles are fairly short
Articles cite sources and provide bibliographies	Articles may include quotations but do not cite sources or provide bibliographies

Older and more current sources.   Most projects can benefit from both older, historical sources and more current ones. Some older sources are classics, essential for understanding later scholarship. Others are simply dated. Whether a source appeared hundreds of years ago or this morning, evaluate it carefully to determine how useful it will be for you.

13b   Use the library to get started.

Many beginning researchers are tempted to assume that all the information they could possibly need is readily available on the Internet from a home connection. However, it is a good idea to begin almost any research project with the sources available in your college library.

Reference librarians.   The purpose of a college reference library is to help students find information—and the staff of your library, especially reference librarians, will willingly help you figure out how to get started, what resources to choose for your project, and how to research more effectively. When in doubt, ask your librarian! You can make an appointment to talk with a librarian about your research project and get specific recommendations about databases and other helpful places to begin your research. In addition, many libraries have online tours and chat environments where students can ask questions about their research.

Catalogs and databases.   Your library's computers hold many resources not accessible to students except through the library's system. In addition to the library's own catalog of books and other holdings, most college libraries also subscribe to a large number of databases—electronic collections of information, such as indexes to journal and magazine articles, texts of news stories and legal cases, lists of sources on particular topics, and compilations of statistics—that students can access for free.

Reference works.   Consulting general reference works is another good way to get started on a research project. These works are especially helpful for getting an overview of a topic, identifying subtopics, finding more specialized sources, and identifying useful keywords for electronic searches.

ENCYCLOPEDIAS. Encyclopedias offer general background on a subject and often include bibliographies that can point you to more specialized sources. Remember that encyclopedias will serve as a place to start your research — not as major sources for a research project.

BIOGRAPHICAL RESOURCES. The lives and the historical settings of famous people are the topics of biographical dictionaries and indexes.

BIBLIOGRAPHIES. Bibliographies are collections of resources available on a subject — for example, Shakespeare or World War II. Bibliographies may be databases or bound collections, and they may list books alone, both books and articles, or media such as film or video. A bibliography may simply list or describe each resource it includes, or it may include analysis of the resources.

ALMANACS, YEARBOOKS, AND ATLASES. Almanacs and yearbooks contain data on current events and statistical information. Look in an atlas for maps and other geographic data.

13c Find library resources.

The library is one of a researcher's best friends, especially in an age of digital communication. Your college library houses a great number of print materials and gives you access to electronic catalogs, indexes, and databases that are not available to you on the Internet. Check your library's Web site or ask a librarian for an introduction to the available resources.

Search options. The most important tools your library offers are its online catalog and databases. Searching these tools will always be easier and more efficient if you use carefully chosen words to limit the scope of your research.

SUBJECT WORD SEARCHING. Catalogs and databases usually index their contents not only by author and title but also by subject headings — standardized words and phrases used to classify the subject matter of books and articles. (For books, most U.S. academic libraries use the *Library of Congress Subject Headings*, or LCSH, for this purpose.) When you search the catalog by subject, you need to use the exact subject words.

Advanced search page from a library catalog that incorporates
Boolean operators

KEYWORD SEARCHING. Searches using keywords, on the other hand, make use of the computer's ability to look for any term in any field of the electronic record, including not just subject but also author, title, series, and notes. In article databases, a keyword search will look in abstracts and summaries of articles as well. Keyword searching is less restrictive, but it requires you to put some thought into choosing your search terms in order to get the best results.

ADVANCED SEARCHING. Many library catalogs and database search engines offer advanced search options (sometimes on a separate page) to help you combine keywords, search for an exact phrase, or exclude items containing particular keywords. Often they limit your search in other ways as well, such as by date, language, country of origin, or location of the keyword within a site.

Many catalogs and databases offer a search option using the Boolean operators AND, OR, and NOT, and some allow you to use parentheses to refine your search or wildcards to expand it. Note that much Boolean decision making is done for you when you use an advanced search option (as on the advanced search page shown above). Note, too, that search engines vary in the exact terms and symbols they use to refine searches, so check before you search.

- **AND limits your search.** If you enter the terms *messaging* AND *language* AND *literacy*, the search engine will retrieve only those items that contain *all* the terms. Some search engines use a plus sign (+) instead of AND.

- **OR expands your search.** If you enter the terms *messaging* OR *language*, the computer will retrieve every item that contains the term *messaging* and every item that contains the term *language*.

- **NOT limits your search.** If you enter the terms *messaging* NOT *language*, the search engine will retrieve every item that contains *messaging* except those that also contain the term *language*. Some search engines use a minus sign (−) or AND NOT instead of NOT.

- **Parentheses customize your search.** Entering *messaging* AND *(literacy* OR *linguistics)*, for example, will locate items that mention either of those terms in connection with messaging.

- **Wildcards expand your search.** Use a wildcard, usually an asterisk (*) or a question mark (?), to find related words that begin with the same letters. Entering *messag** will locate *message*, *messages*, and *messaging*.

- **Quotation marks narrow your search.** Most search engines interpret words within quotation marks as a phrase that must appear with the words in that exact order.

Books.   The library catalog lists all the library's books.

CATALOG INFORMATION. Library catalogs follow a standard pattern of organization, with each holding identified by three kinds of entries: one headed by the *author's name*, one by the *title*, and one or (usually) more by the *subject*. If you can't find a particular source under any of these headings, you can search the catalog by using a combination of subject headings and keywords. Such searches may turn up other useful titles as well.

Catalog entries for books list not only the author, title, subject, and publication information but also a call number that indicates how the book is classified and where it is shelved. Many online catalogs allow you to save the information about the book while you continue searching and then retrieve the call numbers for all of the books you want to find in one list. Once you have the call number for a book, look for a library map or shelving plan to tell you where the book is housed. Take the time to browse through the books near the call number you are looking for. Often you will find other books related to your topic nearby.

Following is a page of results for noted linguist and author David Crystal. Many electronic catalogs indicate whether a book has been checked out and, if so, when it is due to be returned. Sometimes you must click on a link to check the availability of the book.

Total number of items in catalog for author David Crystal

Items on this catalog page

Call number

Location

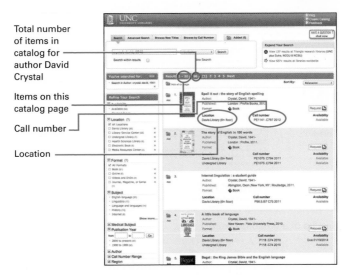

Results for author search in library database

BOOK INDEXES. Indexes can help you quickly locate complete bibliographic information on a book when you know only one piece of it—the author's last name, perhaps, or the title. Indexes can also alert you to other works by a particular author or on a particular subject. If you are looking for an older book, you may find the information you need in a print index rather than in an electronic database.

REVIEW INDEXES. A review index will help you find reviews of books you are interested in so that you can check the relevance of a source or get a thumbnail sketch of its contents before you track it down. For reviews more than ten years old, you will generally need to consult the print version of the index.

Periodical articles. Titles of periodicals held by a library appear in its catalog, but the titles of individual articles do not. To find the contents of periodicals, you will need to use an index source.

PERIODICAL INDEXES. Periodical indexes are databases or print volumes that hold information about articles published in newspapers, magazines, and scholarly journals. Different indexes cover different groups of periodicals. Ask a reference librarian for guidance about the most relevant index for your topic.

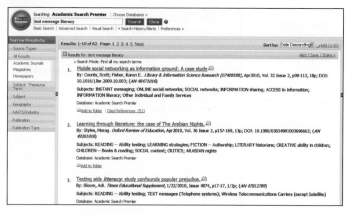

Results of a database search

General indexes of periodicals list articles from general-interest magazines (such as *Time* or *Newsweek*), newspapers, or a combination of these. General indexes usually provide current sources on a topic, but you may need to look further for more in-depth articles.

Many disciplines have *specialized indexes and abstracts* to help researchers find detailed information. To use these resources most efficiently, ask a reference librarian for help.

Some electronic periodical indexes offer the full text of articles, and some offer abstracts (short summaries) of the articles. Be sure not to confuse an abstract with a complete article. Full-text databases can be extremely convenient—you can read and print out articles directly from the computer, without the extra step of tracking down the periodical in question. However, don't limit yourself to full-text databases, which may not include the sources that would benefit your research most. Databases that offer abstracts give you an overview of the article's contents, which can help you decide whether you need to spend time finding and reading the full text.

To locate an indexed article that seems promising for your research project, you can check the library catalog to see whether the periodical is available electronically and, if so, whether your library has access to it. Using the library computer network for access can help you avoid paying to view the text of an article that is available online only for subscribers or for a fee.

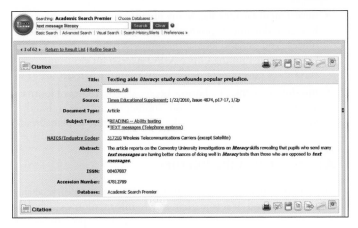

Article page with abstract

If the periodical is not available electronically (some scholarly journals, for example, are not), the library catalog also will tell you whether a print version is available in your library's periodicals room. This room probably has recent issues of hundreds or even thousands of newspapers, magazines, and scholarly journals, and it may also contain bound volumes of past issues and microfilm copies of older newspapers.

Bibliographies.   Bibliographies (lists of sources) in books or articles you are using for your research can lead you to other valuable resources. In addition, check with a reference librarian to find out whether your library has more extensive bibliographies devoted to the area of your research.

Other library resources.   In addition to books and periodicals, libraries give you access to many other useful materials that might be appropriate for your research.

- **Special collections and archives.** Your library may house archives (collections of valuable papers) and other special materials that are often available to student researchers.
- **Audio, video, multimedia, and art collections.** Many libraries have areas devoted to media and art, where they collect films, videos, paintings, and sound recordings.

- **Government documents.** Many libraries have collections of historical documents produced by local or state government offices. You can also look at the online version of the U.S. Government Printing Office (GPO Access) for electronic versions of government publications from the past decade or so.
- **Interlibrary loans.** To borrow books, videos, copies of journal articles, or audio materials from another library, use an interlibrary loan. Some loans can take time, so be sure to plan ahead.

13d Search the Internet.

The Internet is many college students' favorite way of accessing information, and it's true that much information — including authoritative sources identical to those your library provides — can be found online, sometimes for free. However, information in library databases comes from identifiable and professionally edited sources; because no one is responsible for regulating information on the Web, you need to take special care to find out which information online is reliable and which is not. (See Chapter 14 for more on evaluating sources.)

Internet searches. Researchers using a search tool such as Google usually begin with a keyword search. Because the Internet contains vastly more material than the largest library catalog or database, Internet searching requires care in the choice of keywords. For example, if you need information on legal issues regarding the Internet and enter *Internet* and *law* as keywords in your Google search, you will get over three million hits. You may find what you need on the first page of hits, but if not, you will need to choose new keywords that lead to more specific sources.

Bookmarking tools. Today's powerful bookmarking tools can help you browse, sort, and track resources online. Social bookmarking sites allow users to tag information and share it with others. Once you register on a social bookmarking site, you can tag an online resource with any words you choose. Users' tags are visible to all other users. If you find a helpful site, you can check to see how others have tagged it and quickly browse similar tags to find related information. You can sort and group information according to your tags. Fellow users whose tags you like and trust can become part of your network so that you can follow their sites of interest.

Web browsers can also help you to bookmark and return to online resources that you have found. However, unlike the bookmarking tools in a Web browser, which are tied to one machine, social bookmarking tools are available from any computer with an Internet connection.

Authoritative sources online.   You can find many sources online that are authoritative and reliable. For example, the Internet enables you to enter virtual libraries that allow access to some collections in libraries other than your own. Online collections housed in government sites can also be reliable and useful sources. The Library of Congress, the National Institutes of Health, and the U.S. Census Bureau, for example, have large online collections of articles. For current national news, consult online versions of reputable newspapers such as the *Washington Post* or the *Chicago Tribune,* or electronic sites for news services such as C-SPAN. To limit your searches to scholarly works, try Google Scholar.

Some scholarly journals (such as those from Berkeley Electronic Press) and general-interest magazines (including *Slate* and *Salon*) are published only on the Web, and many other publications, like *Newsweek,* the *New Yorker,* and the *New Republic,* make at least some of their content available online for free.

13e   Conduct field research.

For many research projects, particularly those in the social sciences and business, you will need to collect field data. The "field" may be many things—a classroom, a church, a laboratory, or the corner grocery store. As a field researcher, you will need to discover *where* you can find relevant information, *how* to gather it, and *who* might be your best providers of information.

Interviewing.   Some information is best obtained by asking direct questions of other people. If you can talk with an expert—in person, on the telephone, or via the Internet—you might get information you could not obtain through any other kind of research. In addition to getting an expert opinion, you might ask for firsthand accounts or suggestions of other places to look or other people to consult.

CHECKLIST

Conducting an Interview

1. Determine your purpose, and be sure it relates to your research question and your hypothesis.

2. Set up the interview well in advance. Specify how long it will take, and if you wish to record the session, ask permission to do so.

3. Prepare a written list of factual and open-ended questions. Brainstorming or freewriting can help you come up with questions (5a). Leave plenty of space for notes after each question. If the interview proceeds in a direction that seems fruitful, do not feel that you have to ask all of your prepared questions.

4. Record the subject, date, time, and place of the interview.

5. Thank those you interview, either in person or in a letter or email.

Observing. Trained observers report that making a faithful record of an observation requires intense concentration and mental agility. Moreover, an observer is never neutral—he or she always has an angle on what is being observed.

CHECKLIST

Conducting an Observation

1. Determine the purpose of the observation, and be sure it relates to your research question and hypothesis.

2. Brainstorm about what you are looking for, but don't be rigidly bound to your expectations.

3. Develop an appropriate system for recording data. Consider using a split notebook or page: on one side, record your observations directly; on the other, record your thoughts and interpretations.

4. Record the date, time, and place of the observation.

Conducting surveys. Surveys usually depend on questionnaires. On any questionnaire, the questions should be clear and easy to understand and designed so that you can analyze the answers easily. Questions that ask respondents to say *yes* or *no* or to rank items on a scale are particularly easy to tabulate:

The parking facilities on our campus are adequate.

⊙ Strongly agree ⊙ Somewhat agree ⊙ Unsure ⊙ Somewhat disagree ⊙ Strongly disagree

---

CHECKLIST

Designing a Survey Questionnaire

1. Write out your purpose, and review your research question and hypothesis to determine the kinds of questions to ask.

2. Figure out how to reach the respondents you need.

3. Draft potential questions, and make sure that each question calls for a short, specific answer.

4. Test the questions on several people, and revise any that seem unfair, ambiguous, too hard, or too time consuming.

5. For a questionnaire that is to be mailed or emailed, draft a cover letter explaining your purpose.

6. On the final version of the questionnaire, leave adequate space for answers.

7. Proofread the questionnaire carefully.

Analyzing, synthesizing, and interpreting data from field research. To make sense of your data, find a focus for your analysis, since you can't pay attention to everything. Then synthesize the data by looking for recurring words or ideas that fall into patterns. Establish a system for coding your information, labeling each pattern you identify—a plus sign for every positive response, for example. Finally, interpret your data by summing up the meaning of what you have found. What is the significance of your findings? Be careful not to make large generalizations.

EXERCISE 13.1: THINKING CRITICALLY

Begin to analyze the research project you are now working on by examining the ways in which you conducted your research: What use did you make of primary and secondary sources? What library, online, and field research did you carry out? What aspect of the research process was most satisfying? What was most disappointing or irritating? How could you do research more efficiently? Bring your answers to these questions to class.

14 Evaluating Sources and Taking Notes

The difference between a useful source and a poor one depends to a great extent on your topic, purpose, and audience. On almost any topic you can imagine (Why do mosquitoes bite? Who reads fan fiction? What musicians influenced Sonic Youth?), you will need research—looking into sources, gathering data, and thinking critically about these sources—to answer the question. With most topics, in fact, your problem will not be so much finding sources as figuring out *which* sources to consult in the limited time you have available. Learning how to tell which sources are best for you allows you to use your time wisely, and taking effective notes allows you to put the sources to work for you.

14a Understand the purpose of sources.

Why do writers decide to use one source rather than another? Sources serve different purposes, so part of evaluating them involves deciding what you need the source to provide for your research projects. You may need background information or context that your audience will need to follow your writing; explanations of concepts unfamiliar to your audience; verbal and visual emphasis for your points; authority or evidence for your claims, which can help you create your own authority; other perspectives on your topic; or counter-examples or counter-evidence that you need to consider.

As you begin to work with your sources, make notes in your research log about why you plan to use a particular source. You should also begin your working bibliography.

14b Create a working bibliography.

A working bibliography is a list of sources that you may potentially use for your project. As you find and begin to evaluate research sources—articles, books, Web sites, and so on—you should record source information for every source you think you might use. (Relevant information includes everything you need to find the source again and cite it correctly; the information you will need varies based on the type of source, whether you found it in a library or not, and whether you consulted it in print or online.) The emphasis here is on *working* because the list will probably include materials that end up not being useful. For this reason, you don't absolutely need to put all entries into the documentation style you will use (see Chapters 49–52). If you do follow the required documentation style, however, that part of your work will be done when you prepare the final draft.

The following chart will help you keep track of the sorts of information you should try to find:

Type of Source	Information to Collect (if applicable)
Print book	Library call number, author(s) or editor(s), title and subtitle, place of publication, publisher, year of publication, any other information (translator, edition, volume)
Part of a book	Call number, author(s) of part, title of part, author(s) or editor(s) of book, title of book, place of publication, publisher, year of publication, inclusive page numbers for part
Print periodical article	Call number of periodical, author(s) of article, title of article, name of periodical, volume number, issue number, date of issue, inclusive page numbers for article
Online source	Author(s), title of document, title of site, editor(s) of site, sponsor of site, publication information for print version of source, name of database or online service, date of electronic publication or last update, date you accessed the source, URL

For other kinds of sources (such as films, recordings, visuals), you should also list the information required by the documentation style you are using (see Chapters 49–52), and note where you found the information.

Annotated bibliography.   You might wish to annotate your working bibliography to include your own description and comments as well as publishing information (whether or not annotations are required), because annotating can help you understand and remember what the source says. If your instructor requires an annotated bibliography, be sure to ask for the specific guidelines you are to follow in creating the bibliography.

Annotations can sometimes be very detailed and may include summaries of the main points in a source and evaluations of the source's usefulness. However, most annotations students do on their own include fairly brief descriptions and comments.

ANNOTATED BIBLIOGRAPHY ENTRY

Gere, Anne Ruggles. "Kitchen Tables and Rented Rooms: The Extracurriculum of Composition." *Literacy: A Critical Sourcebook.* Ed. Ellen Cushman, Eugene R. Kintgen, Barry M. Kroll, and Mike Rose. Boston: Bedford, 2001. 275–89. Print. This history of writing instruction argues that people teach writing and learn to write—and always have—more often in informal places like kitchens than in traditional writing classrooms. Gere presents numerous examples and comments on their importance to the study of writing today.

14c   Evaluate a source's usefulness and credibility.

Since you want the information and ideas you glean from sources to be reliable and persuasive, you must evaluate each potential source carefully. The following guidelines can help you assess the usefulness and credibility of sources you are considering:

• **Your purpose.** What will this source add to your research project? Does it help you support a major point, demonstrate that you have thoroughly researched your topic, or help establish your own credibility through its authority?

- **Relevance.** How closely related is the source to the narrowed topic you are pursuing? You may need to read beyond the title and opening paragraph to check for relevance.

- **Level of specialization and audience.** General sources can be helpful as you begin your research, but you may then need the authority or currency of more specialized sources. On the other hand, extremely specialized works may be very hard to understand. Who was the source originally written for — the general public? experts in the field? advocates or opponents? How does this fit with your concept of your own audience?

- **Credentials of the publisher or sponsor.** What can you learn about the publisher or sponsor of the source you are using? For example, is it a newspaper known for integrity, or is it a tabloid? Is it a popular source, or is it sponsored by a professional or governmental organization or academic institution? If you're evaluating a book, is the publisher one you recognize or can find described on its own Web site? No hard and fast rules exist for deciding what kind of source to use. But knowing the sponsor's or publisher's credentials can help you determine whether a source is appropriate for your research project.

- **Credentials of the author.** As you do your research, note names that come up from one source to another, since these references may indicate that the author is influential in the field. An author's credentials may also be presented in the article, book, or Web site, or you can search the Internet for information about the author. In U.S. academic writing, experts and those with significant experience in a field have more authority on the subject than others.

- **Date of publication.** Recent sources are often more useful than older ones, particularly in the sciences or other fields that change rapidly. However, in some fields — such as the humanities — the most authoritative works may be older ones. The publication dates of Internet sites can often be difficult to pin down. And even for sites that include dates of posting, remember that the material posted may have been composed some time earlier.

- **Accuracy of the source.** How accurate and complete is the information in the source? How thorough is the bibliography or list of works cited that accompanies the source? Can you find other sources that corroborate what your source is saying?

- **Stance of the source.** Identify the source's point of view or rhetorical stance, and scrutinize it carefully. Does the source present facts, or does it interpret or evaluate them? If it presents facts, what is included and what is omitted, and why? If it interprets or evaluates information that is not disputed, the source's stance may be obvious, but at other times, you will need to think carefully about the source's goals (14d). What does the author or sponsoring group want? to convince you of an idea? sell you something? call you to action in some way?

- **Cross-references to the source.** Is the source cited in other works? If you see your source cited by others, notice how they cite it and what they say about it to find additional clues to its credibility.

For more on evaluating Web sources and periodical articles, see the Source Maps on pp. 174–77.

14d   Read critically, and interpret sources.

For those sources that you want to analyze more closely, reading with a critical eye can make your research process more efficient. Use the following tips to guide your critical reading.

Your research question.   As you read, keep your research question in mind, and ask yourself the following questions:

- How does this material address your research question and support your hypothesis?

- What quotations from this source might help support your thesis?

- Does the source include counterarguments to your hypothesis that you will need to answer? If so, what answers can you provide?

CHECKLIST

Guidelines for Examining Potential Sources

Looking quickly at the various parts of a source can provide useful information and help you decide whether to explore that particular source more thoroughly. You are already familiar with some of these basic elements: title and subtitle, title page and copyright page, home page, table of contents, index, footnotes, and bibliography. Be sure to check other items as well.

✔ *Abstracts* — concise summaries of articles and books — routinely precede journal articles and are often included in indexes and databases.

✔ A *preface* or *foreword* generally discusses the writer's purpose and thesis.

✔ *Subheadings* within the text can alert you to how much detail is given on a topic.

✔ A *conclusion* or *afterword* may summarize or draw the strands of an argument together.

✔ For a digital source, click on some of the *links* to see if they're useful, and see if the overall *design* of the site is easy to navigate.

The author's stance and tone.   Even a seemingly factual report, such as an encyclopedia article, is filled with judgments, often unstated. Read with an eye for the author's overall rhetorical stance, or perspective, as well as for facts or explicit opinions. Also pay attention to the author's tone, the way his or her attitude toward the topic and audience is conveyed. The following questions can help:

• Is the author a strong advocate or opponent of something? a skeptical critic? a specialist in the field?

• Are there any clues to why the author takes this stance?

• How does this stance affect the author's presentation and your reaction to it?

• What facts does the author include? Can you think of any important fact that is omitted?

• What is the author's tone? Is it cautious, angry, flippant, serious, impassioned? What words indicate this tone?

SOURCE MAP: Evaluating Web Sources

Is the sponsor credible?

1 Who is the **sponsor or publisher** of the source? See what information you can get from the URL. The domain names for government sites may end in *.gov* or *.mil* and for educational sites in *.edu*. The ending *.org* may — but does not always — indicate a nonprofit organization. If you see a tilde (~) or percent sign (%) followed by a name, or if you see a word such as *users* or *members*, the page's creator may be an individual, not an institution. In addition, check the header and footer, where the sponsor may be identified. The page shown here, from the domain **nieman.harvard.edu /reports**, is from a site sponsored by the nonprofit Nieman Foundation for Journalism at Harvard University.

2 Look for an *About* **page** or a link to a home page for background information on the sponsor. Is a mission statement included? What are the sponsoring organization's purpose and point of view? Does the mission statement seem balanced? What is the purpose of the site (to inform, to persuade, to advocate for a cause, to advertise, or something else)? Does the information on the site come directly from the sponsor, or is the material reprinted from another source? If it is reprinted, check the original.

Is the author credible?

3 What are the **author's credentials**? Look for information accompanying the material on the page. You can also run a search on the author to find out more. Does the author seem qualified to write about this topic?

Is the information credible and current?

4 When was the information **posted or last updated**? Is it recent enough to be useful?

5 Does the page document sources with **footnotes or links**? If so, do the sources seem credible and current? Does the author include any additional resources for further information? Look for ways to corroborate the information the author provides.

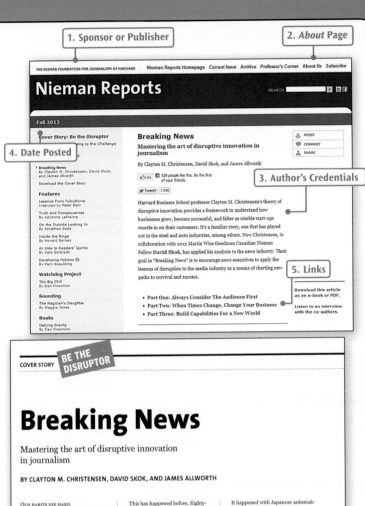

1. Sponsor or Publisher

2. *About* Page

4. Date Posted

3. Author's Credentials

5. Links

THE NIEMAN FOUNDATION FOR JOURNALISM AT HARVARD   Nieman Reports Homepage   Current Issue   Archive   Professor's Corner   About Us   Subscribe

Nieman Reports

SEARCH

Fall 2012

Cover Story: Be the Disruptor
...ing to the Challenge

▸ **Breaking News**
By Clayton M. Christensen, David Skok, and James Allworth

Download the Cover Story

Features

Lessons From Fukushima
Interview by Peter Behr

Truth and Consequences
By Adrienne LaFrance

On the Outside Looking In
By Jonathan Seitz

Inside the Rings
By Howard Berkes

An Ode to Readers' Quirks
By Kate Galbraith

Developing Notions
By Pam Spaulding

Watchdog Project

The Big Chill
By Dan Froomkin

Sounding

The Magician's Daughter
By Maggie Jones

Books

Defying Gravity
By Dan Froomkin

Breaking News

Mastering the art of disruptive innovation in journalism

By Clayton M. Christensen, David Skok, and James Allworth

Like   529 people like this. Be the first of your friends.

Tweet   1,046

Harvard Business School professor Clayton M. Christensen's theory of disruptive innovation provides a framework to understand how businesses grow, become successful, and falter as nimble start-ups muscle in on their customers. It's a familiar story, one that has played out in the steel and auto industries, among others. Now Christensen, in collaboration with 2012 Martin Wise Goodman Canadian Nieman Fellow David Skok, has applied his analysis to the news industry. Their goal in "Breaking News" is to encourage news executives to apply the lessons of disruption to the media industry as a means of charting new paths to survival and success.

- Part One: Always Consider The Audience First
- Part Two: When Times Change, Change Your Business
- Part Three: Build Capabilities For a New World

PRINT
COMMENT
SHARE

Download this article as an e-book or PDF.

Listen to an interview with the co-authors.

COVER STORY **BE THE DISRUPTOR**

Breaking News

Mastering the art of disruptive innovation
in journalism

BY CLAYTON M. CHRISTENSEN, DAVID SKOK, AND JAMES ALLWORTH

OLD HABITS DIE HARD.
Four years after the 2008 financial crisis, traditional news organizations continue to see their newsrooms shrink or close. Those that survive remain mired in the innovator's dilemma: A false choice between today's revenues and tomorrow's digital promise. The problem is a profound one: A study in March by the Pew Research Center's Project for Excellence in Journalism showed that newspapers have been, on average, losing print advertising dollars at seven times the rate they have been growing digital ad revenue.

Journalism institutions play a vital role in the democratic process and we are ...ing for their survival. But only the

This has happened before. Eighty-nine years ago, Henry Luce started Time as a weekly magazine summarizing the news. All 28 pages of the black-and-white weekly were filled with advertisements and aggregation. This wasn't just rewrites of the week's news; it was rip-and-read copy from the day's major publications—The Atlantic Monthly, The Christian Science Monitor, and the New York World, to name a few.

Today Time, with its print and online properties, confronts the challenges posed by the digital age, but reaches a global audience of 25 million.

With history as our guide, it shouldn't be a surprise when new entrants like The Huffington Post and BuzzFeed

It happened with Japanese automakers: They started with cheap subcompacts that were widely considered a joke. Now they make Lexuses that challenge the best of what Europe can offer.

It happened in the steel industry, where minimills began as a cheap, lower-quality alternative to established integrated mills, then moved their way up, pushing aside the industry's giants.

In the news business, newcomers are doing the same thing: delivering a product that is faster and more personalized than that provided by the bigger, more established news organizations. The newcomers aren't burdened by the expensive overheads of legacy organizations that are a function of life in the old

SOURCE MAP: Evaluating Articles

Determine the relevance of the source.

1 Look for an **abstract**, which provides a summary of the entire article. Is this source directly related to your research? Does it provide useful information and insights? Will your readers consider it persuasive support for your thesis?

Determine the credibility of the publication.

2 Consider the **publication's title**. Words in the title such as *Journal*, *Review*, and *Quarterly* may indicate that the periodical is a scholarly source. Most research projects rely on authorities in a particular field, whose work usually appears in scholarly journals. For more on distinguishing between scholarly and popular sources, see 13a.

3 Try to determine the **publisher or sponsor**. This journal is published by Johns Hopkins University Press. Academic presses such as this one generally review articles carefully before publishing them and bear the authority of their academic sponsors.

Determine the credibility of the author.

4 Evaluate the **author's credentials**. In this case, they are given in a note, which indicates that the author is a college professor and has written at least two books on related topics.

Determine the currency of the article.

5 Look at the **publication date**, and think about whether your topic and your credibility depend on your use of very current sources.

Determine the accuracy of the article.

6 Look at the **sources cited** by the author of the article. Here, they are documented in footnotes. Ask yourself whether the works the author has cited seem credible and current. Are any of these works cited in other articles you've considered?

In addition, consider the following questions:

- What is the article's stance or point of view? What are the author's goals? What does the author want you to know or believe?

- How does this source fit in with your other sources? Does any of the information it provides contradict or challenge other sources?

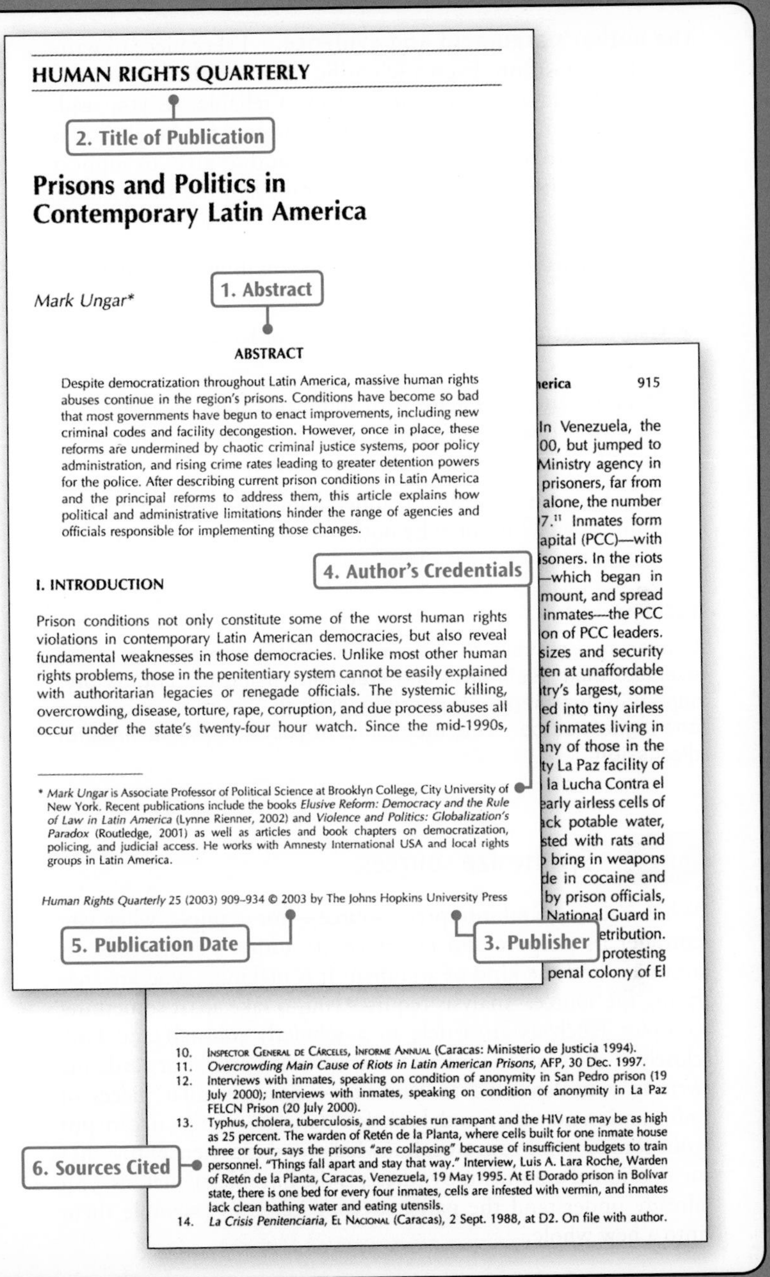

HUMAN RIGHTS QUARTERLY

Prisons and Politics in Contemporary Latin America

*Mark Ungar**

ABSTRACT

Despite democratization throughout Latin America, massive human rights abuses continue in the region's prisons. Conditions have become so bad that most governments have begun to enact improvements, including new criminal codes and facility decongestion. However, once in place, these reforms are undermined by chaotic criminal justice systems, poor policy administration, and rising crime rates leading to greater detention powers for the police. After describing current prison conditions in Latin America and the principal reforms to address them, this article explains how political and administrative limitations hinder the range of agencies and officials responsible for implementing those changes.

I. INTRODUCTION

Prison conditions not only constitute some of the worst human rights violations in contemporary Latin American democracies, but also reveal fundamental weaknesses in those democracies. Unlike most other human rights problems, those in the penitentiary system cannot be easily explained with authoritarian legacies or renegade officials. The systemic killing, overcrowding, disease, torture, rape, corruption, and due process abuses all occur under the state's twenty-four hour watch. Since the mid-1990s,

* *Mark Ungar* is Associate Professor of Political Science at Brooklyn College, City University of New York. Recent publications include the books *Elusive Reform: Democracy and the Rule of Law in Latin America* (Lynne Rienner, 2002) and *Violence and Politics: Globalization's Paradox* (Routledge, 2001) as well as articles and book chapters on democratization, policing, and judicial access. He works with Amnesty International USA and local rights groups in Latin America.

Human Rights Quarterly 25 (2003) 909–934 © 2003 by The Johns Hopkins University Press

erica 915

In Venezuela, the
00, but jumped to
Ministry agency in
prisoners, far from
alone, the number
7.[11] Inmates form
apital (PCC)—with
soners. In the riots
—which began in
mount, and spread
inmates—the PCC
on of PCC leaders.
sizes and security
ten at unaffordable
try's largest, some
ed into tiny airless
of inmates living in
ny of those in the
ty La Paz facility of
la Lucha Contra el
early airless cells of
ck potable water,
sted with rats and
bring in weapons
de in cocaine and
by prison officials,
National Guard in
etribution.
protesting
penal colony of El

10. Inspector General de Cárceles, Informe Annual (Caracas: Ministerio de Justicia 1994).
11. *Overcrowding Main Cause of Riots in Latin American Prisons*, AFP, 30 Dec. 1997.
12. Interviews with inmates, speaking on condition of anonymity in San Pedro prison (19 July 2000); Interviews with inmates, speaking on condition of anonymity in La Paz FELCN Prison (20 July 2000).
13. Typhus, cholera, tuberculosis, and scabies run rampant and the HIV rate may be as high as 25 percent. The warden of Retén de la Planta, where cells built for one inmate house three or four, says the prisons "are collapsing" because of insufficient budgets to train personnel. "Things fall apart and stay that way." Interview, Luis A. Lara Roche, Warden of Retén de la Planta, Caracas, Venezuela, 19 May 1995. At El Dorado prison in Bolívar state, there is one bed for every four inmates, cells are infested with vermin, and inmates lack clean bathing water and eating utensils.
14. *La Crisis Penitenciaria*, El Nacional (Caracas), 2 Sept. 1988, at D2. On file with author.

2. Title of Publication
1. Abstract
4. Author's Credentials
5. Publication Date
3. Publisher
6. Sources Cited

The author's argument and evidence. Every piece of writing takes a position. Even a scientific report implicitly "argues" that we should accept it and its data as reliable. As you read, look for the main point or the main argument the author is making. Try to identify the reasons the author gives to support his or her position. Then try to determine *why* the author takes this position.

- How persuasive is the evidence? Can you think of a way to refute it?

- Can you detect any questionable logic or fallacious thinking (10e)?

- Does this author disagree with arguments you have read elsewhere? If so, what causes the disagreements—differences about facts or about how to interpret facts?

- Does the author consider counterarguments or alternative points of view? If not, why not?

EXERCISE 14.1

Choose two sources that seem well suited to your topic, and evaluate their usefulness and credibility using the criteria presented in this chapter. If possible, analyze one print source and one digital source. Bring the results of your analysis to class for discussion.

14e Synthesize sources.

When you read and interpret a source—for example, when you consider its purpose and relevance, its author's credentials, its accuracy, and the kind of argument it is making—you are analyzing the source. Analysis requires you to take apart something complex (such as an article in a scholarly journal) and look closely at the parts to understand the whole better. For academic writing you also need to *synthesize*—group similar pieces of information together and look for patterns—so you can put your sources (and your own knowledge and experience) together in an original argument. Synthesis is the flip side of analysis: you already understand the parts, so your job is to assemble them into a new whole.

To synthesize sources for a research project, try the following tips:

- **Read the material carefully.** For tips on reading with a critical eye, see Chapter 9.
- **Determine the important ideas in each source.** Take notes on each source (14f). Identify and summarize the key ideas of each piece.
- **Formulate a position.** Review the key ideas of each source and figure out how they fit together. Look for patterns: discussions of causes and effects, specific parts of a larger issue, background information, and so on. Be sure to consider the complexity of the issue, and demonstrate that you have considered more than one perspective.
- **Summon evidence to support your position.** You might use paraphrases, summaries, or direct quotations from your sources as evidence (15a), or your personal experience or prior knowledge. Integrate quotations properly (15b), and keep your ideas central to the piece of writing.
- **Deal with counterarguments.** You don't have to use every idea or every source available—some will be more useful than others. However, ignoring evidence that opposes your position makes your argument weaker. You should acknowledge the existence of valid opinions that differ from yours, and try to explain why they are incorrect or incomplete.
- **Combine your source materials effectively.** Be careful to avoid simply summarizing or listing your research. Think carefully about how the ideas in your reading support your argument. Try to weave the various sources together rather than discussing your sources one by one.

14f Take notes and annotate sources.

Note-taking methods vary greatly from one researcher to another, so you may decide to use a computer file, a notebook, or index cards. Regardless of the method, however, you should (1) record enough information to help you recall the major points of the source; (2) put the information in the form in which you are most likely to incorporate it into your research essay, whether a summary, a paraphrase, or a quotation; and (3) note all the information you will need to cite the source accurately. The following example shows the major items a note should include:

Elements of an Accurate Note

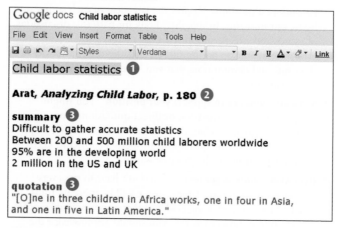

Google docs Child labor statistics

File Edit View Insert Format Table Tools Help

Styles ▾ Verdana ▾ ▾ **B** *I* <u>U</u> <u>A</u>▾ ⍵▾ Link

Child labor statistics ①

Arat, *Analyzing Child Labor*, p. 180 ②

summary ③
Difficult to gather accurate statistics
Between 200 and 500 million child laborers worldwide
95% are in the developing world
2 million in the US and UK

quotation ③
"[O]ne in three children in Africa works, one in four in Asia, and one in five in Latin America."

① **Use a subject heading.** Label each note with a brief but descriptive subject heading so that you can group similar subtopics together.

② **Identify the source.** List the author's name and a shortened title of the source, and a page number, if available. Your working-bibliography entry (14b) for the source will contain the full bibliographic information, so you don't need to repeat it in each note.

③ **Indicate whether the note is a direct quotation, paraphrase, or summary.** Make sure quotations are copied accurately. Put square brackets around any change you make, and use ellipses if you omit material.

Taking complete notes will help you digest the source information as you read and incorporate the material into your text without inadvertently plagiarizing the source (see Chapter 15). Be sure to reread each note carefully, and recheck it against the source to make sure quotations, statistics, and specific facts are accurate.

Quoting. Some of the notes you take will contain quotations, which give the *exact words* of a source. Here, for example, is a note with a quotation that David Craig planned to use in his research paper (see 49e):

Quotation Note

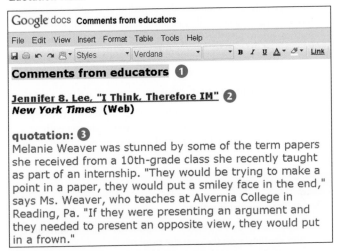

① Subject heading

② Author and short title of source (no page number for electronic source)

③ Direct quotation

Paraphrasing. A paraphrase accurately states all the relevant information from a passage *in your own words and sentence structures*, without any additional comments or elaborations. A paraphrase is useful when the main points of a passage, their order, and at least some details are important but—unlike passages worth quoting—the particular wording is not. Unlike a summary, a paraphrase always restates *all* the main points of a passage in the same order and often in about the same number of words.

ORIGINAL

Language play, the arguments suggest, will help the development of pronunciation ability through its focus on the properties of sounds and sound contrasts, such as rhyming. Playing with

word endings and decoding the syntax of riddles will help
the acquisition of grammar. Readiness to play with words
and names, to exchange puns and to engage in nonsense
talk, promotes links with semantic development. The kinds
of dialogue interaction illustrated above are likely to have
consequences for the development of conversational skills. And
language play, by its nature, also contributes greatly to what in
recent years has been called *metalinguistic awareness*, which is
turning out to be of critical importance in the development of
language skills in general and of literacy skills in particular.

　　　　　　　　　　　— David Crystal, *Language Play* (180)

UNACCEPTABLE PARAPHRASE: STRAYING FROM THE AUTHOR'S IDEAS

Crystal argues that playing with language — creating rhymes,
figuring out how riddles work, making puns, playing with
names, using invented words, and so on — helps children figure

---

CHECKLIST

Guidelines for Taking Notes

✔ Copy quotations carefully, with punctuation, capitalization,
and spelling *exactly* as in the original.

✔ Enclose the quotation in quotation marks; don't rely on
your memory to distinguish your own words from those of
the source.

✔ Use square brackets if you introduce words of your own
into a quotation or make changes in it, and use ellipses if
you omit material. If you later incorporate the quotation
into your essay, copy it faithfully — brackets, ellipses, and
all. (40b)

✔ Record the author's name, the shortened title, and the page
number(s) on which the quotation appears in the source.
If the note refers to more than one page, use a slash (/)
within the quotation to indicate where one page ends and
another begins. For sources without page numbers, record
the paragraph or other section number(s), if any.

✔ Make sure you have a corresponding working-bibliography
entry with complete source information. (14b)

✔ Label the note with a subject heading, and identify it as a
quotation.

out a great deal about language, from the basics of pronunciation and grammar to how to carry on a conversation. Increasing their understanding of how language works in turn helps them become more interested in learning new languages and in pursuing education (180).

This paraphrase starts off well enough, but it moves away from paraphrasing the original to inserting the writer's ideas; Crystal says nothing about learning new languages or pursuing education.

UNACCEPTABLE PARAPHRASE: USING THE AUTHOR'S WORDS

Crystal suggests that language play, including rhyme, helps children improve pronunciation ability, that looking at word endings and decoding the syntax of riddles allows them to understand grammar, and that other kinds of dialogue interaction teach conversation. Overall, language play may be of critical importance in the development of language and literacy skills (180).

Because the highlighted phrases are either borrowed from the original without quotation marks or changed only superficially, this paraphrase plagiarizes.

UNACCEPTABLE PARAPHRASE: USING THE AUTHOR'S SENTENCE STRUCTURES

Language play, Crystal suggests, will improve pronunciation by zeroing in on sounds such as rhymes. Having fun with word endings and analyzing riddle structure will help a person acquire grammar. Being prepared to play with language, to use puns and talk nonsense, improves the ability to use semantics. These playful methods of communication are likely to influence a person's ability to talk to others. And language play inherently adds enormously to what has recently been known as *metalinguistic awareness*, a concept of great magnitude in developing speech abilities generally and literacy abilities particularly (180).

Here is a paraphrase of the same passage that expresses the author's ideas accurately and acceptably:

ACCEPTABLE PARAPHRASE: IN THE STUDENT WRITER'S OWN WORDS

Crystal argues that playing with language—creating rhymes, figuring out riddles, making puns, playing with names, using invented words, and so on—helps children figure out a great

> ## CHECKLIST
>
> ### Guidelines for Paraphrasing
>
> ✔ Include all main points and any important details from the original source, in the same order in which the author presents them.
>
> ✔ State the meaning in your own words and sentence structures. If you want to include especially memorable language from the original, enclose it in quotation marks.
>
> ✔ Save your comments, elaborations, or reactions on another note.
>
> ✔ Record the author's name, the shortened title, and the page number(s) on which the original material appears. For sources without page numbers, record the paragraph, screen, or other section number(s), if any.
>
> ✔ Make sure you have a corresponding working-bibliography entry with complete source information. (14b)
>
> ✔ Label the note with a subject heading, and identify it as a paraphrase.

deal, from the basics of pronunciation and grammar to how to carry on a conversation. This kind of play allows children to understand the overall concept of how language works, a concept that is key to learning to use—and read—language effectively (180).

Summarizing.   A summary is a significantly shortened version of a passage or even of a whole chapter or work that captures main ideas *in your own words.* Unlike a paraphrase, a summary uses just enough information to record the main points you wish to emphasize. To summarize a short passage, read it carefully and, without looking at the text, write a one- or two-sentence summary. On p. 185 is David Craig's note recording a summary of the Crystal passage on pp. 181–82. Notice that the summary note states the author's main points selectively—and without using his words.

For a long passage or an entire chapter, skim the headings and topic sentences, and make notes of each; then write your summary

Summary Note

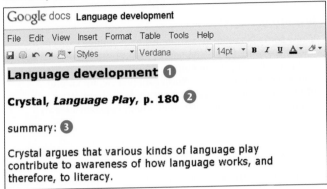

❶ Subject heading

❷ Author, title, page reference

❸ Summary of source

CHECKLIST

Guidelines for Summarizing

✔ Include just enough information to recount the main points you want to cite. A summary is usually far shorter than the original.

✔ Use your own words. If you include any language from the original, enclose it in quotation marks.

✔ Record the author's name, the shortened title, and the page number(s) on which the original material appeared. For sources without page numbers, record the paragraph, screen, or other section number(s), if any.

✔ Make sure you have a corresponding working-bibliography entry with complete source information. (14b)

✔ Label the note with a subject heading, and identify it as a summary.

in a paragraph or two. For a whole book, you may want to refer to the preface and introduction as well as chapter titles, headings, and topic sentences—and your summary may extend to a page or more.

FOR MULTILINGUAL WRITERS

Identifying Sources

While some language communities and cultures expect audiences to recognize the sources of important documents and texts, thereby eliminating the need to cite them directly, conventions for writing in North America call for careful attribution of any quoted, paraphrased, or summarized material in your project. When in doubt, explicitly identify your sources.

Annotating sources.   Sometimes you may photocopy or print out a source you intend to use. In such cases, you can annotate the photocopies or printouts with your thoughts and questions and highlight interesting quotations and key terms.

You can copy online sources electronically, paste them into a computer file, and annotate them there. Try not to rely too heavily on copying or printing out whole pieces, however; you still need to read the material very carefully. And resist the temptation to treat copied material as notes, an action that could lead to inadvertent plagiarizing (15g). (In a computer file, using a different color for text pasted from a source will help to prevent this problem.)

EXERCISE 14.2

Choose an online source you are sure you will use in your research project. Then download and print out the source, record all essential publication information for it, and annotate it as you read it.

EXERCISE 14.3: THINKING CRITICALLY

Take a careful look at the sources you have gathered for your research project. How many make points that support your own point of view? How many provide counterarguments to your point of view? Which sources are you relying on most — and why? Which sources seem most credible to you — and why? Which sources, if any, are you suspicious of or worried about? Bring the results of this investigation to class for discussion.

15   Integrating Sources and Avoiding Plagiarism

In some ways, there really is nothing new under the sun, in writing and research as well as in life. Whatever writing you do has been influenced by what you have already read and experienced. As you work on your research project, you will be joining a scholarly conversation and responding to the work of others. Thus you will need to know how to use, integrate, and acknowledge the work of others.

Integrating sources into your writing can be quite a challenge. In fact, as a beginning researcher, you might do what Professor Rebecca Howard calls "patchwriting": that is, rather than integrate the sources smoothly and accurately, you patch together words, phrases, and even structures from sources into your own writing, sometimes without citation. The author of this textbook remembers doing just such "patchwriting" for a report in middle school on her hero, Dr. Albert Schweitzer. Luckily, she had a teacher who sat patiently with her, showing her how to paraphrase and summarize and quote from the sources correctly and effectively. So it takes time and effort—and good instruction—to learn to integrate sources appropriately into your writing rather than patchwriting, which is sometimes considered plagiarism even if you didn't mean to plagiarize.

All writers need to understand current definitions of plagiarism (which have changed over time and differ from culture to culture) as well as the concept of intellectual property—the works protected by copyright and other laws—so they can give credit where credit is due.

15a   Decide whether to quote, paraphrase, or summarize.

You tentatively decided to quote, paraphrase, or summarize material when you took notes on your sources (14f). As you choose some of these sources for your research project and decide how to use them, however, you may reevaluate those decisions. The following guidelines can help you decide whether to quote, paraphrase, or summarize.

CHECKLIST

When to Quote, Paraphrase, or Summarize
QUOTE

✔ wording that is so memorable or powerful, or expresses a point so perfectly, that you cannot change it without weakening its meaning

✔ authors' opinions you wish to emphasize

✔ authors' words that show you are considering varying perspectives

✔ respected authorities whose opinions support your ideas

✔ authors whose opinions challenge or vary greatly from those of others in the field

PARAPHRASE

✔ passages you do not wish to quote but that use details important to your point

SUMMARIZE

✔ long passages in which the main point is important to your point but the details are not

---

15b Integrate quotations, paraphrases, and summaries effectively.

Here are some general guidelines for integrating source materials into your writing.

Incorporating quotations. Quotations from respected authorities can help establish your credibility and show that you are considering various perspectives. However, because your essay is primarily your own work, limit your use of quotations.

BRIEF QUOTATIONS. Short quotations should run in with your text, enclosed by quotation marks (39a).

> In Miss Eckhart, Welty recognizes a character who shares with her "the love of her art and the love of giving it, the desire to give it until there is no more left" (10).

LONG QUOTATIONS. If you are following the style of the Modern Language Association (MLA), set off a prose quotation longer than four lines. If you are following the style of the American Psychological Association (APA), set off a quotation of more than forty words or more than one paragraph. If you are following *Chicago* style, set off a quotation of more than one hundred words or more than one paragraph. Begin such a quotation on a new line. For MLA style, indent every line one inch; for APA style, five to seven spaces. For *Chicago* style, indent the text or use a smaller font (check your instructor's preference). Quotation marks are unnecessary. Introduce long quotations with a signal phrase or a sentence followed by a colon.

The following long quotation follows MLA style:

A good seating arrangement can prevent problems; however, *withitness*, as defined by Woolfolk, works even better:

> Withitness is the ability to communicate to students that you are aware of what is happening in the classroom, that you "don't miss anything." With-it teachers seem to have "eyes in the back of their heads." They avoid becoming too absorbed with a few students, since this allows the rest of the class to wander. (359)

This technique works, however, only if students actually believe that their teacher will know everything that goes on.

INTEGRATING QUOTATIONS SMOOTHLY INTO YOUR TEXT. Carefully integrate quotations into your text so that they flow smoothly and clearly into the surrounding sentences. Use a signal phrase or verb, such as those identified in the following examples and the list on p. 190.

> As Eudora Welty notes, "learning stamps you with its moments. Childhood's learning," she continues, "is made up of moments. It isn't steady. It's a pulse" (9).

> In her essay, Haraway strongly opposes those who condemn technology outright, arguing that we must not indulge in a "demonology of technology" (181).

Notice that the examples alert readers to the quotations by using signal phrases that include the author's name. When you cite a quotation in this way, you need put only the page number in parentheses.

SIGNAL VERBS

acknowledges	concludes	emphasizes	replies
advises	concurs	expresses	reports
agrees	confirms	interprets	responds
allows	criticizes	lists	reveals
answers	declares	objects	says
asserts	describes	observes	states
believes	disagrees	offers	suggests
charges	discusses	opposes	thinks
claims	disputes	remarks	writes

BRACKETS AND ELLIPSES. In direct quotations, enclose in brackets any words you change or add, and indicate any deletions with ellipsis points (40f).

> "There is something wrong in the [Three Mile Island] area," one farmer told the Nuclear Regulatory Commission after the plant accident ("Legacy" 33).

> Economist John Kenneth Galbraith has pointed out that "large corporations cannot afford to compete with one another. . . . In a truly competitive market someone loses" (qtd. in Key 17).

Incorporating paraphrases and summaries. Introduce paraphrases and summaries clearly, usually with a signal phrase that includes the author of the source, as the highlighted words in this example indicate.

> Professor of linguistics Deborah Tannen says that she offers her book *That's Not What I Meant!* to "women and men everywhere who are trying their best to talk to each other" (19). Tannen goes on to illustrate how communication between women and men breaks down and then to suggest that a full awareness of "genderlects" can improve relationships (297).

EXERCISE 15.1

Take a source-based piece of writing you have done recently or a research project you are working on now, and examine it to see how successfully you have integrated quotations. Have you used accurate signal verbs and introduced the sources of the quotations? Have you used square brackets and ellipses accurately to indicate changes in quotations?

EXERCISE 15.2

Read the brief original passage that follows, and then look closely at the five attempts to quote or paraphrase it. Decide which attempts are acceptable and which plagiarize, prepare notes on what supports your decision in each case, and bring your notes to class for discussion.

> The strange thing about plagiarism is that it's almost always pointless. The writers who stand accused, from Laurence Sterne to Samuel Taylor Coleridge to Susan Sontag, tend to be more talented than the writers they lift from.
> — Malcolm Jones, "Have You Read This Story Somewhere?"

1. According to Malcolm Jones, writers accused of plagiarism are always better writers than those they are supposed to have plagiarized.

2. According to Malcolm Jones, writers accused of plagiarism "tend to be more talented than the writers they lift from."

3. Plagiarism is usually pointless, says writer Malcolm Jones.

4. Those who stand accused of plagiarism, such as Senator Joseph Biden, tend to be better writers than those whose work they use.

5. According to Malcolm Jones, "plagiarism is . . . almost always pointless."

15c   Integrate visuals and media effectively.

Choose visuals and media wisely, whether you use video, audio, photographs, illustrations, charts and graphs, or other kinds of images. Integrate all visuals and media smoothly into your text.

- **Does each visual or media file make a strong contribution to the written message?** Tangential or purely decorative visuals and media may weaken the power of your writing.

- **Is each visual or media file appropriate and fair to your subject?** An obviously biased perspective may seem unfair or manipulative to your audience.

---

e bedfordstmartins.com/wia
Exercise > Research: Integrating sources

- **Is each visual or media file appropriate for and fair to your audience?** Visuals and media should appeal to various members of your likely audience.

Whenever you post documents containing visuals or media to the Web, make sure you check for copyright information. While it is considered "fair use" to use such materials in an essay or other project for a college class, once that project is published on the Web, you might infringe on copyright protections if you do not ask the copyright holder for permission to use the visual or media file. U.S. copyright law considers the reproduction of works for purposes of teaching and scholarship to be "fair use" not bound by copyright, but the law is open to multiple interpretations. If you have questions about whether your work might infringe on copyright, ask your instructor for help.

Just like quotations, paraphrases, and summaries, visuals and media need to be introduced and commented on in some way.

- Refer to the visual, audio, or video in the text (*As Fig. 3 demonstrates . . .*), and position it as close as possible after the first reference.

- Explain or comment on the relevance of the visual or media file. This can be done after the insertion point.

- Check the documentation system you are using to make sure you label visuals and media appropriately; MLA, for instance, asks that you number and title tables and figures (*Table 1: Average Amount of Rainfall by Region*).

- If you are posting your document or essay on a Web site, make sure you have permission to use any visuals or media files that are covered by copyright.

For more on using visuals, see 8d.

15d Check for excessive use of source material.

Your text needs to synthesize your research in support of your own argument; it should not be a patchwork of quotations, paraphrases, and summaries from other people. You need a rhetorical stance that represents you as the author. If you cite too many sources, your own voice will disappear, a problem the following passage demonstrates:

The United States is one of the countries with the most rapid population growth. In fact, rapid population increase has been a "prominent feature of American life since the founding of the republic" (Day 31). In the past, the cause of the high rate of population growth was the combination of large-scale immigration and a high birth rate. As Day notes, "Two facts stand out in the demographic history of the United States: first, the single position as a receiver of immigrants; second, our high rate of growth from natural increase" (31).

Nevertheless, American population density is not as high as in most European countries. Day points out that the Netherlands, with a density of 906 persons per square mile, is more crowded than even the most densely populated American states (33).

15e ## Understand why you should acknowledge your sources.

Acknowledging sources says to your reader that you have done your homework, that you have gained expertise on your topic, and that you are credible. Acknowledging sources can also demonstrate fairness—that you have considered several points of view. In addition, recognizing your sources can help provide background for your research by placing it in the context of other thinking. Most of all, you should acknowledge sources to help your readers follow your thoughts, understand how your ideas relate to the thoughts of others, and know where to go to find more information on your topic.

15f ## Know which sources to acknowledge.

As you carry out research, it is important to understand the distinction between materials that require acknowledgment (in in-text citations, footnotes, or endnotes, and in the works-cited list or bibliography) and those that do not.

Materials that do not require acknowledgment

- **Common knowledge.** If most readers already know a fact, you probably do not need to cite a source for it. You do not need to credit a source for the statement that Barack Obama was reelected in 2012, for example.

- **Facts available in a wide variety of sources.** If a number of encyclopedias, almanacs, textbooks, or reliable Web sources include a certain piece of information, you usually need not cite a specific source for it.
- **Your own findings from field research.** If you conduct observations or surveys, simply announce your findings as your own. Acknowledge people you interview as individuals rather than as part of a survey.

Materials that require acknowledgment. Some of the information you use may need to be credited to a source.

- **Quotations, paraphrases, and summaries.** Whenever you use another person's words, ideas, or opinions, credit the source. Even though the wording of a paraphrase or summary is your own, you should still acknowledge the source.
- **Facts not widely known or claims that are arguable.** If your readers would be unlikely to know a fact, or if an author presents as fact a claim that may or may not be true, cite the source. If you are not sure whether a fact will be familiar to your readers or whether a statement is arguable, cite the source.
- **Visuals from any source.** Credit all visual and statistical material not derived from your own field research, even if you yourself create a graph or table from the data provided in a source.
- **Help provided by others.** If an instructor gave you a good idea or if friends responded to your draft or helped you conduct surveys, give credit.

15g　Uphold your academic integrity and avoid plagiarism.

One of the cornerstones of intellectual work is academic integrity. This principle accounts for our being able to trust those sources we use and to demonstrate that our own work is equally trustworthy. While there are many ways to damage academic integrity, two that are especially important are inaccurate or incomplete acknowledgment of sources in citations—sometimes referred to as unintentional

FOR MULTILINGUAL WRITERS

Plagiarism as a Cultural Concept

Many cultures do not recognize Western notions of plagiarism, which rest on a belief that language and ideas can be owned by writers. Indeed, in many countries other than the United States, and even within some communities in the United States, using the words and ideas of others without attribution is considered a sign of deep respect as well as an indication of knowledge. In academic writing in the United States, however, you should credit all materials except those that are common knowledge, that are available in a wide variety of sources, or that are your own creations (photographs, drawings, and so on) or your own findings from field research.

plagiarism—and plagiarism that is deliberately intended to pass off one writer's work as another's.

Whether it is intentional or not, plagiarism can result in serious consequences. At some colleges, students who plagiarize fail the course automatically; at others, they are expelled. Instructors who plagiarize, even inadvertently, have had their degrees revoked and their books withdrawn from publication. And outside academic life, eminent political, business, and scientific leaders have been stripped of candidacies, positions, and awards because of plagiarism.

Inaccurate or incomplete citation of sources.   If your paraphrase is too close to the wording or sentence structure of a source (even if you identify the source), if you do not identify the source of a quotation (even if you include the quotation marks), or if you fail to indicate clearly the source of an idea that you obviously did not come up with on your own, you may be accused of plagiarism even if your intent was not to plagiarize. Inaccurate or incomplete acknowledgment of sources often results either from carelessness or from not learning how to borrow material properly in the first place. Still, because the costs of even unintentional plagiarism can be severe, it's important to understand how it can happen and how you can guard against it.

As a writer of academic integrity, you will want to take responsibility for your research and for acknowledging all your sources

---

CHECKLIST

Avoiding Plagiarism

✔ Maintain an accurate and thorough working bibliography. (14b)

✔ Establish a consistent note-taking system, listing sources and page numbers and clearly identifying all quotations, paraphrases, summaries, statistics, and visuals. (14f)

✔ Identify all quotations with quotation marks — both in your notes and in your essay. Be sure your summaries and paraphrases use your own words and sentence structures. (15b)

✔ Give a citation or note for each quotation, paraphrase, summary, arguable assertion or opinion, statistic, and visual that is from a source. Prepare an accurate and complete list of sources cited according to the required documentation style. (See Chapters 49–52.)

✔ Plan ahead on writing assignments so that you can avoid the temptation to take shortcuts.

---

accurately. One easy way to keep track is to keep photocopies or printouts as you do your research; then you can identify needed quotations right on the copy.

Deliberate plagiarism.   Deliberate plagiarism — handing in an essay written by a friend or purchased (or simply downloaded) from an essay-writing company; cutting and pasting passages directly from source materials without marking them with quotation marks and acknowledging your sources; failing to credit the source of an idea or concept in your text — is what most people think of when they hear the word *plagiarism*. This form of plagiarism is particularly troubling because it represents dishonesty and deception: those who intentionally plagiarize present the hard thinking and hard work of someone else as their own, and they claim knowledge they really don't have, thereby deceiving their readers.

Deliberate plagiarism is also fairly simple to spot: your instructor will be well acquainted with your writing and likely to notice any sudden shifts in the style or quality of your work. In addition, by typing a few words from an essay into a search engine, your instructor can identify "matches" very easily.

EXERCISE 15.3: THINKING CRITICALLY

Look at a recent piece of your writing that incorporates material from sources, and try to determine how completely and accurately you acknowledged them. Did you properly cite every quotation, paraphrase, and summary? every opinion or other idea from a source? every source you used to create visuals? Did you unintentionally plagiarize someone else's words or ideas? Make notes, and bring them to class for discussion.

16 Writing a Research Project

Everyday decisions often call for research and writing. In trying to choose between colleges in different towns, for example, one student made a long list of questions to answer: Which location had the lower cost of living? Which school offered more financial aid? Which program would be more likely to help graduates find a job? After conducting careful research, he was able to write a letter of acceptance to one place and a letter of regret to the other. In much the same way, when you are working on an academic project, there comes a time to draw the strands of your research together and articulate your conclusions in writing.

16a Refine your writing plans.

You should by now have notes containing facts, opinions, paraphrases, summaries, quotations, and other material; you probably have some images or media to include as well. You may also have ideas about how to synthesize these many pieces of information. And you should have some sense of whether your hypothesis has sufficient support. Now is the time to reconsider your purpose, audience, stance, and working thesis.

- What is your central purpose? What other purposes, if any, do you have?

- What is your stance toward your topic? Are you an advocate, a critic, a reporter, an observer?

- What audience(s) are you addressing?
- How much background information or context does your audience need?
- What supporting information will your readers find most convincing—examples? quotations from authorities? statistics? graphs, charts, or other visuals? data from your field research?
- Should your tone be that of a colleague, an expert, or a student?
- How can you establish common ground with your readers and show them that you have considered points of view other than your own? (See 11e and Chapter 18.)
- What is your working thesis trying to establish? Will your audience accept it?

Developing an explicit thesis.   Writing out an explicit thesis statement allows you to articulate your major points and to see how well they carry out your purpose and appeal to your audience. Before you begin a full draft, then, try to develop your working thesis into an explicit statement.

David Craig developed the explicit thesis statement below (49e):

> Instant messaging seems to be a positive force in the development of youth literacy because it promotes regular contact with words, the use of a written medium for communication, and the development of an alternative form of literacy.

Testing your thesis.   Although writing out an explicit thesis will often confirm your research, you may find that your hypothesis is invalid, inadequately supported, or insufficiently focused. In such cases, you will need to rethink your original research question and

---

FOR MULTILINGUAL WRITERS

Asking Experienced Writers to Review a Thesis

You might find it helpful to ask one or two classmates who have more experience with the particular type of academic writing to look at your explicit thesis. Ask if the thesis is as direct and clear as it can be, and revise accordingly.

perhaps do further research. To test your thesis, consider the following questions:

- How can you state your thesis more precisely or more clearly (5b)? Should the wording be more specific?
- In what ways will your thesis interest your audience? What can you do to increase that interest?
- Will your thesis be manageable, given your limits of time and knowledge? If not, what can you do to make it more manageable?
- What evidence from your research supports each aspect of your thesis? What additional evidence do you need?

EXERCISE 16.1

Take the thesis from your current research project, and test it against the questions provided in 16a. Make revisions if your analysis reveals weaknesses in your thesis.

Considering design. As you move toward producing a draft, take some time to think about how you want your research essay or project to look. What font size will you use? Should you use color? Do you plan to insert text boxes, visuals, or media files? Will you need headings and subheadings? (See Chapter 8.)

16b Organize and draft.

Experienced writers differ considerably in the ways they go about organizing ideas and information, and you will want to experiment until you find a method that works well for you. (For more on organizational strategies, see 5d.)

Organizing by subject. You may find it useful to have physical notes to arrange—note cards or sticky notes, for example, or printouts of your slides or of notes you have been keeping online that you mark in some way to make the subject categories easy to identify. You can group the pieces around subject headings and reorder the parts until they seem to make sense. Shuqiao Song organized the plans for her PowerPoint presentation (6b) by moving sticky notes around on her window.

Grouping your notes will help you see how well you can support your thesis and whether you have missed any essential points. Do you need to omit ideas or sources? Do you need to find additional evidence for a main or supporting point? Once you have gathered everything together and organized your materials, you can see how the many small pieces of your research fit together. Make sure that your evidence supports your explicit thesis; if not, you may need to revise it or do some additional research — or both.

Once you have established initial groups, skim through the notes and look for ways to organize your draft. Figure out what background your audience needs, what points you need to make first, how much detail and support to offer for each of your points, and so on.

Outlining. You can use outlines in various ways and at various stages. Some writers group their notes, write a draft, and then outline the draft to study its tentative structure. Others develop an informal working outline from their notes and revise it as they go along. Still other writers prefer to plot out their organization early on in a formal outline. (For more on outlines, see 5d.)

Drafting. For most college research projects, drafting should begin *at least* two weeks before the instructor's deadline in case you need to gather more information or do more drafting. Set a deadline for having a complete draft, and structure your work with that date in mind. Gather your notes, outline, and sources, and read through them, getting involved in your topic. Most writers find that some sustained work (two or three hours at a time) pays off at this point. Begin drafting a section that you feel confident about. For example, if you are not sure how you want to introduce the draft but do know how you want to approach a particular point, begin with that, and return to the introduction later. The most important thing is to get started.

WORKING TITLE AND INTRODUCTION. The title and introduction play special roles, for they set the stage for what is to come. Ideally, the title announces the subject of the research essay or project in an intriguing or memorable way. The introduction should draw readers in and provide any background they will need to under-

stand your discussion. Here are some tips for drafting an introduction to a research essay:

- It is often effective to *open with a question*, especially your
  research question. Next, you might explain what you will
  do to answer the question. Then *end with your explicit thesis
  statement*—in essence, the answer.
- Help readers by *forecasting your main points*.
- *Establish your own credibility* by revealing how you have
  become knowledgeable about the topic.
- A quotation can be a good attention-getter, but you may
  not want to open with a quotation if doing so will give that
  source too much emphasis.

CONCLUSION. A good conclusion to a research project helps readers
identify what they have learned. Its job is not to persuade (the
body of the essay or project should already have done that) but to
contribute to the overall effectiveness of your argument. Here are
some strategies that may help:

- Refer to your thesis, and then expand to a more general
  conclusion that reminds readers of the significance of your
  discussion.
- If you have covered several main points, you may want to
  remind readers of them. Be careful, however, to provide more
  than a mere summary.
- Try to end with something that will have an impact—a
  provocative quotation or question, a vivid image, a call for
  action, or a warning. But guard against sounding preachy.

16c   Incorporate source materials.

When you reach the point of drafting your research project, a new
task awaits: weaving your source materials into your writing. The
challenge is to use your sources yet remain the author—to quote,
paraphrase, and summarize other voices while remaining the
major voice in your work. (See Chapter 15 for tips on integrating
sources.)

16d   Review and get responses to your draft.

Once you've completed your draft, reread it slowly. As you do so, answer the following questions, and use them as a starting point for revision:

- What do you now see as its *purpose?* How does this compare with your original purpose? Does the draft do what your assignment requires?
- What *audience* does your essay address?
- What is your *stance* toward the topic?
- What is your *thesis?* Is it clearly stated?
- What *evidence* supports your thesis? Is the evidence sufficient?

Next, ask friends, classmates, and, if possible, your instructor to read and respond to your draft. Asking specific questions of your readers will result in the most helpful advice. (See 5f and 5g.)

16e   Revise and edit your draft.

When you have considered your reviewers' responses and your own analysis, you can turn to revising and editing. See the Checklist on pp. 203–4 and sections 5g and 5h for more information.

16f   Prepare a list of sources.

Once you have your final draft and source materials in place, you are ready to prepare a list of sources. Create an entry for each source used in your essay. Then double-check your essay against your list of sources cited; be sure that you have listed every source mentioned in the in-text citations or notes and that you have not listed any sources not cited in your essay. (For guidelines on documentation styles, see Chapters 49–52.)

16g   Prepare and proofread your final copy.

To make sure that the final version of your project puts your best foot forward, proofread it carefully. Work with a hard copy, since reading onscreen often leads to inaccuracies and missed typos.

CHECKLIST

Guidelines for Revising a Research Project

✔ **Take responses into account.** Look at specific problems that reviewers think you need to solve or strengths you might capitalize on. For example, if reviewers showed great interest in one point but no interest in another, consider expanding the first and deleting the second.

✔ **Reconsider your original purpose, audience, and stance. Have you achieved your purpose?** If not, consider how you can. How well have you appealed to your readers? Make sure you satisfy any special concerns of your reviewers. If your rhetorical stance toward your topic has changed, does your draft need to change, too?

✔ **Assess your research.** Think about whether you have investigated the topic thoroughly and consulted materials with more than one point of view. Have you left out any important sources? Are the sources you use reliable and appropriate for your topic? Have you synthesized your research findings and drawn warranted conclusions?

✔ **Assess your use of visuals and media.** Make sure that each one supports your argument, is clearly labeled, and is cited appropriately.

✔ **Gather additional material.** If you need to strengthen any points, first check your notes to see whether you already have the necessary information. In some instances, you may need to do more research.

✔ **Decide what changes you need to make.** List everything you must do to perfect your draft. With your deadline in mind, plan your revision.

✔ **Rewrite your draft.** Many writers prefer to revise first on paper rather than on a computer. However you revise, be sure to save copies of each draft. Begin with the major changes, such as adding content or reorganizing. Then turn to sentence-level problems and word choice. Can you sharpen the work's dominant impression?

✔ **Reevaluate the title, introduction, and conclusion. Is your title specific and engaging?** Does the introduction capture readers' attention and indicate what the work discusses? Does your conclusion help readers see the significance of your argument?

Continued

CHECKLIST (*Continued*)

✔ **Check your documentation.** Make sure you've included a citation in your text for every quotation, paraphrase, summary, visual, and media file you incorporated, following your documentation style consistently.

✔ **Edit your draft.** Check grammar, usage, spelling, punctuation, and mechanics. Consider the advice of computer spell checkers (20e) and grammar checkers carefully before accepting it.

Proofread once for typographical and grammatical errors and once again to make sure you haven't introduced new errors. (To locate examples of student writing in this book and on the Web site, see the Directory of Student Writing at the back of this book.)

EXERCISE 16.2: THINKING CRITICALLY

Reflect on the research project you have completed. How did you go about organizing your information? What would you do to improve this process? What problems did you encounter in drafting? How did you solve these problems? How many quotations did you use, and how did you integrate them into your text? When and why did you use summaries and paraphrases? If you used visuals, how effective were they in supporting your points? What did you learn from revising?

Language

17 Writing to the World

People today often communicate instantaneously across vast distances and cultures. Businesspeople complete multinational transactions with a single click, students in Ohio take online classes at MIT or chat with hundreds of Facebook friends, and bloggers in Baghdad find readers in Atlanta.

Who will read what you write? What choices do you need to make in your writing to have the desired effect on your audience? When the whole world can potentially read your work, it's time to step back and think about how to communicate successfully with such a diverse group—how to become a world writer.

17a Think about what seems "normal."

Your judgment on what's "normal" may be based on assumptions you are not even aware of. But remember: behavior that is considered out of place in one context may appear perfectly normal in another. What's considered "normal" in a text message would be anything but in a request for an internship with a law firm. If you want to communicate with people across cultures, try to learn something about the norms in those cultures and be aware of the norms that guide your own behavior.

Like most people, you may tend to see your own way as the "normal" way to do things. How do your own values and assumptions guide your thinking and behavior? Keep in mind that if your ways seem inherently right, then—even without thinking about it—you may assume that other ways are somehow less than right.

- Know that most ways of communicating are influenced by cultural contexts and differ widely from one culture to the next.

- Pay close attention to the ways that people from cultures other than your own communicate, and be respectful and flexible.

- Pay attention to and respect the differences among individual people within a given culture. Don't assume that all members of a community behave in the same way or value the same things.

- Remember that your audience may be made up of people from many backgrounds who have very different concepts about what is appropriate or "normal." So don't assume unanimity!

CHECKLIST

Communicating across Cultures

✔ Recognize what you consider "normal." Examine your own customary behaviors and assumptions, and think about how they may affect what you think and say (and write). (17a)

✔ Listen closely to someone from another culture, and ask for clarification if needed. Carefully define your terms. (17b)

✔ Think about your audience's expectations. How much authority should you have? What kind of evidence will count most with your audience? (17c)

✔ Organize your writing with your audience's expectations in mind. If in doubt, use formal style. (17c)

17b Clarify meaning.

When an instructor called for "originality" in his students' essays, what did he mean? A Filipina student thought *originality* meant going to an original source and explaining it; a student from Massachusetts thought *originality* meant coming up with an idea entirely on her own. The professor, however, expected students to read multiple sources and develop a critical point of their own about those sources. In subsequent classes, this professor defined *originality* as he was using it in his classes, and he gave examples of student work he judged "original."

This brief example points to the challenges all writers face in trying to communicate across space, across languages, across cultures. While there are no foolproof rules, here are some tips for communicating with people from cultures other than your own:

- Listen carefully. Don't hesitate to ask people to explain or even repeat a point if you're not absolutely sure you understand.

- Take care to be explicit about the meanings of the words you use.

- Invite response—ask whether you're making yourself clear. This kind of back-and-forth is particularly easy (and necessary) in electronic communication like email or texting.

- Remember that sometimes a picture is worth a thousand words. A visual may help make your meaning absolutely clear.

17c Meet audience expectations.

When you do your best to meet an audience's expectations about how a text should work, your writing is more likely to have the desired effect. In practice, figuring out what audiences want, need, or expect can be difficult—especially when you are writing in public spaces online and your audiences can be composed of anyone, anywhere. If you do know something about your readers' expectations, use what you know to present your work effectively. If you know little about your potential audiences, however, carefully examine your assumptions about your readers.

Expectations about your authority as a writer.　　In the United States, students are often asked to establish authority in their writing—by drawing on certain kinds of personal experience, by reporting on research they or others have conducted, or by taking a position for which they can offer strong evidence and support. But this expectation about writerly authority is by no means universal. Indeed, some cultures view student writers as novices whose job is to reflect what they learn from their teachers. One Japanese student, for example, said he was taught that it's rude to challenge a teacher: "Are you ever so smart that you should challenge the wisdom of the ages?"

As this student's comment reveals, a writer's tone also depends on his or her relationship with listeners and readers. As a world writer, you need to remember that those you're addressing may hold a wide range of attitudes about authority.

- What is your relationship to those you are addressing?

- What knowledge are you expected to have? Is it appropriate for or expected of you to demonstrate that knowledge—and if so, how?

- What is your goal—to answer a question? to make a point? to agree? something else?

- What tone is appropriate? If in doubt, show respect: politeness is rarely if ever inappropriate.

- What level of control do you have over your writing? In a report, you may have the final say. But if you are writing on a wiki, where you share control with others, sensitivity to communal standards is key.

Expectations about persuasive evidence. How do you decide what evidence will best support your ideas? The answer depends, in large part, on the audience you want to persuade. American academics generally give great weight to factual evidence.

Differing concepts of what counts as evidence can lead to arguments that go nowhere. Consider, for example, how rare it is for a believer in creationism to be persuaded by what the theory of evolution presents as evidence—or for a supporter of evolutionary theory to be convinced by what creationists present as evidence. Think carefully about how you use evidence in writing, and pay attention to what counts as evidence to members of other groups you are trying to persuade.

- Should you rely on facts? concrete examples? firsthand experience? religious or philosophical texts? other sources?

- Should you include the testimony of experts? Which experts are valued most, and why?

- Should you use analogies as support? How much will they count?

- When does evidence from unedited Web sites such as blogs offer credible support, and when should you question or reject it?

Once you determine what counts as evidence in your own thinking and writing, think about where you learned to use and value this kind of evidence. You can ask these same questions about the use of evidence by members of other cultures.

Expectations about organization. As you make choices about how to organize your writing, remember that the patterns you find pleasing are likely to be ones that are deeply embedded in your own culture. For example, the organizational pattern favored by U.S. engineers, highly explicit and leaving little or nothing unsaid or unexplained, is probably familiar to most U.S. students: introduction and thesis, necessary background, overview of the parts to follow, systematic presentation of evidence, consideration of other viewpoints, and conclusion. If a piece of writing follows this pattern, American readers ordinarily find it well organized and coherent.

In the United States, many audiences (especially those in the academic and business worlds) expect a writer to get to the point as directly as possible and to take on the major responsibility of articulating that point efficiently and unambiguously. But not all audiences have such expectations. For instance, a Chinese student with an excellent command of English heard from her U.S. teachers that her writing was "vague," with too much "beating around the bush." As it turned out, her teachers in China had prized this kind of indirectness, expecting audiences to read between the lines.

When writing for audiences who may not share your expectations, then, think about how you can organize material to get your message across effectively. There are no hard and fast rules to help you organize your writing for effectiveness across cultures, but here are a few options to consider:

- Determine when to state your thesis — at the beginning? at the end? somewhere else? not at all?

- Consider whether digressions are a good idea, a requirement, or best avoided with your intended audience.

- Remember that electronic communication may call for certain ways of organizing. In messages or postings, you need to place the most important information first and be as succinct as possible. Or you may need to follow a template, as in submitting a résumé online.

Expectations about style.   As with beauty, good style is most definitely in the eye of the beholder — and thus is always affected by language, culture, and rhetorical tradition. In fact, what constitutes effective style varies broadly across cultures and depends on the rhetorical situation — purpose, audience, and so on (see Chapter 4). Even so, there is one important style question to consider when writing across cultures: what level of formality is most appropriate? In most writing to a general audience in the United States, a fairly informal style is often acceptable, even appreciated. Many cultures, however, tend to value a more formal approach. When in doubt, it may be wise to err on the side of formality in writing to people from other cultures, especially to elders or to those in authority.

- Be careful to use proper titles:
  Dr. Atul Gawande   Professor Jaime Mejía
- Avoid slang and informal structures such as fragments.
- Do not use first names of people you do not know in correspondence (even in text messages) unless invited to do so. Note, however, that an invitation to use a first name could come indirectly; if someone signs a message to you with his or her first name, you are implicitly invited to use the first name as a term of address. (See 2f for more on electronic communication.)
- For business correspondence, use complete sentences and words; avoid contractions. Open with the salutation "Dear Mr./Ms." or the person's title, if you know it. Write dates with the day before the month, and spell out the name of the month: *7 June 2013*.

Beyond formality, other stylistic preferences vary widely, and context matters. Long, complex sentences and ornate language may be exactly what some audiences are looking for. On Twitter, on the other hand, writers have to limit their message to 140 characters—so using abbreviated words, symbols, and fragments is expected, even desirable.

World writers, then, should take very little about language for granted. To be an effective world writer, aim to recognize and respect stylistic differences as you move from community to community and to meet expectations whenever you can.

EXERCISE 17.1: THINKING CRITICALLY

Choose one or two recent essays or other pieces of writing, and examine them carefully, noting what you assume about what counts as persuasive evidence, good organization, and effective style. How do you represent yourself in relation to your audience? What assumptions do you make about the audience, and are such assumptions warranted? What other unstated assumptions about good writing can you identify?

18 Language That Builds Common Ground

The golden rule of language use might be "Speak to others the way you want them to speak to you." The words we select have power: they can praise, delight, inspire — and also hurt, offend, or even destroy. Words that offend prevent others from identifying with you and thus damage your credibility. Few absolute guidelines exist for using words that respect differences and build common ground. Two rules, however, can help: consider carefully the sensitivities and preferences of others, and watch for words that betray your assumptions, even when you have not directly stated them.

18a Examine assumptions and avoid stereotypes.

Unstated assumptions that enter into thinking and writing can destroy common ground by ignoring important differences between others and ourselves. For example, a student in a religion seminar who uses *we* to refer to Christians and *they* to refer to members of other religions had better be sure that everyone in the class identifies as Christian, or some may feel left out of the discussion.

CHECKLIST

Using Language That Builds Common Ground

✔ Check for stereotypes and other assumptions that might come between you and your readers. Look, for instance, for language implying approval or disapproval and for the ways you use *we*, *you*, and *they*. (18a)

✔ Avoid potentially sexist language. (18b)

✔ Make sure your references to race, religion, sexual orientation, and so on are relevant or necessary to your discussion. If they are not, leave them out. (18c and d)

✔ Check that the terms you use to refer to groups are accurate and acceptable. (18c and d)

At the same time, don't overgeneralize about or stereotype a group of people. Because stereotypes are often based on half-truths, misunderstandings, and hand-me-down prejudices, they can lead to intolerance, bias, and bigotry.

Sometimes stereotypes and assumptions lead writers to call special attention to a group affiliation when it is not relevant to the point, as in *a woman plumber* or *a white basketball player*. Even seemingly positive stereotypes — for example, *Jewish doctors are the best* — or neutral ones — *all college students like pizza* — can hurt, for they inevitably ignore the uniqueness of an individual. Careful writers make sure that their language doesn't stereotype any group or individual.

18b   Examine assumptions about gender.

Powerful gender-related words can subtly affect our thinking and our behavior. For instance, at one time many young women were discouraged from pursuing careers in medicine or engineering at least partially because speakers commonly referred to hypothetical doctors or engineers as *he* (and then labeled a woman who worked as a doctor *a woman doctor*, as if to say, "She's an exception; doctors are normally men"). Similarly, a label like *male nurse* may offend by reflecting stereotyped assumptions about proper roles for men. Equally problematic is the traditional use of *man* and *mankind* to refer to people of both sexes and the use of *he* and *him* to refer generally to any human being. Because such usage ignores half of the people on earth, it hardly helps a writer build common ground.

Sexist language, those words and phrases that stereotype or ignore members of either sex or that unnecessarily call attention to gender, can usually be revised fairly easily. There are several alternatives to using masculine pronouns to refer to persons whose gender is unknown to the writer. One option is to recast the sentence using plural forms.

▶ Lawyers
  A lawyer must pass the bar exam before ~~he~~ they can begin to practice.

Another option is to substitute pairs of pronouns such as *he or she, him or her*, and so on.

▶ A lawyer must pass the bar exam before he or she can begin to

practice.

Yet another way to revise the sentence is to eliminate the pronouns.

▶ A lawyer must pass the bar exam before ~~he can begin~~ beginning to practice.

Beyond the pronoun issue, try to eliminate sexist nouns from your writing.

INSTEAD OF	TRY USING
anchorman, anchorwoman	anchor
businessman	businessperson, business executive
chairman, chairwoman	chair, chairperson
congressman	member of Congress, representative
fireman	firefighter
mailman	mail carrier
male nurse	nurse
man, mankind	humans, human beings, humanity, the human race, humankind
manpower	workers, personnel
mothering	parenting
policeman, policewoman	police officer
salesman	salesperson, sales associate
woman engineer	engineer

EXERCISE 18.1

The following excerpt is taken from the 1948 edition of Dr. Benjamin Spock's *Baby and Child Care*. Read it carefully, noting any language we might now consider sexist. Then try bringing it up-to-date by revising the passage, substituting nonsexist language as necessary.

When you suggest something that doesn't appeal to your baby, he feels he *must* assert himself. His nature tells him to. He just says "no" in words or actions, even about things that he likes to do. The psychologists call it "negativism"; mothers call it "that terrible *no* stage." But stop and think what would happen to him if he never felt like saying "no." He'd become a robot, a mechanical man. You wouldn't be able to resist the temptation to boss him all the time, and he'd stop learning and developing. When he was old enough to go out into the world, to school and later to work, everybody else would take advantage of him, too. He'd never be good for anything.

18c Examine assumptions about race and ethnicity.

In building common ground, writers must watch for any words that ignore differences not only among individual members of a race or ethnic group but also among subgroups. Writers must be aware, for instance, of the many nations to which American Indians belong and of the diverse places from which Americans of Spanish-speaking ancestry have emigrated.

Preferred terms. Identifying preferred terms is sometimes not an easy task, for they can change often and vary widely.

The word *colored*, for example, was once widely used in the United States to refer to Americans of African ancestry. By the 1950s, the preferred term had become *Negro*. This changed in the 1960s, however, as *black* came to be preferred by most, though certainly not all, members of that community. Then, in the late 1980s, some leaders of the American black community urged that *black* be replaced by *African American*.

The word *Oriental*, once used to refer to people of East Asian descent, is now often considered offensive. At the University of California at Berkeley, the Oriental Languages Department is now known as the East Asian Languages Department. One advocate of the change explained that *Oriental* is appropriate for objects—like rugs—but not for people.

Once widely preferred, the term *Native American* is being challenged by those who argue that the most appropriate way to refer to indigenous people is by the specific name of the tribe or pueblo, such as *Chippewa* or *Tesuque*. In Alaska and parts of Canada, many indigenous peoples once referred to as *Eskimos* now prefer *Inuit* or a specific term such as *Tlingit*. It has also become fairly common for tribal groups to refer to themselves as *Indians* or *Indian tribes*.

Among Americans of Spanish-speaking descent, the preferred terms of reference are many: *Chicano/Chicana, Hispanic, Latin American, Latino/Latina, Mexican American, Dominican,* and *Puerto Rican*, to name but a few.

Clearly, then, ethnic terminology changes often enough to challenge even the most careful writers — including writers who belong to the groups they are writing about. The best advice may be to consider your words carefully, to *listen* for the way members of groups refer to themselves (or *ask* about preferences), and to check any term you're unsure of in a current dictionary.

18d   Consider other kinds of difference.

Age.   Mention age if it is relevant, but be aware that age-related terms (*matronly*, *well-preserved*, and so on) can carry derogatory connotations. Describing Mr. Fry as *elderly but still active* may sound polite to you, but chances are Mr. Fry would prefer being called *an active seventy-eight-year-old* — or just *a seventy-eight-year-old*, which eliminates the unstated assumption of surprise that he is active at his age.

Class.   Take special care to examine your words for assumptions about class. As a writer, you should not assume that all your readers share your background or values — that your classmates all own cars, for instance. And avoid using any words — *redneck*, *blueblood*, and the like — that might alienate members of your audience.

Geographical area.   You should not assume that geography determines personality or lifestyle. New Englanders are not all thrifty and tight-lipped; people in "red states" may hold liberal views; midwesterners are not always polite. Be careful not to make simplistic assumptions.

Check also that you use geographical terms accurately.

AMERICA, AMERICAN Although many people use these words to refer to the United States alone, such usage will not necessarily be acceptable to people from Canada, Mexico, and Central or South America.

BRITISH, ENGLISH Use *British* to refer to the island of Great Britain, which includes England, Scotland, and Wales, or to the United Kingdom of Great Britain and Northern Ireland. In general, do not use *English* for these broader senses.

ARAB This term refers only to people of Arabic-speaking descent. Note that Iran is not an Arab nation; its people speak Farsi, not

CONSIDERING DISABILITIES

Knowing Your Readers

Nearly 10 percent of first-year college students—about 155,000—identify themselves as having one or more disabilities. That's no small number. Effective writers consider their own and their readers' disabilities so that they can find ways to build common ground.

Arabic. Note also that *Arab* is not synonymous with *Muslim* or *Moslem* (a believer in Islam). Most (but not all) Arabs are Muslim, but many Muslims (those in Pakistan, for example) are not Arab.

Physical ability or health.   When writing about a person with a serious illness or physical disability, ask yourself whether mentioning the disability is relevant to your discussion and whether the words you use carry negative connotations. You might choose, for example, to say someone *uses* a wheelchair rather than to say he or she is *confined to* one. Similarly, you might note a subtle but meaningful difference in calling someone a *person with AIDS* rather than an *AIDS victim*. Mentioning the person first and the disability second, such as referring to a *child with diabetes* rather than a *diabetic child* or a *diabetic*, is always a good idea.

Religion.   Assumptions about religious groups are very often inaccurate and unfair. For example, Roman Catholics hold a wide spectrum of views on abortion, Muslim women do not all wear veils, and many Baptists are not fundamentalists. In fact, many people do not believe in or practice a religion at all, so be careful of such assumptions. As in other cases, do not use religious labels without considering their relevance to your point.

Sexual orientation.   If you wish to build common ground, do not assume that readers all share one sexual orientation. As with any label, reference to sexual orientation should be governed by context. Someone writing about former representative Barney Frank's legislative record would probably have little if any reason to refer to his sexual orientation. On the other hand, someone writing about diversity in U.S. government might find it important to note that Frank was the first U.S. congressman to voluntarily make his homosexuality public.

EXERCISE 18.2: THINKING CRITICALLY

Writer and filmmaker Ruth Ozeki has written widely on issues related to the environment. In this June 2009 posting from her blog, Ozeki appeals to readers to step back and cultivate silence as a necessary prelude to making difficult decisions. Who is the "we" that Ozeki addresses? What views and values do you think she expects her readers to share with her? Note the strategies the writer uses to establish common ground with readers in this paragraph.

> I'm more and more convinced that we need to cultivate mindful silence, and share it with others whenever possible, if we are going to be able to make the careful and difficult choices we will need to make in order to survive in a wired and warming world. This seems to me to be a key piece of activism and eco-pedagogy that we can all learn to cultivate.   —Ruth Ozeki, *Ozekiland*

19   Language Variety

Comedian Dave Chappelle has said, "Every black American is bilingual. We speak street vernacular, and we speak job interview." As Chappelle understands, English comes in many varieties that differ from one another in pronunciation, vocabulary, usage, and grammar. You probably already adjust the variety of language you use depending on how well — and how formally — you know the audience you are addressing. Adding language variety to your writing can improve your communication with your audience if you think carefully about the effect you want to achieve.

19a   Use standard varieties of English appropriately.

How do writers decide when to use another language or switch from one variety of English to another? Even writers who are perfectly fluent in several languages must think for a moment before switching linguistic gears. The key to shifting among varieties of English and

> ### CHECKLIST
>
> **Language Variety**
>
> You can use different varieties of language to good effect for the following purposes:
>
> ✔ to repeat someone's exact words
>
> ✔ to evoke a person, place, or activity
>
> ✔ to establish your credibility and build common ground with an audience
>
> ✔ to make a strong point
>
> ✔ to connect with an audience

among languages is appropriateness: you need to consider when such shifts will help your audience appreciate your message and when shifts may be a mistake. Used appropriately and wisely, *any* variety of English can serve a good purpose.

One variety of English, often referred to as the "standard" or "standard academic," is that taught prescriptively in schools, represented in this and most other textbooks, used in the national media, and written and spoken widely by those wielding social and economic power. As the language used in business and most public institutions, standard English is a variety you will want to be completely familiar with. Standard English, however, is only one of many effective varieties of English and itself varies according to purpose and audience, from the more formal style used in academic writing to the informal style characteristic of casual conversation.

19b Use varieties of English to evoke a place or community.

> "Ever'body says words different," said Ivy. "Arkansas folks says 'em different, and Oklahomy folks says 'em different. And we seen a lady from Massachusetts, an' she said 'em differentest of all. Couldn' hardly make out what she was sayin'."
>
> —John Steinbeck, *The Grapes of Wrath*

Using the language of a local community is an effective way to evoke a character or place. Author and radio host Garrison Keillor,

FOR MULTILINGUAL WRITERS

Global Varieties of English

Like other world languages, English is used in many countries, so it has many global varieties. For example, British English differs somewhat from U.S. English in certain vocabulary (*bonnet* for hood of a car), syntax (*to hospital* rather than *to the hospital*), spelling (*centre* rather than *center*), and pronunciation. If you have learned a non-American variety of English, you will want to recognize, and to appreciate, the ways in which it differs from the variety widely used in U.S. academic settings.

for example, peppers his tales of his native Minnesota with the homespun English spoken there: "I once was a tall dark heartbreaker who, when I slouched into a room, women jumped up and asked if they could get me something, and now they only smile and say, 'My mother is a big fan of yours. You sure are a day-brightener for her. You sure make her chuckle.'"

Weaving together regionalisms and standard English can also be effective in creating a sense of place for your audience. Here, an anthropologist writing about one Carolina community takes particular care to let the residents speak their minds—and in their own words:

> For Roadville, schooling is something most folks have not gotten enough of, but everybody believes will do something toward helping an individual "get on." In the words of one oldtime resident, "Folks that ain't got no schooling don't get to be nobody nowadays."
>
> —Shirley Brice Heath, *Ways with Words*

Varieties of language can also help writers evoke other kinds of communities. In the panel from *One! Hundred! Demons!* on the opposite page, Lynda Barry uses playground language to present a vivid image of remembered childhood games. See how kids' use of slang ("Dag") and colloquialisms ("Whose up is it?") helps readers join in the experience.

19c   Use varieties of English to build credibility with a community.

Whether you are American Indian or trace your ancestry back to Europe, Asia, Latin America, Africa, or elsewhere, your heritage lives on in the diversity of the English language.

See how one Hawaiian writer uses a local variety of English to paint a picture of young teens hearing a "chicken skin" story from their grandmother.

> "—So, rather dan being rid of da shark, da people were stuck with many little ones, for dere mistake."
>
> Then Grandma Wong wen' pause, for dramatic effect, I guess, and she wen' add, "Dis is one of dose times. . . . Da time of da sharks."
>
> Those words ended another of Grandma's chicken skin stories. The stories she told us had been passed on to her by her grandmother, who had heard them from her grandmother. Always skipping a generation.
>
> —Rodney Morales, "When the Shark Bites"

Notice how the narrator of the story uses both standard and non-standard varieties of English—presenting information necessary to the story line mostly in standard English and then using a local, ethnic variety to represent spoken language. One important reason for the shift from standard English is to demonstrate that the writer is a member of the community whose language he is representing and thus to build credibility with others in the community.

Take care, however, in using the language of communities other than your own. When used inappropriately, such language can have an opposite effect, perhaps destroying your credibility and alienating your audience.

EXERCISE 19.1

Identify the purpose and audience for one of this chapter's examples of regional, ethnic, or communal varieties of English. Then rewrite the passage to remove all evidence of any variety of English other than the "standard." Compare your revised version with the original and with those produced by some of your classmates. What differences do you notice in tone (is it more formal? more distant? something else?) and in overall impression? Which version seems most appropriate for the intended audience and purpose? Which do you prefer, and why?

19d Bring in other languages appropriately.

You might use a language other than English for the same reasons you might use different varieties of English: to represent the actual words of a speaker, to make a point, to connect with your audience, or to get their attention. See how Gerald Haslam uses Spanish to capture his great-grandmother's words and to make a point about his relationship to her.

> *"Expectoran su sangre!"* exclaimed Great-grandma when I showed her the small horned toad I had removed from my breast pocket. I turned toward my mother, who translated: "They spit blood."
>
> *"De los ojos,"* Grandma added. "From their eyes," mother explained, herself uncomfortable in the presence of the small beast.
>
> I grinned, "Awwwwwww."
>
> But my Great-grandmother did not smile. *"Son muy tóxicos,"* she nodded with finality. Mother moved back an involuntary step, her hands suddenly busy at her breast. "Put that thing down," she ordered.
>
> "His name's John," I said.
>
> —Gerald Haslam, *California Childhood*

20 Word Choice and Spelling

Deciding which word is the right word can be a challenge. It's not unusual to find many words that have similar but subtly different meanings, and each makes a different impression on your audience. For instance, the "pasta with marinara sauce" presented in a restaurant may look and taste much like the "macaroni and gravy" served at an Italian family dinner, but the choice of one label rather than the other tells us not only about the food but also about the people serving it and the people they expect to serve it to.

Ensuring that you choose the correct spelling for the word you want to use is also important. Spell checkers can help you to avoid some errors, but they can also make other mistakes more likely, including word choice errors, so you should use them with care (see 20e).

20a Choose appropriate formality.

Choose a level of formality that matches your audience, purpose, and topic. In an email or letter to a friend or close associate, informal language is often appropriate. For most academic and professional writing, however, more formal language is appropriate because you are addressing people you do not know well. Compare the following responses to a request for information about a job candidate:

EMAIL TO SOMEONE YOU KNOW WELL

Maisha is great — hire her if you can!

LETTER OF RECOMMENDATION TO SOMEONE YOU DO NOT KNOW

I am pleased to recommend Maisha Fisher. She will bring good ideas and extraordinary energy to your organization.

Slang and colloquial language. Slang, or extremely informal language, is often confined to a relatively small group and usually

> ## CHECKLIST
>
> **Editing for Appropriate Language and Spelling**
>
> ✔ Check to see that your language reflects the appropriate level of formality for your audience, purpose, and topic. (20a)
>
> ✔ Unless you are writing for a specialized audience that will understand jargon, either define technical terms or replace them with words that are easy to understand. (20a)
>
> ✔ Consider the connotations of words carefully. If you say someone is *pushy*, be sure you mean to be critical; otherwise, use a word like *assertive*. (20b)
>
> ✔ Use both general and specific words. If you are writing about the general category *beds*, for example, do you give enough concrete detail (*an antique four-poster bed*)? (20c)
>
> ✔ Look for clichés, and replace them with fresher language. (20d)
>
> ✔ Use spell checkers with care. (20e)

becomes obsolete rather quickly, though some slang gains wide use (*workaholic, duh*). Colloquial language, such as *a lot, in a bind*, or *snooze*, is less informal, more widely used, and longer lasting than most slang.

Writers who use slang and colloquial language run the risk of not being understood or of not being taken seriously. If you are writing for a general audience about gun-control legislation, for example, and you use the term *gat* to refer to a weapon, some readers may not know what you mean, and others may be irritated by what they see as a frivolous reference to a deadly serious subject.

EXERCISE 20.1

Choose something or someone to describe—a favorite cousin, a stranger on the bus, an automobile, a musical instrument, or whatever strikes your fancy. Describe your subject using colloquial language and slang. Then rewrite the description, this time using neither of these. Read the two passages aloud, and note what different effects each version creates.

Jargon. Jargon is the special vocabulary of a trade or profession, enabling members to speak and write concisely to one another. Reserve jargon for an audience that will understand your terms. The example that follows, from a blog about fonts and typefaces, uses jargon appropriately for an interested and knowledgeable audience.

The Modern typeface classification is usually associated with Didones and display faces that often have too much contrast for text use. The Ingeborg family was designed with the intent of producing a Modern face that was readable at any size. Its roots might well be historic, but its approach is very contemporary. The three text weights (Regular, Bold, and Heavy) are functional and discreet while the Display weights (Fat and Block) catch the reader's eye with a dynamic form and a whole lot of ink on the paper. The family includes a boatload of extras like unicase alternates, swash caps, and a lined fill.
— fontshop.com blog

Depending on the needs of the audience, jargon can be irritating and incomprehensible—or extremely helpful. Terms that begin as jargon for specialists (such as *asynchronous* or *vertical integration*) can quickly become part of the mainstream if they provide a useful shorthand for an otherwise lengthy explanation. Before you use technical jargon, remember your readers: if they will not understand the terms, or if you don't know them well enough to judge, then say what you need to say in everyday language.

Pompous language, euphemisms, and doublespeak.   Stuffy or pompous language is unnecessarily formal for the purpose, audience, or topic. It often gives writing an insincere or unintentionally humorous tone, making a writer's ideas seem insignificant or even unbelievable.

POMPOUS

Pursuant to the August 9 memorandum regarding the increased unit cost of automotive fuels, it is incumbent upon us to endeavor to make maximal utilization of electronic or telephonic communication in lieu of personal visitation.

FOR MULTILINGUAL WRITERS

Avoiding Fancy Language

In writing standard academic English, which is fairly formal, students are often tempted to use many "big words" instead of simple language. Although learning impressive words can be a good way to expand your vocabulary, it is usually best to avoid flowery or fancy language in college writing. Academic writing at U.S. universities tends to value clear, concise prose.

REVISED

As noted in the August 9 memo, higher gasoline prices require us to email or telephone whenever possible rather than make personal visits.

As the following examples illustrate, some writers will use words in an attempt to sound expert, and these puffed-up words can easily backfire.

INSTEAD OF	TRY USING	INSTEAD OF	TRY USING
ascertain	find out	optimal	best
commence	begin	parameters	boundaries
finalize	finish, complete	peruse	look at
impact (as verb)	affect	ramp up	increase
methodology	method	utilize	use

Euphemisms are words and phrases that make unpleasant ideas seem less harsh. *Your position is being eliminated* seeks to soften the blow of being fired or laid off. Other euphemisms include *pass on* or *pass away* for *die* and *plus-sized* for *fat*. Although euphemisms can sometimes appeal to an audience by showing that you are considerate of people's feelings, they can also sound insincere or evasive.

Doublespeak is language used to hide or distort the truth. During massive layoffs and cutbacks in the business world, companies speak of firings as *employee repositioning* or *proactive downsizing*, and of unpaid time off as a *furlough*. The public — and particularly those who lose their jobs — recognize these terms for what they are.

EXERCISE 20.2

Revise each of these sentences to use formal language consistently. Example:

> Although   be enthusiastic   as soon as
> I can ~~get all enthused~~ about writing, ~~but~~ I sit down to write,
>   ^   ^   ^
>   blank.
> ~~and~~ my mind goes ~~right to sleep.~~
>   ^

1. In Shakespeare's *Othello*, Desdemona just lies down like some kind of wimp and accepts her death as inevitable.

2. The budget office doesn't want to cough up the cash to replace the drafty windows, but cranking up the heat in the building all winter doesn't come cheap.

3. Finding all that bling in King Tut's tomb was one of the biggest archeological scores of the twentieth century.

4. In unfamiliar settings or with people he did not know well, Duncan often came off as kind of snooty, but in reality he was scared to death.

5. My family lived in Trinidad for the first ten years of my life, and we went through a lot of bad stuff there, but when we came to the United States, we thought we finally had it made.

20b   Consider denotation and connotation.

Thinking of a stone tossed into a pool and ripples spreading out from it can help you understand the distinction between *denotation*, the dictionary meaning of a word (the stone), and *connotation*, the associations that accompany the word (the ripples). The words *enthusiasm*, *passion*, and *obsession*, for instance, all carry roughly the same denotation. But the connotations are quite different: an *enthusiasm* is a pleasurable and absorbing interest; a *passion* has a strong emotional component and may affect someone positively or negatively; an *obsession* is an unhealthy attachment that excludes other interests.

Note the differences in connotation among the following three statements:

▶ Students Against Racism (SAR) erected a temporary barrier on the campus oval. They say it symbolizes "the many barriers to those discriminated against by university policies."

▶ Left-wing agitators threw up an eyesore on the oval to stampede the university into giving in to their demands.

▶ Supporters of human rights for all students challenged the university's investment in racism by erecting a protest barrier on campus.

The first statement is the most neutral, merely stating facts; the second, using words with negative connotations (*agitators*, *eyesore*, *stampede*), is strongly critical; the third, using a phrase with positive connotations (*supporters of human rights*) and presenting assertions as facts (*the university's investment in racism*), gives a favorable slant to the story.

20c Use general and specific language effectively.

Effective writers balance general words, which name or describe groups or classes, with specific words, which identify individual and particular things. Some general words are abstract; they refer to things we cannot perceive through our five senses. Specific words are usually concrete; they name things we can see, hear, touch, taste, or smell. We can seldom draw a clear-cut line between general or abstract words on the one hand and specific or concrete words on the other, however. Instead, most words fall somewhere in between.

GENERAL	LESS GENERAL	SPECIFIC	MORE SPECIFIC
book	dictionary	abridged dictionary	the fourth edition of *The American Heritage College Dictionary*

ABSTRACT	LESS ABSTRACT	CONCRETE	MORE CONCRETE
culture	visual art	painting	van Gogh's *Starry Night*

EXERCISE 20.3

From the parentheses, choose the word with the denotation that makes most sense in the context of the sentence. Use a dictionary if necessary.

1. She listened (*apprehensively/attentively*) to the long lecture and took notes.

2. The telemarketers were told to (*empathize/emphasize*) more expensive items.

3. The interns were (*conscientious/conscious*) workers who listened carefully and learned fast.

4. Franklin advised his readers to be both frugal and (*industrial/industrious*).

5. All (*proceedings/proceeds*) from the bake sale went to the athletics program.

EXERCISE 20.4

Rewrite each of the following sentences to be more specific and concrete.

1. The entryway of the building was dirty.

2. The sounds at dawn are memorable.

3. Our holiday dinner tasted good.

4. The attendant came toward my car.

5. I woke up.

20d   Use figurative language effectively.

Figurative language, or figures of speech, can paint pictures in a reader's mind, allowing one to "see" a point readily and clearly. Far from being merely decorative, such language can be crucial to understanding.

Similes, metaphors, and analogies.   Similes use *like*, *as*, *as if*, or *as though* to make explicit the similarity between two seemingly different things.

▶ You can tell the graphic-novels section in a bookstore from afar, by the young bodies sprawled around it like casualties of a localized disaster. —Peter Schjeldahl

▶ The comb felt as if it was raking my skin off.

—Malcolm X, "My First Conk"

Metaphors are implicit comparisons, omitting the *like*, *as*, *as if*, or *as though* of similes.

► The Internet is the new town square.   —Jeb Hensarling

Mixed metaphors make comparisons that are inconsistent.

► The lectures were like brilliant comets streaking through the
                    dazzling
   night sky, ~~showering~~ listeners with ~~a torrential rain~~ of insights.
                                            flashes
   The images of streaking light and heavy precipitation are inconsistent; in the revised sentence, all of the images relate to light.

Analogies compare similar features of two dissimilar things; they explain something unfamiliar by relating it to something familiar.

► One way to establish that peace-preserving threat of mutual assured destruction is to commit yourself beforehand, which helps explain why so many retailers promise to match any competitor's advertised price. Consumers view these guarantees as conducive to lower prices. But in fact offering a price-matching guarantee should make it less likely that competitors will slash prices, since they know that any cuts they make will immediately be matched. It's the retail version of the doomsday machine.

                                            — James Surowiecki

► One Hundred and Twenty-fifth Street was to Harlem what the Mississippi was to the South, a long traveling river always going somewhere, carrying something.

                                            — Maya Angelou, *The Heart of a Woman*

Clichés.   A cliché is a frequently used expression such as *busy as a bee*. By definition, we use clichés all the time, especially in speech, and many serve usefully as shorthand for familiar ideas or as a way of connecting to an audience. But if you use too many clichés in your writing, readers may conclude that what you are saying is not very new or interesting — or true. To check for clichés, use this rule of thumb: if you can predict exactly what the next word in a phrase will be, the phrase stands a good chance of being a cliché.

EXERCISE 20.5

Return to the description that you wrote in Exercise 20.1. Note any words that carry strong connotations, and identify the concrete and abstract language as well as any use of figurative language. Revise any inappropriate language you find.

20e Make spell checkers work for you.

Research conducted for this textbook shows that spelling errors have changed dramatically in the past twenty years — and the reason is spell checkers. Although these programs have weeded out many once-common misspellings, they are not foolproof. Spell checkers still allow typical kinds of errors that you should look out for.

Common errors with spell checkers

- **Homonyms.** Spell checkers cannot distinguish between words such as *affect* and *effect* that sound alike but are spelled differently.

- **Proper nouns.** A spell checker cannot tell you when you have misspelled a proper name. Proofread names with special care.

- **Compound words written as two words.** Spell checkers will not see a problem if *nowhere* is incorrectly written as *no where*. When in doubt, check a dictionary.

- **Typos.** The spell checker will not flag *heat* even if you meant to type *heart*.

Spell checker use. To make spell checkers work best for you, you need to learn to adapt them to your own needs.

- Always proofread carefully, even after you have used the spell checker. The more important the message or document, the more careful you should be about its accuracy and clarity.

- Use a dictionary to look up any word the spell checker highlights that you are not sure of.

- If your spell checker's dictionary allows you to add new words, enter proper names, non-English words, or specialized language you use regularly and have trouble spelling. Be careful to enter the correct spelling!

- If you know that you mix up certain homonyms, such as *there* and *their*, check for them after running your spell checker.

- Remember that spell checkers are not sensitive to capitalization. If you write "the united states," the spell checker won't question it.

- Do *not* automatically accept the spell checker's suggestions; you may end up with a word you don't really want.

EXERCISE 20.6

The paragraph below has been checked with a spell checker. Proofread carefully and correct any errors the spell checker missed.

I see that you have send me a warning about a computer virus that can destroy my hard drive, mangle my soft ware, and generally reek havoc on my computer. How ever, you may not be aware oft he fact that warnings like this one are almost never real. When a message axes you to foreword it to every one in you're address book, you should know immediately that its a hoax. User who send false warnings about viruses to hundreds of there friends are not doing any one a favor; instead, they are simple slowing down traffic on line and creating problems that maybe worst then any technical difficulties cause by the virus — if the virus even exist. Please insure that warnings contain a grain of true before you past them on. If your worried that my computer might be in danger, set you mind at easy. I will except responsibility if the machine goes hay wire.

Homonyms.   A relatively small number of homonyms — just eight groups — cause writers the most frequent trouble.

accept (to take or receive)
except (to leave out)

affect (an emotion; to have an influence)
effect (a result; to cause to happen)

its (possessive of *it*)
it's (contraction of *it is* or *it has*)

their (possessive of *they*)
there (in that place)
they're (contraction of *they are*)

to (in the direction of)
too (in addition; excessive)
two (number between *one* and *three*)

weather (climatic conditions)
whether (if)

who's (contraction of *who is* or *who has*)
whose (possessive of *who*)

your (possessive of *you*)
you're (contraction of *you are*)

If you tend to confuse particular homonyms, try creating a special memory device to help you remember the differences between the words. For example, "*We* all complain about the *weather*" will remind you that *weather* (the climate) starts with *we*.

In addition, pay close attention to homonyms that may be spelled as one word or two, depending on the meaning.

▶ Of course, they did not wear *everyday* clothes *every day*.

▶ Before the six lawyers were *all ready* to negotiate, it was *already* May.

▶ The director *may be* on time. But *maybe* she'll be late.

FOR MULTILINGUAL WRITERS

Recognizing American Spellings

Different varieties of English often use different spelling conventions. If you have learned British or Indian English, for example, you will want to be aware of some of the more common spelling differences in American English. For example, words ending in *-yse* or *-ise* in British/Indian English (*analyse, criticise*) usually end in *-yze* or *-ize* in American English (*analyze, criticize*); words ending in *-our* in British/ Indian English (*labour, colour*) usually end in *-or* in American English (*labor, color*); and words ending in *-re* in British/Indian English (*theatre, centre*) usually end in *-er* in American English (*theater, center*).

For additional advice on commonly confused words, see the glossary of usage in Chapter 21.

EXERCISE 20.7

Choose the appropriate word in parentheses to fill each blank.

If _____ (*your/you're*) looking for some summer fun, _____ (*accept/except*) the friendly _____ (*advice/advise*) of thousands of happy adventurers: spend three _____ (*weaks/weeks*) kayaking _____ (*thorough/threw/through*) the inside passage _____ (*to/too/two*) Alaska. For ten years, Outings, Inc., has _____ (*lead/led*) groups of new kayakers _____ (*passed/past*) some of the most breathtaking scenery in North America. The group's goal is simple: to give participants the time of _____ (*their/there/they're*) lives and show them things they don't see _____ (*every day/everyday*). As one of last year's adventurers said, "_____ (*Its/It's*) a trip that is _____ (*already/all ready*) one of my favorite memories. The trip _____ (*affected/effected*) me powerfully."

20f Master spelling rules.

General spelling rules can help writers enormously, but many rules have exceptions. When in doubt, consult a dictionary.

i **before** *e* **except after** *c*.   Here is a slightly expanded version of the "*i* before *e*" rule:

I BEFORE *E*	ach*ie*ve, br*ie*f, f*ie*ld, fr*ie*nd
EXCEPT AFTER *C*	c*ei*ling, perc*ei*ve, rec*ei*pt
OR WHEN PRONOUNCED *AY*	*ei*ghth, n*ei*ghbor, r*ei*gn, w*ei*gh
OR IN WEIRD EXCEPTIONS	*ei*ther, for*ei*gn, h*ei*ght, l*ei*sure, n*ei*ther, s*ei*ze

Word endings (suffixes)

FINAL SILENT *E*.   Drop the final silent *e* when you add an ending that starts with a vowel.

imagine + -able = imaginable   exercise + -ing = exercising

Generally, keep the final *e* if the ending starts with a consonant. Common exceptions include *argument, judgment, noticeable,* and *truly.*

force + -ful = forceful   state + -ly = stately

FINAL *Y*.   When adding an ending to a word that ends in a consonant plus *y*, change the *y* to an *i* in most cases.

try, tried   busy, busily

Keep the *y* if it is part of a proper name or if the ending begins with *i*.

Kennedy, Kennedyesque   dry, drying

FINAL CONSONANTS.   When adding an ending beginning with a vowel to a word that ends with a vowel and a consonant, double the final consonant if the original word is one syllable or if the accent is on the same syllable in both the original and the new word.

stop, stopped   begin, beginner   refer, referral

Otherwise, do not double the final consonant.

bait, baiting   start, started   refer, reference

Plurals

ADDING -*S* OR -*ES*.   For most nouns, add -*s*. For words ending in *s*, *ch*, *sh*, *x*, or *z*, add -*es*.

pencil, pencils   church, churches   bus, buses

CONSIDERING DISABILITIES

Spelling

Spelling is especially difficult for people who have trouble processing letters and sounds in sequence. Technology can help: "talking pens" can scan words and read them aloud, and voice-recognition programs can transcribe dictated text.

In general, add *-s* to nouns ending in *o* if the *o* is preceded by a vowel. Add *-es* if the *o* is preceded by a consonant.

> rodeo, rodeos   patio, patios   potato, potatoes   hero, heroes

For some nouns ending in *f* or *fe*, change *f* to *v*, and add *-s* or *-es*.

> calf, calves   life, lives   hoof, hooves

For compound nouns written as separate or hyphenated words, make the most important part plural, whether or not it is the last part of the compound.

> lieutenant governors   brothers-in-law

For plurals of numbers and words used as terms, see 38c.

21 Glossary of Usage

Conventions of usage might be called the "good manners" of discourse. And just as manners vary from culture to culture and time to time, so do conventions of usage. Matters of usage, like other language choices you must make, depend on what your purpose is and on what is appropriate for a particular audience at a particular time.

a, an Use *a* with a word that begins with a consonant (*a book*), a consonant sound such as "y" or "w" (*a euphoric moment*, *a one-sided match*), or a sounded *h* (*a hemisphere*). Use *an* with a word that begins with a vowel (*an umbrella*), a vowel sound (*an X-ray*), or a silent *h* (*an honor*).

accept, except The verb *accept* means "receive" or "agree to." *Except* is usually a preposition that means "aside from" or "excluding." *All the plaintiffs except Mr. Kim decided to accept the settlement.*

advice, advise The noun *advice* means "opinion" or "suggestion"; the verb *advise* means "offer advice." *Doctors <u>advise</u> everyone not to smoke, but many people ignore the <u>advice</u>.*

affect, effect As a verb, *affect* means "influence" or "move the emotions of"; as a noun, it means "emotions" or "feelings." *Effect* is a noun meaning "result"; less commonly, it is a verb meaning "bring about." *The storm <u>affected</u> a large area. Its <u>effects</u> included widespread power failures. The drug <u>effected</u> a major change in the patient's <u>affect</u>.*

aggravate The formal meaning is "make worse." *Having another mouth to feed <u>aggravated</u> their poverty.* In academic and professional writing, avoid using *aggravate* to mean "irritate" or "annoy."

all ready, already *All ready* means "fully prepared." *Already* means "previously." *We were <u>all ready</u> for Lucy's party when we learned that she had <u>already</u> left.*

all right, alright Avoid the spelling *alright*.

all together, altogether *All together* means "all in a group" or "gathered in one place." *Altogether* means "completely" or "everything considered." *When the board members were <u>all together</u>, their mutual distrust was <u>altogether</u> obvious.*

allude, elude *Allude* means "refer indirectly." *Elude* means "avoid" or "escape from." *The candidate did not even <u>allude</u> to her opponent. The suspect <u>eluded</u> the police for several days.*

allusion, illusion An *allusion* is an indirect reference. An *illusion* is a false or misleading appearance. *The speaker's <u>allusion</u> to the Bible created an <u>illusion</u> of piety.*

a lot Avoid the spelling *alot*.

already See *all ready, already*.

alright See *all right, alright*.

altogether See *all together, altogether*.

among, between In referring to two things or people, use *between*. In referring to three or more, use *among*. *The relationship <u>between</u> the twins is different from that <u>among</u> the other three children.*

amount, number Use *amount* with quantities you cannot count; use *number* for quantities you can count. *A small <u>number</u> of volunteers cleared a large <u>amount</u> of brush.*

an See *a, an*.

and/or Avoid this term except in business or legal writing. Instead of *fat and/or protein*, write *fat, protein, or both.*

any body, anybody, any one, anyone *Anybody* and *anyone* are pronouns meaning "any person." *Anyone* [or *anybody*] *would enjoy this film. Any body* is an adjective modifying a noun. *Any body of water has its own ecology. Any one* is two adjectives or a pronoun modified by an adjective. *Customers could buy only two sale items at any one time. The winner could choose any one of the prizes.*

anyplace In academic and professional discourse, use *anywhere* instead.

anyway, anyways In writing, use *anyway*, not *anyways.*

apt, liable, likely *Likely to* means "probably will," and *apt to* means "inclines or tends to." In many instances, they are interchangeable. *Liable* often carries a more negative sense and is also a legal term meaning "obligated" or "responsible."

as Avoid sentences in which it is not clear if *as* means "when" or "because." For example, does *Carl left town as his father was arriving* mean "at the same time as his father was arriving" or "because his father was arriving"?

as, as if, like In academic and professional writing, use *as* or *as if* instead of *like* to introduce a clause. *The dog howled as if* [not *like*] *it were in pain. She did as* [not *like*] *I suggested.*

assure, ensure, insure *Assure* means "convince" or "promise"; its direct object is usually a person or persons. *She assured voters she would not raise taxes. Ensure* and *insure* both mean "make certain," but *insure* usually refers specifically to protection against financial loss. *When the city rationed water to ensure that the supply would last, the Browns could no longer afford to insure their car-wash business.*

as to Do not use *as to* as a substitute for *about. Karen was unsure about* [not *as to*] *Bruce's intentions.*

at, where See *where.*

a while, awhile Always use *a while* after a preposition such as *for, in,* or *after. We drove awhile and then stopped for a while.*

bad, badly Use *bad* after a linking verb such as *be, feel,* or *seem.* Use *badly* to modify an action verb, an adjective, or another verb. *The hostess felt bad because the dinner was badly prepared.*

bare, bear Use *bare* to mean "uncovered" and *bear* to refer to the animal or to mean "carry" or "endure": *The walls were <u>bare</u>. The emptiness was hard to <u>bear</u>.*

because of, due to Use *due to* when the effect, stated as a noun, appears before the verb *be*. *His illness was <u>due to</u> malnutrition.* (*Illness*, a noun, is the effect.) Use *because of* when the effect is stated as a clause. *He was sick <u>because of</u> malnutrition.* (*He was sick*, a clause, is the effect.)

being as, being that In academic and professional writing, use *because* or *since* instead of these expressions. *<u>Because</u>* [not *being as*] *Romeo killed Tybalt, he was banished to Padua.*

beside, besides *Beside* is a preposition meaning "next to." *Besides* can be a preposition meaning "other than" or an adverb meaning "in addition." *No one <u>besides</u> Francesca would sit <u>beside</u> him.*

between See *among, between.*

brake, break *Brake* means "to stop" and also refers to a stopping mechanism: *Check the <u>brakes</u>. Break* means "fracture" or an interruption: *The coffee <u>break</u> was too short.*

breath, breathe *Breath* is a noun; *breathe*, a verb. "*<u>Breathe</u>,*" said the nurse, so June took a deep <u>breath</u>.*

bring, take Use *bring* when an object is moved from a farther to a nearer place; use *take* when the opposite is true. *<u>Take</u> the box to the post office; <u>bring</u> back my mail.*

but that, but what Avoid using these as substitutes for *that* in expressions of doubt. *Hercule Poirot never doubted <u>that</u>* [not *but that*] *he would solve the case.*

but yet Do not use these words together. *He is strong <u>but</u>* [not *but yet*] *gentle.*

can, may *Can* refers to ability and *may* to possibility or permission. *Since I <u>can</u> ski the slalom well, I <u>may</u> win the race.*

can't hardly *Hardly* has a negative meaning; therefore, *can't hardly* is a double negative. This expression is commonly used in some varieties of English but is not used in academic English. *Tim <u>can</u>* [not *can't*] *<u>hardly</u> wait.*

can't help but This expression is redundant. Use *I can't help going* rather than *I can't help but go.*

censor, censure *Censor* means "remove that which is considered offensive." *Censure* means "formally reprimand." *The newspaper* <u>*censored*</u> *stories that offended advertisers. The legislature* <u>*censured*</u> *the official for misconduct.*

compare to, compare with *Compare to* means "regard as similar." *Jamie* <u>*compared*</u> *the loss* <u>*to*</u> *a kick in the head. Compare with* means "examine to find differences or similarities." <u>*Compare*</u> *Tim Burton's films* <u>*with*</u> *David Lynch's.*

complement, compliment *Complement* means "go well with." *Compliment* means "praise." *Guests* <u>*complimented*</u> *her on how her earrings* <u>*complemented*</u> *her gown.*

comprise, compose *Comprise* means "contain." *Compose* means "make up." *The class* <u>*comprises*</u> *twenty students. Twenty students* <u>*compose*</u> *the class.*

conscience, conscious *Conscience* means "a sense of right and wrong." *Conscious* means "awake" or "aware." *Lisa was* <u>*conscious*</u> *of a guilty* <u>*conscience*</u>.

consensus of opinion Use *consensus* rather than this redundant phrase. *The family* <u>*consensus*</u> *was to sell the old house.*

consequently, subsequently *Consequently* means "as a result"; *subsequently* means "then." *He quit, and* <u>*subsequently*</u> *his wife lost her job;* <u>*consequently*</u>, *they had to sell their house.*

continual, continuous *Continual* means "repeated at regular or frequent intervals." *Continuous* means "continuing or connected without a break." *The damage done by* <u>*continuous*</u> *erosion was increased by the* <u>*continual*</u> *storms.*

could of *Have*, not *of*, should follow *could, would, should,* or *might.* *We could* <u>*have*</u> *[not* of*] invited them.*

criteria, criterion *Criterion* means "standard of judgment" or "necessary qualification." *Criteria* is the plural form. *Image is the wrong* <u>*criterion*</u> *for choosing a president.*

data *Data* is the plural form of the Latin word *datum*, meaning "fact." Although *data* is used informally as either singular or plural, in academic or professional writing, treat *data* as plural. *These* <u>*data*</u> *indicate that fewer people are smoking.*

different from, different than *Different from* is generally preferred in academic and professional writing, although both of these phrases are widely used. *Her lab results were no **different from** [not than] his.*

discreet, discrete *Discreet* means "tactful" or "prudent." *Discrete* means "separate" or "distinct." *The leader's **discreet** efforts kept all the **discrete** factions unified.*

disinterested, uninterested *Disinterested* means "unbiased." *Uninterested* means "indifferent." *Finding **disinterested** jurors was difficult. She was **uninterested** in the verdict.*

distinct, distinctive *Distinct* means "separate" or "well defined." *Distinctive* means "characteristic." *Germany includes many **distinct** regions, each with a **distinctive** accent.*

doesn't, don't *Doesn't* is the contraction for *does not*. Use it with *he, she, it,* and singular nouns. *Don't* stands for *do not*; use it with *I, you, we, they,* and plural nouns.

due to See *because of, due to.*

each other, one another Use *each other* in sentences that involve two subjects and *one another* in sentences that involve more than two.

effect See *affect, effect.*

elicit, illicit The verb *elicit* means "draw out." The adjective *illicit* means "illegal." *The police **elicited** from the criminal the names of others involved in **illicit** activities.*

elude See *allude, elude.*

emigrate from, immigrate to *Emigrate from* means "move away from one's country." *Immigrate to* means "move to another country." *We **emigrated from** Norway in 1999. We **immigrated to** the United States.*

ensure See *assure, ensure, insure.*

enthused, enthusiastic Use *enthusiastic* rather than *enthused* in academic and professional writing.

equally as good Replace this redundant phrase with *equally good* or *as good.*

every day, everyday *Everyday* is an adjective meaning "ordinary." *Every day* is an adjective and a noun, meaning "each day." *I wore **everyday** clothes almost **every day**.*

every one, everyone *Everyone* is a pronoun. *Every one* is an adjective and a pronoun, referring to each member of a group. *Because* *he began after* <u>*everyone*</u> *else, David could not finish* <u>*every one*</u> *of the problems.*

except See *accept, except.*

explicit, implicit *Explicit* means "directly or openly expressed." *Implicit* means "indirectly expressed or implied." *The* <u>*explicit*</u> *message of the ad urged consumers to buy the product, while the* <u>*implicit*</u> *message promised popularity if they did so.*

farther, further *Farther* refers to physical distance. *How much* <u>*farther*</u> *is it to Munich? Further* refers to time or degree. *I want to avoid* <u>*further*</u> *delays.*

fewer, less Use *fewer* with nouns that can be counted. Use *less* with general amounts that you cannot count. *The world needs* <u>*fewer*</u> *bombs and* <u>*less*</u> *hostility.*

finalize *Finalize* is a pretentious way of saying "end" or "make final." *We* <u>*closed*</u> [not *finalized*] *the deal.*

firstly, secondly, etc. *First, second,* etc., are more common in U.S. English.

flaunt, flout *Flaunt* means to "show off." *Flout* means to "mock" or "scorn." *The drug dealers* <u>*flouted*</u> *authority by* <u>*flaunting*</u> *their wealth.*

former, latter *Former* refers to the first and *latter* to the second of two things previously mentioned. *Kathy and Anna are athletes; the* <u>*former*</u> *plays tennis, and the* <u>*latter*</u> *runs.*

further See *farther, further.*

good, well *Good* is an adjective and should not be used as a substitute for the adverb *well. Gabriel is a* <u>*good*</u> *host who cooks* <u>*well*</u>.

good and *Good and* is colloquial for "very"; avoid it in academic and professional writing.

hanged, hung *Hanged* refers to executions; *hung* is used for all other meanings.

hardly See *can't hardly.*

herself, himself, myself, yourself Do not use these reflexive pronouns as subjects or as objects unless they are necessary. *Jane and I* [not *myself*] *agree. They invited John and me* [not *myself*].

he/she, his/her Better solutions for avoiding sexist language are to write out *he or she,* to eliminate pronouns entirely, or to make the subject plural. Instead of writing *Everyone should carry* <u>*his/her*</u>

driver's license, try *Drivers should carry their licenses* or *People should carry their driver's licenses.*

himself See *herself, himself, myself, yourself.*

hisself Use *himself* instead in academic or professional writing.

hopefully *Hopefully* is often used informally to mean "it is hoped," but its formal meaning is "with hope." *Sam watched the roulette wheel hopefully* [not *Hopefully, Sam will win*].

hung See *hanged, hung.*

illicit See *elicit, illicit.*

illusion See *allusion, illusion.*

immigrate to See *emigrate from, immigrate to.*

impact Some readers object to the colloquial use of *impact* or *impact on* as a verb meaning "affect." *Population control may reduce* [not *impact*] *world hunger.*

implicit See *explicit, implicit.*

imply, infer To *imply* is to suggest indirectly. To *infer* is to guess or conclude on the basis of an indirect suggestion. *The note implied they were planning a small wedding; we inferred we would not be invited.*

inside of, outside of Use *inside* and *outside* instead. *The class regularly met outside* [not *outside of*] *the building.*

insure See *assure, ensure, insure.*

interact, interface *Interact* is a vague word meaning "do something that somehow involves another person." *Interface* is computer jargon; when used as a verb, it means "discuss" or "communicate." Avoid both verbs in academic and professional writing.

irregardless, regardless *Irregardless* is a double negative. Use *regardless.*

is when, is where These vague expressions are often incorrectly used in definitions. *Schizophrenia is a psychotic condition in which* [not *is when* or *is where*] *a person withdraws from reality.*

its, it's *Its* is the possessive form of *it. It's* is a contraction for *it is* or *it has. It's important to observe the rat before it eats its meal.*

kind, sort, type These singular nouns should be modified with *this* or *that*, not *these* or *those*, and followed by other singular nouns, not plural nouns. *Wear this kind of dress* [not *those kind of dresses*].

kind of, sort of Avoid these colloquialisms. *Amy was somewhat* [not *kind of*] *tired.*

know, no Use *know* to mean "understand." *No* is the opposite of *yes.*

later, latter *Later* means "after some time." *Latter* refers to the second of two items named. *Juan and Chad won all their early matches, but the latter was injured later in the season.*

latter See *former, latter* and *later, latter.*

lay, lie *Lay* means "place" or "put." Its main forms are *lay, laid, laid.* It generally has a direct object, specifying what has been placed. *She laid her books on the desk.* *Lie* means "recline" or "be positioned" and does not take a direct object. Its main forms are *lie, lay, lain. She lay awake until two.*

leave, let *Leave* means "go away." *Let* means "allow." *Leave alone* and *let alone* are interchangeable. *Let me leave now, and leave* [or *let*] *me alone from now on!*

lend, loan In academic and professional writing, do not use *loan* as a verb; use *lend* instead. *Please lend me your pen so that I may fill out this application for a loan.*

less See *fewer, less.*

let See *leave, let.*

liable See *apt, liable, likely.*

lie See *lay, lie.*

like See *as, as if, like.*

likely See *apt, liable, likely.*

literally *Literally* means "actually" or "exactly as stated." Use it to stress the truth of a statement that might otherwise be understood as figurative. Do not use *literally* as an intensifier in a figurative statement. *Mirna was literally at the edge of her seat* may be accurate, but *Mirna is so hungry that she could literally eat a horse* is not.

loan See *lend, loan.*

loose, lose *Lose* is a verb meaning "misplace." *Loose* is an adjective that means "not securely attached." *Sew on that loose button before you lose it.*

lots, lots of Avoid these informal expressions meaning "much" or "many" in academic or professional discourse.

man, mankind Replace these terms with *people, humans, humankind, men and women*, or similar wording.

may See *can, may.*

may be, maybe *May be* is a verb phrase. *Maybe* is an adverb that means "perhaps." *He <u>may be</u> the head of the organization, but <u>maybe</u> someone else would handle a crisis better.*

media *Media* is the plural form of the noun *medium* and takes a plural verb. *The <u>media are</u>* [not *is*] *obsessed with scandals.*

might of See *could of.*

moral, morale A *moral* is a succinct lesson. *The <u>moral</u> of the story is that generosity is rewarded. Morale* means "spirit" or "mood." *Office <u>morale</u> was low.*

myself See *herself, himself, myself, yourself.*

no See *know, no.*

nor, or Use *either* with *or* and *neither* with *nor.*

number See *amount, number.*

off, of Use *off* without *of. The spaghetti slipped <u>off</u>* [not *off of*] *the plate.*

OK, O.K., okay All are acceptable spellings, but avoid the term in academic and professional discourse.

on account of Use this substitute for *because of* sparingly or not at all.

one another See *each other, one another.*

or See *nor, or.*

outside of See *inside of, outside of.*

owing to the fact that Avoid this and other wordy expressions for *because.*

passed, past Use *passed* to mean "went by" or "received a passing grade": *The marching band <u>passed</u> the reviewing stand.* Use *past* to refer to a time before the present: *Historians study the <u>past</u>.*

per Use the Latin *per* only in standard technical phrases such as *miles per hour.* Otherwise, find English equivalents. *As mentioned in* [not *As per*] *the latest report, the country's average food consumption each day* [not *per day*] *is only 2,000 calories.*

percent, percentage Use *percent* with a specific number; use *percentage* with an adjective such as *large* or *small*. *Last year, 80 percent of the members were female. A large percentage of the members are women.*

plenty *Plenty* means "enough" or "a great abundance." *They told us America was a land of plenty.* Colloquially, it is used to mean "very," a usage you should avoid in academic and professional writing. *He was very [not plenty] tired.*

plus *Plus* means "in addition to." *Your salary plus mine will cover our expenses.* In academic writing, do not use *plus* to mean "besides" or "moreover." *That dress does not fit me. Besides [not Plus], it is the wrong color.*

precede, proceed *Precede* means "come before"; *proceed* means "go forward." *Despite the storm that preceded the ceremony, the wedding proceeded on schedule.*

pretty Except in informal situations, avoid using *pretty* as a substitute for "rather," "somewhat," or "quite." *Bill was quite [not pretty] disagreeable.*

principal, principle When used as a noun, *principal* refers to a head official or an amount of money; when used as an adjective, it means "most significant." *Principle* means "fundamental law or belief." *Albert went to the principal and defended himself with the principle of free speech.*

proceed See *precede, proceed.*

quotation, quote *Quote* is a verb, while *quotation* is a noun. *He quoted the president, and the quotation [not quote] was preserved in history books.*

raise, rise *Raise* means "lift" or "move upward." (Referring to children, it means "bring up.") It takes a direct object; someone raises something. *The guests raised their glasses to toast.* *Rise* means "go upward." It does not take a direct object; something rises by itself. *She saw the steam rise from the pan.*

rarely ever Use *rarely* by itself, or use *hardly ever.* *When we were poor, we rarely went to the movies.*

real, really *Real* is an adjective, and *really* is an adverb. Do not substitute *real* for *really.* In academic and professional writing, do not use *real* or *really* to mean "very." *The old man walked very [not real or really] slowly.*

reason is because Use either *the reason is that* or *because* — not both. *The <u>reason</u> the copier stopped <u>is that</u>* [not *is because*] *the paper jammed.*

reason why This expression is redundant. *The <u>reason</u>* [not *reason why*] *this book is short is market demand.*

regardless See *irregardless, regardless.*

respectfully, respectively *Respectfully* means "with respect." *Respectively* means "in the order given." *Karen and David are, <u>respectively</u>, a juggler and an acrobat. The children treated their grandparents <u>respectfully</u>.*

rise See *raise, rise.*

set, sit *Set* usually means "put" or "place" and takes a direct object. *Sit* refers to taking a seat and does not take an object. *<u>Set</u> your cup on the table, and <u>sit</u> down.*

should of See *could of.*

since Be careful not to use *since* ambiguously. In *<u>Since</u> I broke my leg, I've stayed home,* the word *since* might be understood to mean either "because" or "ever since."

sit See *set, sit.*

so In academic and professional writing, avoid using *so* alone to mean "very." Instead, follow *so* with *that* to show how the intensified condition leads to a result. *Aaron was <u>so</u> tired <u>that</u> he fell asleep at the wheel.*

someplace Use *somewhere* instead in academic and professional writing.

some time, sometime, sometimes *Some time* refers to a length of time. *Please leave me <u>some time</u> to dress. Sometime* means "at some indefinite later time." *<u>Sometime</u> I will take you to London. Sometimes* means "occasionally." *<u>Sometimes</u> I eat sushi.*

sort See *kind, sort, type.*

sort of See *kind of, sort of.*

stationary, stationery *Stationary* means "standing still"; *stationery* means "writing paper." *When the bus was <u>stationary</u>, Pat took out <u>stationery</u> and wrote a note.*

subsequently See *consequently, subsequently.*

supposed to, used to Be careful to include the final *-d* in these expressions. *He is <u>supposed to</u> attend.*

sure, surely Avoid using *sure* as an intensifier. Instead, use *certainly*. *I was <u>certainly</u> glad to see you.*

take See *bring, take.*

than, then Use *than* in comparative statements. *The cat was bigger <u>than</u> the dog.* Use *then* when referring to a sequence of events. *I won, and <u>then</u> I cried.*

that, which A clause beginning with *that* singles out the item being described. *The book <u>that</u> is on the table is a good one* specifies the book on the table as opposed to some other book. A clause beginning with *which* may or may not single out the item, although some writers use *which* clauses only to add more information about an item being described. *The book, <u>which</u> is on the table, is a good one* contains a *which* clause between the commas. The clause simply adds extra, nonessential information about the book; it does not specify which book.

theirselves Use *themselves* instead in academic and professional writing.

then See *than, then.*

thorough, threw, through *Thorough* means "complete": *After a <u>thorough</u> inspection, the restaurant reopened.* *Threw* is the past tense of *throw*, and *through* means "in one side and out the other": *He <u>threw</u> the ball <u>through</u> a window.*

to, too, two *To* generally shows direction. *Too* means "also." *Two* is the number. *We, <u>too</u>, are going <u>to</u> the meeting in <u>two</u> hours.* Avoid using *to* after *where. Where are you flying* [not *flying to*]?

two See *to, too, two.*

type See *kind, sort, type.*

uninterested See *disinterested, uninterested.*

unique Some people argue that *unique* means "one and only" and object to usage that suggests it means merely "unusual." In formal writing, avoid constructions such as *quite unique.*

used to See *supposed to, used to.*

very Avoid using *very* to intensify a weak adjective or adverb; instead, replace the adjective or adverb with a stronger, more precise, or more colorful word. Instead of *very nice*, for example, use *kind, warm, sensitive, endearing,* or *friendly.*

way, ways When referring to distance, use *way. Graduation was a long <u>way</u>* [not *ways*] *off.*

well See *good, well.*

where Use *where* alone, not with words such as *at* and *to. <u>Where</u> are you going* [not *going to*]?

which See *that, which.*

who, whom Use *who* if the word is the subject of the clause and *whom* if the word is the object of the clause. *Monica, <u>who</u> smokes incessantly, is my godmother.* (*Who* is the subject of the clause; the verb is *smokes.*) *Monica, <u>whom</u> I saw last winter, lives in Tucson.* (*Whom* is the object of the verb *saw.*)

who's, whose *Who's* is a contraction for *who is* or *who has. <u>Who's</u> on the patio? Whose* is a possessive form. *<u>Whose</u> sculpture is in the garden? <u>Whose</u> is on the patio?*

would of See *could of.*

yet See *but yet.*

your, you're *Your* shows possession. *Bring <u>your</u> sleeping bag along. You're* is the contraction for *you are. <u>You're</u> in the wrong sleeping bag.*

yourself See *herself, himself, myself, yourself.*

Sentence Grammar

22 Basic Grammar

The grammar of our first language comes to us almost automatically, without our thinking much about it or even being aware of it. Listen in, for instance, on a conversation between a six-year-old and her sister.

> AUDREY: My new bike that Daddy got me has a pink basket and a loud horn, and I love it.
>
> LILA: Can I ride it?
>
> AUDREY: Sure, as soon as you get big enough.

This simple conversation features sophisticated grammar, used effortlessly. Every language has grammar (basic structures), and native speakers understand and use these structures long before they learn what to call parts of a sentence or the different options for putting the pieces of sentences together effectively. Thinking carefully about the basic structures of English can help you make wise choices for your audience and your rhetorical situation.

22a The basic grammar of sentences

A sentence is a grammatically complete group of words that expresses a thought. In standard English, a grammatically complete sentence must contain a subject, which identifies what the sentence is about, and a predicate, which says or asks something about the subject or tells the subject to do something.

SUBJECT	PREDICATE
I	have a dream.
The rain in Spain	stays mainly in the plain.
Stephen Colbert, who hosts a cable TV show,	pretends to be a conservative.

Some sentences have only a one-word predicate with an implied, or understood, subject (for example, *Stop!*). Most sentences, however, contain additional words that expand the basic subject and predicate. In the preceding example, for instance, the subject might have been simply *Stephen Colbert*; the words *who hosts a cable TV show* tell us more about the subject. Similarly, the predicate of that sentence could grammatically be *pretends*; the words *to be a conservative* expand the predicate by telling us what Colbert pretends.

EXERCISE 22.1

Identify the subject and the predicate in each of the following sentences, underlining the subject once and the predicate twice. Example:

> The roaring lion at the beginning of old MGM films is part of
>
> movie history.

1. Scientific experiments on human subjects are now carefully regulated.
2. Her first afternoon as a kindergarten teacher had left her exhausted.
3. The Croatian news media is almost entirely owned by the state.
4. Our office manager, a stern taskmaster with a fondness for Chanel suits, has been terrifying interns since 1992.
5. Reading edited prose shows writers how to communicate.
6. The security officer at the border questioned everyone suspiciously.
7. People in the nineteenth century communicated with each other constantly through letters.
8. Disease killed off a large number of the tomato plants in the northeastern United States last year.
9. What do scientists know about dinosaurs?
10. The hula-hoop craze of the 1960s has made a comeback among adults looking for fun ways to exercise.

Parts of Speech

All English words belong to one or more of eight grammatical categories called parts of speech: verbs, nouns, pronouns, adjectives, adverbs, prepositions, conjunctions, and interjections. Many English words regularly function as more than one part of speech. Take the word *book*, for example: when you *book a flight*, it is a verb; when you *take a good book to the beach*, it is a noun; and when you *have book knowledge*, it is an adjective.

22b Verbs

Verbs are among the most important words because they move the meanings of sentences along. Verbs show actions of body or mind (*skip*, *speculate*), occurrences (*become*, *happen*), or states of being (*be*, *seem*). They can also change form to show *time*, *person*, *number*, *voice*, and *mood*.

TIME	we work, we worked
PERSON	I work, she works
NUMBER	one person works, two people work
VOICE	she asks, she is asked
MOOD	we see, if we saw

Helping verbs (also called auxiliary verbs) combine with other verbs (often called main verbs) to create verb phrases. Helping verbs include the various forms of *be*, *do*, and *have* (which can also function as main verbs) and the words *can*, *could*, *may*, *might*, *must*, *shall*, *should*, *will*, and *would*.

▶ You do need some sleep tonight!

▶ I could have danced all night.

▶ She would prefer to learn Italian rather than Spanish.

See Chapters 23 and 24 for a complete discussion of verbs.

EXERCISE 22.2

Underline each verb or verb phrase in the following sentences. Example:

Drivers should expect weather-related delays.

1. The story was released to the press late on Friday evening.
2. Most athletes will be arriving well before the games.
3. Housing prices have fallen considerably in the past year.
4. No one spoke in the room where the students were taking the exam.
5. The suspect has been fingerprinted and is waiting now for his lawyer.

22c Nouns

A noun names a person (*aviator, child*), place (*lake, library*), thing (*truck, suitcase*), or concept (*happiness, balance*). Proper nouns name specific people, places, things, and concepts: *Bill, Iowa, Supreme Court, Buddhism*. Collective nouns name groups: *team, flock, jury* (24c).

You can change most nouns from singular (one) to plural (more than one) by adding *-s* or *-es*: *horse, horses; kiss, kisses*. Some nouns, however, have irregular plural forms: *woman, women; alumnus, alumni; mouse, mice; deer, deer*. Noncount nouns—such as *dust, peace*, and *prosperity*—do not have a plural form because they name something that cannot easily be counted (46a).

To show ownership, nouns take the possessive form by adding an apostrophe plus *-s* to a singular noun or just an apostrophe to a plural noun: *the horse's owner, the boys' dilemma* (38a).

FOR MULTILINGUAL WRITERS

Using Count and Noncount Nouns

Do people conduct *research* or *researches*? See 46a for a discussion of count and noncount nouns.

EXERCISE 22.3

Identify the nouns and the articles in each of the following sentences. Underline the nouns once and the articles twice. Example:

The Puritans hoped for a different king, but Charles II regained his father's throne.

1. On Halloween, the children got sick from eating so much candy.
2. Although June is technically the driest month, severe flooding has occurred in the late spring.
3. Baking is no longer a common activity in most households around the country.
4. A sudden frost turned the ground into a field of ice.
5. The cyclist swerved to avoid an oncoming car that had run a red light.

22d Pronouns

Pronouns often take the place of nouns, other pronouns, or other words functioning as a noun. Pronouns serve as short forms so that you do not have to repeat a word or group of words you have already mentioned. A word or group of words that a pronoun replaces or refers to is called the antecedent of the pronoun. (See Chapter 27.)

ANTECEDENT   PRONOUN

▶ *Caitlin* refused the invitation even though *she* wanted to go.

Here are the categories of pronouns:

PERSONAL PRONOUNS. Personal pronouns refer to specific persons or things.

I, me, you, he, she, him, her, it, we, us, they, them

▶ When Keisha saw the dogs, she called them, and they ran to her.

POSSESSIVE PRONOUNS. Possessive pronouns are personal pronouns that indicate ownership.

my, mine, your, yours, her, hers, his, its, our, ours, their, theirs

▶ My roommate lost her keys.

REFLEXIVE PRONOUNS. Reflexive pronouns refer back to the subject of the sentence and end in *-self* or *-selves*.

myself, yourself, himself, herself, itself, oneself, ourselves, yourselves, themselves

▶ The seals sunned themselves on the warm rocks.

INTENSIVE PRONOUNS. Intensive pronouns have the same form as reflexive pronouns. They emphasize a noun or another pronoun.

▶ He decided to paint the apartment himself.

INDEFINITE PRONOUNS. Indefinite pronouns do not refer to specific nouns, although they may refer to identifiable persons or things. The following is a partial list:

all, another, anybody, both, each, either, everything, few, many, most, neither, none, no one, nothing, one, some, something

▶ **Everybody** screamed, and **someone** fainted, when the lights went out.

DEMONSTRATIVE PRONOUNS. Demonstrative pronouns point to specific nouns.

> *this, that, these, those*

▶ **These** are Peter's books.

INTERROGATIVE PRONOUNS. Interrogative pronouns are used to ask questions.

> *who, which, what*

▶ **Who** can help set up the chairs for the meeting?

RELATIVE PRONOUNS. Relative pronouns both introduce dependent clauses and relate the information to the rest of the sentence (22m). The interrogative pronoun *who* and the relative pronouns *who* and *whoever* have different forms depending on how they are used in a sentence (27a).

> *who, which, that, what, whoever, whichever, whatever*

▶ Maya, **who** hires interns, is the manager **whom** you should contact.

RECIPROCAL PRONOUNS. Reciprocal pronouns refer to individual parts of a plural antecedent.

> *each other, one another*

▶ The business failed because the partners distrusted **each other**.

EXERCISE 22.4

Identify the pronouns and any antecedents in each of the following sentences, underlining the pronouns once and any antecedents twice. Example:

> As identical <u><u>twins</u></u>, <u>they</u> really do understand <u>each other</u>.

1. He told the volunteers to help themselves to the leftovers.
2. There are two kinds of people: those who divide people into two kinds and those who don't.

3. Who is going to buy the jeans and wear them if the designer himself finds them uncomfortable?

4. Before an annual performance review, employees are asked to take a hard look at themselves and their work habits.

5. Forwarding an email warning about a computer virus to everyone in your address book is never a good idea.

22e Adjectives

Adjectives modify nouns and pronouns, usually by describing, identifying, or limiting those words. Some people refer to the identifying or quantifying adjectives as *determiners* (46b).

▶ The **red** Corvette ran off the road. [describes]

▶ **That** Corvette needs to be repaired. [identifies]

▶ We saw **several** Corvettes race by. [quantifies]

In addition to their basic forms, most descriptive adjectives have other forms that allow you to make comparisons: *small, smaller, smallest; foolish, more foolish, most foolish, less foolish, least foolish* (25b). Many words that function in some sentences as pronouns (22d) can function as identifying adjectives when they are followed by a noun.

▶ **That** is a dangerous intersection. [pronoun]

▶ **That** intersection is dangerous. [identifying adjective]

Adjectives usually precede the words they modify, though they may follow linking verbs: *The car was defective.*

Other kinds of identifying or quantifying adjectives are articles (*a, an, the*) and numbers (*three, sixty-fifth*).

FOR MULTILINGUAL WRITERS

Deciding When Articles Are Necessary

Do you say "I'm working on *a* paper" or "I'm working on *the* paper"? Deciding when to use the articles *a*, *an*, and *the* can be challenging for multilingual writers since many languages have nothing directly comparable to them. For help using articles, see 46c.

Proper adjectives are adjectives formed from or related to proper nouns (*British*, *Emersonian*). Proper adjectives are capitalized (41b).

22f Adverbs

Adverbs modify verbs, adjectives, other adverbs, or entire clauses. They often answer the questions *when? where? why? to what extent?* Many adverbs have an *-ly* ending, though some do not (*always, never, very, well*), and some words that end in *-ly* are not adverbs but adjectives (*scholarly, lovely*). One of the most common adverbs is *not*.

▶ Jabari recently visited his roommate's family in Maine. [modifies the verb *visited*]

▶ It was an unexpectedly exciting trip. [modifies the adjective *exciting*]

▶ The visit ended too soon. [modifies the adverb *soon*]

▶ Frankly, he would have liked to stay another month. [modifies the independent clause that makes up the rest of the sentence]

Many adverbs, like many adjectives, take other forms when making comparisons: *forcefully, more forcefully, most forcefully, less forcefully, least forcefully* (25b).

Conjunctive adverbs modify an entire clause and help connect the meaning between that clause and the preceding clause (or sentence). Examples of conjunctive adverbs include *however, furthermore, therefore,* and *likewise* (22h).

EXERCISE 22.5

Identify the adjectives and adverbs in each of the following sentences, underlining the adjectives once and the adverbs twice. Remember that articles and some pronouns are used as adjectives. Example:

Inadvertently, the two agents misquoted their major client.

1. The small, frightened child firmly squeezed my hand and refused to take another step forward.

2. Meanwhile, she learned that the financial records had been completely false.

3. Koalas are generally quiet creatures that make loud grunting noises during mating season.

4. The huge red tomatoes looked lovely, but they tasted disappointingly like cardboard.

5. The youngest dancer in the troupe performed a brilliant solo.

22g Prepositions

Prepositions are important structural words that express relationships — in time, space, or other senses — between nouns or pronouns and other words in a sentence.

▶ We did not want to leave during the game.

▶ The contestants waited nervously for the announcement.

▶ Drive across the bridge, and go down the avenue past three stoplights.

SOME COMMON PREPOSITIONS

about	at	down	near	since
above	before	during	of	through
across	behind	except	off	toward
after	below	for	on	under
against	beneath	from	onto	until
along	beside	in	out	up
among	between	inside	over	upon
around	beyond	into	past	with
as	by	like	regarding	without

SOME COMPOUND PREPOSITIONS

according to	except for	instead of
as well as	in addition to	next to
because of	in front of	out of
by way of	in place of	with regard to
due to	in spite of	

Research for this book shows that many writers today — even native speakers of English — have trouble using prepositions idiomatically. If you aren't sure which preposition to use, consult a dictionary.

EXERCISE 22.6

Identify and underline the prepositions in the following sentences. Example:

> In the dim interior of the hut crouched an old man.

1. The supervisor of the night shift requested that all available personnel work extra hours from October through December.

2. The hatchlings emerged from their shells, crawled across the sand, and swam into the sea.

3. Instead of creating a peaceful new beginning, the tribunal factions are constantly fighting among themselves.

4. After some hard thinking on a weeklong camping trip, I decided I would quit my job and join the Peace Corps for two years.

5. The nuclear power plant about ten miles from the city has the worst safety record of any plant in the country.

22h Conjunctions

Conjunctions connect words or groups of words to each other and tell something about the relationship between these words.

Coordinating conjunctions. Coordinating conjunctions (31a) join equivalent structures: two or more nouns, pronouns, verbs, adjectives, adverbs, prepositions, conjunctions, phrases, or clauses.

▶ A strong but warm breeze blew across the desert.

▶ Please print or type the information on the application form.

▶ Taiwo worked two shifts today, so she is tired tonight.

COORDINATING CONJUNCTIONS

and	for	or	yet
but	nor	so	

Correlative conjunctions. Correlative conjunctions join equal elements, and they come in pairs.

▶ Both Bechtel and Kaiser submitted bids on the project.

▶ Jeff not only sent a card but also visited me in the hospital.

CORRELATIVE CONJUNCTIONS

| both . . . and | just as . . . so | not only . . . but also |
| either . . . or | neither . . . nor | whether . . . or |

Subordinating conjunctions.   Subordinating conjunctions introduce adverb clauses and signal the relationship between an adverb clause and another clause. For instance, in the following sentence, the subordinating conjunction *while* signals that the two events in the sentence happened simultaneously:

▶ **Sweat ran down my face while I frantically searched for my child.**

SOME SUBORDINATING CONJUNCTIONS

after	if	unless
although	in order that	until
as	once	when
as if	since	where
because	so that	whether
before	than	while
even though	though	

Conjunctive adverbs.   Conjunctive adverbs signal a logical relationship between parts of a sentence and, when used with a semicolon, can link independent clauses (22m).

▶ **The cider tasted bitter; however, each of us drank a tall glass of it.**

▶ **The cider tasted bitter; each of us, however, drank a tall glass of it.**

SOME CONJUNCTIVE ADVERBS

also	however	moreover	similarly
anyway	incidentally	namely	still
besides	indeed	nevertheless	then
certainly	instead	next	therefore
finally	likewise	now	thus
furthermore	meanwhile	otherwise	undoubtedly

EXERCISE 22.7

Underline the coordinating, correlative, and subordinating conjunctions as well as the conjunctive adverbs in each of the following sentences. Example:

> We used sleeping bags, <u>even though</u> the cabin had sheets <u>and</u> blankets.

1. After waiting for an hour and a half, both Jenny and I were disgruntled, so we went home.
2. The facilities were not only uncomfortable but also dangerous.
3. I usually get a bonus each January; however, sales were down this year, so the company did not give us any extra money.
4. Although I had completed a six-week training regimen of running, swimming, and cycling, I did not feel ready, so I withdrew from the competition.
5. Enrique was not qualified for the job because he knew one of the programming languages but not the other; still, the interview encouraged him.

22i   Interjections

Interjections express surprise or emotion: *oh*, *ouch*, *ah*, *hey*. Interjections often stand alone. Even when interjections are part of a sentence, they do not relate grammatically to the rest of the sentence.

▶ Hey, no one suggested that we would find an easy solution.

Parts of Sentences

Knowing a word's part of speech helps you understand how to use that word. But you also need to look at the part the word plays in a particular sentence. Consider, for instance, the word *description*.

SUBJECT
▶ This *description* conveys the ecology of the Everglades.

DIRECT OBJECT
▶ I read a *description* of the ecology of the Everglades.

Description is a noun in both sentences, yet in the first it serves as the subject of the verb *conveys*, while in the second it serves as the direct object of the verb *read*.

CHECKLIST

Basic Sentence Patterns

1. subject/verb

        S   V
   ▶ Babies drool.

2. subject/verb/subject complement

        S   V   SC
   ▶ Babies smell sweet.

3. subject/verb/direct object

        S   V   DO
   ▶ Babies drink milk.

4. subject/verb/indirect object/direct object

        S   V   IO   DO
   ▶ Babies give grandparents pleasure.

5. subject/verb/direct object/object complement

        S   V   DO   OC
   ▶ Babies keep parents awake.

22j Subjects

The subject of a sentence identifies what the sentence is about. The simple subject consists of one or more nouns or pronouns; the complete subject consists of the simple subject with all of its modifiers.

▶ **Baseball** is a summer game.

  ┌──── COMPLETE SUBJECT ────┐
▶ Sailing over the fence, the **ball** crashed through Mr. Wilson's window.

  ┌──── COMPLETE SUBJECT ────┐
▶ **Those** who sit in the bleachers have the most fun.

A compound subject contains two or more simple subjects that are joined with either a coordinating conjunction (*and, but, or*) or a correlative conjunction (*both . . . and, either . . . or, neither . . . nor*). (See 22h.)

▶ **Baseball and softball** developed from cricket.
▶ **Both baseball and softball** developed from cricket.

The subject usually comes before the predicate, or verb, but sometimes writers reverse this order to achieve a special effect.

▶ Up to the plate stepped **Casey**.

In imperative sentences, which express requests or commands, the subject *you* is usually implied but not stated.

▶ **(You)** Keep your eye on the ball.

In questions and certain other constructions, the subject usually appears between the auxiliary verb (22b) and the main verb.

▶ Did **Casey** save the game?

In sentences beginning with *there* or *here* followed by a form of *be*, the subject always follows the verb. *There* and *here* are never the subject.

▶ There was no **joy** in Mudville.

EXERCISE 22.8

Identify the complete subject and the simple subject in each sentence. Underline the complete subject once and the simple subject twice. Example:

The tall, powerful woman defiantly blocked the doorway.

1. That container of fried rice has spent six weeks in the back of the refrigerator.

2. Did the new tour guide remember to stop in the ancient Greek gallery?

3. There was one student still taking the exam when the bell rang.

4. Japanese animation, with its cutting-edge graphics and futuristic plots, has earned many American admirers.

5. Sniffer dogs trained to detect drugs, blood, and explosives can help solve crimes and save lives.

22k   Predicates

In addition to a subject, every sentence has a predicate, which asserts or asks something about the subject or tells the subject to do something. The hinge, or key word, of a predicate is the verb. The simple predicate of a sentence consists of the main verb and any auxiliaries (22b); the complete predicate includes the simple predicate plus any modifiers of the verb and any objects or complements and their modifiers.

┌──── COMPLETE PREDICATE ────┐
▶ Both of us are planning to major in history.

A compound predicate contains two or more verbs that have the same subject, usually joined by a coordinating or a correlative conjunction.

┌──────── COMPOUND PREDICATE ────────┐
▶ Omar shut the book, put it back on the shelf, and sighed.

┌──── COMPOUND PREDICATE ────┐
▶ The Amish neither drive cars nor use electricity.

On the basis of how they function in predicates, verbs can be divided into three categories: linking, transitive, and intransitive.

Linking verbs.   A linking verb links, or joins, a subject with a subject complement (sc), a word or group of words that identifies or describes the subject.

┌──── SC ────┐
▶ Nastassia is a single mother.

  SC
▶ She is patient.

If it identifies the subject, the complement is a noun or pronoun (*a single mother*). If it describes the subject, the complement is an adjective (*patient*).

   The forms of *be*, when used as main verbs rather than as auxiliary verbs, are linking verbs (like *are* in this sentence). Other verbs—such as *appear, become, feel, grow, look, make, seem, smell,* and *sound*—can also function as linking verbs, depending on the sense of the sentence.

Transitive verbs.   A transitive verb expresses action that is directed toward a noun or pronoun, called the direct object (DO) of the verb.

▸ He peeled ⌐—— DO ——⌐ all the rutabagas.

In the preceding example, the subject and verb do not express a complete thought. The direct object completes the thought by saying *what* he peeled.

A direct object may be followed by an object complement (OC), a word or word group that describes or identifies the direct object. Object complements may be adjectives, as in the next example, or nouns, as in the second example.

▸ I find ⌐———— DO ————⌐ ⌐—— OC ——⌐ cell-phone conversations in restaurants very annoying.

▸ Alana considers DO Keyshawn ⌐—— OC ——⌐ her best friend.

A transitive verb may also be followed by an indirect object (IO), which tells to whom or what, or for whom or what, the verb's action is done. You might say the indirect object is the recipient of the direct object.

▸ The sound of the traffic gave IO me ⌐—— DO ——⌐ a splitting headache.

Intransitive verbs.   An intransitive verb expresses action that is not directed toward an object. Therefore, an intransitive verb does not have a direct object.

▸ The Red Sox persevered.

▸ Their fans watched anxiously.

The verb *persevered* has no object (it makes no sense to ask, *persevered what?*), and the verb *watched* has an object that is implied but not expressed.

Some verbs that express action can be only transitive or only intransitive, but most can be used either way, with or without a direct object.

▸ A maid wearing a uniform opened ⌐— DO —⌐ the door.

The verb *opened* is transitive here.

▶ The door opened silently.

The verb *opened* is intransitive here.

EXERCISE 22.9

Underline the predicate in each of the following sentences. Then label each verb as linking (LV), transitive (TV), or intransitive (IV). Finally, label all subject and object complements and all direct and indirect objects. Example:

TV ┌─ DO ┐ OC
We considered city life unbearable.

1. He is proud of his heritage.
2. The horrifying news story made me angry.
3. The old house looks deserted.
4. Rock and roll will never die.
5. Chloe's boss offered her a promotion.

22l Phrases

A phrase is a group of words that lacks either a subject or a predicate or both.

Noun phrases. A noun phrase consists of a noun and all its modifiers. In a sentence, a noun phrase can play the role of a subject, object, or complement.

┌──────── SUBJECT ────────┐
▶ Delicious, gooey peanut butter is surprisingly healthful.

┌─ OBJECT ─┐
▶ Dieters prefer green salad.

┌─ COMPLEMENT ─┐
▶ A tuna sandwich is a popular lunch.

Verb phrases. A main verb and its auxiliary verbs make up a verb phrase, which can function only one way in a sentence: as a predicate.

▶ I can swim for a long time.
▶ His headaches might have been caused by tension.

Prepositional phrases. A prepositional phrase includes a preposition, a noun or pronoun (called the object of the preposition), and any modifiers of the object. Prepositional phrases usually serve as adjectives or adverbs.

ADJECTIVE	Our house in Maine is a cabin.
ADVERB	From Cadillac Mountain, you can see the Northern Lights.

Verbal phrases. Verbals are verb forms that do not function as verbs. Instead, they stand in for nouns, adjectives, or adverbs. A verbal phrase is made up of a verbal and any modifiers, objects, or complements. There are three kinds of verbals: participles, gerunds, and infinitives.

PARTICIPIAL PHRASES. A participial phrase always functions as an adjective and can include either a present participle (the *crying* child) or a past participle (the *spoken* word).

▶ A dog howling at the moon kept me awake.

▶ Irritated by the delay, Louise complained.

GERUND PHRASES. A gerund has the same form as a present participle, ending in -*ing*. But a gerund or a gerund phrase always functions as a noun.

SUBJECT
▶ Recycling is not always easy.

DIRECT OBJECT
▶ He ignored the loud wailing from the sandbox.

INFINITIVE PHRASES. An infinitive phrase can function as a noun, an adjective, or an adverb. The infinitive is the *to* form of a verb: *to be, to write.*

ADJECTIVE
▶ A vote would be a good way to end the meeting.

ADVERB
▶ To perfect a draft, always proofread carefully.

NOUN
▶ My goal is to be a biology teacher.

Absolute phrases. An absolute phrase usually includes a noun or pronoun and a participle. It modifies an entire sentence rather than a particular word and is usually set off from the rest of the sentence with commas (35a).

▶ I stood on the deck, the wind whipping my hair.

▶ My fears laid to rest, I climbed into the plane for my first solo flight.

Appositive phrases. A noun phrase that renames the noun or pronoun immediately preceding it is referred to as an appositive phrase.

▶ The report, a hefty three-volume work, included sixty recommendations.

▶ A single desire, to change the corporation's policies, guided our actions.

EXERCISE 22.10

Read the following sentences, and identify and label all of the prepositional, verbal, absolute, and appositive phrases. Notice that one kind of phrase may appear within another kind. Example:

```
           ──────── ABSOLUTE ────────        ──── PREP ────
His voice breaking with emotion, Ed thanked us for the award.
           └──── PREP ────┘
```

1. Chantelle, the motel clerk, hopes to be certified as a river guide.
2. Carpets made by hand are usually the most valuable.
3. My stomach doing flips, I answered the door.
4. Floating on my back, I ignored my practice requirements.
5. Driving across town during rush hour can take thirty minutes or more.

22m Clauses

A clause is a group of words containing a subject and a predicate. There are two kinds of clauses: independent and dependent.

Independent clauses (also known as main clauses) can stand alone as complete sentences: *The window is open.* Pairs of independent clauses may be joined with a comma and a coordinating conjunction (*and*, *but*, *for*, *or*, *nor*, *so*, or *yet*).

▶ The window is open, *so* we'd better be quiet.

Like independent clauses, dependent clauses (also known as subordinate clauses) contain a subject and a predicate, but they cannot stand alone as complete sentences because they begin with a subordinating word (31b). Dependent clauses function as nouns, adjectives, or adverbs.

▶ Because the window is open, the room feels cool.

In this combination, the subordinating conjunction *because* transforms the independent clause *the window is open* into a dependent clause. In doing so, it indicates a causal relationship between the two clauses.

Noun clauses.   Noun clauses can function as subjects, direct objects, subject complements, or objects of prepositions. A noun clause is always contained within another clause. Noun clauses usually begin with a relative pronoun (*that*, *which*, *what*, *who*, *whom*, *whose*, *whatever*, *whoever*, *whomever*, *whichever*) or with *when*, *where*, *whether*, *why*, or *how*.

┌──── S ────┐
▶ That she had a good job was important to him.

┌──── DO ────┐
▶ He asked where she went to college.

┌──── SC ────┐
▶ The real question was why he wanted to know.

┌──── OBJ OF PREP ────┐
▶ He was looking for whatever information was available.

Notice that in each of these sentences the noun clause is an integral part of the independent clause that makes up the sentence. For example, in the second sentence, the independent clause is not just *he asked* but *he asked where she went to college*.

Adjective clauses.   Adjective clauses modify nouns and pronouns in other clauses. Usually adjective clauses immediately follow the words they modify. Most of these clauses begin with the relative pronoun *who, whom, whose, that,* or *which*. Some begin with *when, where,* or *why*.

▶ The surgery, which took three hours, was a complete success.

▶ It was performed by the surgeon who had developed the procedure.

▶ The hospital was the one where I was born.

Sometimes the relative pronoun introducing an adjective clause may be omitted.

▶ That is one book [that] I intend to read.

Adverb clauses. Adverb clauses modify verbs, adjectives, or other adverbs. They begin with a subordinating conjunction (22h) and, like adverbs, usually tell when, where, why, how, or to what extent.

▶ We hiked where there were few other hikers.

▶ My backpack felt heavier than it ever had.

▶ I climbed as swiftly as I could under the weight of my backpack.

EXERCISE 22.11

Identify the independent and dependent clauses and any subordinating conjunctions and relative pronouns in each of the following sentences. Example:

┌──────── DEPENDENT CLAUSE ────────┐ ┌── INDEPENDENT CLAUSE ──
If I were going on a really long hike, I would carry a lightweight

stove.

If is a subordinating conjunction.

1. The hockey game was postponed because one of the players collapsed on the bench.

2. She eventually discovered the secret admirer who had been leaving notes in her locker.

3. After he completed three advanced drawing classes, Jason was admitted into the fine arts program, and he immediately rented a small studio space.

4. The test was easier than I had expected.

5. I could tell that it was going to rain, so I tried to get home quickly.

EXERCISE 22.12

Expand each of the following sentences by adding at least one dependent clause to it. Be prepared to explain how your addition improves the sentence. Example:

> *As the earth continued to shake, the*
> ~~The~~ books tumbled from the shelves.
> ^

1. The economy gradually began to recover.
2. Simone waited nervously by the phone.
3. New school safety rules were instituted this fall.
4. Rob always borrowed money from friends.
5. The crowd grew louder and more disorderly.

Types of Sentences

Like words, sentences can be classified in different ways: grammatically and functionally.

22n Grammatical classifications

Grammatically, sentences may be classified as simple, compound, complex, and compound-complex.

Simple sentences.   A simple sentence consists of one independent clause and no dependent clause.

┌─────────────── INDEPENDENT CLAUSE ───────────────┐
▶ The trailer is surrounded by a wooden deck.

┌─────────────── INDEPENDENT CLAUSE ───────────────┐
▶ Both my roommate and I left our keys in the room.

Compound sentences. A compound sentence consists of two or more independent clauses and no dependent clause. The clauses may be joined by a comma and a coordinating conjunction (*and, but, or, nor, for, so, yet*) or by a semicolon.

┌─────── IND CLAUSE ───────┐   ┌─── IND CLAUSE ───┐
▶ Occasionally, a car goes up the dirt trail, and dust flies everywhere.

┌─────── IND CLAUSE ───────┐ ┌─── IND CLAUSE ───┐
▶ Angelo is obsessed with soccer; he eats, breathes, and lives

┌────┐
the game.

Complex sentences. A complex sentence consists of one independent clause and at least one dependent clause.

┌─── IND CLAUSE ───┐ ┌─────── DEP CLAUSE ───────┐
▶ Many people believe that anyone can earn a living.

Compound-complex sentences. A compound-complex sentence consists of two or more independent clauses and at least one dependent clause.

┌─── IND CLAUSE ───┐ ┌──── DEP CLAUSE ────┐
▶ I complimented Luis when he finished the job, and

┌─── IND CLAUSE ───┐
he seemed pleased.

┌─────────── IND CLAUSE ───────────┐   ┌────┐
▶ Sister Lucy tried her best to help Martin, but he was an

┌── IND CLAUSE ──┐┌─────── DEP CLAUSE ───────┐
undisciplined boy who drove many teachers to despair.

22o   Functional classifications

In terms of function, sentences can be classified as declarative (making a statement), interrogative (asking a question), imperative (giving a command), or exclamatory (expressing strong feeling).

DECLARATIVE   He sings with the Carolina Boys' Choir.

INTERROGATIVE   How long has he sung with them?

| IMPERATIVE | Comb his hair before the performance starts. |
| EXCLAMATORY | What voices those boys have! |

EXERCISE 22.13

Classify each of the following sentences as simple, compound, complex, or compound-complex. In addition, note any sentence that may be classified as interrogative, imperative, or exclamatory.

1. The boat rocked and lurched over the rough surf as the passengers groaned in agony.

2. Is this the coldest winter on record, or was last year even worse?

3. After waiting for over an hour, I was examined by the doctor for only three minutes!

4. Keeping in mind the terrain, the weather, and the length of the hike, decide what you need to take.

5. The former prisoner, who was cleared by DNA evidence, has lost six years of his life, and he needs a job right away.

EXERCISE 22.14: THINKING CRITICALLY

The following sentences come from the openings of well-known works. Identify the independent and dependent clauses in each sentence. Then choose one sentence, and write a sentence of your own imitating its structure, clause for clause and phrase for phrase. Example:

> Ten days after the war ended, my sister Laura drove a car off a bridge. —Margaret Atwood, *The Blind Assassin*

> A few minutes before the detectives arrived, our friend Nastassia found a passageway behind the wall.

1. We observe today not a victory of party but a celebration of freedom, symbolizing an end as well as a beginning, signifying renewal as well as change.
> —John F. Kennedy, Inaugural Address

2. Once in a long while, four times so far for me, my mother brings out the metal tube that holds her medical diploma.
> —Maxine Hong Kingston, "Photographs of My Parents"

23 Verbs

One famous restaurant in Boston offers to bake, broil, pan-fry, deep-fry, poach, sauté, fricassee, blacken, or scallop any of the fish entrées on its menu. To someone ordering—or cooking—at this restaurant, the important distinctions lie entirely in the verbs.

23a Use regular and irregular verb forms.

The past tense and past participle of a regular verb are formed by adding *-ed* or *-d* to the base form.

BASE FORM	PAST TENSE	PAST PARTICIPLE
love	loved	loved
honor	honored	honored
obey	obeyed	obeyed

An irregular verb does not follow the *-ed* or *-d* pattern. If you are unsure about whether a verb is regular or irregular, or what the correct form is, consult the following list or a dictionary. Dictionaries list any irregular forms under the entry for the base form.

Some common irregular verbs

BASE FORM	PAST TENSE	PAST PARTICIPLE
arise	arose	arisen
be	was/were	been
beat	beat	beaten
become	became	become
begin	began	begun
bite	bit	bitten, bit
blow	blew	blown
break	broke	broken
bring	brought	brought
build	built	built
burn	burned, burnt	burned, burnt

BASE FORM	PAST TENSE	PAST PARTICIPLE
burst	burst	burst
buy	bought	bought
catch	caught	caught
choose	chose	chosen
come	came	come
cost	cost	cost
cut	cut	cut
dig	dug	dug
dive	dived, dove	dived
do	did	done
draw	drew	drawn
dream	dreamed, dreamt	dreamed, dreamt
drink	drank	drunk
drive	drove	driven
eat	ate	eaten
fall	fell	fallen
feel	felt	felt
fight	fought	fought
find	found	found
fly	flew	flown
forget	forgot	forgotten, forgot
freeze	froze	frozen
get	got	gotten, got
give	gave	given
go	went	gone
grow	grew	grown
hang (suspend)[1]	hung	hung
have	had	had
hear	heard	heard
hide	hid	hidden
hit	hit	hit
keep	kept	kept
know	knew	known
lay	laid	laid

[1] *Hang* meaning "execute by hanging" is regular: *hang, hanged, hanged.*

BASE FORM	PAST TENSE	PAST PARTICIPLE
lead	led	led
leave	left	left
lend	lent	lent
let	let	let
lie (recline)[2]	lay	lain
lose	lost	lost
make	made	made
mean	meant	meant
meet	met	met
pay	paid	paid
prove	proved	proved, proven
put	put	put
read	read	read
ride	rode	ridden
ring	rang	rung
rise	rose	risen
run	ran	run
say	said	said
see	saw	seen
send	sent	sent
set	set	set
shake	shook	shaken
shoot	shot	shot
show	showed	showed, shown
shrink	shrank	shrunk
sing	sang	sung
sink	sank	sunk
sit	sat	sat
sleep	slept	slept
speak	spoke	spoken
spend	spent	spent
spread	spread	spread
spring	sprang, sprung	sprung
stand	stood	stood

[2]*Lie* meaning "tell a falsehood" is regular: *lie, lied, lied.*

BASE FORM	PAST TENSE	PAST PARTICIPLE
steal	stole	stolen
strike	struck	struck, stricken
swim	swam	swum
swing	swung	swung
take	took	taken
teach	taught	taught
tear	tore	torn
tell	told	told
think	thought	thought
throw	threw	thrown
wake	woke, waked	waked, woken
wear	wore	worn
win	won	won
write	wrote	written

CHECKLIST

Editing the Verbs in Your Writing

✔ Check verb endings that cause you trouble. (23a)

✔ Double-check forms of *lie* and *lay*, *sit* and *set*, *rise* and *raise*. (23b)

✔ Refer to action in a literary work in the present tense. (23c)

✔ Check that verb tenses in your writing express meaning accurately. (23c and 23d)

✔ Use passive voice appropriately. (23e)

EXERCISE 23.1

Complete each of the following sentences by filling in each blank with the past tense or past participle of the verb listed in parentheses. Example:

They had already *eaten* (eat) the entrée; later they *ate* (eat) the dessert.

1. The babysitter _____ (let) the children play with my schoolbooks, and before I _____ (come) home, they had _____ (tear) out several pages.

2. After they had _____ (review) the evidence, the jury _____ (find) the defendant not guilty.

3. Hypnosis _____ (work) only on willing participants.

4. My parents _____ (plant) a tree for me in the town where I was born, but I have never _____ (go) back to see it.

5. Some residents _____ (know) that the levee was leaking long before the storms, but authorities _____ (ignore) the complaints.

6. I _____ (paint) a picture from a photograph my sister had _____ (take) at the beach.

7. When the buzzer sounded, the racers _____ (spring) into the water and _____ (swim) toward the far end of the pool.

8. We had _____ (assume) for some time that surgery was a possibility, and we had _____ (find) an excellent facility.

9. Once the storm had _____ (pass), we could see that the old oak tree had _____ (fall).

10. Some high-level employees _____ (decide) to speak publicly about the cover-up before the company's official story had _____ (be) released to the media.

23b Use *lie* and *lay*, *sit* and *set*, *rise* and *raise*.

These pairs of verbs cause confusion because both verbs in each pair have similar-sounding forms and somewhat related meanings. In each pair, one verb is transitive, meaning that it is followed by a direct object (*I lay the package on the counter*). The other is intransitive, meaning that it does not have an object (*He lies on the floor unable to move*). The best way to avoid confusing these verbs is to memorize their forms and meanings.

BASE FORM	PAST TENSE	PAST PARTICIPLE	PRESENT PARTICIPLE	-S FORM
lie (recline)	lay	lain	lying	lies
lay (put)	laid	laid	laying	lays
sit (be seated)	sat	sat	sitting	sits
set (put)	set	set	setting	sets
rise (get up)	rose	risen	rising	rises
raise (lift)	raised	raised	raising	raises

▶ The doctor asked the patient to ~~lay~~ ^{lie} on his side.

▶ She ~~sat~~ ^{set} the vase on the table.

▶ He ~~rose~~ ^{raised} himself to a sitting position.

EXERCISE 23.2

Underline the appropriate verb form in each of the following sentences. Example:

The guests (*raised*/*rose*) their glasses to the happy couple.

1. That cat (*lies*/*lays*) on the sofa all morning.
2. The chef (*lay*/*laid*) his knives carefully on the counter.
3. The two-year-old walked carefully across the room and (*set*/*sat*) the glass ornament on the table.
4. Grandpa used to love (*sitting*/*setting*) on the front porch and telling stories of his childhood.
5. Almost immediately, the dough (*sitting*/*setting*) by the warm oven began to (*raise*/*rise*).

23c Use verb tenses.

Tenses show when the verb's action takes place. The three simple tenses are the present tense, the past tense, and the future tense.

PRESENT TENSE	I ask, write
PAST TENSE	I asked, wrote
FUTURE TENSE	I will ask, will write

More complex aspects of time are expressed through progressive, perfect, and perfect progressive forms of the simple tenses.

PRESENT PROGRESSIVE	she is asking, is writing
PAST PROGRESSIVE	she was asking, was writing
FUTURE PROGRESSIVE	she will be asking, will be writing
PRESENT PERFECT	she has asked, has written

PAST PERFECT	she had asked, had written
FUTURE PERFECT	she will have asked, will have written
PRESENT PERFECT PROGRESSIVE	she has been asking, has been writing
PAST PERFECT PROGRESSIVE	she had been asking, had been writing
FUTURE PERFECT PROGRESSIVE	she will have been asking, will have been writing

The simple tenses locate an action only within the three basic time frames of present, past, and future. Progressive forms express continuing actions; perfect forms express completed actions; perfect progressive forms express actions that continue up to some point in the present, past, or future.

Special purposes of the present tense.   When writing about action in literary works, use the present tense.

▶ Ishmael slowly ~~realized~~ realizes all that ~~was~~ is at stake in the search for the white whale.

General truths or scientific facts should be written in the present tense, even when the predicate in the main clause is in the past tense.

▶ Pasteur demonstrated that his boiling process ~~made~~ makes milk safe.

In general, when you are quoting, summarizing, or paraphrasing a work, use the present tense.

▶ Keith Walters ~~wrote~~ writes that the "reputed consequences and promised blessings of literacy are legion."

But when using APA (American Psychological Association) style, report the results of your experiments or another researcher's work in the past tense (*wrote, noted*) or the present perfect (*has discovered*). (For more on APA style, see Chapter 50.)

► Comer (1995) ~~notes~~ ^noted^ that protesters who deprive themselves of

food are seen not as dysfunctional but rather as "caring,

sacrificing, even heroic" (p. 5).

23d Sequence verb tenses.

Careful and accurate use of tenses is important for clear writing. When you use the appropriate tense for each action, readers can follow time changes easily.

► By the time he lent her the money, she ^had^ declared bankruptcy.

The revised sentence makes clear that the bankruptcy occurred before the loan.

EXERCISE 23.3

Fill in the blank in each sentence with an appropriate form of the verb in parentheses. If more than one form is acceptable, be ready to explain your choices. Example:

The supply of a product _rises_ (rise) when the demand is great.

1. History _____ (show) that crime usually decreases as the economy improves.
2. Ever since the first nuclear power plants were built, opponents _____ (fear) disaster.
3. Thousands of Irish peasants _____ (immigrate) to America after the potato famine of the 1840s.
4. The soap opera *General Hospital* _____ (be) on the air since 1963.
5. Olivia _____ (direct) the play next year.
6. While they _____ (eat) in a local café, they witnessed a minor accident.
7. By this time next week, each of your clients _____ (receive) an invitation to the opening.
8. By the time a child born today enters first grade, he or she _____ (watch) thousands of television commercials.

9. In one of the novel's most memorable scenes, Huck _____ (express) his willingness to go to hell rather than report Jim as an escaped slave.

10. A cold typically _____ (last) for about a week and a half.

EXERCISE 23.4

Edit each sentence to create the appropriate sequence of tenses. Example:

> have sent
> He needs to ~~send~~ in his application before today.
>   ^

1. When she saw *Chicago*, it had made her want to become an actress even more.

2. Leaving England in December, the settlers arrived in Virginia in May.

3. I hoped to make the football team, but injuries prevented me from trying out.

4. Working with great dedication as a summer intern at the magazine, Mohan called his former supervisor in the fall to ask about a permanent position.

5. As we waited for the bus, we would watch the taxis pass by.

23e Use active and passive voice.

Voice tells whether a subject is acting (*He questions us*) or being acted upon (*He is questioned*). When the subject is acting, the verb is in the active voice; when the subject is being acted upon, the verb is in the passive voice. Most contemporary writers use the active voice as much as possible because it makes their prose stronger and livelier. To shift a sentence from passive to active voice, make the performer of the action the subject of the sentence.

> My sister took the
> ▸ ~~The~~ prizewinning photograph. ~~was taken by my sister.~~
>   ^   ^

Use the passive voice when you want to emphasize the recipient of an action rather than the performer of the action.

▸ Colonel Muammar al-Qaddafi was killed during an uprising in his hometown of Surt.

In scientific and technical writing, use the passive voice to focus attention on what is being studied.

▶ The volunteers' food intake **was** closely **monitored**.

23f Use mood effectively.

The mood of a verb indicates the writer's attitude toward what he or she is saying. The indicative mood states facts or opinions and asks questions: *I did the right thing.* The imperative mood gives commands and instructions: *Do the right thing.* The subjunctive mood (used primarily in dependent clauses beginning with *that* or *if*) expresses wishes and conditions that are contrary to fact: *If I were doing the right thing, I'd know it.*

The present subjunctive uses the base form of the verb with all subjects.

▶ It is important that children **be** psychologically ready for a new sibling.

The past subjunctive is the same as the simple past except for the verb *be*, which uses *were* for all subjects.

▶ He spent money as if he **had** infinite credit.
▶ If the store **were** better located, it would attract more customers.

Because the subjunctive creates a rather formal tone, many people today substitute the indicative mood in informal conversation.

INFORMAL

▶ If the store **was** better located, it would attract more customers.

For academic or professional writing, use the subjunctive in the following contexts:

CLAUSES EXPRESSING A WISH

▶ He wished that his brother ~~was~~ ^{were} still living nearby.

THAT CLAUSES EXPRESSING A REQUEST OR DEMAND

▶ The plant inspector insists that a supervisor ~~is~~ ^{be} on site at all times.

IF CLAUSES EXPRESSING A CONDITION THAT DOES NOT EXIST

▶ If public transportation ~~was~~ ^{were} widely available, fewer Americans would commute by car.

One common error is to use *would* in both clauses. Use the subjunctive in the *if* clause and *would* in the other clause.

▶ If I ~~would have~~ ^{had} played harder, I would have won.

EXERCISE 23.5

Revise any of the following sentences that do not use the appropriate subjunctive verb forms required in formal writing. Example:

I saw how carefully he moved, as if he ~~was~~ ^{were} holding an infant.

1. Josh kept spending money as if he was still earning high commissions.
2. She wished that she was able to take her daughter along on the business trip.
3. Protesters demanded that the senator resign from her post.
4. If the vaccine was more readily available, the county health department would recommend that everyone receive the shot.
5. It is critical that the liquid remains at room temperature for seven hours.

EXERCISE 23.6: THINKING CRITICALLY

Thinking about Your Own Use of Verbs

Writing that relies too heavily on the verbs *be*, *do*, and *have* almost always bores readers. Look at something you've written recently to see whether you rely too heavily on these verbs, and revise accordingly.

24 Subject-Verb Agreement

In everyday terms, the word *agreement* refers to an accord of some sort: you reach an agreement with your boss about salary; friends agree to go to a movie; the members of a family agree to share household chores. This meaning covers grammatical agreement as well. Verbs must agree with their subjects in number (singular or plural) and in person (first, second, or third).

To make a verb in the present tense agree with a third-person singular subject, add *-s* or *-es* to the base form.

▶ A vegetarian diet lowers the risk of heart disease.

To make a verb in the present tense agree with any other subject, use the base form of the verb.

▶ I miss my family.
▶ They live in another state.

Have and *be* do not follow the *-s* or *-es* pattern with third-person singular subjects. *Have* changes to *has*; *be* has irregular forms in both the present tense and the past tense.

▶ War is hell.
▶ The soldier was brave beyond the call of duty.

24a   Check words between subject and verb.

Make sure the verb agrees with the subject and not with another noun that falls in between.

                                                                    have
▶ Many books on the best-seller list ~~has~~ little literary value.
                                                                               ^
    The simple subject is *books*, not *list.*

Be careful when you use *as well as, along with, in addition to, together with,* and similar phrases. They do not make a singular subject plural.

                                                                       was
▶ A passenger, as well as the driver, ~~were~~ injured in the accident.
                                                                ^
    Though this sentence has a grammatically singular subject, it would be clearer with a compound subject: *The driver and a passenger were injured in the accident.*

EXERCISE 24.1

Underline the appropriate verb form in each of the following sentences. Example:

> The benefits of family planning (*is*/are) not apparent to many peasants.

1. Soldiers who are injured while fighting bravely for their country (*deserves*/*deserve*) complete medical coverage.

2. The dog, followed by his owner, (*races*/*race*) wildly down the street every afternoon.

3. Just when I think I can go home, yet another pile of invoices (*appears*/*appear*) on my desk.

4. The pattern of secrecy and lies (*needs*/*need*) to stop in order for counseling to be successful.

5. A substance abuser often (*hides*/*hide*) the truth to cover up his or her addiction.

6. The police chief, in addition to several soldiers and two civilians, (*was*/*were*) injured in the explosion.

7. Garlic's therapeutic value as well as its flavor (*comes*/*come*) from sulfur compounds.

8. The fiber content of cereal (*contributes*/*contribute*) to its nutritional value.

9. The graphics on this computer game often (*causes*/*cause*) my system to crash.

10. Current research on AIDS, in spite of the best efforts of hundreds of scientists, (*leaves*/*leave*) serious questions unanswered.

24b Check agreement with compound subjects.

Compound subjects joined by *and* are generally plural.

> A backpack, a canteen, and a rifle ~~was~~ issued to each recruit.
>
> *were*

When subjects joined by *and* are considered a single unit or refer to the same person or thing, they take a singular verb form.

> The lead singer and chief songwriter wants to make the new
>
> songs available online.

CHECKLIST

Editing for Subject-Verb Agreement

✔ Identify the subject that goes with each verb to check for agreement problems. (24a)

✔ Check compound subjects joined by *and, or,* and *nor.* (24b)

✔ Check collective-noun subjects to determine whether they refer to a group as a single unit or as multiple members. (24c)

✔ Check indefinite-pronoun subjects. Most take a plural verb. (24d)

---

remains

▶ Drinking and driving ~~remain~~ a major cause of highway

accidents and fatalities.

In this sentence, *drinking and driving* is considered a single activity, so a singular verb is used.

With subjects joined by *or* or *nor*, the verb agrees with the part closer to the verb.

▶ Neither my roommate nor my neighbors *like* my loud music.

▶ Either the witnesses or the defendant *is* lying.

If you find this sentence awkward, put the plural noun closer to the verb: *Either the defendant or the witnesses <u>are</u> lying.*

24c Make verbs agree with collective nouns.

Collective nouns—such as *family, team, audience, group, jury, crowd, band, class,* and *committee*—and fractions can take either singular or plural verbs, depending on whether they refer to the group as a single unit or to the multiple members of the group. The meaning of a sentence as a whole is your guide.

▶ After deliberating, the jury *reports* its verdict.

The jury acts as a single unit.

▶ The jury still *disagree* on a number of counts.

The members of the jury act as multiple individuals.

▶ Two-thirds of the park ~~have~~ ^{has} burned.

   Two-thirds refers to the single portion of the park that burned.

▶ One-third of the student body ~~was~~ ^{were} commuters.

   One-third here refers to the students who commuted as individuals.

Treat phrases starting with *the number of* as singular and with *a number of* as plural.

SINGULAR	The number of applicants for the internship *was* unbelievable.
PLURAL	A number of them *were* put on the wait list.

24d   Make verbs agree with indefinite pronouns.

Indefinite pronouns do not refer to specific persons or things. Most take singular verb forms.

SOME COMMON INDEFINITE PRONOUNS

another	each	much	one
any	either	neither	other
anybody	everybody	nobody	somebody
anyone	everyone	no one	someone
anything	everything	nothing	something

▶ Of the two jobs, neither holds much appeal.

▶ Each of the plays ~~depict~~ ^{depicts} a hero undone by a tragic flaw.

Both, few, many, others, and *several* are plural.

▶ Though many apply, few are chosen.

All, any, enough, more, most, none, and *some* can be singular or plural, depending on the noun they refer to.

▶ All of the cake *was* eaten.

▶ All of the candidates *promise* to improve the schools.

24e   Make verbs agree with *who*, *which*, and *that*.

When the relative pronouns *who*, *which*, and *that* are used as subjects, the verb agrees with the antecedent of the pronoun (27b).

▶ Fear is an ingredient that goes into creating stereotypes.

▶ Guilt and fear are ingredients that go into creating stereotypes.

Problems often occur with the words *one of the.* In general, *one of the* takes a plural verb, while *the only one of the* takes a singular verb.

▶ Carla is one of the employees who always ~~works~~ work overtime.

work

Some employees always work overtime. Carla is among them. Thus *who* refers to *employees*, and the verb is plural.

▶ Ming is the only one of the employees who always ~~work~~ works overtime.

works

Only one employee always works overtime, and that employee is Ming. Thus *one*, and not *employees*, is the antecedent of *who,* and the verb form must be singular.

24f   Make linking verbs agree with subjects.

A linking verb should agree with its subject, which usually precedes the verb, not with the subject complement, which follows it.

▶ These three key treaties ~~is~~ are the topic of my talk.

are

The subject is *treaties*, not *topic.*

▶ Nero Wolfe's passion ~~were~~ was orchids.

was

The subject is *passion*, not *orchids.*

24g   Make verbs agree with subjects that end in -s.

Some words that end in -s seem to be plural but are singular in meaning and thus take singular verb forms.

> strikes
> Measles still ~~strike~~ many Americans.
>   ^

Some nouns of this kind (such as *statistics* and *politics*) may be either singular or plural, depending on context.

| SINGULAR | Statistics *is* a course I really dread. |
| PLURAL | The statistics in that study *are* questionable. |

24h Check for subjects that follow the verb.

In English, verbs usually follow subjects. When this order is reversed, make the verb agree with the subject, not with a noun that happens to precede it.

> stand
> Beside the barn ~~stands~~ silos filled with grain.
>   ^

The subject, *silos*, is plural, so the verb must be *stand*.

In sentences beginning with *there is* or *there are* (or *there was* or *there were*), *there* serves only as an introductory word; the subject follows the verb.

> There are five basic positions in classical ballet.

24i Make verbs agree with titles and words used as words.

Titles and words used as words always take singular verb forms, even if their own forms are plural.

> describes
> *One Writer's Beginnings* ~~describe~~ Eudora Welty's childhood.
>   ^

> is
> *Steroids* ~~are~~ a little word that packs a big punch in the
>   ^
> world of sports.

24j Consider spoken forms of *be*.

Conventions for subject-verb agreement with *be* in spoken or vernacular varieties of English may differ from those of academic English. For instance, an Appalachian speaker might say "I been down" rather than "I have been down"; a speaker of African American vernacular might say "He be at work" rather than "He is at work." You may want to quote such spoken phrases in your writing, but for most academic and professional writing, follow the conventions of academic English. (For information on using varieties of English appropriately, see Chapter 19.)

EXERCISE 24.2

Revise any of the following sentences as necessary to establish subject-verb agreement. (Some of the sentences do not require any change.) Example:

> *darts*
> Into the shadows ~~dart~~ the frightened raccoon.
> ^

1. Room and board are the most expensive part of my college education.
2. *Three Cups of Tea* tell the story of one man's mission to establish schools in poor, remote areas of Pakistan.
3. Hanging near the *Mona Lisa* is many more Renaissance paintings.
4. Most of the students oppose the shortened dining hall hours.
5. Each of the security workers are considered trained after viewing a twenty-minute videotape.
6. Neither his expensive clothes nor his charm were enough to get him the job.
7. The committee were expected to produce its annual report two weeks early.
8. My grandmother is the only one of my relatives who still goes to church.
9. Sweden was one of the few European countries that was neutral in 1943.
10. Economics involve the study of the distribution of goods and services.

EXERCISE 24.3: THINKING CRITICALLY

Thinking about Your Own Use of Subject-Verb Agreement

Visiting relatives is/are treacherous. Either verb makes a grammatically acceptable sentence, yet the verbs result in two very different statements. Write a brief explanation of the two possible meanings. Then write a paragraph or two about visiting relatives. Using the information in this chapter, examine each subject and its verb. Do you maintain subject-verb agreement throughout? Revise to correct any errors you find. If you find any patterns, make a note to yourself of things to look for routinely as you revise your writing.

25   Adjectives and Adverbs

Adjectives and adverbs frequently add indispensable differences in meaning to the words they modify (describe). In basketball, for example, there is an important difference between a *flagrant* foul and a *technical* foul, a layup and a *reverse* layup, and an *angry* coach and an *abusively angry* coach. In each instance, the modifiers are crucial to accurate communication.

Adjectives modify nouns and pronouns; they answer the questions *which? how many?* and *what kind?* Adverbs modify verbs, adjectives, and other adverbs; they answer the questions *how? when? where?* and *to what extent?* Many adverbs are formed by adding -*ly* to adjectives (*slight, slightly*), but some are formed in other ways (*outdoors*) or have forms of their own (*very*).

25a   Use adjectives after linking verbs.

When adjectives come after linking verbs (such as *is*), they usually describe the subject: *I am patient.* Note that in specific sentences, some verbs may or may not be linking verbs—*appear, become, feel, grow, look, make, prove, seem, smell, sound,* and *taste,* for instance. When a word following one of these verbs modifies the subject, use an adjective; when it modifies the verb, use an adverb.

ADJECTIVE	Fluffy looked angry.
ADVERB	Fluffy looked angrily at the poodle.

Linking verbs suggest a state of being, not an action. In the preceding examples, *looked angry* suggests the state of being angry; *looked angrily* suggests an angry action.

:e **bedfordstmartins.com/wia**
Exercise > Adjectives and adverbs

In everyday conversation, you will often hear (and perhaps use) adjectives in place of adverbs. For example, people often say *go quick* instead of *go quickly*. When you write in academic and professional English, however, use adverbs to modify verbs, adjectives, and other adverbs.

▶ You can feel the song's meter if you listen ~~careful~~. *carefully.*

▶ The audience was ~~real~~ disappointed by the show. *really*

Good, *well*, *bad*, and *badly*.   The modifiers *good, well, bad,* and *badly* cause problems for many writers because the distinctions between *good* and *well* and between *bad* and *badly* are often not observed in conversation. Problems also arise because *well* can function as either an adjective or an adverb.

▶ I look ~~well~~ in blue. *good*

▶ Now that the fever has broken, I feel ~~good~~ again. *well*

▶ He plays the trumpet ~~good~~. *well.*

▶ I feel ~~badly~~ for the Toronto fans. *bad*

▶ Their team played ~~bad~~. *badly.*

25b   Use comparatives and superlatives.

Most adjectives and adverbs have three forms: positive, comparative, and superlative. You usually form the comparative and superlative of one- or two-syllable adjectives by adding *-er* and *-est*: *short, shorter, shortest*. With some two-syllable adjectives, longer adjectives, and most adverbs, use *more* and *most* (or *less* and *least*): *scientific, more scientific, most scientific; elegantly, more elegantly, most elegantly.* Some short adjectives and adverbs have irregular comparative and superlative forms: *good, better, best; badly, worse, worst.*

Comparatives versus superlatives.   In academic writing, use the comparative to compare two things; use the superlative to compare three or more things.

▶ Rome is a much *older* city than New York.

▶ Damascus is one of the ~~older~~ cities in the world.
          oldest ^

Double comparatives and superlatives. Double comparatives and superlatives are those that unnecessarily use both the *-er* or *-est* ending and *more* or *most*. Occasionally, these forms can add a special emphasis, as in the title of Spike Lee's movie *Mo' Better Blues*. In academic and professional writing, however, do not use *more* or *most* before adjectives or adverbs ending in *-er* or *-est*.

▶ Paris is the ~~most~~ loveliest city in the world.

Absolute concepts. Some readers consider modifiers such as *perfect* and *unique* to be absolute concepts; according to this view, a thing is either unique or it isn't, so modified forms of the concept don't make sense. However, many seemingly absolute words have multiple meanings, all of which are widely accepted as correct. For example, *unique* may mean *one of a kind* or *unequaled*, but it can also simply mean *distinctive* or *unusual*.

If you think your readers will object to a construction such as *more perfect* (which appears in the U.S. Constitution), then avoid such uses.

FOR MULTILINGUAL WRITERS

Using Adjectives with Plural Nouns

In Spanish, Russian, and many other languages, adjectives agree in number with the nouns they modify. In English, adjectives do not change number in this way: *the kittens are cute* (not *cutes*).

EXERCISE 25.1

Revise each of the following sentences to use modifiers correctly, clearly, and effectively. Many of the sentences can be revised in more than one way. Example:

He is sponsoring a housing project. ~~financial plan approval bill.~~
          bill to approve a financial plan for the
                              ^   ^

1. Alicia speaks both Russian and German, but she speaks Russian best.

2. The summers are more rainier in New York than they are in Seattle.

3. He glanced at the menu and ordered the expensivest wine on the list.

4. Most of the elderly are women because women tend to live longer.

5. Minneapolis is the largest of the Twin Cities.

6. She came up with the most silliest plan for revenge.

7. Our theater company has produced several of the famousest classical Greek plays.

8. The student cafeteria is operated by a college food service system chain.

9. It is safer to jog in daylight.

10. Evan argued that subtitled films are boringer to watch than films dubbed in English.

EXERCISE 25.2: THINKING CRITICALLY

Reading with an Eye for Adjectives and Adverbs

> Gwendolyn Brooks "describes the 'graceful life' as one where people glide over floors in softly glowing rooms, smile correctly over trays of silver, cinnamon, and cream, and retire in quiet elegance."
>
> —Mary Helen Washington, "Taming All That Anger Down"

Identify the adjectives and adverbs in the preceding passage, and comment on what they add to the writing. What would be lost if they were removed?

Thinking about Your Own Use of Adjectives and Adverbs

Take a few minutes to study something you can observe or examine closely. In a paragraph or two, describe your subject for someone who has never seen it. Using the guidelines in this chapter, check your use of adjectives and adverbs, and revise your paragraphs. How would you characterize your use of adjectives and adverbs?

26 Modifier Placement

To be effective, modifiers should clearly refer to the words they modify and be positioned close to those words. Consider this command:

DO NOT USE THE ELEVATORS IN CASE OF FIRE.

Should we avoid the elevators altogether, or only in case there is a fire? Repositioning the modifier *in case of fire* eliminates such confusion—and makes clear that we are to avoid the elevators only if there is a fire: IN CASE OF FIRE, DO NOT USE THE ELEVATORS.

26a Revise misplaced modifiers.

Modifiers can cause confusion or ambiguity if they are not close enough to the words they modify or if they seem to modify more than one word in the sentence.

▶ She teaches a seminar this term ~~on voodoo~~ *on voodoo* at Skyline College.

The voodoo is not at the college; the seminar is.

▶ ~~Billowing from the window, he~~ *He* saw clouds of smoke/ *billowing from the window.*

People cannot billow from windows.

▶ *After he lost the 1962 race,* Nixon told reporters that he planned to get out of politics. ~~after he lost the 1962 race.~~

The unedited sentence implies that Nixon planned to lose the race.

Limiting modifiers. Be especially careful with the placement of limiting modifiers such as *almost, even, just, merely,* and *only.* In general, these modifiers should be placed right before or after the words they modify. Putting them in other positions may produce not just ambiguity but a completely different meaning.

AMBIGUOUS	The court *only* hears civil cases on Tuesdays.
CLEAR	The court hears only civil cases on Tuesdays.
CLEAR	The court hears civil cases on Tuesdays only.

Squinting modifiers. If a modifier can refer either to the word before it or to the word after it, it is a squinting modifier. Put the modifier where it clearly relates to only a single word.

SQUINTING	Students who practice writing *often* will benefit.
REVISED	Students who often practice writing will benefit.
REVISED	Students who practice writing will often benefit.

EXERCISE 26.1

Revise each of the following sentences by moving any misplaced modifiers so that they clearly modify the words they should. Example:

When they propose sensible plans, politicians
~~Politicians~~ earn support from the people. ~~when they propose~~
^   ^

~~sensible plans.~~

1. The comedian had the audience doubled over with laughter relating her stories in a deadpan voice.

2. News reports can increase a listener's irrational fears that emphasize random crime or rare diseases.

3. Studying legal documents and court records from hundreds of years ago, ordinary people in the Middle Ages teach us about everyday life at that time.

4. Risking their lives in war zones, civilians learn about the conflict from the firsthand accounts of journalists abroad.

5. Charlotte and Devon saw lions in the wild on a safari in Africa last spring.

6. Doctors recommend a new test for cancer, which is painless.

7. Every afternoon I find flyers for free pizza left on my windshield.

8. Screeching strings told the audience that the killer was coming after the opening credits.

9. The coach awarded a medal to the most valuable player made of solid brass.

10. Hanging on by a thread, the five-year-old finally lost her tooth.

26b Revise disruptive modifiers.

Disruptive modifiers interrupt the connections between parts of a sentence, making it hard for readers to follow the progress of the thought.

If they are cooked too long, vegetables will
▶ ~~Vegetables will, if they are cooked too long,~~ lose most
^

of their nutritional value.

Split infinitives.   In general, do not place a modifier between the *to* and the verb of an infinitive (*to often complain*). Doing so makes it hard for readers to recognize that the two go together.

> surrender
> ► Hitler expected the British to fairly quickly. ~~surrender.~~
>   ^   ^

In some sentences, however, a modifier sounds awkward if it does not split the infinitive. Most language experts consider split infinitives acceptable in such cases. Another option is to reword the sentence to eliminate the infinitive altogether.

SPLIT	I hope *to* almost *equal* my last year's income.
REVISED	I hope that I will earn almost as much as I did last year.

EXERCISE 26.2

Revise each of the following sentences by moving the disruptive modifier so that the sentence reads smoothly. Example:

> During the recent economic depression, many
> ~~Many~~ unemployed college graduates ~~during the recent~~
> ^
> ~~economic depression~~ attended graduate school.

1. Strong economic times have, statistics tell us, led to increases in the college dropout rate.
2. During finals an otherwise honest student, facing high levels of stress, may consider cheating to achieve a higher grade.
3. The director encouraged us to loudly and enthusiastically applaud after each scene.
4. Michael Jordan earned, at the pinnacle of his career, roughly $40 million a year in endorsements.
5. The stock exchange became, because of the sudden trading, a chaotic circus.

26c Revise dangling modifiers.

Dangling modifiers are words or phrases that modify nothing else in the rest of a sentence. They often *seem* to modify something that is implied but not actually present in the sentence. Dangling modifiers frequently appear at the beginnings or ends of sentences.

DANGLING	Driving nonstop, Salishan Lodge is two hours from Portland.

| REVISED | Driving nonstop from Portland, you can reach Salishan Lodge in two hours. |

To revise a dangling modifier, often you need to add a subject that the modifier clearly refers to; sometimes you have to turn the modifier into a phrase or a clause.

▶ Reluctantly, the hound ~~was given~~ to a neighbor. *our family gave*

In the original sentence, was the dog reluctant, or was someone else who is not mentioned reluctant?

▶ ~~As~~ a young boy, his grandmother told stories of her years *When he was*

as a migrant worker.

His grandmother was never a young boy.

▶ ~~Thumbing through the magazine, my~~ eyes automatically *My* *as I was thumbing through the magazine.* noticed the perfume ads/

Eyes cannot thumb through a magazine.

EXERCISE 26.3

Revise each of the following sentences to correct the dangling phrase. Example:

Watching television news, an impression ~~is given~~ of constant *a viewer gets*

disaster.

1. No longer obsessed with being the first to report a story, information is now presented as entertainment.
2. Trying to attract younger viewers, news is blended with comedy on late-night talk shows.
3. Highlighting local events, important international news stories may get overlooked.
4. Chosen for their looks, the journalistic credentials of newscasters may be weak.
5. As an interactive medium, people can find information online that reinforces views they already hold.

EXERCISE 26.4: THINKING CRITICALLY

Reading with an Eye for Modifiers

Look at the limiting modifier italicized in the following passage. Identify which word or words it modifies. Then try moving the modifier to some other spot in the sentence, and consider how the meaning of the sentence changes as a result.

> It was, among other things, the sort of railroad you would occasionally ride *just* for the hell of it, a higher existence into which you would escape unconsciously and without hesitation.

—E. B. White, "Progress and Change"

Thinking about Your Own Use of Modifiers

As you examine two pages of a draft, check for clear and effective modifiers. Can you identify any misplaced, disruptive, or dangling modifiers? Using the guidelines in this chapter, revise as need be. Then look for patterns—in the kinds of modifiers you use and in any problems you have placing them. Make a note of what you find.

27 Pronouns

As words that stand in for nouns, pronouns carry a lot of weight in everyday discourse. These directions show why it's important for a pronoun to refer clearly to a specific noun or pronoun antecedent:

▶ When you see a dirt road on the left side of Winston Lane, follow it for two more miles.

The word *it* could mean either the dirt road or Winston Lane.

27a Consider a pronoun's role in the sentence.

Most speakers of English know intuitively when to use *I*, *me*, and *my*. The choices reflect differences in case, the form a pronoun takes to indicate its function in a sentence. Pronouns functioning as subjects or subject complements are in the subjective case (*I*); those functioning as objects are in the objective case (*me*); those functioning as possessives are in the possessive case (*my*).

SUBJECTIVE	OBJECTIVE	POSSESSIVE
I	me	my/mine
we	us	our/ours
you	you	your/yours
he/she/it	him/her/it	his/her/hers/its
they	them	their/theirs
who/whoever	whom/whomever	whose

Problems tend to occur in the following situations.

In subject complements.   Americans routinely use the objective case for subject complements in conversation: *Who's there? It's me.* If the subjective case for a subject complement sounds stilted or awkward (*It's I*), try rewriting the sentence using the pronoun as the subject (*I'm here*).

► ~~The~~ first person to see Kishore after the awards. ~~was she.~~
   She was the

Before gerunds.   Pronouns before a gerund should be in the possessive case.

► The doctor argued for ~~him~~ writing a living will.
   his

With *who*, *whoever*, *whom*, and *whomever*.   Today's speakers tend not to use *whom* and *whomever*, which can create a very formal tone. But for academic and professional writing in which formality is appropriate, remember that problems distinguishing between *who* and *whom* occur most often in two situations: when they begin a question, and when they introduce a dependent clause (29c). You can determine whether to use *who* or *whom* at the beginning of a question by answering the question using a personal pronoun. If the answer is in the subjective case, use *who*; if it is in the objective case, use *whom*.

► ~~Who~~ did you visit?
   Whom
   I visited *them*. *Them* is objective, so *whom* is correct.

► ~~Whom~~ do you think wrote the story?
   Who
   I think *she* wrote the story. *She* is subjective, so *who* is correct.

> **CHECKLIST**
>
> **Editing Pronouns**
>
> ✔ Make sure all pronouns in subject complements are in the subjective case. (27a)
>
> ✔ Check for correct use of *who, whoever, whom,* and *whomever.* (27a)
>
> ✔ In compound structures, check that pronouns are in the same case they would be in if used alone. (27a)
>
> ✔ When a pronoun follows *than* or *as,* complete the sentence mentally to determine whether the pronoun should be in the subjective or objective case. (27a)
>
> ✔ Check that pronouns agree with indefinite-pronoun antecedents, and revise sexist pronouns. (27b)
>
> ✔ Identify the antecedent that a pronoun refers to. Supply one if none appears in the sentence. If more than one possible antecedent is present, revise the sentence. (27c)

If the pronoun acts as a subject or subject complement in the clause, use *who* or *whoever.* If the pronoun acts as an object in the clause, use *whom* or *whomever.*

>   *who*
> ▶ Anyone can hypnotize a person ~~whom~~ wants to be
>
> hypnotized.
>
> The verb of the clause is *wants,* and its subject is *who.*

>   *Whomever*
> ▶ ~~Whoever~~ the party suspected of disloyalty was executed.
>
> *Whomever* is the object of *suspected* in the clause *whomever the party suspected of disloyalty.*

EXERCISE 27.1

Insert *who, whoever, whom,* or *whomever* appropriately in the blank in each of the following sentences. Example:

> She is someone _who_ will go far.

1. _____ did you say was our most likely suspect?
2. _____ the audience chooses will move up to the next level.

3. The awards banquet will recognize _____ made the honor roll.

4. Professor Quiñones asked _____ we wanted to collaborate with.

5. _____ received the highest score?

In compound structures. When a pronoun is part of a compound subject, complement, or object, put it in the same case you would use if the pronoun were alone.

▶ When ~~him~~ and Zelda were first married, they lived in New York.
  ^{he}

▶ The boss invited ~~she~~ and her family to dinner.
  ^{her}

▶ This morning saw yet another conflict between my sister and ~~I.~~
  ^{me.}

In elliptical constructions. Elliptical constructions are sentences in which some words are understood but left out. When an elliptical construction ends in a pronoun, put the pronoun in the case it would be in if the construction were complete.

▶ His sister has always been more athletic than *he* [is].

In some elliptical constructions, the case of the pronoun depends on the meaning intended.

▶ Willie likes Lily more than *she* [likes Lily].

   She is the subject of the omitted verb *likes*.

▶ Willie likes Lily more than [he likes] *her*.

   Her is the object of the omitted verb *likes*.

With *we* and *us* before a noun. If you are unsure about whether to use *we* or *us* before a noun, use whichever pronoun would be correct if the noun were omitted.

▶ ~~Us~~ fans never give up hope.
  ^{We}

   Without *fans*, *we* would be the subject.

▶ The Rangers depend on ~~we~~ fans.
  ^{us}

   Without *fans*, *us* would be the object of the preposition *on*.

EXERCISE 27.2

Underline the appropriate pronoun from the pair in parentheses in each of the following sentences. Example:

> The possibility of (*their/them*) succeeding never occurred to me.

1. Max has had more car accidents than Gabriella, but he still insists he is a better driver than (*she/her*).
2. Fixing the dock with Hank and (*they/them*) reminded me of our summers at the lake.
3. The coach gave honorable-mention ribbons to the two who didn't win any races—Aiden and (*I/me*).
4. There seemed to be no reason at all for (*them/their*) voluntarily studying on a Saturday night.
5. Tomorrow (*we/us*) recruits will have our first on-the-job test.

27b Make pronouns agree with antecedents.

The antecedent of a pronoun is the word the pronoun refers to. Pronouns and antecedents are said to agree when they match up in person, number, and gender.

SINGULAR	The choirmaster raised *his* baton.
PLURAL	The boys picked up *their* music.

Compound antecedents. Whenever a compound antecedent is joined by *or* or *nor*, the pronoun agrees with the nearer or nearest antecedent. If the parts of the antecedent are of different genders, however, this kind of sentence can be awkward and may need to be revised.

AWKWARD	Neither Annie nor Henry got *his* work done.
REVISED	Annie didn't get *her* work done, and neither did Henry.

When a compound antecedent contains singular and plural parts, the sentence may sound awkward unless the plural comes last.

▶ Neither the newspaper nor the radio stations would reveal their sources.

Collective-noun antecedents. A collective noun such as *herd*, *team*, or *audience* may refer to a group as a single unit. If so, use a singular pronoun.

▶ The *committee* presented *its* findings to the board.

When a collective noun refers to the members of the group as individuals, however, use a plural pronoun.

▶ The *herd* stamped *their* hooves and snorted nervously.

Indefinite-pronoun antecedents. Indefinite pronouns do not refer to specific persons or things. Most indefinite pronouns are always singular; a few are always plural. Some can be singular or plural depending on the context.

▶ One of the ballerinas lost her balance.

▶ Many in the audience jumped to their feet.

SINGULAR *Some* of the furniture was showing *its* age.

PLURAL *Some* of the farmers abandoned *their* land.

Sexist pronouns. Pronouns often refer to antecedents that may be either male or female. Writers used to use a masculine pronoun, known as the "generic *he*," to refer to such antecedents: *Everyone should know his legal rights.* However, such wording ignores or even excludes females—and therefore should be revised: *Everyone should know his or her legal rights*, for example, or *People should know their legal rights.*

EXERCISE 27.3
Revise the following sentences when needed to create pronoun-antecedent agreement and to eliminate the generic *he* and any awkward pronoun references. Some can be revised in more than one way. Example:

or her
Every graduate submitted his diploma card.

All graduates their cards.
~~Every graduate~~ submitted ~~his~~ diploma ~~card.~~

1. While shopping for a new computer for school, I noticed that a laptop costs much less than they used to.

2. Congress usually resists a president's attempt to encroach on what they consider their authority.

3. Marco and Ellen were each given a chance to voice their opinion.

4. An emergency room doctor needs to be swift and decisive; he also needs to be calm and careful.

5. Every dog and cat has their own personality.

27c Make pronouns refer to clear antecedents.

If a pronoun does not refer clearly to a specific antecedent, readers will have trouble making the connection between the two.

Ambiguous antecedents. When a pronoun can refer to more than one antecedent, revise the sentence to make the meaning clear.

▶ The car went over the bridge just before ~~it~~ the bridge fell into the water.

What fell into the water—the car or the bridge? The revision makes the meaning clear.

▶ Kerry told Ellen, "I ~~that she~~ should be ready soon."

Reporting Kerry's words directly, in quotation marks, eliminates the ambiguity.

Vague use of *it*, *this*, *that*, and *which*. The words *it*, *this*, *that*, and *which* often function as a shortcut for referring to something mentioned earlier. Like other pronouns, each must refer to a specific antecedent.

▶ When the senators realized the bill would be defeated, they tried to postpone the vote but failed. ~~It~~ The entire effort was a fiasco.

▶ Nancy just found out that she won the lottery, ~~which~~ and her sudden wealth explains her resignation.

Indefinite use of *you*, *it*, and *they*. In everyday conversation, we frequently use *you*, *it*, and *they* in an indefinite sense in such expressions as *you never know* and *on television, they said.*

In academic and professional writing, however, use *you* only to mean "you, the reader," and *they* or *it* only to refer to a clear antecedent.

▶ Commercials try to make ~~you~~ people buy without thinking.

▶ ~~On the~~ The Weather Channel,/ ~~it~~ reported a powerful earthquake in China.

▶ ~~In France, they~~ Many restaurants in France allow dogs. ~~in many restaurants.~~

Implied antecedents. A pronoun may suggest a noun antecedent that is implied but not present in the sentence.

▶ Detention centers routinely blocked efforts by ~~detainees'~~ detainees. families and lawyers to locate ~~them.~~

EXERCISE 27.4

Revise each of the following items to clarify pronoun reference. Most of the items can be revised in more than one way. If a pronoun refers ambiguously to more than one possible antecedent, revise the sentence to reflect each possible meaning. Example:

~~After~~ Miranda found Jane's keys after Jane left,/. ~~Miranda found her keys.~~

~~After~~ Miranda found her own keys after Jane left,/. ~~Miranda found her keys.~~

1. All scholarship applicants must fill out a financial aid form, meet with the dean, and write a letter to the committee members. The deadline is October 24, so they should start the process as soon as possible.

2. Patients on medication may relate better to their therapists, be less vulnerable to what disturbs them, and be more responsive to them.

3. Ms. Dunbar wanted to speak to my mother before she spoke to me.

4. In Texas, you often hear about the influence of big oil corporations.

5. A small band of protestors picketed the new shopping center, which outraged many residents.

EXERCISE 27.5

Revise the following paragraph to establish a clear antecedent for every pronoun that needs one.

> In the summer of 2005, the NCAA banned the use of mascots that could be considered offensive to American Indians at any of their championship games. In order to understand this, it is important to consider that movies and television programs for years portrayed them as savage warriors that were feared and misunderstood. That is why some schools have chosen to use Indians as their mascot, a role typically played by wild animals or fictional beasts. You would not tolerate derogatory terms for other ethnic groups being used for school mascots. In the NCAA's new ruling, they ask schools to eliminate mascots that may be hurtful or offensive to America's Indian population.

EXERCISE 27.6: THINKING CRITICALLY

Turn to a recent piece of your writing (something at least two pages long), and analyze your use of pronouns. Look carefully at the pronoun case you tend to use most; if it is first person, ask whether *I* is used too much. And if you find that you rely heavily on any one case (*you*, for example), decide whether your writing seems monotonous as a result. Take a look as well at whether you tend to use masculine pronouns exclusively to refer to people generally; if so, ask whether you would be more inclusive if you used both masculine and feminine pronouns or if you should revise to use plural pronouns that are not marked as either masculine or feminine (such as *we* or *they*). Finally, check to make sure that your pronouns and their antecedents agree and that the pronouns refer clearly and directly to antecedents.

28   Comma Splices and Fused Sentences

A comma splice results from placing only a comma between independent clauses—groups of words that can stand alone as a sentence. We often see comma splices used to give slogans a catchy rhythm.

bedfordstmartins.com/wia
LearningCurve > Comma splices and fused sentences

▶ **Dogs have owners, cats have staff.**   —Bumper sticker

A related construction is a fused sentence, or run-on, which results from joining two independent clauses with no punctuation or connecting word between them. The bumper sticker as a fused sentence would be "Dogs have owners cats have staff."

In academic and professional English, using comma splices or fused sentences will almost always be identified as an error.

28a   Separate the clauses into two sentences.

The simplest way to revise comma splices or fused sentences is to separate them into two sentences.

COMMA SPLICE   My mother spends long hours every spring

tilling the soil and moving manure,.

T
this part of gardening is nauseating.
∧

If the two clauses are very short, making them two sentences may sound abrupt and terse, so some other method of revision is probably preferable.

28b   Link the clauses with a comma and a coordinating conjunction.

If the two clauses are closely related and equally important, join them with a comma and a coordinating conjunction (*and, but, or, nor, for, so,* or *yet*).

                                    so
FUSED   Interest rates fell, people began borrowing
SENTENCE   ∧

more money.

28c   Link the clauses with a semicolon.

If the ideas in the two clauses are closely related and you want to give them equal emphasis, link them with a semicolon.

COMMA SPLICE   This photograph is not at all realistic,; it uses
                                              ∧

dreamlike images to convey its message.

Be careful when you link clauses with a conjunctive adverb like *however* or *therefore* or with a transition like *in fact.* In such sentences, the two clauses must be separated by a semicolon or by a comma and a coordinating conjunction.

> COMMA SPLICE   Many developing countries have high
>
> birthrates/; therefore, most of their citizens
>
> are young.

28d Rewrite the two clauses as one independent clause.

Sometimes you can reduce two spliced or fused independent clauses to a single independent clause.

> FUSED   Most
> SENTENCE   A large part of my mail is advertisements
>   and
>   most of the rest is bills.

28e Rewrite one independent clause as a dependent clause.

When one independent clause is more important than the other, try converting the less important one to a dependent clause by adding an appropriate subordinating conjunction.

> COMMA   Although
> SPLICE   Zora Neale Hurston is regarded as one of
>
>   America's major novelists, she died in obscurity.

FOR MULTILINGUAL WRITERS

Judging Sentence Length

In U.S. academic contexts, readers sometimes find a series of short sentences "choppy" and undesirable. If you want to connect two independent clauses into one sentence, join them using one of the methods discussed in this chapter to avoid creating a comma splice or fused sentence. Another useful tip for writing in American English is to avoid writing several very long sentences in a row. If you find this pattern in your writing, try breaking it up by including a shorter sentence occasionally.

In the revision, the writer emphasizes the second clause and makes the first one into a dependent clause by adding the subordinating conjunction *although*.

FUSED
SENTENCE

The arts and crafts movement called for , which reacted against mass production,

handmade objects. ~~it reacted against mass~~

~~production.~~

In the revision, the writer chooses to emphasize the first clause (the one describing what the movement advocated) and make the second clause into a dependent clause.

28f Link the two clauses with a dash.

In informal writing, you can use a dash to join the two clauses, especially when the second clause elaborates on the first clause.

COMMA
SPLICE

Exercise trends come and go, this year yoga is hot.

EXERCISE 28.1

Using two of the methods discussed in this chapter, revise each item to correct its comma splice or fused sentence. Use each of the methods at least once. Example:

so
I had misgivings about the marriage, I did not attend the ceremony.

Because
I had misgivings about the marriage, I did not attend the ceremony.

1. Many motorists are unaware of the dangers of texting while driving, lawmakers have taken the matter into their own hands.

2. The tallest human on record was Robert Wadlow he reached an amazing height of eight feet, eleven inches.

3. Some employers provide on-site care for the children of their employees, others reimburse workers for day-care costs.

4. The number of vaccine manufacturers has plummeted the industry has been hit with a flood of lawsuits.

5. Most crustaceans live in the ocean, some also live on land or in freshwater habitats.

6. She inherited some tribal customs from her grandmother, she knows the sewing technique called Seminole patchwork.

7. Don't throw your soda cans in the trash recycle them.

8. My West Indian neighbor has lived in New England for years, nevertheless, she always feels betrayed by winter.

9. The Hope diamond in the Smithsonian Institution is impressive in fact, it looks even larger in person than online.

10. You signed up for the course now you'll have to do the work.

EXERCISE 28.2

Revise the following paragraph, eliminating all comma splices by using a period or a semicolon. Then revise the paragraph again, this time using any of the other methods discussed in this chapter. Comment on the two revisions. What differences in rhythm do you detect? Which version do you prefer, and why?

> We may disagree on the causes of global warming, however, we cannot ignore that it is happening. Of course we still experience cold winters, on the other hand, average global temperatures have risen drastically for the last three decades. Polar ice caps are melting, as a result, sea levels are rising. Scientists predict more extreme weather in the coming decades, droughts will probably be more common, in addition, flooding and tropical storm activity may increase. Some experts fear that rising temperatures may cause large amounts of methane gases to be released, this could be disastrous for our atmosphere. Climate change may have human causes, it might be a natural occurrence, nevertheless, we must find ways to save our planet.

EXERCISE 28.3: THINKING CRITICALLY

Thinking about Any Comma Splices and Fused Sentences in Your Own Writing

Go through some essays you have written, checking for comma splices and fused sentences. Revise any that you find, using the methods discussed in this chapter. Comment on your chosen methods.

29 Sentence Fragments

Sentence fragments are often used to make writing sound conversational, as in this Facebook status update:

> Realizing that there are no edible bagels in this part of Oregon. Sigh.

Fragments—groups of words that are punctuated as sentences but are not sentences—are often seen in intentionally informal writing and in public writing, such as advertising, that aims to attract attention or give a phrase special emphasis. But you should think carefully before using fragments in academic or professional writing, where readers might regard them as errors.

29a   Revise phrase fragments.

A phrase is a group of words that lacks a subject, a verb, or both. When a phrase is punctuated like a sentence, it becomes a fragment. To revise a phrase fragment, attach it to an independent clause, or make it a separate sentence.

▶ NBC is broadcasting the debates./ ~~With~~ ^{with} discussions

afterward.

> *With discussions afterward* is a prepositional phrase, not a sentence. The editing combines the phrase with an independent clause.

▶ The town's growth is controlled by zoning laws/, ^a A~~ ~~strict set of

regulations for builders and corporations.

> *A strict set of regulations for builders and corporations* is a phrase renaming *zoning laws.* The editing attaches the fragment to the sentence containing that noun.

▶ Kamika stayed out of school for three months after Linda was

born. ^{She did so to} ~~To~~ recuperate and to take care of her baby.

> The revision—adding a subject (*she*) and a verb (*did*)—turns the fragment into a separate sentence.

Fragments beginning with transitions.   If you introduce an example or explanation with a transitional word or phrase like *also, for example, such as,* or *that,* be certain you write a sentence, not a fragment.

▶ Joan Didion has written on many subjects/, ~~Such~~ as the
                                            ^such

Hoover Dam and migraine headaches.

The second word group is a phrase, not a sentence. The editing
combines it with an independent clause.

29b Revise compound-predicate fragments.

A fragment occurs when one part of a compound predicate lacks
a subject but is punctuated as a separate sentence. Such a fragment usually begins with *and*, *but*, or *or*. You can revise it by
attaching it to the independent clause that contains the rest of
the predicate.

▶ They sold their house/ ~~And~~ moved into an apartment.
                         ^and

EXERCISE 29.1

Revise each of the following items to eliminate any sentence fragments, either by combining fragments with independent clauses
or by rewriting them as separate sentences. Example:

~~Zoe looked close to tears.~~ Standing with her head bowed/,
                                                            ^ *Zoe looked close to tears.*

Zoe looked close to tears. ~~Standing~~ with her head bowed.
                           ^ *She was standing*

1. Long stretches of white beaches and shady palm trees. Give
   tourists the impression of an island paradise.

2. Forgetting to study for an exam. That is what many college students are afraid of.

3. Much of New Orleans is below sea level. Making it susceptible
   to flooding.

4. Uncle Ron forgot to bring his clarinet to the party. Fortunately
   for us.

5. Oscar night is an occasion for celebrating the film industry. And
   criticizing the fashion industry.

6. Diners in Creole restaurants might try shrimp gumbo. Or order
   turtle soup.

7. In the late 1940s, women began hosting Tupperware parties.
   Casual gatherings in which the hosts act as salespersons.

8. Attempting to lose ten pounds in less than a week. I ate only cottage cheese and grapefruit.

9. Our parents did not realize that we were hoarding our candy. Under our beds.

10. Thomas Edison was famous for his inventions. For example, the phonograph and the first practical lightbulb.

29c Revise clause fragments.

A dependent clause contains both a subject and a verb, but it cannot stand alone as a sentence; it depends on an independent clause to complete its meaning. A dependent clause usually begins with a subordinating conjunction, such as *after, because, before, if, since, though, unless, until, when, where, which, while, who,* or *that.* You can usually combine dependent-clause fragments with a nearby independent clause.

▶ When I decided to switch to part-time work/ I gave up

a lot of my earning potential.

If you cannot smoothly attach a clause to a nearby independent clause, try deleting the opening subordinating word and turning the dependent clause into a sentence.

▶ Most injuries in automobile accidents occur in two ways.
An
~~When an~~ occupant either is hurt by something inside the car

or is thrown from the car.

EXERCISE 29.2
Identify all of the sentence fragments in the following items, and explain why each is grammatically incomplete. Then revise each one in at least two ways. Example:

Controlling my temper/ ~~That~~ has been one of my goals this year.

One of my goals this year has been controlling
~~Controlling~~ my temper. ~~That has been one of my goals this year.~~

1. As soon as the seventy-five-year-old cellist walked onstage. The audience burst into applause.

2. The patient has only one intention. To smoke behind the doctor's back.

3. Some reality shows feature people working in dangerous situations. Such as fishing for Alaskan king crab or logging in swamps.

4. After writing and rewriting for almost three years. She finally felt that her novel was complete.

5. In the wake of the earthquake. Relief workers tried to provide food and shelter to victims.

6. Forster stopped writing novels after *A Passage to India*. Which is one of the greatest novels of the twentieth century.

7. Because only two students signed up. The class was canceled this semester.

8. I started running in April. And ran my first marathon in September.

9. We sat stunned as she delivered her monologue. A ten-minute speech about everything we had done to annoy her.

10. All primates have opposable thumbs. Which sets them apart from other mammals.

EXERCISE 29.3: THINKING CRITICALLY

Reading with an Eye for Fragments

Identify the fragments in the following passage. What effect does the writer achieve by using fragments rather than complete sentences?

> On Sundays, for religion, we went up on the hill. Skipping along the hexagon-shaped tile in Colonial Park. Darting up the steps to Edgecomb Avenue. Stopping in the candy store on St. Nicholas to load up. Leaning forward for leverage to finish the climb up to the church. I was always impressed by this particular house of the Lord.   —Keith Gilyard, *Voices of the Self*

Thinking about Any Fragments in Your Own Writing

Read through some essays you have written. Using the guidelines in this chapter, see whether you find any sentence fragments. If so, do you recognize any patterns? Do you write fragments when you're attempting to add emphasis? Are all of them dependent clauses? phrases? Note any patterns you discover, and make a point of routinely checking your writing for fragments. Finally, revise any fragments to form complete sentences.

7

Sentence Style

30 Consistency and Completeness

If you listen carefully to the conversations around you, you will hear inconsistent and incomplete structures all the time. For instance, during an interview with journalist Bill Moyers, Jon Stewart discussed the supposed objectivity of news reporting:

> But news has never been objective. It's always . . . what does every newscast start with? "Our top stories tonight." That's a list. That's a subjective . . . some editor made a decision: "Here's our top stories. Number one: There's a fire in the Bronx."

Because Stewart is talking casually, some of his sentences begin one way but then move in another direction. The mixed structures pose no problem for the viewer, but sentences such as these can be confusing in writing.

30a Revise faulty sentence structure.

Beginning a sentence with one grammatical pattern and then switching to another one confuses readers.

> **MIXED**   The fact that I get up at 5:00 AM, a wake-up time that explains why I'm always tired in the evening.

The sentence starts out with a subject (*The fact*) followed by a dependent clause (*that I get up at 5:00 AM*). The sentence needs a predicate to complete the independent clause, but instead it moves to another phrase followed by a dependent clause (*a wake-up time that explains why I'm always tired in the evening*), and a fragment results.

> **REVISED**   The fact that I get up at 5:00 AM explains why I'm always tired in the evening.

Deleting *a wake-up time that* changes the rest of the sentence into a predicate.

> **REVISED**   I get up at 5:00 AM, a wake-up time that explains why I'm always tired in the evening.

Deleting *The fact that* turns the beginning of the sentence into an independent clause.

30b Match subjects and predicates.

Another kind of mixed structure, called faulty predication, occurs when a subject and predicate do not fit together grammatically or simply do not make sense together.

▶ A characteristic that I admire is ~~a person who is generous.~~ generosity.

A person is not a characteristic.

▶ The rules of the corporation ~~expect~~ require that employees ~~to~~ be on time.

Rules cannot expect anything.

Is when, is where, the reason . . . is because. Although you will often hear these expressions in everyday use, such constructions are inappropriate in academic or professional writing.

▶ A stereotype is ~~when someone characterizes~~ an unfair characterization of a group~~. unfairly.~~

▶ Spamming is ~~where companies send~~ the practice of sending electronic junk mail.

▶ ~~The reason~~ I like to play soccer ~~is~~ because it provides

aerobic exercise.

EXERCISE 30.1

Revise each of the following sentences in two ways to make its structures consistent in grammar and meaning. Example:

~~The fact that~~ Because our room was cold, we put a heater between

our beds.

The fact that our room was cold, led us to ~~we~~ put a heater between

our beds.

1. To enroll in film school being my primary goal, so I am always saving my money and watching for scholarship opportunities.

2. The reason air-pollution standards should not be relaxed is because many people would suffer.
3. By turning off the water when you brush your teeth, saving up to eight gallons of water per day.
4. Irony is when you expect one thing and get something else.
5. The best meal I've ever eaten was sitting by a river eating bread and cheese from a farmers' market.

30c Use consistent compound structures.

Sometimes writers omit certain words in compound structures. If the omitted word does not fit grammatically with other parts of the compound, the omission can be inappropriate.

▶ His skills are weak, and his performance only *is* average.

The omitted verb *is* does not match the verb in the other part of the compound (*are*), so the writer needs to include it.

30d Make complete comparisons.

When you compare two or more things, the comparison must be complete and clear.

▶ I was embarrassed because my parents were so different/ *from my friends' parents.*

Adding *from my friends' parents* completes the comparison.

UNCLEAR	Aneil always felt more affection for his brother than his sister.
CLEAR	Aneil always felt more affection for his brother than his sister did.
CLEAR	Aneil always felt more affection for his brother than he did for his sister.

EXERCISE 30.2

Revise each of the following sentences to eliminate any inappropriate compound constructions; to make comparisons complete, logically consistent, and clear; and to supply any other omitted words that are necessary for meaning. Example:

Most of the candidates are bright, and one *is* brilliant.

1. Convection ovens cook more quickly and with less power.
2. Argentina and Peru were colonized by Spain, and Brazil by Portugal.
3. She argued that children are even more important for men than women.
4. Do you think the barbecue sauce in Memphis is better than North Carolina?
5. The equipment in our new warehouse is guaranteed to last longer than our current facility.

EXERCISE 30.3: THINKING CRITICALLY

Read over three or four paragraphs from a draft or completed essay you have written recently. Check for mixed sentences and incomplete or missing structures. Revise the paragraphs to correct any problems you find. If you find any, do you recognize any patterns? If so, make a note of them for future reference.

31 Coordination and Subordination

You may notice a difference between your spoken and your written language. In speech, people tend to use *and* and *so* as all-purpose connectors.

> He enjoys psychology, and he has to study hard.

The meaning of this sentence may be perfectly clear in speech, which provides clues with voice, facial expressions, and gestures. But in writing, the sentence could have more than one meaning.

> Although he enjoys psychology, he has to study hard.

> He enjoys psychology although he has to study hard.

The first sentence links two ideas with a coordinating conjunction, *and*; the other two sentences link ideas with a subordinating conjunction, *although*. A coordinating conjunction gives the ideas equal emphasis, and a subordinating conjunction emphasizes one idea more than another.

 bedfordstmartins.com/wia
Exercise > Coordination and subordination
LearningCurve > Coordination and subordination

31a Relate equal ideas.

When you want to give equal emphasis to different ideas in a sentence, link them with a coordinating conjunction (*and, but, for, nor, or, so,* or *yet*) or a semicolon.

▶ They acquired horses, **and** their ancient nomadic spirit was suddenly free of the ground.

▶ There is perfect freedom in the mountains, **but** it belongs to the eagle and the elk, the badger and the bear.

—N. Scott Momaday, The Way to Rainy Mountain

Coordination can help make explicit the relationship between two separate ideas.

▶ My son watches *The Simpsons* religiously~~,~~; ~~Forced~~ ^{forced} to choose,

he would probably take Homer Simpson over his sister.

Connecting these two sentences with a semicolon strengthens the connection between two closely related ideas.

When you connect ideas in a sentence, make sure that the relationship between the ideas is clear.

▶ Surfing the Internet is a common way to spend leisure time,

~~and~~ ^{but} it should not replace human contact.

What does being a common form of leisure have to do with replacing human contact? Changing *and* to *but* better relates the two ideas.

EXERCISE 31.1

Using coordination to signal equal importance or to create special effects, combine and revise the following fourteen short sentences into several longer and more effective ones. Add or delete words as necessary.

The auditorium was filled with people. The sea of faces did not intimidate me. I had decided to appear in a musical with my local community theater group. There was no going back now. I reminded myself of how I had gotten here. It took hard work. I refused to doubt my abilities. Besides, the director and her staff had held auditions. I had read the heroine's part. I had sung a song. They had chosen me for the role. I was untrained. My skills as an actor would now be judged publicly. I felt ready to rise to the challenge.

31b Distinguish main ideas.

Subordination allows you to distinguish between major points and minor points or to bring in supporting details. If, for instance, you put your main idea in an independent clause, you might then put any less significant ideas in dependent clauses, phrases, or even single words. The following sentence highlights the subordinated point:

▶ Mrs. Viola Cullinan was a plump woman who lived in a three-bedroom house somewhere behind the post office.

—Maya Angelou, "My Name Is Margaret"

The dependent clause adds important information about Mrs. Cullinan, but it is subordinate to the independent clause.

Notice that the choice of what to subordinate rests with the writer and depends on the intended meaning. Angelou might have given the same basic information differently.

▶ Mrs. Viola Cullinan, a plump woman, lived in a three-bedroom house somewhere behind the post office.

Subordinating the information about Mrs. Cullinan's size to that about her house would suggest a slightly different meaning, of course. As a writer, you must think carefully about what you want to emphasize and must subordinate information accordingly.

Subordination can also establish logical relationships among ideas. These relationships are often specified by subordinating conjunctions.

SOME COMMON SUBORDINATING CONJUNCTIONS

after	if	though
although	in order that	unless
as	once	until
as if	since	when
because	so that	where
before	than	while
even though	that	

In the following sentence, the subordinate clause is highlighted and the subordinating word underlined.

▶ She usually rested her smile until late afternoon <u>when</u> her women friends dropped in and Miss Glory, the cook, served them cold drinks on the closed-in porch.

—Maya Angelou, "My Name Is Margaret"

Using too many coordinate structures can be monotonous and can make it hard for readers to recognize the most important ideas. Subordinating lesser ideas can help highlight the main ideas.

▶ Many people check email in the evening, and so they turn on the computer. ~~They~~ Though they may intend to respond only to urgent messages, a friend sends a link to a blog post, ~~and~~ which they decide to read ~~it~~ for just a short while/. ~~and~~ Eventually, they get engrossed in Facebook, and they end up spending the whole evening in front of the screen.

Determining what to subordinate

▶ ~~Our~~ Although our new boss can be difficult, ~~although~~ she has revived and maybe even saved the division.

The editing puts the more important information—that the new boss has saved part of the company—in an independent clause and subordinates the rest.

Avoiding excessive subordination. When too many subordinate clauses are strung together, readers may have trouble keeping track of the main idea expressed in the independent clause.

TOO MUCH SUBORDINATION

▶ Philip II sent the Spanish Armada to conquer England, which was ruled by Elizabeth, who had executed Mary because she was plotting to overthrow Elizabeth, who was a Protestant, whereas Mary and Philip were Roman Catholics.

REVISED

▶ Philip II sent the Spanish Armada to conquer England, which was ruled by Elizabeth, a Protestant. She had executed Mary, a Roman Catholic like Philip, because Mary was plotting to overthrow her.

Putting the facts about Elizabeth executing Mary into an independent clause makes key information easier to recognize.

EXERCISE 31.2

Combine each of the following sets of sentences into one sentence that uses subordination to signal the relationships among ideas. Example:

I was looking through the cupboard.
I noticed the cookies were gone.
This snack is a favorite of my roommate.

While I was looking through the cupboard, I noticed that the cookies, one of my roommate's favorite snacks, were gone.

1. The original *Star Trek* television show ran from 1966 to 1969.
   It was critically acclaimed.
   It had low ratings and was canceled by the network.

2. Athena was the goddess of wisdom.
   Ancient Greeks relied on Athena to protect the city of Athens.
   Athens was named in Athena's honor.

3. Harry Potter is a fictional wizard.
   He turns eleven years old.
   He is taken to Hogwarts School of Witchcraft and Wizardry.

4. Flappers seemed rebellious to their parents' generation.
   They broke with 1920s social conventions.
   They cut their hair short and smoked in public.

5. Skateboarding originated in Venice, California.
   The time was the mid-seventies.
   There was a drought.
   The swimming pools were empty.

EXERCISE 31.3

Revise each of the following sentences to highlight what you take to be the main or most climactic order, or the order that increases in importance or emphasis. Example:

Theories about dinosaurs have run the gamut—simple lizards, hybrids of cold-blooded capabilities,

fully adapted warm-blooded creatures, ~~hybrids of cold-blooded~~
~~capabilities.~~

1. The president persuaded the American people, his staff, and Congress.

2. We can expect a decade of record-breaking tropical storms and hurricanes, if meteorologists are correct in their predictions.

3. From the sightseeing boat, we saw a whale dive toward us and then, before crashing its tail on the waves, lift itself out of the water.

4. I did not realize that living in the city would mean eating canned soup every night, selling my car, and losing half my closet space.

5. Jake experienced several side effects from the medication, including dizziness, severe abdominal pain, and dry mouth.

EXERCISE 31.4: THINKING CRITICALLY

Analyze two paragraphs from one of your drafts. Do the independent clauses contain the main ideas? How many dependent clauses do you find? Should the ideas in the dependent clauses be subordinate to those in the independent clauses? Revise the paragraphs to use coordination and subordination effectively. What conclusions can you draw about your use of coordination and subordination?

32 Conciseness

If you have a Twitter account, you already know a lot about being concise—that is, about getting messages across in no more than 140 characters. Recently, *New York Times* editor Bill Keller tweeted, "Twitter makes you stupid. Discuss." That little comment drew a large number of responses, including one from his wife that read, "I don't know if Twitter makes you stupid, but it's making you late for dinner. Come home."

No matter how you feel about the effects of Twitter on the brain (or stomach!), you can make any writing more effective by choosing words that convey exactly what you mean to say.

32a Eliminate redundant words.

Sometimes writers add words for emphasis, saying that something is large *in size* or red *in color* or that two ingredients should be combined *together*. The italicized words are redundant (unnecessary for meaning), as are the deleted words in the following examples.

▶ ~~Compulsory~~ A̖ttendance at assemblies is required.

▶ The auction featured ~~contemporary~~ "antiques" made recently.

▶ Many different forms of hazing occur, such as physical ~~abuse~~

   and mental abuse.

32b Eliminate empty words.

Words that contribute little or no meaning to a sentence include vague nouns like *area*, *kind*, *situation*, and *thing* as well as vague modifiers like *definitely*, *major*, *really*, and *very*. Delete such words, or find a more specific way to say what you mean.

▶ ~~The~~ H̖ousing ~~situation~~ can ~~have a really significant impact~~ strongly influence
   ~~on the social aspect of~~ a student's life. social

32c Replace wordy phrases.

Many common phrases can be reduced to a word or two with no loss in meaning.

WORDY	CONCISE
at all times	always
at that point in time	then
at the present time	now/today
due to the fact that	because
for the purpose of	for
in order to	to
in spite of the fact that	although
in the event that	if

32d Simplify sentence structure.

Using the simplest grammatical structures can tighten and strengthen your sentences considerably.

▶ Hurricane Sandy, ~~which was certainly~~ one of the most powerful
    widespread
    storms ever to hit the New York area, caused damage. ~~to a~~

    ~~very wide area.~~

Strong verbs.   *Be* verbs (*is, are, was, were, been*) often result in wordiness.

                                       harms
▶ A high-fat, high-cholesterol diet ~~is bad for~~ your heart.
                                       ^

Expletives.   Sometimes expletive constructions such as *there is, there are,* and *it is* introduce a topic effectively; often, however, your writing will be better without them.

       M
▶ ~~There are m~~any people ~~who~~ fear success because they believe
       ^
    they do not deserve it.

       P   need
▶ ~~It is necessary for~~ presidential candidates to perform well on
       ^   ^
    television.

Active voice.   Some writing situations call for the passive voice, but it is always wordier than the active—and often makes for dull or even difficult reading (see 23e).

    Gower
▶ ~~In Gower's research, it was~~ found that pythons often dwell
    ^
    in trees.

EXERCISE 32.1

Look at the following sentences, which use the passive voice. Then rewrite each sentence in the active voice, and decide which version you prefer and why. Example:

    I   you
    ~~You are~~ hereby relieved of your duties. ~~by me.~~
    ^   ^   ^

1. Mistakes were made.
2. Musical legends such as Ray Charles, Billie Holiday, and Johnny Cash have all influenced Norah Jones.
3. Numerous reports of loud music from bars and shouting neighbors were taken by the city's new noise-complaint hotline.
4. The violin solo was performed by an eight-year-old.
5. In a patient with celiac disease, intestinal damage can be caused by the body's immunological response to gluten.

EXERCISE 32.2

Revise the following paragraph to eliminate unnecessary words, nominalizations, expletives, and inappropriate use of the passive voice.

As dogs became tamed and domesticated by humans over many thousands of years, the canine species underwent an evolution into hundreds of breeds designed to perform particular, specific tasks, such as pulling sleds and guarding sheep. Over time, there was a decreased need for many breeds. For example, as humans evolved from hunter-gatherers into farmers, it was no longer at all necessary for them to own hunting dogs. Later, as farming societies became industrialized, there was a disappearance of herd animals, and fewer shepherds watching sheep meant that there were fewer sheepdogs. But by this time humans had grown accustomed to dogs' companionship, and breeding continued. Today, most dogs are kept by their owners simply as companions, but some dogs still do the work they were intentionally bred for, such as following a scent, guarding a home, or leading the blind.

EXERCISE 32.3: THINKING CRITICALLY

Reading with an Eye for Conciseness

Bring two pieces of writing to class: one that is not just short but concise—wasting no words but conveying its meaning clearly—and one that uses too many words to say too little. Bring both of these pieces to class to compare with those chosen by your classmates.

Thinking about Conciseness in Your Own Writing

Find two or three paragraphs you have written recently, and study them with an eye for empty words. Eliminate meaningless words such as *quite* and *very*. Compare notes with one or two classmates to see what empty words, if any, you tend to use. Finally, make a note of the empty words you use, and try to avoid them in the future.

33 Parallelism

If you look and listen, you will see parallel grammatical structures in everyday use. Bumper stickers often use parallelism to make their messages memorable (*Minds are like parachutes; both work best when open*), as do song lyrics and jump-rope rhymes. In addition to creating pleasing rhythmic effects, parallelism helps clarify meaning.

33a   Make items in a series or list parallel.

All items in a series should be in parallel form—all nouns, all verbs, all prepositional phrases, and so on. Parallelism makes a series both graceful and easy to follow.

▶ In the eighteenth century, armed forces could fight in open fields and on the high seas. Today, they can clash on the ground anywhere, on the sea, under the sea, and in the air.
  —Donald Snow and Eugene Brown, *The Contours of Power*

The parallel structure of the phrases, and of the sentences themselves, highlights the contrast between the eighteenth century and today.

▶ The quarter horse skipped, pranced, and ~~was sashaying~~ onto ^sashayed^ the track.

▶ The children ran down the hill, skipped over the lawn, and ^jumped^ into the swimming pool.

▶ The duties of the job include babysitting, housecleaning, and ^preparing^ ~~preparation of~~ meals.

Items in a list, in a formal outline, and in headings should all be parallel.

▶ Kitchen rules: (1) Coffee to be made only by library staff.
  (2) Coffee service to be closed at 4:00 PM. (3) Doughnuts to be kept in cabinet. (4) ^Coffee materials not to be handled by faculty.^ ~~No faculty members should handle coffee materials.~~

33b   Make paired ideas parallel.

Parallel structures can help you pair two ideas effectively. The more nearly parallel the two structures are, the stronger the connection between the ideas will be.

▶ I type in one place, but I write all over the house.

—Toni Morrison

▶ Writers are often more interesting on the page than they are
the flesh.
in ~~person.~~
              ^

In these examples, the parallel structures help readers see an important contrast between two ideas or acts.

With conjunctions.   When you link ideas with *and, but, or, nor, for, so,* or *yet,* make the ideas parallel in structure. Always use the same structure after both parts of a correlative conjunction: *either . . . or, both . . . and, neither . . . nor, not . . . but, not only . . . but also, just as . . . so,* and *whether . . . or.*

                    who is
▶ Consult a friend in your class or who is excellent at
                       ^
chemistry.
                                        accepts
▶ The wise politician promises the possible and ~~should accept~~
                                             ^
the inevitable.
                                        live in
▶ I wanted not only to go away to school but also to New England.
                                             ^

EXERCISE 33.1

Complete the following sentences, using parallel words or phrases in each case. Example:

The wise politician *promises the possible, faces the unavoidable*, and *accepts the inevitable.*

1. Before buying a used car, you should ____, ____, and ____.
2. Three activities I'd like to try are ____, ____, and ____.
3. Working in a restaurant taught me not only ____ but also ____.

4. We must either ____ or ____.

5. To pass the time in the waiting room, I ____, ____, and ____.

EXERCISE 33.2

Revise the following sentences as necessary to eliminate any errors in parallel structure. Example:

> I enjoy skiing, playing the guitar, and ~~I walk~~ on the beach in
>   ^walking
> warm weather.

1. I remember watching it the first time, realizing I'd never seen anything like it, and immediately vowed never to miss an episode of *The Daily Show.*

2. A crowd stood outside the school and were watching as the graduates paraded by.

3. An effective Web site is well designed, provides useful information, and links are given to other relevant sites.

4. It is impossible to watch *The Office* and not seeing a little of yourself in one of the characters.

5. Lila was the winner not only of the pie-eating contest but also won the yodeling competition.

33c Use words necessary for clarity.

In addition to making parallel elements grammatically similar, be sure to include any words—prepositions, articles, verb forms, and so on—that are necessary for clarity.

> ▶ We'll move to a city in the Southwest or Mexico.
>   ^in
>
> To a city in Mexico or to Mexico in general? The editing clarifies the meaning.

EXERCISE 33.3: THINKING CRITICALLY

Thinking about Your Own Use of Parallelism

Read carefully several paragraphs from a draft you have recently written, noting any series of words, phrases, or clauses. Using the guidelines in this chapter, determine whether the series are parallel, and if not, revise them for parallelism. Then reread the paragraphs, looking for places where parallel structures would add emphasis or clarity, and revise accordingly. Can you draw any conclusions about your use of parallelism?

34 Shifts

A shift in writing is an abrupt change that results in inconsistency. Sometimes a writer or speaker will shift deliberately, as linguist Geneva Smitherman does in this passage from *Word from the Mother*: "There are days when I optimistically predict that Hip Hop will survive—and thrive. . . . In the larger realm of Hip Hop culture, there is cause for optimism as we witness Hip Hop youn-guns tryna git they political activist game togetha."

This shift from formal academic language to vernacular speech calls out for and holds our attention. Although writers make shifts for good rhetorical reasons, unintentional shifts can be confusing.

34a Revise shifts in tense.

If the verbs in a passage refer to actions occurring at different times, they may require different tenses. Be careful, however, not to change tenses without a good reason.

► A few countries produce almost all of the world's illegal drugs,
    but addiction ~~affected~~ *affects* many countries.

34b Revise shifts in voice.

Do not shift between the active voice (she *sold* it) and the passive voice (it *was sold*) without a reason. Sometimes a shift in voice is justified, but often it only confuses readers.

► Two youths approached ~~me,~~ *me* and ~~I was~~ asked for my wallet.

The original sentence shifts from active to passive voice (23e), so it is unclear who asked for the wallet.

bedfordstmartins.com/wia
Exercise > Verb tense shifts
LearningCurve > Active and passive voice

34c   Revise shifts in point of view.

Unnecessary shifts in point of view between first person (*I* or *we*), second person (*you*), and third person (*he*, *she*, *it*, *one*, or *they*), or between singular and plural subjects, can be very confusing to readers.

<blockquote>

You
▶ ~~One~~ can do well on this job if you budget your time.
   ^

Is the writer making a general statement or giving advice to someone? Revising the shift eliminates this confusion.
</blockquote>

34d   Revise shifts between direct and indirect discourse.

When you quote someone's exact words, you are using direct discourse: *She said, "I'm an editor."* When you report what someone says without repeating the exact words, you are using indirect discourse: *She said she was an editor.* Shifting between direct and indirect discourse in the same sentence can cause problems, especially with questions.

<blockquote>

              he
▶ Bob asked what could ~~he~~ do to help~~?~~.
             ^   ^

The editing eliminates an awkward shift by reporting Bob's question indirectly. It could also be edited to quote Bob directly: *Bob asked, "What can I do to help?"*
</blockquote>

EXERCISE 34.1

Revise the following sentences to eliminate unnecessary shifts in tense, voice, or point of view and between direct and indirect discourse. Most of the items can be revised in more than one way. Examples:

> When a person goes to college, you face many new situations.
>
> When a <u>person</u> goes to college, <u>he or she</u> faces many new situations.
>
> When <u>people</u> go to college, <u>they</u> face many new situations.

1. The greed of the 1980s gave way to the occupational insecurity of the 1990s, which in turn gives way to reinforced family ties in the early 2000s.

2. The instructor grabbed her coat, wondered why was the substitute late, and ran out of the room.

3. Suddenly, we heard an explosion of wings off to our right, and you could see a hundred or more ducks lifting off from the water.

4. In my previous job, I sold the most advertising spots and was given a sales excellence award.

5. A cloud of snow powder rose as skis and poles fly in every direction.

6. The flight attendant said, "Please turn off all electronic devices," but that we could use them again after takeoff.

7. The real estate market was softer than it had been for a decade, and a buyer could practically name their price.

8. The freezing weather is threatening crops such as citrus fruits, which were sensitive to cold.

34e Revise shifts in tone and diction.

Watch out for shifts in your tone (overall attitude toward a topic or audience) and word choice. These shifts can confuse readers and leave them wondering what your real attitude is.

INCONSISTENT TONE

The question of child care forces a society to make profound decisions about its values. If some conservatives had their way, June Cleaver would still be in the kitchen baking cookies for Wally and the Beaver and waiting for Ward to bring home the bacon, but with only one income, the Cleavers would be lucky to afford hot dogs.

REVISED

The question of child care forces a society to make profound decisions about its values. Some conservatives believe that women with young children should not work outside the home, but many mothers are forced to do so for financial reasons.

The shift in diction from formal to informal makes readers wonder whether the writer is presenting a serious analysis or a humorous satire. As revised, the passage makes more sense because the words are consistently formal.

EXERCISE 34.2: THINKING CRITICALLY

Thinking about Any Shifts in Your Own Writing

Find an article about a well-known person you admire. Then write a paragraph or two about him or her, making a point of using both direct and indirect discourse. Using the information in 34d, check your writing for any inappropriate shifts between direct and indirect discourse, and revise as necessary.

Punctuation and Mechanics

35 Commas

It's hard to go through a day without encountering directions of some kind, and commas often play a crucial role in how you interpret instructions. See how important the comma is in the following directions for making hot cereal:

> Add Cream of Wheat slowly, stirring constantly.

That sentence tells the cook to *add the cereal slowly.* If the comma came before the word *slowly,* however, the cook might add all of the cereal at once and *stir slowly.*

35a Set off introductory elements.

In general, use a comma after any word, phrase, or clause that precedes the subject of the sentence.

▶ However, health care costs keep rising.

▶ Wearing new running shoes, Audrey prepared for the race.

▶ To win the game, Connor needed skill and luck.

▶ Fingers on the keyboard, Maya waited for the test to begin.

▶ While her friends watched, Lila practiced her gymnastics
   routine.

Some writers omit the comma after a short introductory element that does not seem to require a pause after it. However, you will never be wrong if you use a comma.

EXERCISE 35.1

In the following sentences, add any commas that are needed after the introductory element. Example:

> To find a good day-care provider, parents usually need both
> time and money.

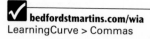
bedfordstmartins.com/wia
LearningCurve > Commas

1. After the concession speech the senator's supporters drifted out of the room.

2. To our surprise the charity auction raised enough money to build a new technology center.

3. Unaware that the microphone was on the candidate made an offensive comment.

4. Whenever someone rings the doorbell her dog goes berserk.

5. Therefore Sasha must take a summer course to receive her diploma.

6. With the fifth century came the fall of the Roman Empire.

7. A tray of shrimp in one hand and a pile of napkins in the other the waiter avoided me.

8. Toward the rapids floated an empty rubber raft.

9. When they woke up the exhausted campers no longer wanted to hike.

10. Tears in his eyes Keflezighi won the marathon.

35b Separate clauses in compound sentences.

A comma usually precedes a coordinating conjunction (*and*, *but*, *or*, *nor*, *for*, *so*, or *yet*) that joins two independent clauses in a compound sentence.

▶ The climbers must reach the summit today, or they will have to turn back.

With very short clauses, you can sometimes omit the comma (*she saw her chance and she took it*). But always use the comma if there is a chance the sentence will be misread without it.

▶ I opened the junk drawer, and the cabinet door jammed.

Use a semicolon rather than a comma when the clauses are long and complex or contain their own commas.

▶ When these early migrations took place, the ice was still confined to the lands in the far north; but eight hundred thousand years ago, when man was already established in the temperate latitudes, the ice moved southward until it covered large parts of Europe and Asia.

—Robert Jastrow, *Until the Sun Dies*

CHECKLIST

Editing for Commas

Research for this book shows that five of the most common errors in college writing involve commas.

✔ Check that a comma separates an introductory word, phrase, or clause from the main part of the sentence. (35a)

✔ Look at every sentence that contains a coordinating conjunction (*and, but, for, nor, or, so,* or *yet*). If the groups of words before and after this conjunction both function as complete sentences, use a comma before the conjunction. (35b)

✔ Look at each adjective clause beginning with *which, who, whom, whose, when,* or *where* and at each phrase and appositive. If the rest of the sentence would have a different meaning without the clause, phrase, or appositive, do not set off the element with commas. (35c)

✔ Make sure that adjective clauses beginning with *that* are not set off with commas. Do not use commas between subjects and verbs, verbs and objects or complements, or prepositions and objects; to separate parts of compound constructions other than compound sentences; to set off restrictive clauses; or before the first or after the last item in a series. (35i)

✔ Do not use a comma alone to separate sentences. (See Chapter 28.)

EXERCISE 35.2

Use a comma and a coordinating conjunction (*and, but, for, nor, or, so,* or *yet*) to combine each of the following pairs of sentences into one sentence. Delete or rearrange words if necessary. Example:

I had finished studying for the test ͪ, I went to bed.

1. The chef did not want to serve a heavy dessert. She was planning to have a rich stew for the main course.

2. My mother rarely allowed us to eat sweets. Halloween was a special exception.

3. Scientists have mapped the human genome. They learn more every day about how genes affect an individual's health.

4. Perhaps I will change my name when I get married. Maybe I will keep my maiden name.

5. Penguins cannot fly. They cannot walk the way other birds do.

35c   Set off nonrestrictive elements.

Nonrestrictive elements are word groups that do not limit, or restrict, the meaning of the noun or pronoun they modify. Setting nonrestrictive elements off with commas shows your readers that the information is not essential to the meaning of the sentence. Restrictive elements, on the other hand, *are* essential to the meaning and should *not* be set off with commas. The same sentence may mean different things with and without the commas:

▶ The bus drivers rejecting the management offer remained on strike.

▶ The bus drivers, rejecting the management offer, remained on strike.

The first sentence says that only *some* bus drivers, the ones rejecting the offer, remained on strike. The second says that *all* the drivers did.

Since the decision to include or omit commas affects how readers interpret your sentence, you should think especially carefully about what you mean and then use commas (or omit them) accordingly.

RESTRICTIVE   Drivers *who have been convicted of drunken driving* should lose their licenses.

In the preceding sentence, the clause *who have been convicted of drunken driving* is essential because it explains that only drivers who have been convicted of drunken driving should lose their licenses. Therefore, it is *not* set off with commas.

NONRESTRICTIVE   The two drivers involved in the accident, *who have been convicted of drunken driving*, should lose their licenses.

In this sentence, however, the clause *who have been convicted of drunken driving* is not essential to the meaning because it does not limit what it modifies, *The two drivers involved in the accident*, but merely provides additional information about the drivers. Therefore, the clause *is* set off with commas.

To decide whether an element is restrictive or nonrestrictive, mentally delete the element, and see if the deletion changes the meaning of the rest of the sentence. If the deletion *does* change the meaning, you should probably not set the element off with commas. If it *does not* change the meaning, the element probably requires commas.

Adjective and adverb clauses.   An adjective clause that begins with *that* is always restrictive; do not set it off with commas. An adjective clause beginning with *which* may be either restrictive or nonrestrictive; however, some writers prefer to use *which* only for nonrestrictive clauses, which they set off with commas.

RESTRICTIVE CLAUSES

▶ The claim *that men like seriously to battle one another to some sort of finish* is a myth.

> —John McMurtry, "Kill 'Em! Crush 'Em! Eat 'Em Raw!"

The adjective clause is necessary to the meaning because it explains which claim is a myth; therefore, the clause is not set off with commas.

▶ The man⁄who rescued Jana's puppy⁄won her eternal gratitude.

The adjective clause is necessary to the meaning because it identifies the man, so it takes no commas.

NONRESTRICTIVE CLAUSES

▶ I borrowed books from the rental library of Shakespeare and Company, *which was the library and bookstore of Sylvia Beach at 12 rue de l'Odeon.*   —Ernest Hemingway, *A Moveable Feast*

The adjective clause is not necessary to the meaning of the independent clause and therefore is set off with a comma.

An adverb clause that follows a main clause does *not* usually require a comma to set it off unless the adverb clause expresses contrast.

▶ The park became a popular gathering place, although nearby residents complained about the noise.

The adverb clause expresses contrast; therefore, it is set off with a comma.

Phrases.   Participial phrases may be restrictive or nonrestrictive. Prepositional phrases are usually restrictive, but sometimes they are not essential to the meaning of a sentence and thus are set off with commas.

NONRESTRICTIVE PHRASES

► The singer's children, refusing to be ignored, interrupted

the recital.

Using commas around the participial phrase makes it nonrestrictive, telling us that all of the children interrupted.

Appositives.   An appositive is a noun or noun phrase that renames a nearby noun. When an appositive is not essential to identify what it renames, it is set off with commas.

NONRESTRICTIVE APPOSITIVES

► Savion Glover, the award-winning dancer, taps like

poetry in motion.

Savion Glover's name identifies him; the appositive *the award-winning dancer* provides extra information.

RESTRICTIVE APPOSITIVES

► Mozart's opera/ *The Marriage of Figaro/* was considered

revolutionary.

The phrase is restrictive because Mozart wrote more than one opera. Therefore, it is *not* set off with commas.

EXERCISE 35.3

Use commas to set off all nonrestrictive clauses, phrases, and appositives in any of the following sentences that contain such elements.

1. What can you buy for the person who has everything?
2. Embalming is a technique that preserves a cadaver.
3. The enormous new house which was the largest in the neighborhood had replaced a much smaller old home.

4. The rescue workers exhausted and discouraged stared ahead without speaking.

5. The new mall has the same stores and restaurants as all the other malls in town.

6. Viruses unlike bacteria can reproduce only by infecting live cells.

7. Napoléon was imprisoned following his defeat at the battle of Waterloo.

8. Hammurabi an ancient Babylonian king created laws that were carved on a stone for public display.

9. Birds' hearts have four chambers whereas reptiles' have three.

10. A female cheetah hisses and swats if another animal gets too close to her young.

35d Separate items in a series.

▶ **He has plundered our seas, ravaged our coasts, burnt our towns, and destroyed the lives of our people.**

—Declaration of Independence

You may see a series with no comma after the next-to-last item, particularly in newspaper writing. Occasionally, however, omitting the comma can cause confusion.

▶ **All the cafeteria's vegetables — broccoli, green beans,**

peas, and carrots — were cooked to a gray mush.

Without the comma after *peas,* you wouldn't know if there were three choices (the third being a *mixture* of peas and carrots) or four.

Coordinate adjectives — two or more adjectives that relate equally to the noun they modify — should be separated by commas.

▶ **The long, twisting, muddy road led to a shack in the woods.**

In a sentence like *The cracked bathroom mirror reflected his face,* however, *cracked* and *bathroom* are not coordinate because *bathroom mirror* is the equivalent of a single word, which is modified by *cracked.* Hence, they are *not* separated by commas.

You can usually determine whether adjectives are coordinate by inserting *and* between them. If the sentence makes sense with the *and,* the adjectives are coordinate and should be separated by commas.

▶ **They are sincere *and* talented *and* inquisitive researchers.**

The sentence makes sense with the *and*s, so the adjectives should be separated by commas: *They are sincere, talented, inquisitive researchers.*

▶ **Byron carried an elegant ~~and~~ pocket watch.**

The sentence does not make sense with *and*, so the adjectives *elegant* and *pocket* should not be separated by a comma: *Byron carried an elegant pocket watch.*

EXERCISE 35.4

Revise any of the following sentences that require commas to set off words, phrases, or clauses in a series.

1. The students donated clothing school supplies and nonperishable food.

2. The hot humid weather did not stop the fans from flocking to the free outdoor concert.

3. The ball sailed over the fence across the yard and through the Wilsons' window.

4. Several art historians carefully inspected each of the Chinese terra-cotta figures.

5. The young athletes' parents insist on calling every play judging every move and telling everyone within earshot exactly what is wrong with the team.

35e Set off parenthetical and transitional expressions.

Parenthetical expressions add comments or information. Because they often interrupt the flow of a sentence, they are usually set off with commas.

▶ **Some studies have shown that chocolate, of all things, helps**

prevent tooth decay.

Transitions (such as *as a result*), conjunctive adverbs (such as *however*), and other expressions used to connect parts of sentences are usually set off with commas.

▶ **Ozone is a by-product of dry cleaning, for example.**

35f Set off contrasting elements, interjections, direct address, and tag questions.

▶ I asked you, *not your brother*, to sweep the porch.

▶ *Holy cow*, did you see that?

▶ Remember, *sir*, that you are under oath.

▶ The governor did not veto the bill, *did she*?

EXERCISE 35.5

Revise each of the following sentences, using commas to set off parenthetical and transitional expressions, contrasting elements, interjections, words used in direct address, and tag questions.

1. One must consider the society as a whole not just its parts.
2. Drinking caffeinated beverages can in fact be good for your health.
3. You don't expect me to read this speech do you?
4. Coming in ahead of schedule and under budget it appears is the only way to keep this client happy.
5. Believe me Jenna I had no idea things would turn out this way.

35g Set off parts of dates and addresses.

Dates. Use a comma between the day of the week and the month, between the day of the month and the year, and between the year and the rest of the sentence, if any.

▶ On Wednesday, November 26, 2008, gunmen arrived in

Mumbai by boat.

Do not use commas with dates in inverted order or with dates consisting of only the month and the year.

▶ She dated the letter 5 August 2013.

▶ Thousands of Germans swarmed over the wall in November 1989.

Addresses and place names. Use a comma after each part of an address or a place name, including the state if there is no ZIP code. Do not precede a ZIP code with a comma.

▶ Forward my mail to the Department of English, The Ohio State
  University, Columbus, Ohio 43210.
▶ Portland, Oregon, is much larger than Portland, Maine.

EXERCISE 35.6
Revise each of the following sentences, using commas appropriately with dates, addresses, place names, titles, and numbers.

1. The city of Dublin Ireland has a population of over 500000.
2. I rode a total of almost 1200 miles on my bike in 2009.
3. New Delhi India and Islamabad Pakistan became the capitals of two independent nations at midnight on August 15 1947.
4. MLA headquarters are located at 26 Broadway New York New York 10004.
5. I was convinced that the nameplate I. M. Well MD was one of my sister's pranks.

35h Set off quotations.

Commas set off a quotation from words used to introduce or identify the source of the quotation. A comma following a quotation goes *inside* the closing quotation mark.

▶ A German proverb warns, "Go to law for a sheep, and lose your cow."
▶ "All I know about grammar," said Joan Didion, "is its infinite power."

Do not use a comma after a question mark or an exclamation point.

▶ "Out, damned spot!/" cries Lady Macbeth.

Do not use a comma to introduce a quotation with *that* or when you do not quote a speaker's exact words.

▶ The writer of Ecclesiastes concludes that/ "all is vanity."
▶ Patrick Henry declared/ that he wanted either liberty or death.

EXERCISE 35.7

Insert a comma in any of the following sentences that require one.

1. "The public be damned!" William Henry Vanderbilt was reported to have said. "I'm working for my stockholders."

2. My mother was fond of telling me "You'd make coffee nervous!"

3. I refuse to believe the old saying that "nice guys finish last."

4. "Learning without thought is labor lost; thought without learning is perilous" Confucius argued.

5. "Do you have any idea who I am?" the well-dressed man asked belligerently.

35i   Avoid unnecessary commas.

Excessive use of commas can spoil an otherwise fine sentence.

Around restrictive elements.   Do not use commas to set off restrictive elements—elements that limit, or define, the meaning of the words they modify or refer to (35c).

▸ I don't let my children watch movies/ that are violent.

▸ The actor/ Joaquin Phoenix/ might win the award.

Between subjects and verbs, verbs and objects or complements, and prepositions and objects.   Do not use a comma between a subject and its verb, a verb and its object or complement, or a preposition and its object.

▸ Watching movies late at night/ allows me to relax.

▸ Parents must decide/ what time their children should go to bed.

▸ The winner of/ the prize for community service stepped forward.

In compound constructions.   In compound constructions other than compound sentences, do not use a comma before or after a coordinating conjunction that joins the two parts.

▸ Improved health care/ and more free trade were two of the

administration's goals.

  The *and* joins parts of a compound subject, which should not be separated by a comma.

▶ Mark Twain trained as a printer/ and worked as a steamboat

pilot.

The *and* joins parts of a compound predicate, which should not be separated by a comma.

In a series.   Do not use a comma before the first or after the last item in a series.

▶ The auction included/ furniture, paintings, and china.

▶ The swimmer took slow, elegant, powerful/ strokes.

EXERCISE 35.8: THINKING CRITICALLY

Thinking about Your Own Use of Commas

Choose a paragraph that you have written. Remove all of the commas, and read it aloud. What is the effect of leaving out the commas? Now, punctuate the passage with commas, consulting this chapter. Did you replace all of your original commas? Did you add any new ones? Explain why you added the commas you did.

36   Semicolons

The following public-service announcement, posted in New York City subway cars, reminded commuters what to do with a used newspaper at the end of the ride:

Please put it in a trash can; that's good news for everyone.

The semicolon in the subway announcement separates two clauses that could have been written as separate sentences. Semicolons, which create a pause stronger than that of a comma but not as strong as the full pause of a period, show close connections between related ideas.

36a   Link independent clauses.

Though a comma and a coordinating conjunction often join independent clauses (35b), semicolons provide writers with subtler ways of signaling closely related clauses. The clause following a semicolon often restates an idea expressed in the first clause; it sometimes expands on or presents a contrast to the first.

▶ **Immigration acts were passed; newcomers had to prove, besides moral correctness and financial solvency, their ability to read.**

—Mary Gordon, "More Than Just a Shrine"

Gordon uses a semicolon to join the two clauses, giving the sentence an abrupt rhythm that suits the topic: laws that imposed strict requirements.

If two independent clauses joined by a coordinating conjunction contain commas, you may use a semicolon instead of a comma before the conjunction to make the sentence easier to read.

▶ **Every year, whether the Republican or the Democratic party is in office, more and more power drains away from the individual to feed vast reservoirs in far-off places; and we have less and less say about the shape of events which shape our future.**

—William F. Buckley Jr., "Why Don't We Complain?"

A semicolon should link independent clauses joined by a conjunctive adverb such as *however* or *therefore* or a transition such as *as a result* or *for example*.

▶ **The circus comes as close to being the world in microcosm as anything I know; in a way, it puts all the rest of show business in the shade.** —E. B. White, "The Ring of Time"

EXERCISE 36.1

Combine each of the following pairs of sentences into one sentence by using a semicolon. Example:

Take the bus to Henderson Street; ~~Meet~~ meet me under the clock.

1. Abalone fishing in California is strictly regulated. A person is allowed to harvest only twenty-four of these large mollusks per year.

2. City life offers many advantages. In many ways, however, life in a small town is much more pleasant.

3. The door contains an inflatable slide that can be used in an emergency. In addition, each of the seats can become a flotation device.

4. Most car accidents occur within twenty-five miles of the home. Therefore, you should wear a seat belt on every trip.

5. Involvement in team sports provides more than just health benefits for young girls. It also increases their self-confidence.

36b Separate items in a series containing other punctuation.

Ordinarily, commas separate items in a series (35d). But when the items themselves contain commas or other punctuation, semicolons make the sentence clearer.

▸ Anthropology encompasses archaeology, the study of ancient civilizations through artifacts,**;** linguistics, the study of the structure and development of language,**;** and cultural anthropology, the study of language, customs, and behavior.

36c Avoid misused semicolons.

Use a comma, not a semicolon, to separate an independent clause from a dependent clause or phrase.

▸ The police found fingerprints**;,** which they used to identify the thief.

▸ The new system would encourage students to register for courses online**;,** thus streamlining registration.

Use a colon, not a semicolon, to introduce a series or list.

▸ The reunion tour includes the following bands**;:** Urban Waste, Murphy's Law, Rapid Deployment, and Ism.

EXERCISE 36.2

Revise the following passage, eliminating any misused or overused semicolons and, if necessary, replacing them with different punctuation.

> Hosting your first dinner party can be very stressful; but careful planning and preparation can make it a success. The guest list must contain the right mix of people; everyone should feel comfortable; good talkers and good listeners are both important; while they don't need to agree on everything, you don't want them to have fistfights, either. Then you need to plan the menu; which should steer clear of problem areas; for vegans; no pork chops; for guests with shellfish allergies, no lobster; for teetotalers; no tequila. In addition; make sure your home is clean and neat, and check that you have enough chairs; dishes; glasses; napkins; and silverware. Leave enough time to socialize with your guests; and save a little energy to clean up when it's over!

EXERCISE 36.3: THINKING CRITICALLY

Thinking about Your Own Use of Semicolons

Think of something that you might take five or ten minutes to observe—a football game, a brewing storm, an argument between friends—and then write a paragraph describing your observations point by point and using semicolons to separate each point. Then, look at the way you used semicolons. Are there places where a period or a comma and a coordinating conjunction would better serve your meaning? Revise appropriately. What can you conclude about effective ways of using semicolons?

37 End Punctuation

Periods, question marks, and exclamation points often appear in advertising to create special effects:

> You have a choice to make.
> Where can you turn for advice?
> Ask our experts today!

End punctuation tells us how to read each sentence—as a matter-of-fact statement, a question for the reader, or an enthusiastic exclamation.

37a Use periods.

Use a period to close sentences that make statements or give mild commands.

▶ **All books are either dreams or swords.** —Amy Lowell

▶ **Don't use a fancy word if a simpler word will do.**

—George Orwell, "Politics and the English Language"

A period also closes indirect questions, which report rather than ask questions.

▶ **I asked how old the child was.**

In American English, periods are used with most abbreviations. However, more and more abbreviations are appearing without periods.

Mr.	MD	BCE *or* B.C.E.
Ms.	PhD	AD *or* A.D.
Sen.	Jr.	PM *or* p.m.

Some abbreviations rarely if ever appear with periods. These include the postal abbreviations of state names, such as *FL* and *TN*, and most groups of initials (*GE, CIA, AIDS, YMCA, UNICEF*). If you are not sure whether a particular abbreviation should include periods, check a dictionary or follow the style guidelines you are using for a research paper. (For more about abbreviations, see Chapter 42.)

Do not use an additional period when a sentence ends with an abbreviation that has its own period.

▶ **The social worker referred me to John Pintz Jr./**

37b Use question marks.

Use question marks to close sentences that ask direct questions.

▶ **How is the human mind like a computer, and how is it different?**

—Kathleen Stassen Berger and Ross A. Thompson,
The Developing Person through Childhood and Adolescence

Question marks do not close indirect questions, which report rather than ask questions.

▶ She asked whether I opposed his nomination?.
                                              ∧

37c   Use exclamation points.

Use an exclamation point to show surprise or strong emotion. Use these marks sparingly because they can distract your readers or suggest that you are exaggerating.

▶ **In those few moments of geologic time will be the story of all that has happened since we became a nation. And what a story it will be!**   —James Rettie, "But a Watch in the Night"

EXERCISE 37.1

Revise each of the following sentences, adding appropriate punctuation and deleting any unnecessary punctuation you find. Example:

She asked the travel agent, "What is the air fare to Greece?"/

1. Social scientists face difficult questions: should they use their knowledge to shape society, merely describe human behavior, or try to do both.

2. The court denied a New Jersey woman's petition to continue raising tigers in her backyard!

3. I screamed at Jamie, "You rat. You tricked me."

4. The reporter wondered whether anything more could have been done to save lives?

5. Zane called every store within fifty miles and asked if they had the Wii game he wanted

6. "Have you seen the new George Clooney film?," Mia asked.

EXERCISE 37.2: THINKING CRITICALLY

Thinking about Your Own Use of End Punctuation

Look through something you have written recently, noting its end punctuation. Using the guidelines in this chapter, see if your use of end punctuation follows any patterns. Then, try revising the end punctuation in a paragraph or two in order to emphasize (or de-emphasize) some point. What conclusions can you draw about ways of using end punctuation to draw attention to (or away from) a sentence?

38 Apostrophes

The little apostrophe can make a big difference in meaning. The following sign at a neighborhood swimming pool, for instance, says something different from what the writer probably intended:

> Please deposit your garbage (and your guests) in the trash receptacles before leaving the pool area.

The sign indicates that guests, not their garbage, should be deposited in trash receptacles. Adding a single apostrophe would offer a more neighborly statement: *Please deposit your garbage (and your guests') in the trash receptacles before leaving the pool area.*

38a Signal possessive case.

The possessive case denotes ownership or possession. Add an apostrophe and *-s* to form the possessive of most singular nouns, including those that end in *-s*, and of indefinite pronouns (24d). The possessive forms of personal pronouns do not take apostrophes: *mine, yours, his, hers, its, ours, theirs.*

▶ The **bus's** fumes overpowered her.
▶ George **Lucas's** movies have been wildly popular.
▶ **Anyone's** guess is as good as mine.

Plural nouns. To form the possessive case of plural nouns not ending in *-s*, add an apostrophe and *-s*. For plural nouns ending in *-s*, add only the apostrophe.

▶ The **men's** department sells business attire.
▶ The **clowns'** costumes were bright green and orange.

Compound nouns. For compound nouns, make the last word in the group possessive.

▶ Both her **daughters-in-law's** birthdays fall in July.

bedfordstmartins.com/wia
LearningCurve > Apostrophes

Two or more nouns.   To signal individual possession by two or more owners, make each noun possessive.

▶ **Great differences exist between Jerry Bruckheimer's and Ridley Scott's films.**

Bruckheimer and Scott produce different films.

To signal joint possession, make only the last noun possessive.

▶ **Wallace and Gromit's creator is Nick Park.**

Wallace and Gromit have the same creator.

EXERCISE 38.1

Complete each of the following sentences by inserting 's or an apostrophe alone to form the possessive case for the italicized words. Example:

A.J. older *brother* name is Griffin.

1. Grammar is not *everybody* favorite subject.
2. An *ibis* wingspan is about half as long as a *flamingo*.
3. *Charles and Camilla* first visit to the United States as a married couple included a stop at the White House.
4. The long debate over *states* rights culminated in the Civil War.
5. *Kobe Bryant and Tiger Woods* personal crises have threatened to overshadow their athletic careers.
6. She insists that her personal life is *nobody* business.
7. Parents often question *their children* choice of friends.
8. This dog has a *beagle* ears and a *St. Bernard* face.
9. All of the sidewalk smokers disregarded the *surgeon generals* warnings.
10. *Anna and Tobias* income dropped dramatically after Anna lost her job.

38b   Signal contractions.

Contractions are two-word combinations formed by leaving out certain letters, which are replaced by an apostrophe (*it is, it has/it's; will not/won't*).

Contractions are common in conversation and informal writing. Academic and professional work, however, often calls for greater formality.

Distinguishing *its* and *it's*.   *Its* is a possessive pronoun—the possessive form of *it*. *It's* is a contraction for *it is* or *it has*.

▶ This disease is unusual; its symptoms vary from person to person.

▶ It's a difficult disease to diagnose.

38c   Understand apostrophes and plural forms.

Many style guides now advise against using apostrophes for any plurals.

▶ The gymnasts need marks of 8s and 9s to qualify for the finals.

Other guidelines call for an apostrophe and *-s* to form the plural of numbers, letters, and words referred to as terms. Check your instructor's preference.

EXERCISE 38.2

The following sentences, from which all apostrophes have been deleted, appear in Langston Hughes's "Salvation." Insert apostrophes where appropriate. Example:

"Sister Reed, what is this child's name?"
                                        ^

1. There was a big revival at my Auntie Reeds church.
2. I heard the songs and then the minister saying: "Why dont you come?"
3. Finally Westley said to me in a whisper: . . . "Im tired o sitting here. Lets get up and be saved."
4. So I decided that maybe to save further trouble, Id better lie. . . .
5. That night . . . I cried, in bed alone, and couldnt stop.

EXERCISE 38.3: THINKING CRITICALLY

Write a brief paragraph, beginning "I've always been amused by my neighbor's (or roommate's) _____." Then note every use of an apostrophe. Use the guidelines in this chapter to check that you have used apostrophes correctly.

39   Quotation Marks

"Hilarious!" "A great family movie!" "A must see!" The quotation marks are a key component of statements like these from movie ads; they make the praise more believable by indicating that it comes from people other than the movie promoter. Quotation marks identify a speaker's exact words or the titles of short works.

39a   Signal direct quotation.

▶ The crowd chanted "Yes, we can" as they waited for the speech to begin.

▶ She smiled and said, "Son, this is one incident that I will never forget."

Use quotation marks to enclose the words of each speaker within running dialogue. Mark each shift in speaker with a new paragraph.

> "I want no proof of their affection," said Elinor; "but of their engagement I do."
> "I am perfectly satisfied of both."
> "Yet not a syllable has been said to you on the subject, by either of them."   —Jane Austen, *Sense and Sensibility*

Single quotation marks.   Single quotation marks enclose a quotation within a quotation. Open and close the quoted passage with double quotation marks, and change any quotation marks that appear *within* the quotation to single quotation marks.

▶ Baldwin says, "The title 'The Uses of the Blues' does not refer to music; I don't know anything about music."

Long quotations.   To quote a passage that is more than four typed lines, set the quotation off by starting it on a new line and indenting it one inch from the left margin. This format, known as block quotation, does not require quotation marks.

In "Suspended," Joy Harjo tells of her first awareness of jazz as a child:

> My rite of passage into the world of humanity occurred then,
> via jazz. The music made a startling bridge between the
> familiar and strange lands, an appropriate vehicle, for . . . we
> were there when jazz was born. I recognized it, that humid
> afternoon in my formative years, as a way to speak beyond
> the confines of ordinary language. I still hear it. (84)

This block quotation, including the ellipsis dots and the page number in parentheses at the end, follows the style of the Modern Language Association (MLA). The American Psychological Association (APA) has different guidelines for setting off block quotations. (See Chapters 49 and 50.)

Poetry.   When quoting poetry, if the quotation is brief (fewer than four lines), include it within your text. Separate the lines of the poem with slashes, each preceded and followed by a space, in order to tell the reader where one line of the poem ends and the next begins.

> In one of his best-known poems, Robert Frost remarks, "Two roads
> diverged in a yellow wood, and I — / I took the one less traveled by /
> And that has made all the difference."

To quote more than three lines of poetry, indent the block one inch from the left margin. Do not use quotation marks. Take care to follow the spacing, capitalization, punctuation, and other features of the original poem.

> The duke in Robert Browning's poem "My Last Duchess" is clearly
> a jealous, vain person, whose arrogance is illustrated through this
> statement:
>
> > She thanked men — good! but thanked
> > Somehow — I know not how — as if she ranked
> > My gift of a nine-hundred-years-old name
> > With anybody's gift. (lines 31–34)

39b   Identify titles of short works and definitions.

Use quotation marks to enclose the titles of short poems, short stories, articles, essays, songs, sections of books, and episodes of television and radio programs. Quotation marks also enclose definitions.

▶ The essay "Big and Bad" analyzes some reasons for the popularity of SUVs.

▶ In social science, the term *sample size* means "the number of individuals being studied in a research project."

—Kathleen Stassen Berger and Ross A. Thompson,
The Developing Person through Childhood and Adolescence

39c   Use quotation marks with other punctuation.

Periods and commas go *inside* closing quotation marks.

▶ "Don't compromise yourself," said Janis Joplin. "You are all you've got."

Colons, semicolons, and footnote numbers go *outside* closing quotation marks.

▶ I felt one emotion after finishing "Eveline": sorrow.

▶ Tragedy is defined by Aristotle as "an imitation of an action that is serious and of a certain magnitude."[1]

Question marks, exclamation points, and dashes go *inside* if they are part of the quoted material, *outside* if they are not.

FOR MULTILINGUAL WRITERS

Quoting in American English

Remember that the way you mark quotations in American English (" ") may not be the same as in other languages. In French, for example, quotations are marked with *guillemets* (« »), while in German, quotations take split-level marks (‚‚ "). American English and British English offer opposite conventions for double and single quotation marks. If you are writing for an American audience, be careful to follow the U.S. conventions governing quotation marks.

PART OF THE QUOTATION

► The cashier asked, "Would you like to supersize that?"

NOT PART OF THE QUOTATION

► What is the theme of "The Birth-Mark"?

39d Avoid misused quotation marks.

Do not use quotation marks for indirect quotations—those that do not use someone's exact words.

► Mother smiled and said that ⁄"she was sure she would

never forget the incident."⁄

Do not use quotation marks just to add emphasis to particular words or phrases.

► The hikers were startled by the appearance of a ⁄"gigantic"⁄

grizzly bear.

Do not use quotation marks around slang or colloquial language; they create the impression that you are apologizing for using those words. If you have a good reason to use slang or a colloquial term, use it without quotation marks.

► After our twenty-mile hike, we were completely exhausted and

ready to ⁄"turn in."⁄

EXERCISE 39.1: THINKING CRITICALLY

Thinking about Your Own Use of Quotation Marks

Choose a topic that is of interest on your campus, and interview one of your friends about it. On the basis of your notes from the interview, write two or three paragraphs about your friend's views, using several direct quotations that support the points you are making. Then see how closely you followed the conventions for quotation marks explained in this chapter. Note any usages that caused you problems.

40   Other Punctuation

Parentheses, brackets, dashes, colons, slashes, and ellipses are everywhere. Every URL includes colons and slashes, many sites use brackets or parentheses to identify updates and embedded media, and dashes and ellipses are increasingly common in writing that expresses conversational informality.

You can also use these punctuation marks for more formal purposes: to signal relationships among parts of sentences, to create particular rhythms, and to help readers follow your thoughts.

40a   Use parentheses.

Use parentheses to enclose material that is of minor or secondary importance in a sentence—material that supplements, clarifies, comments on, or illustrates what precedes or follows it.

▶ Inventors and men of genius have almost always been regarded as fools at the beginning (and very often at the end) of their careers.
—Fyodor Dostoyevsky

▶ During my research, I found problems with the flat-rate income tax (a single-rate tax with no deductions).

Parentheses are also used to enclose textual citations and numbers or letters in a list.

▶ Freud and his followers have had a most significant impact on the ways abnormal functioning is understood and treated (Joseph, 1991).
—Ronald J. Comer, *Abnormal Psychology*

The in-text citation in this sentence shows the style of the American Psychological Association (APA). (See Chapter 50 for more on APA style.)

▶ Five distinct styles can be distinguished: (1) Old New England, (2) Deep South, (3) Middle American, (4) Wild West, and (5) Far West or Californian.

—Alison Lurie, *The Language of Clothes*

With other punctuation.   A period may be placed either inside or outside a closing parenthesis, depending on whether the parenthetical text is part of a larger sentence. A comma, if needed, is always placed *outside* a closing parenthesis (and never before an opening one).

▶ Gene Tunney's single defeat in an eleven-year career was to a flamboyant and dangerous fighter named Harry Greb ("The Human Windmill"), who seems to have been, judging from boxing literature, the dirtiest fighter in history.

— Joyce Carol Oates, "On Boxing"

40b Use brackets.

Use brackets to enclose any parenthetical elements in material that is itself within parentheses. Also use brackets to enclose explanatory words or comments that you are inserting into a quotation.

▶ Eventually, the investigation had to examine the major agencies (including the National Security Agency [NSA]) that were conducting covert operations.

▶ Massing notes that "on average, it [Fox News] attracts more than eight million people daily — more than double the number who watch CNN."

The bracketed words clarify *it* in the original quotation.

In the quotation in the following sentence, the artist Gauguin's name is misspelled. The bracketed word *sic*, which means "so," tells readers that the person being quoted — not the writer who has picked up the quotation — made the mistake, in this case misspelling Gauguin's name.

▶ One admirer wrote, "She was the most striking woman I'd ever seen — a sort of wonderful combination of Mia Farrow and one of Gaugin's [*sic*] Polynesian nymphs."

EXERCISE 40.1

Revise the following sentences, using parentheses and brackets correctly. Example:

She was in fourth grade (or was it third?) when she became
^   ^
blind.

1. The committee was presented with three options to pay for the new park: 1 increase vehicle registration fees, 2 install parking meters downtown, or 3 borrow money from the reserve fund.

2. The FISA statute authorizes government wiretapping only under certain circumstances for instance, the government has to obtain a warrant.

3. The health care expert informed readers that "as we progress through middle age, we experience intimations of our own morality *sic*."

4. Some hospitals train nurses in a pseudoscientific technique called therapeutic touch TT, which has been discredited by many rigorous studies.

5. Because I was carrying an umbrella, which, as it turned out, wasn't even necessary, I was required to enter the stadium through the high-security gate.

40c Use dashes.

Use dashes to insert a comment or to highlight material within a sentence.

▶ The pleasures of reading itself—who doesn't remember?—were like those of Christmas cake, a sweet devouring.

—Eudora Welty, "A Sweet Devouring"

A single dash can be used to emphasize material at the end of a sentence, to mark a sudden change in tone, to indicate hesitation in speech, or to introduce a summary or an explanation.

▶ In the twentieth century it has become almost impossible to moralize about epidemics—except those which are transmitted sexually.   —Susan Sontag, *AIDS and Its Metaphors*

▶ In walking, the average adult person employs a motor mechanism that weighs about eighty pounds—sixty pounds of muscle and twenty pounds of bone.   —Edwin Way Teale

Dashes give more emphasis than parentheses to the material they enclose or set off. Many word-processing programs automatically convert two typed hyphens with no spaces before or after into a solid dash.

EXERCISE 40.2

Punctuate the following sentences with dashes where appropriate. Example:

He is quick, violent, and mean — they don't call him Dirty Harry for nothing — but appealing nonetheless.

1. Most people would say that Labradors are easy dogs to train but they never met our Millie.
2. Even if marijuana is dangerous an assertion disputed by many studies it is certainly no more harmful to human health than alcohol and cigarettes, which remain legal.
3. If too much exposure to negative news stories makes you feel depressed or anxious and why wouldn't it? try going on a media fast.
4. Union Carbide's plant in Bhopal, India, sprang a leak that killed more than 2,000 people and injured an additional 200,000.
5. Refrigerators especially side-by-side models use up a lot more energy than most people realize.

40d Use colons.

Use a colon to introduce an explanation, an example, an appositive, a series, a list, or a quotation.

▶ At the baby's one-month birthday party, Ah Po gave him the Four Valuable Things: ink, inkslab, paper, and brush.
—Maxine Hong Kingston, *China Men*

Use a colon rather than a comma to introduce a quotation when the lead-in is a complete sentence on its own.

▶ The 2013 State of the Union address ended with a bold challenge: "Well into our third century as a nation, it remains the task of us all . . . to be the authors of the next great chapter in our American story."

Colons are also used after salutations in formal letters; with numbers indicating hours, minutes, and seconds; with ratios; with biblical chapters and verses; with titles and subtitles; and in bibliographic entries.

▶ Dear Dr. Ito:
▶ 4:59 PM
▶ a ratio of 5:1
▶ Ecclesiastes 3:1
▶ *The Joy of Insight: Passions of a Physicist*
▶ Boston: Bedford/St. Martin's, 2013

Misused colons. Do not put a colon between a verb and its object or complement (unless the object is a quotation), between a preposition and its object, or after such expressions as *such as*, *especially*, and *including*.

▶ Some natural fibers are⫽ cotton, wool, silk, and linen.

▶ In poetry, additional power may come from devices such as⫽

  simile, metaphor, and alliteration.

EXERCISE 40.3

In the following items, insert a colon in any sentence that needs one, and delete any unnecessary colons. Some sentences may be correct as written. Example:

Images⫽ My Life in Film includes revealing material written by
　　　　＾
Ingmar Bergman.

1. After discussing the case study, the class reached one main conclusion for any business, the most important asset is the customer.

2. Another example is taken from Psalm 139 16.

3. Roberto tried to make healthier choices, such as: eating organic food, walking to work, and getting plenty of rest.

4. A number of quotable movie lines come from *Casablanca*, including "Round up the usual suspects."

5. Sofi rushed to catch the 5 45 express but had to wait for the 6 19.

40e   Use slashes.

Use a slash to separate alternatives.

▶ Then there was Daryl, the cabdriver/bartender.
　　　　　　　　　　—John L'Heureux, *The Handmaid of Desire*

Use a slash, preceded and followed by a space, to divide lines of poetry quoted within running text.

▶ The speaker of Sonnet 130 says of his mistress, "I love to hear her speak, yet well I know / That music hath a far more pleasing sound."

Slashes also separate parts of fractions and Internet addresses.

40f Use ellipses.

Ellipses, or ellipsis points, are three equally spaced dots. Ellipses usually indicate that something has been omitted from a quoted passage. Just as you should carefully use quotation marks around any material that you quote directly from a source, so you should carefully use ellipses to indicate that you have left out some part of a quotation that otherwise appears to be a complete sentence. Ellipses have been used in the following example to indicate two omissions—one in the middle of the sentence and one at the end of the sentence.

ORIGINAL TEXT

▶ The quasi-official division of the population into three economic classes called high-, middle-, and low-income groups rather misses the point, because as a class indicator the amount of money is not as important as the source.

—Paul Fussell, "Notes on Class"

WITH ELLIPSES

▶ As Paul Fussell argues, "The quasi-official division of the population into three economic classes . . . rather misses the point. . . ."

When you omit the last part of a quoted sentence, add a period before the ellipses—for a total of four dots. Be sure a complete sentence comes before the four dots. If your shortened quotation ends with a source citation (such as a page number, a name, or a title), place the documentation source in parentheses after the three ellipsis points and the closing quotation mark but before the period.

▶ Packer argues, "The Administration is right to reconsider its strategy . . . " (34).

You can also use ellipses to indicate a pause or a hesitation in speech in the same way that you can use a dash for that purpose.

▶ Then the voice, husky and familiar, came to wash over us— "The winnah, and still heavyweight champeen of the world . . . Joe Louis."

—Maya Angelou, *I Know Why the Caged Bird Sings*

EXERCISE 40.4

The following sentences use the punctuation marks presented in this chapter very effectively. Read the sentences carefully; then choose one, and use it as a model for writing a sentence of your own, making sure to use the punctuation marks in the same way in your sentence.

1. The dad was—how can you put this gracefully?—a real blimp, a wide load, and the white polyester stretch-pants only emphasized the cargo. —Garrison Keillor, "Happy to Be Here"

2. Not only are the distinctions we draw between male nature and female nature largely arbitrary and often pure superstition: they are completely beside the point.
   —Brigid Brophy, "Women"

3. If no one, including you, liked the soup the first time round (and that's why you've got so much left over), there is no point in freezing it for some hopeful future date when, miraculously, it will taste delicious. But bagging leftovers—say, stews—in single portions can be useful for those evenings when you're eating alone. —Nigella Lawson, *How to Eat*

EXERCISE 40.5: THINKING CRITICALLY

Thinking about Your Own Use of Punctuation

Look through a draft you have recently written or are working on, and then check your use of parentheses, brackets, dashes, colons, slashes, and ellipses. Do you follow the conventions presented in this chapter? If not, revise accordingly. Check the material in parentheses to see if it could use more emphasis and thus be set off instead with dashes. Then check any material in dashes to see if it could do with less emphasis and thus be punctuated with commas or parentheses.

41 Capital Letters

Capital letters are a key signal in everyday life. Look around any store to see their importance: you can shop for Levi's or *any* blue jeans, for Pepsi or *any* cola, for Kleenex or *any* tissue. In each of these instances, the capital letter indicates the name of a particular brand.

bedfordstmartins.com/wia
LearningCurve > Capitalization

41a Capitalize the first word of a sentence.

With very few exceptions, capitalize the first word of a sentence. If you are quoting a full sentence, capitalize its first word.

▶ **Kennedy said, "Let us never negotiate out of fear."**

Capitalization of a nonquoted sentence following a colon is optional.

▶ **Gould cites the work of Darwin: The [*or* the] theory of natural selection incorporates the principle of evolutionary ties among all animals.**

Capitalize a sentence within parentheses unless the parenthetical sentence is inserted into another sentence.

▶ **Gould cites the work of Darwin. (Other researchers cite more recent evolutionary theorists.)**
▶ **Gould cites the work of Darwin (see p. 150).**

When citing poetry, follow the capitalization of the original poem. Though most poets capitalize the first word of each line in a poem, some do not.

▶ **Morning sun heats up the young beech tree**
  leaves and almost lights them into fireflies
                                             —June Jordan, "Aftermath"

41b Capitalize proper nouns and proper adjectives.

Capitalize proper nouns (those naming specific persons, places, and things) and most adjectives formed from proper nouns. All other nouns are common nouns and are not capitalized unless they are used as part of a proper noun: *a street*, but *Elm Street*.

Capitalized nouns and adjectives include personal names; nations, nationalities, and languages; months, days of the week, and holidays (but not seasons of the year); geographical names; structures and monuments; ships, trains, aircraft, and spacecraft; organizations, businesses, and government institutions; academic institutions and courses; historical events and eras; and religions, their deities, followers, and sacred writings. For trade names, follow the capitalization you see in company advertising or on the product itself.

PROPER	COMMON
Alfred Hitchcock, Hitchcockian	a director
Brazil, Brazilian	a nation, a language
Pacific Ocean	an ocean
Challenger	a spaceship
Library of Congress	a federal agency
Political Science 102	a political science course
the Qur'an	a holy book
Catholicism, Catholics	a religion
Cheerios, iPhone	cereal, a smartphone
Halloween	a holiday in the fall

41c   Capitalize titles before proper names.

When used alone or following a proper name, most titles are not capitalized. One common exception is the word *president*, which many writers capitalize whenever it refers to the President of the United States.

Professor Django Paris	my history professor
Dr. Teresa Ramirez	Teresa Ramirez, our doctor

41d   Capitalize titles of works.

Capitalize most words in titles of books, articles, speeches, stories, essays, plays, poems, documents, films, paintings, and musical compositions. Do not capitalize articles (*a*, *an*, *the*), prepositions, conjunctions, and the *to* in an infinitive, unless they are the first or last words in a title or subtitle.

FOR MULTILINGUAL WRITERS

Learning English Capitalization

Capitalization systems vary considerably. Arabic, Chinese, Hebrew, and Hindi, for example, do not use capital letters at all. English may be the only language to capitalize the first-person singular pronoun (*I*), but Dutch and German capitalize some forms of the second-person pronoun (*you*)—and German also capitalizes all nouns.

Walt Whitman: A Life   Declaration of Independence
"As Time Goes By"   *The Producers*
"Crazy in Love"   *The Living Dead*

41e   Revise unnecessary capitalization.

Capitalize compass directions only if the word designates a specific geographical region.

▶ John Muir headed west, motivated by the desire to explore.

▶ Water rights are an increasingly contentious issue in the West.

Capitalize family relationships only if the word is used as part of a name or as a substitute for the name.

▶ When she was a child, my mother shared a room with my aunt.

▶ I could always tell when Mother was annoyed with Aunt Rose.

EXERCISE 41.1

Capitalize words as needed in the following sentences. Example:

> T. S. Eliot,   *The Waste Land,*   Faber
> t.s. eliot, who wrote *the waste land,* was an editor at faber and
> ^   ^   ^
>
> Faber.
> faber.
> ^

1. the town in the south where i was raised had a statue of a civil war soldier in the center of main street.

2. sarah palin, the former governor, frequently complained that the press had treated her harshly before she accepted a position as an analyst for fox news.

3. the corporation for public broadcasting relies on donations as well as on grants from the national endowment for the arts.

4. during the economic recession, companies such as starbucks had to close some of their stores; others, such as circuit city, went completely out of business.

5. most americans remember where they were when they heard about the 9/11 disaster.

6. accepting an award for his score for the john wayne film *the high and the mighty*, dimitri tiomkin thanked beethoven, brahms, wagner, and strauss.

EXERCISE 41.2

Correct any unnecessary or missing capitalization in the following sentences. Some sentences may be correct as written. Example:

> *southern governors*
> A group of ~~Southern Governors~~ meets annually in
> ^
>
> Washington,
> ~~washington,~~ DC.
> ^

1. The Newtown, Connecticut, School Shootings in 2012 prompted a debate about Gun Control Laws in the United States.

2. Every Professor in the department of english has a degree in literature.

3. The Cast included several children, but only two of them had Speaking Roles.

4. Airport checkpoints are the responsibility of the Transportation Security Administration.

5. The price of oil has fluctuated this Winter.

EXERCISE 41.3: THINKING CRITICALLY

The following poem uses unconventional capitalization. Read it over a few times, at least once aloud. What effect does the capitalization have? Why do you think the poet chose to use capitals as she did?

> A little Madness in the Spring
> Is wholesome even for the King,
> But God be with the Clown—
> Who ponders this tremendous scene—
> This whole Experiment of Green—
> As if it were his own!
>
> —Emily Dickinson

42 Abbreviations and Numbers

Anytime you look up an address, you see an abundance of abbreviations and numbers, as in the following listing from a Google map:

Tarrytown Music Hall   13 Main St   Tarrytown, NY

Abbreviations and numbers allow writers to present detailed information in a small amount of space.

42a Use abbreviations.

Certain titles are normally abbreviated.

Ms. Susanna Moller	Henry Louis Gates Jr.
Mr. Mark Otuteye	Cheryl Gold, MD

Religious, academic, and government titles should be spelled out in academic writing but can be abbreviated in other writing when they appear before a full name.

Rev. Fleming Rutledge	Reverend Rutledge
Prof. Jaime Mejía	Professor Mejía
Sen. Barbara Boxer	Senator Boxer

Business, government, and science terms. As long as you can be sure that your readers will understand them, use common abbreviations, such as *PBS*, *NASA*, and *DNA*. If an abbreviation may be unfamiliar, spell out the full term the first time you use it, and give the abbreviation in parentheses; after that, you can use the abbreviation by itself. Use abbreviations such as *Co.*, *Inc.*, *Corp.*, and *&* only if they are part of a company's official name.

▶ The Comprehensive Test Ban (CTB) Treaty was first proposed in the 1950s. For those nations signing it, the CTB would bring to a halt all nuclear weapons testing.

▶ Sears, Roebuck & Co. was the only large ~~corp.~~ *corporation* in town.

With numbers. The following abbreviations are all acceptable with specific years and times.

399 BCE ("before the common era") *or* 399 BC ("before Christ")
49 CE ("common era") *or* AD 49 (*anno Domini*, Latin for "year of our Lord")
11:15 AM (*or* a.m.)
9:00 PM (*or* p.m.)

Symbols such as % and $ are acceptable with figures (*$11*) but not with words (*eleven dollars*). Units of measurement can be abbreviated in charts and graphs (*4 in.*) but not in the body of a paper (*four inches*).

In notes and source citations. Some Latin abbreviations required in notes and in source citations are not appropriate in the body of a paper.

cf.	compare (*confer*)
e.g.	for example (*exempli gratia*)
et al.	and others (*et alia*)
etc.	and so forth (*et cetera*)
i.e.	that is (*id est*)
N.B.	note well (*nota bene*)

In addition, except in notes and source citations, do not abbreviate such terms as *chapter*, *page*, and *volume* or the names of months, states, cities, or countries. Two exceptions are *Washington, D.C.*, and *U.S.* The latter abbreviation is acceptable as an adjective but not as a noun: *U.S. borders* but *in the United States*.

EXERCISE 42.1

Revise each of the following sentences to eliminate any abbreviations that would be inappropriate within most academic writing. Example:

United States

The population of the U̶.̶S̶.̶ grew considerably in the 1980s.

1. Every Fri., my grandmother would walk a mi. to the P.O. and send a care package to her brother in Tenn.

2. The blue whale can grow to be 180 ft. long and can weigh up to 380,000 lbs.

3. Many a Mich.-based auto co., incl. GM, requested financial aid from the govt.

4. A large corp. like AT&T may help finance an employee's MBA.

5. Rosie began by saying, "If you want my two ¢," but she did not wait to see if listeners wanted it or not.

42b   Use numbers.

If you can write out a number in one or two words, do so. Use figures for longer numbers.

> thirty-eight
> ► Her screams were ignored by 3̶8̶ people.

> 216
> ► A baseball is held together by t̶w̶o̶ ̶h̶u̶n̶d̶r̶e̶d̶ ̶s̶i̶x̶t̶e̶e̶n̶ red stitches.

If one of several numbers *of the same kind* in the same sentence requires a figure, you should use figures for all the numbers in that sentence.

▶ An audio system can range in cost from ~~one hundred dollars~~ $100 to $2,599.

When a sentence begins with a number, either spell out the number or rewrite the sentence.

▶ 119 years of CIA labor. ~~cost taxpayers sixteen million dollars.~~
Taxpayers spent sixteen million dollars for

In general, use figures for the following:

ADDRESSES	23 Main Street; 175 Fifth Avenue
DATES	September 17, 1951; 6 June 1983; 4 BCE; the 1860s
DECIMALS AND FRACTIONS	65.34; 8½
EXACT AMOUNTS OF MONEY	$7,348; $1.46 trillion; $2.50; thirty-five (*or* 35) cents
PERCENTAGES	77 percent (*or* 77%)
SCORES AND STATISTICS	an 8–3 Red Sox victory; an average age of 22
TIME OF DAY	6:00 AM (*or* a.m.)

EXERCISE 42.2

Revise the numbers in the following sentences as necessary for correctness and consistency. Some sentences may be correct as written. Example:

Did the ~~21st~~ twenty-first century begin in 2000 or 2001?

1. In the 2000 election, Al Gore carried the popular vote with 50,996,116 votes, but he was still short by 5 electoral votes.
2. 200,000 people perished in the 2010 Haitian earthquake.
3. The senator who voted against the measure received 6817 angry emails and only twelve in support of her decision.
4. Walker signed a three-year, $4.5-million contract.
5. In that age group, the risk is estimated to be about one in 2,500.

EXERCISE 42.3: THINKING CRITICALLY

Thinking about Your Own Use of Abbreviations and Numbers

Look over an essay that you have written, noting all abbreviations and numbers. Check your usage for correctness, consistency, and appropriateness. If you discover a problem with abbreviations or numbers, make a note of it so that you can avoid the error in the future.

43   Italics

The slanted type known as *italics* is more than just a pretty type-face. Indeed, italics give words special meaning or emphasis. In the sentence "Many people read *People* on the subway every day," the italics (and the capital letter) tell us that *People* is a publication. You may use your computer to produce italic type; if not, under-line words that you would otherwise italicize.

43a   Italicize titles.

In general, use italics for titles and subtitles of long works; use quotation marks for shorter works (39b).

BOOKS	*Vietnamerica*
CHOREOGRAPHIC WORKS	Agnes de Mille's *Rodeo*
FILMS AND VIDEOS	*Star Wars*
LONG MUSICAL WORKS	*Brandenburg Concertos*
LONG POEMS	*Bhagavad Gita*
MAGAZINES AND JOURNALS	*Ebony*; the *New England Journal of Medicine*
NEWSPAPERS	the Cleveland *Plain Dealer*
PAINTINGS AND SCULPTURE	Georgia O'Keeffe's *Black Iris*
PAMPHLETS	Thomas Paine's *Common Sense*
PLAYS	*Les Misérables*
RADIO SERIES	*All Things Considered*
RECORDINGS	The Ramones' *Leave Home*
SOFTWARE	*Quicken*

TELEVISION SERIES	*Breaking Bad*
WEB SITES	*Salon*

Do not italicize titles of sacred books, such as the Bible and the Qur'an; public documents, such as the Constitution and the Magna Carta; or your own papers.

43b Italicize words, letters, and numbers used as terms.

▶ On the back of his jersey was the famous *24*.

▶ One characteristic of some New York speech is the absence of postvocalic *r* — for example, pronouncing the word *four* as "fouh."

43c Italicize non-English words.

Italicize words from other languages unless they have become part of English — like the French "bourgeois" or the Italian "pasta," for example. If a word is in an English dictionary, it does not need italics.

▶ At last one of the phantom sleighs gliding along the street would come to a stop, and with gawky haste Mr. Burness in his fox-furred *shapka* would make for our door.

— Vladimir Nabokov, *Speak, Memory*

43d Italicize names of aircraft, ships, and trains.

Spirit of St. Louis   Amtrak's *Silver Star*   USS *Iowa*

43e Use italics for emphasis.

Italics can help create emphasis in writing, but use them sparingly for this purpose. It is usually better to create emphasis with sentence structure and word choice.

▶ Great literature and a class of literate readers are nothing new in India. What is new is the emergence of a gifted generation of Indian writers *working in English*.   — Salman Rushdie

EXERCISE 43.1

In each of the following sentences, underline any words that should be italicized, and circle any italicized words that should not be. Example:

> The film <u>Good Night, and Good Luck</u> tells the story of a CBS newsman who helped to end the career of Senator Joseph McCarthy.

1. One critic claimed that few people listened to *The Velvet Underground & Nico* when the record was issued but that everyone who did formed a band.

2. Homemade *sushi* can be dangerous, but so can deviled eggs kept too long in a picnic basket.

3. The Web site Poisonous Plants and Animals includes tobacco (Nicotiana tobacum) in its list of the most popular poisons in the world.

4. The monster in the Old English epic Beowulf got to tell his own side of the story in John Gardner's novel Grendel.

5. The 2009 film Star Trek imagines the youthful life of James T. Kirk and his early years as a starship captain.

EXERCISE 43.2: THINKING CRITICALLY

Thinking about Your Own Use of Italics

Write a paragraph or two describing the most eccentric person you know, italicizing some words for special emphasis. Read your passage aloud to hear the effect of the italics. Now explain each use of italics. If you find yourself unable to give a reason, ask yourself whether the word should be italicized at all.

Then revise the passage to eliminate *all but one* use of italics. Try revising sentences and choosing more precise words to convey emphasis. Decide which version is more effective. Can you reach any conclusions about using italics for emphasis?

44 Hyphens

Hyphens are undoubtedly confusing to many people—hyphen problems are now one of the twenty most common surface errors in student writing (see p. 11). The confusion is understandable. Over time, the conventions for hyphen use in a given word can change (*tomorrow* was once spelled *to-morrow*). New words, even compounds such as *firewall*, generally don't use hyphens, but controversy continues to rage over whether to hyphenate *email* (or is it *e-mail*?). And some words are hyphenated when they serve one kind of purpose in a sentence and not when they serve another.

44a Use hyphens with compound words.

Compound nouns. Some are one word (*rowboat*), some are separate words (*hard drive*), and some require hyphens (*sister-in-law*). You should consult a dictionary to be sure.

Compound adjectives. Hyphenate most compound adjectives that precede a noun, but not those that follow a noun.

a *well-liked* boss	My boss is *well liked.*
a *six-foot* plank	The plank is *six feet long.*

In general, the reason for hyphenating compound adjectives is to make meaning clear.

▶ Designers often use potted plants as living‸room dividers.

Without the hyphen, *living* may seem to modify *room dividers.*

Never hyphenate an *-ly* adverb and an adjective.

▶ They used a widely⁄distributed mailing list.

CHECKLIST

Editing for Hyphens

✔ Double-check compound words to be sure they are properly closed up, separated, or hyphenated. If in doubt, consult a dictionary. (44a)

✔ Check all terms that have prefixes or suffixes to see whether you need hyphens. (44b)

✔ Do not hyphenate two-word verbs or word groups that serve as subject complements. (44c)

Fractions and compound numbers.   Use a hyphen to write out fractions and to spell out compound numbers from twenty-one to ninety-nine.

one-seventh   three hundred fifty-four thousand

44b   Use hyphens with prefixes and suffixes.

Most words containing prefixes or suffixes are written without any hyphens: *antiwar, Romanesque.* Here are some exceptions:

BEFORE CAPITALIZED BASE WORDS	un-American, non-Catholic
WITH FIGURES	pre-1960, post-1945
WITH CERTAIN PREFIXES AND SUFFIXES	all-state, ex-partner, self-possessed, quasi-legislative, mayor-elect, fifty-odd
WITH COMPOUND BASE WORDS	pre-high school, post-cold war
FOR CLARITY OR EASE OF READING	re-cover, anti-inflation, troll-like

Re-cover means "cover again"; the hyphen distinguishes it from *recover,* meaning "get well." In *anti-inflation* and *troll-like,* the hyphens separate confusing clusters of vowels and consonants.

44c   Avoid unnecessary hyphens.

Unnecessary hyphens are at least as common a problem as omitted ones. Do not hyphenate the parts of a two-word verb such as *depend on, turn off,* or *tune out* (48b).

▶ Each player must pick/up a medical form before foot-

   ball tryouts.

The words *pick up* act as a verb and should not be hyphenated.

However, be careful to check that two words do indeed function as a verb in the sentence; if they function as an adjective, a hyphen may be needed.

▶ Let's sign up for the early class.

The verb *sign up* should not have a hyphen.

▶ **Where is the sign-up sheet?**

The adjective *sign-up*, which modifies the noun *sheet*, needs a hyphen.

Do not hyphenate a subject complement—a word group that follows a linking verb (such as a form of *be* or *seem*) and describes the subject.

▶ **Audrey is almost three/years/old.**

EXERCISE 44.1

Insert or delete hyphens as necessary in the following sentences. Use your dictionary if you are not sure whether or where to hyphenate a word. Example:

The governor-elect joked about the polls.
             ^

1. The group seeks volunteers to set-up chairs in the meeting room before the event.

2. Despite concerns about reliability, police line-ups are still frequently used to identify suspects.

3. I was ill-prepared for my first calculus exam, but I managed to pass anyway.

4. Some passengers were bumped from the over-sold flight.

5. Having an ignore the customer attitude may actually make a service-industry job less pleasant.

6. Both pro- and anti-State Department groups registered complaints.

7. At a yard sale, I found a 1964 pre CBS Fender Stratocaster in mint condition.

8. Applicants who are over fifty-years-old may face age discrimination.

9. Neil Armstrong, a selfproclaimed "nerdy engineer," was the first person to set foot on the moon.

10. Carefully-marketed children's safety products suggest to new parents that the more they spend, the safer their kids will be.

9

Multilingual Writers

45 Sentence Structure

Short phrases, or sound bites, are everywhere—from the Dairy Council's "Got Milk?" to Volkswagen's "Drivers Wanted" ad. These short, simple slogans may be memorable, but they don't say very much. In writing, you usually need more complex sentences to convey meaning. English sentences are put together in ways that may differ from sentence patterns you may find in other languages.

45a Use explicit subjects and objects.

English sentences consist of a subject and a predicate. While many languages can omit a sentence subject, English very rarely allows this. Though you might write *Responsible for analyzing data* on a résumé, in most varieties of spoken and written English you must explicitly state the subject.

▶ They took the Acela Express to Boston because ^it^ was fast.

English even requires a kind of "dummy" subject to fill the subject position in certain kinds of sentences.

▶ It is raining.
▶ There is a strong wind.

Transitive verbs typically require that objects—and sometimes other information—also be explicitly stated. For example, it is not enough to tell someone *Give!* even if it is clear what is to be given to whom. You must say, for example, *Give it to me* or *Give her the passport.*

45b Follow English word order.

In general, subjects, verbs, and objects must be placed in specific positions within a sentence.

SUBJECT VERB OBJECT   ADVERB
▶ Mario left Venice reluctantly.

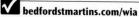 bedfordstmartins.com/wia
LearningCurve > For multilingual writers: Sentence structure

The only word in this sentence that can be moved to different locations is the adverb *reluctantly* (*Mario reluctantly left Venice* or *Reluctantly, Mario left Venice*). The three key elements of subject, verb, and object are moved out of their normal order only to create special effects.

45c   Adapt structures from genres.

If English is not your strongest language, you may find it useful to borrow and adapt transitional devices and pieces of sentence structure from other writing in the genre you are working in. You should not copy the whole structure, however, or your borrowed sentences may seem plagiarized (Chapter 15). Find sample sentence structures from similar genres but on different topics so that you borrow a typical structure (which does not belong to anyone) rather than the idea or the particular phrasing. Write your own sentences first, and then look at other people's sentences only to guide you in your revision.

ABSTRACT FROM A SOCIAL SCIENCE PAPER

Using the interpersonal communications research of J. K. Brilhart and G. J. Galanes, along with T. Hartman's personality assessment, I observed and analyzed the group dynamics of my project collaborators in a communications course. Based on results of the Hartman personality assessment, I predicted that a single leader would emerge. However, complementary individual strengths and gender differences instead encouraged a distributed leadership style.

EFFECTIVE BORROWING OF STRUCTURES

Drawing on the research of Deborah Tannen on conversational styles, I analyzed the conversational styles of six first-year students at DePaul University. Based on Tannen's research, I expected that the three men I observed would use features typical of male conversational style and the three women would use features typical of female conversational style. In general, these predictions were accurate; however, some exceptions were also apparent.

45d Check usage with search engines.

To multilingual writers, search engines such as Google can provide a useful way of checking sentence structure and word usage. For example, if you are not sure whether you should use an infinitive form (*to* + verb) or a gerund (*-ing*) for the verb *confirm* after the main verb *expect* (47b), you can search for both "*expected confirming*" and "*expected to confirm*" to see which search term yields more results. A search for "*expected to confirm*" yields many more hits than a search for "*expected confirming*." These results indicate that *expected to confirm* is the more commonly used expression. Be sure to click through a few pages of the search engine's results to make sure that most results come from ordinary sentences rather than from headlines or phrases that may be constructed differently from standard English.

46 Nouns and Noun Phrases

Everyday life is filled with nouns: orange *juice*, the morning *news*, a *bus* to *work*, *meetings*, *pizza*, *email*, *Diet Coke*, *errands*, *dinner* with *friends*, a *chapter* in a good *book*. No matter what your first language is, it includes nouns. In English, articles (*a* book, *an* email, *the* news) often accompany nouns.

46a Understand count and noncount nouns.

Nouns in English can be either count nouns or noncount nouns. Count nouns refer to distinct individuals or things that can be directly counted: *a doctor, an egg, a child*; *doctors, eggs, children*. Noncount nouns refer to masses, collections, or ideas without distinct parts: *milk, rice, courage*. You cannot count noncount nouns except with a preceding phrase: <u>*a glass of*</u> milk, <u>*three grains of*</u> rice, <u>*a little*</u> courage.

Count nouns usually have singular and plural forms: *tree, trees*. Noncount nouns usually have only a singular form: *grass*.

COUNT	NONCOUNT
people (plural of *person*)	humanity
tables, chairs, beds	furniture
letters	mail
pebbles	gravel
suggestions	advice

Some nouns can be either count or noncount, depending on meaning.

COUNT	Before video games, children played with marbles.
NONCOUNT	The palace floor was made of marble.

When you learn a noun in English, you need to learn whether it is count, noncount, or both. Many dictionaries provide this information.

46b   Use determiners.

Determiners are words that identify or quantify a noun, such as <u>*this*</u> study, <u>*all*</u> people, <u>*his*</u> suggestions.

COMMON DETERMINERS

- the articles *a, an, the*
- *this, these, that, those*
- *my, our, your, his, her, its, their*
- possessive nouns and noun phrases (*Sheila's <u>paper</u>, my friend's <u>book</u>*)
- *whose, which, what*
- *all, both, each, every, some, any, either, no, neither, many, much, (a) few, (a) little, several, enough*
- the numerals *one, two,* etc.

Determiners with singular count nouns.   All singular count nouns must be preceded by a determiner. Place any adjectives between the determiner and the noun.

▶ my sister
  ^

▶ the growing population
  ^

▶ that old neighborhood
  ^

These determiners . . .	. . . can precede these noun types	Examples
a, an, every, each	singular count nouns	a book an American every Buddhist each word
this, that	singular count nouns noncount nouns	this book that milk
(*a*) *little, much*	noncount nouns	a little milk much affection
some, enough	noncount nouns plural count nouns	some milk enough trouble some books enough problems
the	singular count nouns plural count nouns noncount nouns	the doctor the doctors the information
these, those, (*a*) *few, many, both, several*	plural count nouns	these books those plans a few ideas many students both hands several trees

Determiners with plural nouns or noncount nouns.   Noncount and plural nouns sometimes have determiners and sometimes do not. For example, *This research is important* and *Research is important* are both acceptable but have different meanings.

46c   Use articles.

Articles (*a*, *an*, and *the*) are a type of determiner. In English, choosing which article to use — or whether to use an article at all — can be challenging. Although there are exceptions, the following general guidelines can help.

Using *a* or *an*.   Use *a* and *an* (indefinite articles) with singular count nouns. Use *a* before a consonant sound (*a car*) and *an* before a vowel sound (*an uncle*). Consider sound rather than spelling: *a house, an hour.*

A or *an* tells readers they do not have enough information to identify specifically what the noun refers to. Compare these sentences:

▶ I need a new coat for the winter.

▶ I saw a coat that I liked at Dayton's, but it wasn't heavy enough.

The coat in the first sentence is hypothetical rather than actual. Since it is indefinite to the writer and the reader, it is used with *a*, not *the*. The second sentence refers to an actual coat, but since the writer cannot expect the reader to know which one, it is used with *a* rather than *the*.

If you want to speak of an indefinite quantity rather than just one indefinite thing, use *some* or *any* with a noncount noun or a plural count noun. Use *any* in negative sentences.

▶ This stew needs some more salt.

▶ I saw some plates that I liked at Gump's.

▶ This stew doesn't need any more salt.

Using *the*.   Use the definite article *the* with both count and noncount nouns whose identity is known or is about to be made known to readers. The necessary information for identification can come from the noun phrase itself, from elsewhere in the text, from context, from general knowledge, or from a superlative.

▶ Let's meet at ^the^ fountain in front of Dwinelle Hall.

The phrase *in front of Dwinelle Hall* identifies the specific fountain.

▶ Last Saturday, a fire that started in a restaurant spread to a nearby clothing store. ~~Store~~ ^The store^ was saved, although it suffered water damage.

The word *store* is preceded by *the*, which directs our attention to the information in the previous sentence, where the store is first identified.

▶ She asked him to shut ^the^ door when he left her office.

The context shows that she is referring to her office door.

▶ ~~Pope~~ ^The pope^ is expected to visit Africa in October.

There is only one acting pope.

the
▶ Marco is now best singer in the choir.
　　　　　　　　　^
The superlative *best* identifies the noun *singer*.

No article.　Noncount and plural count nouns can be used without an article to make generalizations:

▶ In this world nothing is certain but death and taxes.

　　　　　　　　　　　　　　　　　　　　—Benjamin Franklin

Franklin refers not to a particular death or specific taxes but to death and taxes in general, so no article is used with *death* or with *taxes*.

English differs from many other languages that use the definite article to make generalizations. In English, a sentence like *The ants live in colonies* can refer only to particular, identifiable ants, not to ants in general.

47　Verbs and Verb Phrases

When we must act, verbs tell us what to do—from the street signs that say *stop* or *yield* to email commands such as *send* or *delete*. With a few stylistic exceptions, all written English sentences must include a verb.

47a　Build verb phrases.

Verb phrases can be built up out of a main verb and one or more helping (auxiliary) verbs.

▶ Immigration figures are rising every year.
▶ Immigration figures have risen every year.

Verb phrases have strict rules of order. If you try to rearrange the words in either of these sentences, you will find that most alternatives are impossible. You cannot say *Immigration figures rising are every year.*

	Modal	Perfect *Have*	Progressive *Be*	Passive *Be*	Main Verb	
Sonia	—	has	—	been	invited	to visit a family in Prague.
She	should	—	—	be	finished	with school soon.
The invitation	must	have	—	been	sent	in the spring.
She	—	has	been	—	studying	Czech.
She	may	—	be	—	feeling	nervous.
She	might	have	been	—	expecting	to travel elsewhere.
The trip	will	have	been	—	planned	for a month by the time she leaves.

Putting auxiliary verbs in order.   In the sentence *Immigration figures <u>may have been rising</u>*, the main verb *rising* follows three auxiliaries: *may*, *have*, and *been*. Together these auxiliaries and main verb make up a verb phrase.

- *May* is a modal that indicates possibility; it is followed by the base form of a verb.

- *Have* is an auxiliary verb that in this case indicates the perfect tense; it must be followed by a past participle (*been*).

- Any form of *be*, when it is followed by a present participle ending in *-ing* (such as *rising*), indicates the progressive tense.

- *Be* followed by a past participle, as in *New immigration policies have <u>been passed</u> in recent years*, indicates the passive voice (23e).

As shown in the preceding chart, when two or more auxiliaries appear in a verb phrase, they must follow a particular order based on the type of auxiliary: (1) modal, (2) a form of *have* used to indicate a perfect tense, (3) a form of *be* used to indicate a progressive tense, and (4) a form of *be* used to indicate the passive voice. (Very few sentences include all four kinds of auxiliaries.)

Only one modal is permitted in a verb phrase.

▶ She will <s>can</s> speak Czech much better soon.
       be able to

Forming auxiliary verbs.   Whenever you use an auxiliary, check the form of the word that follows.

MODAL + BASE FORM.   Use the base form of a verb after *can, could, will, would, shall, should, may, might,* and *must*: *Alice <u>can read</u> Latin.* In many other languages, modals like *can* or *must* are followed by the infinitive (*to* + base form). Do not substitute an infinitive for the base form in English.

▶ Alice can <s>to</s> read Latin.

PERFECT *HAVE, HAS,* OR *HAD* + PAST PARTICIPLE.   To form the perfect tenses, use *have, has,* or *had* with a past participle: *Everyone <u>has gone</u> home. They <u>have been</u> working all day.*

PROGRESSIVE *BE* + PRESENT PARTICIPLE.   A progressive form of the verb is signaled by two elements, a form of the auxiliary *be* (*am, is, are, was, were, be,* or *been*) and the *-ing* form of the next word: *The children <u>are studying</u>.* Be sure to include both elements.

▶ The children ^are studying science.

▶ The children are <s>study</s> science.
              studying

Some verbs are rarely used in progressive forms. These are verbs that express unchanging conditions or mental states rather than deliberate actions: *believe, belong, hate, know, like, love, need, own, resemble, understand.*

PASSIVE *BE* + PAST PARTICIPLE.   Use *am, is, are, was, were, being, be,* or *been* with a past participle to form the passive voice.

▶ Tagalog is spoken in the Philippines.

Notice that the word following the progressive *be* (the present participle) ends in *-ing*, but the word following the passive *be* (the past participle) never ends in *-ing*.

| PROGRESSIVE | Thanh is studying music. |
| PASSIVE | Natasha was taught by a famous violinist. |

If the first auxiliary in a verb phrase is a form of *be* or *have*, it must show either present or past tense and must agree with the subject: *Meredith has played in an orchestra.*

47b   Use infinitives and gerunds.

Knowing whether to use an infinitive (*to read*) or a gerund (*reading*) in a sentence may be a challenge.

INFINITIVE

▶ My adviser urged me to apply to several colleges.

GERUND

▶ Applying took a great deal of time.

In general, infinitives tend to represent intentions, desires, or expectations, while gerunds tend to represent facts. The infinitive in the first sentence conveys the message that the act of applying was desired but not yet accomplished, while the gerund in the second sentence calls attention to the fact that the application process was actually carried out.

The association of intention with infinitives and facts with gerunds can often help you decide whether to use an infinitive or a gerund when another verb immediately precedes it.

INFINITIVES

▶ Kumar expected to get a good job after graduation.

▶ Last year, Fatima decided to become a math major.

▶ The strikers have agreed to go back to work.

GERUNDS

▶ Jerzy enjoys going to the theater.

▶ We resumed working after our coffee break.

▶ Kim appreciated getting candy from Sean.

A few verbs can be followed by either an infinitive or a gerund. With some, such as *begin* and *continue*, the choice makes little difference in meaning. With others, however, the difference in meaning is striking.

▶ **Carlos was working as a medical technician, but he stopped to study English.**

The infinitive indicates that Carlos left his job because he intended to study English.

▶ **Carlos stopped studying English when he left the United States.**

The gerund indicates that Carlos actually studied English but then stopped.

The distinction between fact and intention is a tendency, not a rule, and other rules may override it. Always use a gerund—not an infinitive—directly following a preposition.

▶ **This fruit is safe for ~~to eat.~~** eating.

You can also remove the preposition and keep the infinitive.

▶ **This fruit is safe ~~for~~ to eat.**

47c Use conditional sentences appropriately.

English distinguishes among many different types of conditional sentences—sentences that focus on questions and that are introduced by *if* or its equivalent. Each of the following examples makes different assumptions about the likelihood that what is stated in the *if* clause is true.

▶ **If you *practice* (or *have practiced*) writing often, you *learn* (or *have learned*) what your main problems are.**

This sentence assumes that what is stated in the *if* clause may be true; any verb tense that is appropriate in a simple sentence may be used in both the *if* clause and the main clause.

▶ **If you *practice* writing for the rest of this term, you *will* (or *may*) understand the process better.**

This sentence makes a prediction and again assumes that what is stated may turn out to be true. Only the main clause uses the future tense (*will understand*) or a modal that can indicate future time (*may understand*). The *if* clause must use the present tense.

▶ **If you *practiced* (or *were to practice*) writing every day, it *would* eventually *seem* easier.**

This sentence indicates doubt that what is stated will happen. In the *if* clause, the verb is either past—actually, past subjunctive

(23f)—or *were to* + the base form, though it refers to future time. The main clause contains *would* + the base form of the main verb.

▸ **If you *practiced* writing on Mars, you *would find* no one to read your work.**

This sentence imagines an impossible situation. Again, the past subjunctive is used within the *if* clause, although past time is not being referred to, and *would* + the base form is used in the main clause.

▸ **If you *had practiced* writing in ancient Egypt, you *would have used* hieroglyphics.**

This sentence shifts the impossibility back to the past; obviously you won't find yourself in ancient Egypt. But a past impossibility demands a form that is "more past": the past perfect in the *if* clause and *would* + the present perfect form of the main verb in the main clause.

48 Prepositions and Prepositional Phrases

Words such as *to* and *from*, which show the relations between other words, are prepositions. They are one of the more challenging elements of English writing.

48a Choose the right preposition.

Even if you usually know where to use prepositions, you may have difficulty knowing which preposition to use. Each of the most common prepositions has a wide range of different applications, and this range never coincides exactly from one language to another. See, for example, how *in* and *on* are used in English.

▸ The peaches are **in** the refrigerator.

▸ The peaches are **on** the table.

▸ Is that a diamond ring **on** your finger?

✔ **bedfordstmartins.com/wia**
LearningCurve > For multilingual writers: Prepositions

The Spanish translations of these sentences all use the same preposition (*en*), a fact that might lead you astray in English.

There is no easy solution to the challenge of using English prepositions idiomatically, but a few strategies can make it less troublesome.

Know typical examples. The object of the preposition *in* is often a container that encloses something; the object of the preposition *on* is often a horizontal surface that supports something touching it.

> IN   The peaches are *in* the refrigerator.
>
>   There are still some pickles *in* the jar.
>
> ON   The peaches are *on* the table.

Learn related examples. Prepositions that are not used in typical ways may still show some similarities to typical examples.

> IN   You shouldn't drive *in* a snowstorm.
>
> Like a container, the falling snow surrounds the driver. The preposition *in* is used for many weather-related expressions.
>
> ON   Is that a diamond ring *on* your finger?
>
> The preposition *on* is used to describe things you wear.

Use your imagination. Mental images can help you remember figurative uses of prepositions.

> IN   Michael is *in* love.
>
> Imagine a warm bath — or a raging torrent — in which Michael is immersed.
>
> ON   I've just read a book *on* social media.
>
> Imagine the book sitting on a shelf labeled "Social Media."

Learn prepositions as part of a system. In identifying the location of a place or an event, the three prepositions *at, in*, and *on* can be used. *At* specifies the exact point in space or time; *in* is required for expanses of space or time within which a place is located or an event takes place; and *on* must be used with the names of streets (but not exact addresses) and with days of the week or month.

AT	There will be a meeting tomorrow *at* 9:30 AM *at* 160 Main Street.
IN	I arrived *in* the United States *in* January.
ON	The airline's office is *on* Fifth Avenue.
	I'll be moving to my new apartment *on* September 30.

48b   Use two-word verbs idiomatically.

Some words that look like prepositions do not always function as prepositions. Consider the following sentences:

▸ The balloon rose *off* the ground.

▸ The plane took *off* without difficulty.

In the first sentence, *off* is a preposition that introduces the prepositional phrase *off the ground.* In the second sentence, *off* neither functions as a preposition nor introduces a prepositional phrase. Instead, it combines with *took* to form a two-word verb with its own meaning. This kind of verb is called a phrasal verb, and the word *off,* when used in this way, is called an adverbial particle. Many prepositions can function as particles to form phrasal verbs.

The verb + particle combination that makes up a phrasal verb is a single entity that cannot usually be torn apart.

▸ The plane took without difficulty. ~~off.~~ ^{off}

Exceptions include some phrasal verbs that are transitive, meaning that they take a direct object. Some of these verbs have particles that may be separated from the verb by the object.

▸ I *picked up my baggage* at the terminal.

▸ I *picked my baggage up* at the terminal.

If a personal pronoun is used as the direct object, it *must* separate the verb from its particle.

▸ I picked up ~~it~~ at the terminal. ^{it}

In some idiomatic two-word verbs, the second word is a preposition. With such verbs, the preposition can never be separated from the verb.

▶ We *ran into* our neighbor on the train. [not *ran our neighbor into*]

The combination *run + into* has a special meaning (find by chance). Therefore, *run into* is a two-word verb.

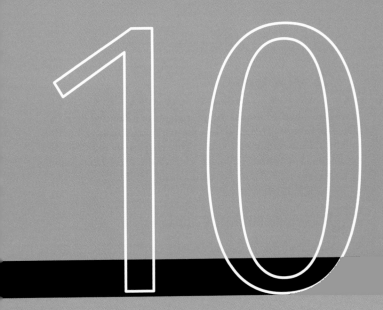

Documentation

49 MLA Style

Many fields in the humanities ask students to follow Modern Language Association (MLA) style to format manuscripts and to document various kinds of sources. This chapter introduces MLA guidelines. For further reference, consult the *MLA Handbook for Writers of Research Papers*, Seventh Edition, 2009.

49a Understand MLA citation style.

Why does academic work call for very careful citation practices when writing for the general public may not? The answer is that readers of your academic work will expect source citations for several reasons:

- Source citations demonstrate that you've done your homework on your topic and are a part of the conversation surrounding it. Careful citation shows your readers what you know, where you stand, and what you think is important.

- Source citations show that you understand the need to give credit when you make use of someone else's intellectual property. Especially in academic writing, when it's better to be safe than sorry, include a citation for any source you think you might need to cite. (See 15f.)

- Source citations give explicit directions to guide readers who want to look for themselves at the works you're using.

The guidelines for MLA style help you with this last purpose, giving you instructions on exactly what information to include in your citation and how to format that information.

Types of sources. Look at the Directory to MLA Style on p. 411 for guidelines on citing various types of sources, including print books, print periodicals (journals, magazines, and newspapers), digital written-word sources, and other sources (films, artwork) that consist mainly of material other than written words. A digital version of a source may include updates or corrections that the print version lacks, so MLA guidelines ask you to indicate the medium and to cite print and digital sources differently. If you can't find a model exactly like the source you've selected, see the Checklist on p. 420.

WEB AND DATABASE SOURCES. MLA asks you to distinguish between Web sources and database sources. Individual researchers almost always gain access to articles in databases through the computer system of a school or public library that pays to subscribe. The easiest way to tell whether a source comes from a database, then, is that its information is *not* generally available to anyone with an Internet connection. Many databases are digital collections of articles that originally appeared in edited print periodicals, ensuring that an authority has vouched for the accuracy of the information. Such sources may have more credibility than free material available on the Web.

SOURCES FOR CONTENT BEYOND THE WRITTEN WORD. Figuring out which model to follow for media sources online can pose questions. Is a video interview posted on YouTube most like a work from a Web site? an online video? an interview? Talk with your instructor about complicated sources, and remember that your ultimate goal is to make the source as accessible as possible to your readers.

Parts of citations. MLA citations appear in two parts of your text—a brief in-text citation in parentheses in the body of your written text, and a full citation in the list of works cited, to which the in-text citation directs readers. A basic in-text citation includes the author's name and the page number (for a print source), but many variations on this format are discussed in 49c.

Explanatory notes. MLA citation style asks you to include explanatory notes for information or comments that don't readily fit into your text but are needed for clarification or further explanation. In addition, MLA permits bibliographic notes for information about or evaluation of a source, or to list multiple sources that relate to a single point. Use superscript numbers in the text to refer readers to the notes, which may appear as endnotes (under the heading *Notes* on a separate page immediately before the list of works cited) or as footnotes at the bottom of each page where a superscript number appears.

becomes *every1*. This type of wordplay has a special importance
in the development of an advanced literacy, and for good reason.
According to David Crystal, an internationally recognized scholar
of linguistics at the University of Wales, as young children
develop and learn how words string together to express ideas,
they go through many phases of language play. The singsong

...in SAT
...Yielding
...results. Reading and Writing Are Causes for concern. New
York: College Board, 2002. Print.

College Board. "2011 SAT Trends." *Collegeboard.org.* College
Board, 14 Sept. 2012. Web. 6 Dec. 2012.

Crystal, David. *Language Play.* Chicago: U of Chicago P, 1998.
Print.

The Discouraging Word. "Re: Messaging and Literacy." Message
to the author. 13 Nov. 2012. E-mail.

Ferguson, Niall. "Texting Makes U Stupid." *Newsweek* 158.12
(2011): 11. *Academic Search Premier.* Web. 7 Dec. 2012.

Leibowitz, Wendy R. "Technology Transforms Writing and the
Teaching of Writing." *Chronicle of Higher Education* 26 Nov.
1999: A67-68. Print.

Lenhart, Amanda. *Teens, Smartphones, & Texting.* Pew Research
Center's Internet & Amer. Life Project, 19 Mar. 2012. PDF
file.

Lenhart, Amanda, Sousan Arafeh, Aaron Smith, and Alexandra
Macgill. *Writing, Technology & Teens.* Pew Research Center's
Internet & Amer. Life Project, 24 Apr. 2008. PDF file.

the Pew Internet & American Life Project, 85 percent of those
aged 12-17 at least occasionally write text messages, instant
messages, or comments on social networking sites (Lenhart,
Arafeh, Smith, and Macgill). In 2001, the most conservative

...ne: The
...Internet's
..., Pew
..., 21 June
2001. PDF file.

EXAMPLE OF SUPERSCRIPT NUMBER IN TEXT

Although messaging relies on the written word, many messagers
disregard standard writing conventions. For example, here is a
snippet from an IM conversation between two teenage girls:[1]

EXAMPLE OF EXPLANATORY NOTE

1. This transcript of an IM conversation was collected on 20 Nov.
2012. The teenagers' names are concealed to protect their privacy.

49b Follow MLA manuscript format.

The MLA recommends the following format for the manuscript of a research paper. However, check with your instructor before preparing the final draft of a print work.

First page and title. The MLA does not require a title page. Type each of the following items on a separate line on the first page, beginning one inch from the top and flush with the left margin: your name, the instructor's name, the course name and number, and the date. Double-space between each item; then double-space again and center the title. Double-space between the title and the beginning of the text.

Margins and spacing. Leave one-inch margins at the top and bottom and on both sides of each page. Double-space the entire text, including set-off quotations, notes, and the list of works cited. Indent the first line of a paragraph one-half inch. Indent set-off quotations one inch.

Page numbers. Include your last name and the page number on each page, one-half inch below the top and flush with the right margin.

Long quotations. To quote a long passage (more than four typed lines), set the quotation off by starting it on a new line and indenting each line one inch, or ten spaces, from the left margin. Do not enclose the passage in quotation marks (39a).

Headings. MLA style allows, but does not require, headings. Many students and instructors find them helpful. (See Chapter 8 for guidelines on using headings and subheadings.)

Visuals. Visuals (photographs, drawings, charts, graphs, and tables) should be placed as near as possible to the relevant text. (See 8d and 15c for guidelines on incorporating visuals into your text.) Tables should have a label and number (*Table 1*) and a clear caption. The label and caption should be aligned on the left, on separate lines. Give the source information below the table. All other visuals should be labeled *Figure* (abbreviated *Fig.*), numbered, and captioned. The label and caption should appear on the same line, followed by source information. Remember to refer to each visual in your text, indicating how it contributes to the point(s) you are making.

49c   Create MLA in-text citations.

MLA style requires a citation in the text of a writing project for every quotation, paraphrase, summary, or other material requiring documentation (see 15f). In-text citations document material from other sources with both signal phrases and parenthetical references. Parenthetical references should include the information your readers need to locate the full reference in the list of works cited at the end of the text. An in-text citation in MLA style gives the reader two kinds of information: (1) it indicates which source on the works-cited page the writer is referring to, and (2) it explains where in the source the material quoted, paraphrased, or summarized can be found, if the source has page numbers or other numbered sections.

The basic MLA in-text citation includes the author's last name either in a signal phrase introducing the source material (see 15b) or in parentheses at the end of the sentence. For print sources, it also includes the page number in parentheses at the end of the sentence.

DIRECTORY TO MLA STYLE

MLA style for in-text citations

SAMPLE CITATION USING A SIGNAL PHRASE

> In his discussion of Monty Python routines, Crystal notes that the group relished "breaking the normal rules" of language (107).

SAMPLE PARENTHETICAL CITATION

> A noted linguist explains that Monty Python humor often relied on "bizarre linguistic interactions" (Crystal 108).

(For digital sources without print page numbers, see model 3.)

Note in the following examples where punctuation is placed in relation to the parentheses.

1. AUTHOR NAMED IN A SIGNAL PHRASE. The MLA recommends using the author's name in a signal phrase to introduce the material and citing the page number(s) in parentheses.

> Lee claims that his comic-book creation, Thor, was "the first regularly published superhero to speak in a consistently archaic manner" (199).

2. AUTHOR NAMED IN A PARENTHETICAL REFERENCE. When you do not mention the author in a signal phrase, include the author's last name before the page number(s) in the parentheses. Use no punctuation between the author's name and the page number(s).

> The word *Bollywood* is sometimes considered an insult because it implies that Indian movies are merely "a derivative of the American film industry" (Chopra 9).

3. DIGITAL OR NONPRINT SOURCE. Give enough information in a signal phrase or in parentheses for readers to locate the source in your list of works cited. Many works found online or in electronic databases lack stable page numbers; you can omit the page number in such cases. However, if you are citing a work with stable pagination, such as an article in PDF format, include the page number in parentheses.

DIGITAL SOURCE WITHOUT STABLE PAGE NUMBERS

> As a *Slate* analysis explains, "Prominent sports psychologists get praised for their successes and don't get grief for their failures" (Engber).

DIGITAL SOURCE WITH STABLE PAGE NUMBERS

> According to Whitmarsh, the British military had experimented with
> using balloons for observation as far back as 1879 (328).

If the source includes numbered sections, paragraphs, or screens, include the abbreviation (*sec.*), paragraph (*par.*), or screen (*scr.*) number in parentheses.

4. TWO OR THREE AUTHORS. Use all the authors' last names in a signal phrase or in parentheses.

> Gortner, Hebrun, and Nicolson maintain that "opinion leaders"
> influence other people in an organization because they are
> respected, not because they hold high positions (175).

5. FOUR OR MORE AUTHORS. Name all the authors in a signal phrase or in parentheses, or use the first author's name and *et al.* ("and others").

> Similarly, as Belenky, Clinchy, Tarule, and Goldberger assert,
> examining the lives of women expands our understanding of human
> development (7).

> Similarly, as Belenky et al. assert, examining the lives of women
> expands our understanding of human development (7).

6. ORGANIZATION AS AUTHOR. Provide the group's full name or a shortened form of it in a signal phrase or in parentheses.

> Any study of social welfare involves a close analysis of "the
> impacts, the benefits, and the costs" of its policies (Social Research
> Corporation iii).

7. UNKNOWN AUTHOR. Give the full title, if it is brief, in your text—or a shortened version of the title in parentheses.

> One analysis defines *hype* as "an artificially engendered atmosphere
> of hysteria" (*Today's Marketplace* 51).

8. AUTHOR OF TWO OR MORE WORKS CITED IN THE SAME PROJECT. If your list of works cited has more than one work by the same author, include a shortened version of the title of the work you are citing in a signal phrase or in parentheses to prevent reader confusion.

> Gardner shows readers their own silliness in his description of a "pointless, ridiculous monster, crouched in the shadows, stinking of dead men, murdered children, and martyred cows" (*Grendel* 2).

9. TWO OR MORE AUTHORS WITH THE SAME LAST NAME. Include the author's first *and* last names in a signal phrase or first initial and last name in a parenthetical reference.

> Children will learn to write if they are allowed to choose their own subjects, James Britton asserts, citing the Schools Council study of the 1960s (37-42).

10. MULTIVOLUME WORK. In a parenthetical reference, note the volume number first and then the page number(s), with a colon and one space between them.

> Modernist writers prized experimentation and gradually even sought to blur the line between poetry and prose, according to Forster (3: 150).

If you name only one volume of the work in your list of works cited, include only the page number in the parentheses.

11. LITERARY WORK. Because literary works are often available in many different editions, cite the page number(s) from the edition you used followed by a semicolon, and then give other identifying information that will lead readers to the passage in any edition. Indicate the act and/or scene in a play (*37; sc. 1*). For a novel, indicate the part or chapter (*175; ch. 4*).

> In utter despair, Dostoyevsky's character Mitya wonders aloud about the "terrible tragedies realism inflicts on people" (376; bk. 8, ch. 2).

For a poem, cite the part (if there is one) and line(s), separated by a period. If you are citing only line numbers, use the word *line(s)* in the first reference (*lines 33-34*).

> Whitman speculates, "All goes onward and outward, nothing collapses, / And to die is different from what anyone supposed, and luckier" (6.129-30).

For a verse play, give only the act, scene, and line numbers, separated by periods.

> The witches greet Banquo as "Lesser than Macbeth, and greater" (1.3.65).

12. WORK IN AN ANTHOLOGY OR A COLLECTION. For an essay, a short story, or other piece of prose reprinted in an anthology, use the name of the author of the work, not the editor of the anthology, but use the page number(s) from the anthology.

> Narratives of captivity play a major role in early writing by women in the United States, as demonstrated by Silko (219).

13. SACRED TEXT. To cite a sacred text such as the Qur'an or the Bible, give the *title* of the edition you used, the book, and the chapter and verse (or their equivalent) separated by a period. In your text, spell out the names of books. In parenthetical references, use abbreviations for books with names of five or more letters (*Gen.* for *Genesis*).

> He ignored the admonition "Pride goes before destruction, and a haughty spirit before a fall" (*New Oxford Annotated Bible,* Prov. 16.18).

14. ENCYCLOPEDIA OR DICTIONARY ENTRY. An entry from a reference work—such as an encyclopedia or a dictionary—without an author will appear on the works-cited list under the entry's title. Enclose the entry title in quotation marks, and place it in parentheses. Omit the page number for print reference works that arrange entries alphabetically.

> The term *prion* was coined by Stanley B. Prusiner from the words *proteinaceous* and *infectious* and a suffix meaning *particle* ("Prion").

15. GOVERNMENT SOURCE WITH NO AUTHOR NAMED. Because entries for sources authored by government agencies will appear on your list of works cited under the name of the country (see 49d, item 73), your in-text citation for such a source should include the name of the country as well as the name of the agency responsible for the source.

To reduce the agricultural runoff into the Chesapeake Bay, the United States Environmental Protection Agency has argued that "[h]igh nutrient loading crops, such as corn and soybean, should be replaced with alternatives in environmentally sensitive areas" (2-26).

16. ENTIRE WORK. Include the reference in the text, without any page numbers.

Jon Krakauer's *Into the Wild* both criticizes and admires the solitary impulses of its young hero, which end up killing him.

17. INDIRECT SOURCE (AUTHOR QUOTING SOMEONE ELSE). Use the abbreviation *qtd. in* to indicate that you are quoting from someone else's report of a source.

As Arthur Miller says, "When somebody is destroyed everybody finally contributes to it, but in Willy's case, the end product would be virtually the same" (qtd. in Martin and Meyer 375).

18. TWO OR MORE SOURCES IN ONE PARENTHETICAL REFERENCE. Separate the information with semicolons.

Economists recommend that *employment* be redefined to include unpaid domestic labor (Clark 148; Nevins 39).

19. VISUAL INCLUDED IN THE TEXT. When you include an image in your text, number it and include a parenthetical reference in your text (*see Fig. 2*). Number figures (photos, drawings, cartoons, maps, graphs, and charts) and tables separately. Each visual should include a caption with the figure or table number and information about the source — either a complete citation or enough information to direct readers to your works-cited entry. (See 8d and 15c.)

This trend is illustrated in a chart distributed by the College Board as part of its 2011 analysis of aggregate SAT data (see Fig. 1).

Soon after the preceding sentence, readers find the following figure and a caption referring them to the entry on the list of works cited (see 49e and the integrated media page at **bedfordstmartins** **.com/wia** to read the student's research paper):

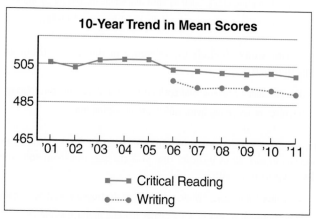

Fig. 1. Ten-year trend in mean SAT reading and writing scores (2001-2011). Source: College Board, "2011 SAT Trends."

An image that you create might appear with a caption like this:

Fig. 4. Young women reading magazines. Personal photograph by author.

49d Create an MLA list of works cited.

A list of works cited is an alphabetical list of the sources that you have referred to in your essay. (If your instructor asks you to list everything you have read as background, call the list *Works Consulted*.)

Guidelines for author listings

The list of works cited is arranged alphabetically. The in-text citations in your writing point readers toward particular sources on the list.

NAME CITED IN SIGNAL PHRASE IN TEXT

Crystal explains . . .

NAME IN PARENTHETICAL CITATION IN TEXT

. . . (Crystal 107).

BEGINNING OF ENTRY IN LIST OF WORKS CITED

Crystal, David.

CHECKLIST

Formatting a List of Works Cited

✔ Start your list on a separate page after the text of your document and any notes.

✔ Continue the consecutive numbering of pages.

✔ Center the heading *Works Cited* (not italicized or in quotation marks) one inch from the top of the page.

✔ Begin each entry flush with the left margin, but indent subsequent lines one-half inch. Double-space the entire list.

✔ List sources alphabetically by the first word. Start with the author's name, if available, or the editor's name. If no author or editor is given, start with the title.

✔ List the author's last name first, followed by a comma and the first name. If a source has multiple authors, subsequent authors' names appear first name first (see model 2).

✔ Capitalize every important word in titles and subtitles. Italicize titles of books and long works, but put titles of shorter works in quotation marks.

✔ In general, use a period and a space after each element of the entry; look at the models in this chapter for information on punctuating particular kinds of entries.

✔ For a book, list the city of publication (add a country abbreviation for non-U.S. cities that may be unfamiliar). Follow it with a colon and a shortened form of the publisher's name—omit *Co.* or *Inc.*, shorten names such as *Simon & Schuster* to *Simon*, and abbreviate *University Press* to *UP*.

✔ List dates of periodical publication or of access to electronic items in day, month, year order, and abbreviate months except for May, June, and July.

✔ Give a medium, such as *Print* or *Web*, for each entry.

✔ List inclusive page numbers for a part of a larger work.

Models 1–5 on pp. 414–15 explain how to arrange author names. The information that follows the name of the author depends on the type of work you are citing—a book (models 6–27); a print periodical (models 28–34); a written text from a digital source, such as an article from a Web site or database (models 35–55); sources from art, film, comics, or other media, including live performances (models 56–71); and academic, government, and legal sources (models 72–79). Consult the model that most closely resembles the kind of source you are using.

1. ONE AUTHOR. Put the last name first, followed by a comma, the first name (and initial, if any), and a period.

Crystal, David.

2. MULTIPLE AUTHORS. List the first author with the last name first (see model 1). Give the names of any other authors with the first name first. Separate authors' names with commas, and include the word *and* before the last person's name.

Martineau, Jane, Desmond Shawe-Taylor, and Jonathan Bate.

For four or more authors, either list all the names or list the first author followed by a comma and *et al.* ("and others").

Lupton, Ellen, Jennifer Tobias, Alicia Imperiale, Grace Jeffers, and Randi Mates.

Lupton, Ellen, et al.

3. ORGANIZATION OR GROUP AUTHOR. Give the name of the group, government agency, corporation, or other organization listed as the author.

Getty Trust.

United States. Government Accountability Office.

4. UNKNOWN AUTHOR. When the author is not identified, begin the entry with the title, and alphabetize by the first important word. Italicize titles of books and long works, but put titles of articles and other short works in quotation marks.

"California Sues EPA over Emissions."

New Concise World Atlas.

5. TWO OR MORE WORKS BY THE SAME AUTHOR. Arrange the entries alphabetically by title. Include the author's name in the first entry, but in subsequent entries, use three hyphens followed by a period. (For the basic format for citing a book, see model 6. For the basic format for citing an article from an online newspaper, see model 38.)

Chopra, Anupama. "Bollywood Princess, Hollywood Hopeful." *New York Times*. New York Times, 10 Feb. 2008. Web. 13 Feb. 2008.

---. *King of Bollywood: Shah Rukh Khan and the Seductive World of Indian Cinema*. New York: Warner, 2007. Print.

Note: Use three hyphens only when the work is by *exactly* the same author(s) as the previous entry.

Print books

6. BASIC FORMAT FOR A BOOK. Begin with the author name(s). (See models 1–5.) Then include the title and subtitle, the city of publication and publisher, the publication year, and finally the medium (*Print*). The source map on pp. 416–17 shows where to find this information in a typical book.

author: last name first — title — city of publication — publisher — date — medium

Crystal, David. *Language Play*. Chicago: U of Chicago P, 1998. Print.

Note: Place a period and a space after the name, title, and date. Place a colon after the city and a comma after the publisher, and shorten the publisher's name—omit *Co.* or *Inc.*, and abbreviate *University Press* to *UP*.

7. AUTHOR AND EDITOR BOTH NAMED

author — title — editor: first name first

Bangs, Lester. *Psychotic Reactions and Carburetor Dung*. Ed. Greil

city of publication — publisher — date — medium

Marcus. New York: Knopf, 1988. Print.

Note: To cite the editor's contribution instead, begin the entry with the editor's name.

Marcus, Greil, ed. *Psychotic Reactions and Carburetor Dung*. By Lester Bangs. New York: Knopf, 1988. Print.

MLA SOURCE MAP: Books

Take information from the book's title page and copyright page (on the reverse side of the title page), not from the book's cover or a library catalog.

1 **Author.** List the last name first. End with a period. For variations, see models 2–5.

2 **Title.** Italicize the title and any subtitle; capitalize all major words. End with a period.

3 **City of publication and publisher.** If more than one city is given, use the first one listed. For foreign cities, add an abbreviation of the country or province (*Cork, Ire.*). Follow it with a colon and a shortened version of the publisher's name (*Oxford UP* for *Oxford University Press*). Follow it with a comma.

4 **Year of publication.** If more than one copyright date is given, use the most recent one. End with a period.

5 **Medium of publication.** End with the medium (*Print*) followed by a period.

A citation for the book on p. 417 would look like this:

    1   2

Patel, Raj. *The Value of Nothing: How to Reshape Market Society and*

                         3   4   5

    Redefine Democracy. New York: Picador, 2009. Print.

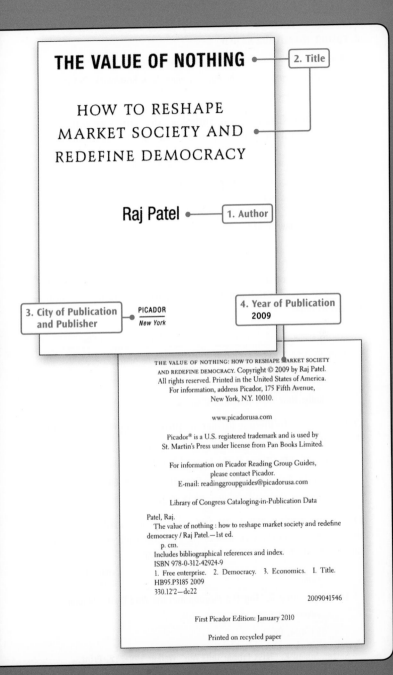

THE VALUE OF NOTHING

2. Title

HOW TO RESHAPE MARKET SOCIETY AND REDEFINE DEMOCRACY

Raj Patel

1. Author

3. City of Publication and Publisher

PICADOR
New York

4. Year of Publication
2009

THE VALUE OF NOTHING: HOW TO RESHAPE MARKET SOCIETY AND REDEFINE DEMOCRACY. Copyright © 2009 by Raj Patel. All rights reserved. Printed in the United States of America. For information, address Picador, 175 Fifth Avenue, New York, N.Y. 10010.

www.picadorusa.com

Picador® is a U.S. registered trademark and is used by St. Martin's Press under license from Pan Books Limited.

For information on Picador Reading Group Guides, please contact Picador.
E-mail: readinggroupguides@picadorusa.com

Library of Congress Cataloging-in-Publication Data

Patel, Raj.
  The value of nothing : how to reshape market society and redefine democracy / Raj Patel.—1st ed.
    p. cm.
  Includes bibliographical references and index.
  ISBN 978-0-312-42924-9
  1. Free enterprise.   2. Democracy.   3. Economics.   I. Title.
HB95.P3185 2009
330.12'2—dc22

                                                    2009041546

First Picador Edition: January 2010

Printed on recycled paper

8. EDITOR, NO AUTHOR NAMED

Wall, Cheryl A., ed. *Changing Our Own Words: Essays on Criticism,*

Theory, and Writing by Black Women. New Brunswick: Rutgers UP,

1989. Print.

9. ANTHOLOGY. Cite an entire anthology the same way you would cite a book with an editor and no named author (see model 8).

editor:
last name first   title and subtitle

Walker, Dale L., ed. *Westward: A Fictional History of the American*

                        city of
                        publication publisher date medium

West. New York: Forge, 2003. Print.

10. WORK IN AN ANTHOLOGY OR CHAPTER IN A BOOK WITH AN EDITOR. List the author(s) of the selection; the selection title, in quotation marks; the title of the book, italicized; the abbreviation *Ed.* and the name(s) of the editor(s); publication information; and the selection's page numbers.

                        title
author   (selection)   title (book)   editor

Komunyakaa, Yusef. "Facing It." *The Seagull Reader*. Ed. Joseph

        city of
        publication publisher   date   page(s) medium

Kelly. New York: Norton, 2000. 126-27. Print.

Note: Use the following format to provide original publication information for a reprinted selection:

Byatt, A. S. "The Thing in the Forest." *New Yorker* 3 June 2002:

80-89. Rpt. in *The O. Henry Prize Stories 2003*. Ed. Laura

Furman. New York: Anchor, 2003. 3-22. Print.

11. TWO OR MORE ITEMS FROM THE SAME ANTHOLOGY. List the anthology as one entry (see model 9). Also list each selection separately with a cross-reference to the anthology.

                                            editor of anthology:
author   title (selection)   last name only

Estleman, Loren D. "Big Tim Magoon and the Wild West." Walker

page(s) medium

391-404. Print.

Salzer, Susan K. "Miss Libbie Tells All." Walker 199-212. Print.

12. TRANSLATION

> Bolaño, Roberto. *2666*. Trans. Natasha Wimmer. New York: Farrar,
>
> > 2008. Print.

13. BOOK WITH BOTH TRANSLATOR AND EDITOR. List the editor's and the translator's names after the title, in the order they appear on the title page.

> Kant, Immanuel. *"Toward Perpetual Peace" and Other Writings on*
>
> > *Politics, Peace, and History*. Ed. Pauline Kleingeld. Trans. David
> >
> > L. Colclasure. New Haven: Yale UP, 2006. Print.

14. TRANSLATION OF A SECTION OF A BOOK. If different translators have worked on various parts of the book, identify the translator of the part you are citing.

> García Lorca, Federico. "The Little Mad Boy." Trans. W. S. Merwin. *The*
>
> > *Selected Poems of Federico García Lorca*. Ed. Francisco García
> >
> > Lorca and Donald M. Allen. London: Penguin, 1969. Print.

15. TRANSLATION OF A BOOK BY AN UNKNOWN AUTHOR

> *Grettir's Saga*. Trans. Denton Fox and Hermann Palsson. Toronto: U of
>
> > Toronto P, 1974. Print.

16. BOOK IN A LANGUAGE OTHER THAN ENGLISH. Include a translation of the title in brackets, if necessary.

> Benedetti, Mario. *La borra del café [The Coffee Grind]*. Buenos Aires:
>
> > Sudamericana, 2000. Print.

17. GRAPHIC NARRATIVE. If the words and images are created by the same person, cite a graphic narrative just as you would a book (model 6).

> Bechdel, Alison. *Fun Home: A Family Tragicomic*. New York: Houghton,
>
> > 2006. Print.

If the work is a collaboration, indicate the author or illustrator who is most important to your research before the title of the work. List other contributors after the title, in the order of their appearance on the title page. Label each person's contribution to the work.

> Stavans, Ilan, writer. *Latino USA: A Cartoon History*. Illus. Lalo
>
> > Arcaraz. New York: Basic, 2000. Print.

CHECKLIST

Combining Parts of Models

What should you do if your source doesn't match the model exactly? Suppose, for instance, that your source is a translated essay that appears in the fifth edition of an anthology.

✔ Identify a basic model to follow. If you decide that your source looks most like an essay in an anthology, you would start with a citation that looks like model 10.

✔ Look for models that show the additional elements in your source. For this example, you would need to add elements of model 14 (for the translation) and model 18 (for an edition other than the first).

✔ Add new elements from other models to your basic model in the order indicated.

✔ If you still aren't sure how to arrange the pieces to create a combination model, ask your instructor.

18. EDITION OTHER THAN THE FIRST

Walker, John A. *Art in the Age of Mass Media*. 3rd ed. London: Pluto,
    2001. Print.

19. ONE VOLUME OF A MULTIVOLUME WORK. Give the number of the volume cited after the title. Including the total number of volumes after the medium is optional.

Ch'oe, Yong-Ho, Peter Lee, and William Theodore De Barry, eds.
    Sources of Korean Tradition. Vol. 2. New York: Columbia UP,
    2000. Print. 2 vols.

20. TWO OR MORE VOLUMES OF A MULTIVOLUME WORK

Ch'oe, Yong-Ho, Peter Lee, and William Theodore De Barry, eds.
    Sources of Korean Tradition. 2 vols. New York: Columbia UP,
    2000. Print.

21. PREFACE, FOREWORD, INTRODUCTION, OR AFTERWORD. After the writer's name, describe the contribution. After the title, indicate the book's author (with *By*) or editor (with *Ed.*).

author:
last name first | book part | title (book)

Atwan, Robert. Foreword. *The Best American Essays 2002.*

editor: in normal order | city of publication | publisher | date | page(s) | medium

Ed. Stephen Jay Gould. Boston: Houghton, 2002. viii-xii. Print.

Moore, Thurston. Introduction. *Confusion Is Next: The Sonic Youth
     Story.* By Alec Foege. New York: St. Martin's, 1994. xi. Print.

22. ENTRY IN A REFERENCE BOOK. For a well-known encyclopedia, note the edition (if identified) and year of publication. If the entries are alphabetized, omit publication information and page number.

Kettering, Alison McNeil. "Art Nouveau." *World Book Encyclopedia.*
     2002 ed. Print.

23. BOOK THAT IS PART OF A SERIES. Cite the series name (and number, if any) from the title page.

Nichanian, Marc, and Vartan Matiossian, eds. *Yeghishe Charents: Poet
     of the Revolution.* Costa Mesa: Mazda, 2003. Print. Armenian
     Studies Ser. 5.

24. REPUBLICATION (MODERN EDITION OF AN OLDER BOOK). Indicate the original publication date after the title.

Austen, Jane. *Sense and Sensibility.* 1813. New York: Dover, 1996. Print.

25. PUBLISHER'S IMPRINT. If the title page gives a publisher's imprint, hyphenate the imprint and the publisher's name.

Hornby, Nick. *About a Boy.* New York: Riverhead-Penguin Putnam,
     1998. Print.

26. BOOK WITH A TITLE WITHIN THE TITLE. Do not italicize a book title within a title. For an article title within a title, italicize as usual and place the article title in quotation marks.

Mullaney, Julie. *Arundhati Roy's* The God of Small Things: *A Reader's
     Guide.* New York: Continuum, 2002. Print.

Rhynes, Martha. *"I, Too, Sing America": The Story of Langston
     Hughes.* Greensboro: Morgan, 2002. Print.

27. SACRED TEXT. To cite individual published editions of sacred books, begin the entry with the title.

> *Qur'an: The Final Testament (Authorized English Version) with Arabic*
>
> *Text.* Trans. Rashad Khalifa. Fremont: Universal Unity, 2000. Print.

Print periodicals

Begin with the author name(s). (See models 1–5.) Then include the article title, the title of the periodical, the date or volume information, the page numbers, and the medium (*Print*). The source map on pp. 424–25 shows where to find this information in a sample periodical.

28. ARTICLE IN A PRINT JOURNAL. Follow the journal title with the volume number, a period, the issue number (if given), and the year (in parentheses).

      author   title and subtitle (article)

Gigante, Denise. "The Monster in the Rainbow: Keats and the Science

              title   volume,
       (periodical) issue, date   page(s) medium

   of Life." *PMLA* 117.3 (2002): 433-48. Print.

29. ARTICLE IN A PRINT MAGAZINE. Provide the date from the magazine cover instead of volume or issue numbers.

                                            date:
                                 title   day + month
      author   title (article)   (magazine) + year

Surowiecki, James. "The Stimulus Strategy." *New Yorker* 25 Feb. 2008:

  page(s) medium

   29. Print.

   Taubin, Amy. "All Talk?" *Film Comment* Nov.-Dec. 2007: 45-47. Print.

30. ARTICLE IN A PRINT NEWSPAPER. Include the edition (if listed) and the section number or letter (if listed).

                                       title
      author   title (article)   (newspaper)

Longman, Jeré. "Kim Jong-il, Sportsman." *New York Times*

       date:
    day + month   name of
     + year   edition page(s) medium

   21 Dec. 2011, late ed.: B12. Print.

Note: For locally published newspapers, add the city in brackets after the name if it is not part of the name: *Globe and Mail [Toronto].*

31. ARTICLE THAT SKIPS PAGES. When an article skips pages, give only the first page number and a plus sign.

> Tyrnauer, Matthew. "Empire by Martha." *Vanity Fair* Sept. 2002: 364+. Print.

32. EDITORIAL OR LETTER TO THE EDITOR. Include the writer's name, if given, and the title, if any, followed by a label for the work.

> "California Dreaming." Editorial. *Nation* 25 Feb. 2008: 4. Print.
>
> Galbraith, James K. "JFK's Plans to Withdraw." Letter. *New York Review of Books* 6 Dec. 2007: 77-78. Print.

33. REVIEW

> Franklin, Nancy. "Teen Spirit." Rev. of *Glee,* by Ryan Murphy, Brad Falchuk, and Ian Brennan. *New Yorker* 10 May 2010: 72-73. Print.
>
> Schwarz, Benjamin. Rev. of *The Second World War: A Short History,* by R. A. C. Parker. *Atlantic Monthly* May 2002: 110-11. Print.

MLA SOURCE MAP: Articles in Print Periodicals

1 **Author.** List the last name first. End with a period. For variations, see models 2–5.

2 **Article title.** Put the title and any subtitle in quotation marks; capitalize all major words. Place a period inside the closing quotation mark.

3 **Periodical title.** Italicize the title; capitalize all major words. Omit any initial *A*, *An*, or *The*.

4 **Volume and issue / Date of publication.** For journals, give the volume number and issue number (if any), separated by a period; then list the year in parentheses and follow it with a colon.

   For magazines, list the day (if given), month, and year.

5 **Page numbers.** List inclusive page numbers. If the article skips pages, put the first page number and a plus sign. End with a period.

6 **Medium.** Give the medium (*Print*). End with a period.

A citation for the article on p. 425 would look like this:

Quart, Alissa. "Lost Media, Found Media: Snapshots from the Future of Writing." *Columbia Journalism Review* May/June 2008: 30-34. Print.

3. Periodical Title

COLUMBIA
JOURNALISM
REVIEW

May / June 2008 • cjr.org

4. Date of Publication
May/June 2008

The Future of
Writing + Reading

2. Article Title

Lost Media,
Found Media

Snapshots from the future of writing

BY ALISSA QUART

1. Author
ALISSA QUART

If there were an ashram for people who worship contemplative long-form journalism, it would be the Nieman Conference on Narrative Journalism. This March, at the Sheraton Boston Hotel, hundreds of journalists, authors, students, and aspirants came for the weekend event. Seated on metal chairs in large conference rooms, we learned about muscular storytelling (the Q-shaped narrative structure—who knew?). We sipped cups of coffee and ate bagels and heard about reporting history through letters and public documents and how to evoke empathy for our subjects, particularly our most marginal ones. As we listened to reporters discussing great feats—exposing Walter Reed's fetid living quarters for wounded soldiers, for instance—we also renewed our pride in our profession. In short, the conference exemplified the best of the older media models, the ones that have so recently fallen into economic turmoil.

Yet even at the weekend's strongest lectures on interview techniques or the long-form profile, we couldn't ignore the digital elephant in the room. We all knew as writers that the kinds of pieces we were discussing require months of work to be both deep and refined, and that we were all hard-pressed for the time and the money to do that. It was always hard for nonfiction writers, but something seems to have changed. For those of us who believed in the value of the journalism and literary nonfiction of the past, we had become like the people at the ashram after the guru has died.

Right now, journalism is more or less divided into two camps, which I will call Lost Media and Found Media. I went to the Nieman conference partially because I wanted to see how the forces creating this new division are affecting and afflicting the Lost Media world that I love best, not on the institutional level, but for reporters and writers themselves. This world includes people who write for all the newspapers and magazines that are currently struggling with layoffs, speedups, hiring freezes, buyouts, the death or shrinkage of film- and book-review sections, limits on expensive investigative work, the erasure of foreign bureaus, and the general narrowing of institutional ambition. It includes freelance writers competing with hordes of ever-younger competitors willing to write and publish online for free, the fade-out of established journalistic career paths, and, perhaps most crucially, a muddled sense of the meritorious, as blogs level and scramble the value and status of print publications, and of professional writers. The glamour and influence once associated with a magazine elite seem to have faded, becoming a sort of pastiche of winsome articles about yearning and boxers and dinners at Elaine's.

Found Media-ites, meanwhile, are the bloggers, the contributors to Huffington Post-type sites that aggregate blogs, as well as other work that somebody else paid for, and the new nonprofits and pay-per-article schemes that aim to save journalism from 20 percent profit-margin demands. Although these elements are often disparate, together they compose the new media landscape. In economic terms, I mean all the outlets for nonfiction writing that seem to be thriving in the new era or striving to fill niches that Lost Media is giving up in a new order. Stylistically, Found Media tends to feel spontaneous, almost accidental. It's a domain dominated by the young, where writers get points not for following traditions or burnishing them but for amateur and hybrid vigor, for creating their own venues and their own genres. It is about public expression and community—not quite John Dewey's Great Community, which the critic Eric Alterman alluded to in a recent *New Yorker* article on newspapers, but rather a fractured form of Dewey's ideal: call it Great Communities.

To be a Found Media journalist or pundit, one need not be elite, expert, or trained; one must simply produce punchy intellectual property that is in conversation with groups of

Illustration by Tomer Hanuka

5. Page Numbers
30-34

34. UNSIGNED ARTICLE

"Performance of the Week." *Time* 6 Oct. 2003: 18. Print.

Digital written-word sources

Digital sources such as Web sites differ from print sources in the ease with which they can be changed, updated, or eliminated. In addition, the various electronic media do not organize their works the same way. The most commonly cited electronic sources are

---

CHECKLIST

Citing Digital Sources

When citing sources accessed online or from an electronic database, give as many of the following elements as you can find:

1. **Author.** Give the author's name, if available.

2. **Title.** Put titles of articles or short works in quotation marks. Italicize book titles.

For works from databases:

3. **Title of periodical,** italicized.

4. **Publication information.** After the volume/issue/year or date, include page numbers (or *n. pag.* if no page numbers are listed).

5. **Name of database,** italicized, if you used a subscription service such as Academic Search Premier.

For works from the Web:

3. **Title of the site,** italicized.

4. **Name of the publisher or sponsor.** This information usually appears at the bottom of the page.

5. **Date of online publication or most recent update.** This information often appears at the bottom of the page. If no date is given, use *n.d.*

6. **Medium of publication.** Use *Web*.

7. **Date of access.** Give the most recent date you accessed the source.

If you think your readers will have difficulty finding the source without a URL, put it after the period following the date of access, inside angle brackets, with a period after the closing bracket.

documents from Web sites and databases. For help determining which is which, see 49a.

35. WORK FROM A DATABASE. The basic format for citing a work from a database appears in the source map on pp. 428–29.

For a periodical article that is available in print but that you access in an online database through a library subscription service such as Academic Search Premier, begin with the author's name (if given); the title of the work, in quotation marks; the title of the periodical, italicized; and the volume / issue number and the date for the print version of the work (see models 28–34). Include the page numbers from the print version; if no page numbers are available, use *n. pag.* Then give the name of the online database, italicized; the medium (*Web*); and your most recent date of access.

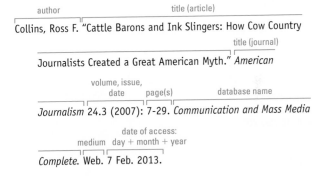

author   title (article)

Collins, Ross F. "Cattle Barons and Ink Slingers: How Cow Country

title (journal)

Journalists Created a Great American Myth." *American*

volume, issue,
date   page(s)   database name

Journalism 24.3 (2007): 7-29. *Communication and Mass Media*

date of access:
medium   day + month + year

Complete. Web. 7 Feb. 2013.

36. ARTICLE FROM THE WEB SITE OF A JOURNAL. Begin an entry for an online journal article as you would one for a print journal article (see model 28). If an article does not have page numbers, use *n. pag.* End with the medium consulted (*Web*) and the date of access.

author   title (article)

Gallagher, Brian. "Greta Garbo Is Sad: Some Historical Reflections on

the Paradoxes of Stardom in the American Film Industry,

title (journal)

1910-1960." *Images: A Journal of Film and Popular Culture*

volume,   date of
date   page(s) medium   access

3 (1997): n. pag. Web. 7 Aug. 2013.

MLA SOURCE MAP: Articles from Databases

Library subscriptions—such as EBSCOhost and Academic Search Premier—provide access to huge databases of articles.

1 **Author.** List the last name first. End with a period. For variations, see models 2–5.

2 **Article title.** Enclose the title and any subtitle in quotation marks.

3 **Periodical title.** Italicize it. Exclude any initial *A*, *An*, or *The*.

4 **Volume and issue / Date of publication.** List the volume and issue number, if any; the date of publication, including the day (if given), month, and year, in that order; and a colon.

5 **Page numbers.** Give the inclusive page numbers. If an article has no page numbers, write *n. pag.*

6 **Database name.** Italicize the name of the database.

7 **Medium.** For an online database, use *Web*.

8 **Date of access.** Give the day, month, and year, then a period.

A citation for the article on p. 429 would look like this:

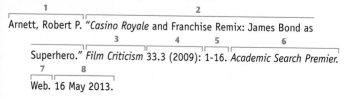

Arnett, Robert P. "*Casino Royale* and Franchise Remix: James Bond as Superhero." *Film Criticism* 33.3 (2009): 1-16. *Academic Search Premier.* Web. 16 May 2013.

2. Article Title

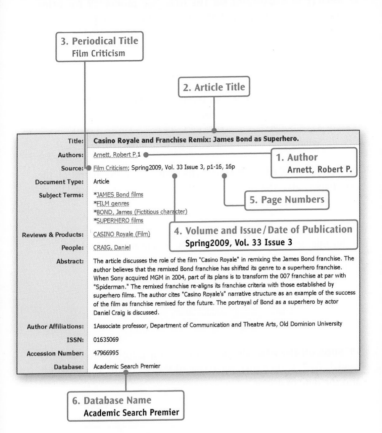

Title:	**Casino Royale and Franchise Remix: James Bond as Superhero.**
Authors:	Arnett, Robert P.1
Source:	Film Criticism; Spring2009, Vol. 33 Issue 3, p1-16, 16p
Document Type:	Article
Subject Terms:	*JAMES Bond films *FILM genres *BOND, James (Fictitious character) *SUPERHERO films
Reviews & Products:	CASINO Royale (Film)
People:	CRAIG, Daniel
Abstract:	The article discusses the role of the film "Casino Royale" in remixing the James Bond franchise. The author believes that the remixed Bond franchise has shifted its genre to a superhero franchise. When Sony acquired MGM in 2004, part of its plans is to transform the 007 franchise at par with "Spiderman." The remixed franchise re-aligns its franchise criteria with those established by superhero films. The author cites "Casino Royale's" narrative structure as an example of the success of the film as franchise remixed for the future. The portrayal of Bond as a superhero by actor Daniel Craig is discussed.
Author Affiliations:	1Associate professor, Department of Communication and Theatre Arts, Old Dominion University
ISSN:	01635069
Accession Number:	47966995
Database:	Academic Search Premier

1. Author
Arnett, Robert P.

5. Page Numbers

4. Volume and Issue / Date of Publication
Spring2009, Vol. 33 Issue 3

6. Database Name
Academic Search Premier

37. ARTICLE IN A MAGAZINE ON THE WEB. See model 29 for print publication information if the article appears in print. After the name of the magazine, give the sponsor of the Web site, the date of publication, the medium (*Web*), and the date of access.

<pre>
                                                                title
    author   title (article)   (magazine)
</pre>
Shapiro, Walter. "The Quest for Universal Healthcare." *Salon.*

<pre>
          sponsor   date of   date of
          of site   publication   medium   access
</pre>
Salon Media Group, 21 Feb. 2008. Web. 2 Mar. 2012.

38. ARTICLE IN A NEWSPAPER ON THE WEB. After the name of the newspaper, give the publisher, publication date, medium (*Web*), and access date.

<pre>
                author(s)   title (article)
</pre>
Bustillo, Miguel, and Carol J. Williams. "Old Guard in Cuba

<pre>
                     title (newspaper)   sponsor of site
</pre>
Keeps Reins." *Los Angeles Times.* Los Angeles Times,

<pre>
     date of   date of
   publication   medium   access
</pre>
25 Feb. 2008. Web. 26 Feb. 2013.

39. BOOK ON THE WEB. Provide information as for a print book (see models 6–27); then give the name of the Web site, the medium, and the date of access.

<pre>
                                                         city of
    author   title (book)   translator publication
</pre>
Euripides. *The Trojan Women.* Trans. Gilbert Murray. New York:

<pre>
     publisher   date   title (Web site)   medium
</pre>
Oxford UP, 1915. *Internet Sacred Text Archive.* Web.

<pre>
  date of access
</pre>
12 Oct. 2013.

Note: Cite a part of an online book as you would a part of a print book (see models 10 and 21). Give the print publication information (if any), the name of the site, the medium (*Web*), and the date of access.

Riis, Jacob. "The Genesis of the Gang." *The Battle with the Slum.*
New York: Macmillan, 1902. N. pag. *Bartleby.com: Great Books Online.* Web. 31 Mar. 2013.

40. POEM ON THE WEB. Include the poet's name, the title of the poem, and the print publication information (if any) as you would for part of an online book (model 39). End with the name of the site, the medium (*Web*), and the date of access.

> Dickinson, Emily. "The Grass." *Poems: Emily Dickinson*. Boston, 1891.
>
> N. pag. *Humanities Text Initiative American Verse Project*. Web.
>
> 6 Jan. 2012.

41. EDITORIAL OR LETTER IN A WEB PERIODICAL. Include the word *Editorial* or *Letter* after the author (if given) and title (if any). End with the periodical name, the sponsor of the Web site, the date of the posting or most recent update, the medium, and the access date.

> "The Funding Gap." Editorial. *Washington Post*. Washington Post, 5
>
> Nov. 2003. Web. 19 Oct. 2012.
>
> Moore, Paula. "Go Vegetarian." Letter. *New York Times*. New
>
> York Times, 25 Feb. 2008. Web. 25 Feb. 2013.

42. REVIEW IN A WEB PERIODICAL. Cite an online review as you would a print review (see model 33). End with the name of the periodical, the sponsor, the date of electronic publication, the medium, and the date of access.

> Seitz, Matt Zoller. "A Modern Horror Film." Rev. of *The Social Network*,
>
> dir. David Fincher. *Salon*. Salon Media Group, 4 Oct. 2010. Web.
>
> 24 May 2013.

43. ENTRY IN A WEB REFERENCE WORK. Cite the entry as you would an entry from a print reference work (see model 22). Follow with the name of the Web site, the sponsor, the date of publication, the medium, and the date of access.

> "Tour de France." *Encyclopaedia Britannica Online*. Encyclopaedia
>
> Britannica, 2006. Web. 21 May 2012.

44. WORK FROM A WEB SITE. For basic information on citing a work from a Web site, see the source map on pp. 434–35. Include all of the following elements that are available: the author; the title of the work in quotation marks; the name of the Web site, italicized; the name of the publisher or sponsor (if none is available, use *N.p.*); the date of publication (if not available, use *n.d.*); the medium (*Web*); and the date of access.

"America: A Center-Left Nation." *Media Matters for America*. Media

Matters for America, 27 May 2009. Web. 31 May 2011.

Stauder, Ellen Keck. "Darkness Audible: Negative Capability and Mark

Doty's 'Nocturne in Black and Gold.'" *Romantic Circles Praxis*

Series. U of Maryland, 2003. Web. 28 Sept. 2013.

45. DOWNLOADED PDF FILE. If you download a PDF file instead of reading the source online, determine what kind of source it is (such as a journal article) and give the information for citing such a source. Use *PDF file* as the medium; omit the access date.

Christenson, Clayton M., David Skok, and James Allworth. "Be the

Disruptor." *Nieman Reports* 66.3 (2012): 8-23. PDF file.

46. ENTIRE WEB SITE. Follow the guidelines for a specific work from the Web, beginning with the name of the author, editor, compiler, director, narrator, or translator, followed by the title of the Web site, italicized; the name of the sponsor or publisher (if none, use *N.p.*); the date of publication or last update; the medium of publication (*Web*); and the date of access.

editor(s)

Bernstein, Charles, Kenneth Goldsmith, Martin Spinelli, and Patrick

                                       title (Web site)   sponsor or   date of
                                                                      publisher publication

Durgin, eds. *Electronic Poetry Corner*. SUNY Buffalo, 2003.

medium date of access

Web. 26 Sept. 2013.

Weather.com. Weather Channel Interactive, 2011. Web. 13 Mar. 2012.

For a personal Web site, include the name of the person who created the site; the title or (if there is no title) a description such as *Home page*, not italicized; the name of the larger site, if different from the personal site's title; the publisher or sponsor of the site (if none, use *N.p.*); the date of the last update; the medium of publication (*Web*); and the date of access.

Ede, Lisa. Home page. *Oregon State*. Oregon State U, 2010. Web.

17 May 2013.

47. ACADEMIC COURSE WEB SITE. For a course site, include the name of the instructor, the title of the course in quotation marks, the title of the site in italics, the department (if relevant) and institution sponsoring the site, the date (or *n.d.*), the medium (*Web*), and the access date.

Creekmur, Corey K., and Philip Lutgendorf. "Topics in Asian Cinema:

Popular Hindi Cinema." *University of Iowa.* Depts. of English,

Cinema, and Comparative Literature, U of Iowa, 2004. Web.

13 Mar. 2012.

For a department Web site, give the department name, the description *Dept. home page*, the institution (in italics), the site sponsor, the date (or *n.d.*), the medium (*Web*), and the access information.

English Dept. home page. *Amherst College.* Amherst Coll., n.d. Web.

5 Apr. 2013.

48. BLOG. For an entire blog, give the author's name; the title of the blog, italicized; the sponsor or publisher of the blog (if there is none, use *N.p.*); the date of the most recent update; the medium (*Web*); and the date of access.

Little Green Footballs. Little Green Footballs, 23 Aug. 2012. Web.

23 Aug. 2012.

Note: To cite a blogger who writes under a pseudonym, begin with the pseudonym and then put the writer's real name (if you know it) in square brackets.

Atrios [Duncan Black]. *Eschaton.* N.p., 27 June 2013. Web.

27 June 2013.

49. PUBLISHED INTERVIEW. List the person interviewed; the title of the interview (if any) or the label *Interview* and the interviewer's name, if relevant. Then provide information about the source, following the appropriate model.

Paretsky, Sara. Interview. *Progressive.* Progressive Magazine, 14 Jan.

2008. Web. 12 Feb. 2011.

Taylor, Max. "Max Taylor on Winning." *Time* 13 Nov. 2000: 66. Print.

50. POST OR COMMENT ON A BLOG. Give the author's name; the title of the post or comment, in quotation marks (if there is no title, use the description *Web log post* or *Web log comment*, not italicized); the title of the blog, italicized; the sponsor of the blog (if there is none, use

You may need to browse other parts of a site to find some of the following elements, and some sites may omit elements. Uncover as much information as you can.

1 **Author.** List the last name first. End with a period. If no author is given, begin with the title. For variations, see models 2–5.

2 **Title of work.** Enclose the title and any subtitle in quotation marks.

3 **Title of Web site.** Give the title of the entire Web site, italicized.

4 **Publisher or sponsor.** Look for the sponsor's name at the bottom of the home page. If no information is available, write *N.p.* Follow it with a comma.

5 **Date of publication or latest update.** Give the most recent date, followed by a period. If no date is available, use *n.d.*

6 **Medium.** Use *Web* and follow it with a period.

7 **Date of access.** Give the date you accessed the work. End with a period.

A citation for the work on p. 435 would look like this:

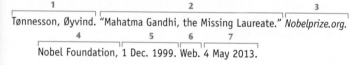

Tønnesson, Øyvind. "Mahatma Gandhi, the Missing Laureate." *Nobelprize.org.*
    Nobel Foundation, 1 Dec. 1999. Web. 4 May 2013.

Nobelprize.org

NOBEL PRIZES   ALFRED NOBEL   PRIZE AWARDERS   NOMINATION   PRIZE ANNOUNCEMENTS   AWARD CEREMONIES   EDUCATIONAL GAMES
By Year   Nobel Prize in Physics   Nobel Prize in Chemistry   Nobel Prize in Medicine   Nobel Prize in Literature   Nobel Peace Prize   Prize in Economics

Mahatma Gandhi, the Missing Laureate

by Øyvind Tønnesson
Nobelprize.org Peace Editor, 1998-2000
1 December 1999

Mohandas Gandhi (1869-1948) has become the strongest symbol of non-violence in the 20th century. It is widely held – in retrospect – that the Indian national leader should have been the very man to be selected for the Nobel Peace Prize. He was nominated several times, but was never awarded the prize. Why?

These questions have been asked frequently: Was the horizon of the Norwegian Nobel Committee too narrow? Were the committee members unable to appreciate the struggle for freedom among non-European peoples?" Or were the Norwegian committee members perhaps afraid to make a prize award which might be detrimental to the relationship between their own country and Great Britain?

When still alive, Mohandas Gandhi had many admirers, both in India and abroad. But his martyrdom in 1948 made him an even greater symbol of peace. Twenty-one years later, he was commemorated on this double-sized United Kingdom postage stamp.
Photo Copyright © Scanpix

Gandhi was nominated in 1937, 1938, 1939, 1947 and, finally, a few days before he was murdered in January 1948. The omission has been publicly regretted by later members of the Nobel Committee; when the Dalai Lama was awarded the Peace Prize in 1989, the

Why Was Gandhi Never Awarded the Nobel Peace Prize?

Up to 1960, the Nobel Peace Prize was awarded almost exclusively to Europeans and Americans. In retrospect, the horizon of the Norwegian Nobel Committee may seem too narrow. Gandhi was very different from earlier Laureates. He was no real politician or proponent of international law, not primarily a humanitarian relief worker and not an organiser of international peace congresses. He would have belonged to a new breed of Laureates.

There is no hint in the archives that the Norwegian Nobel Committee ever took into consideration the possibility of an adverse British reaction to an award to Gandhi. Thus it seems that the hypothesis that the Committee's omission of Gandhi was due to its members' not wanting to provoke British authorities, may be rejected.

In 1947 the conflict between India and Pakistan and Gandhi's prayer-meeting statement, which made people wonder whether he was about to abandon his consistent pacifism, seem to have been the primary reasons why he was not selected by the committee's majority. Unlike the situation today, there was no tradition for the Norwegian Nobel Committee to try to use the Peace Prize as a stimulus for peaceful settlement of regional conflicts.

During the last months of his life, Gandhi worked hard to end the violence between Hindus and Muslims which followed the partition of India. We know little about the Norwegian Nobel Committee's discussions on Gandhi's candidature in 1948 other than the above quoted entry of November 18 in Gunnar Jahn's diary – but it seems clear that they seriously considered a posthumous award. When the committee, for formal reasons, ended up not making such an award, they decided to reserve the prize, and then, one year later, not to spend the prize money for 1948 at all. What many thought should have been Mahatma Gandhi's place on the list of Laureates was silently but respectfully left open.

N.p.); the date of the most recent update; the medium (*Web*); and the date of access.

author   title (post or comment)   title (blog)   sponsor

Marcotte, Amanda. "Standing Up to Sexism Works." *Raw Story*. N.p.,

date of
publication   medium   date of
access

    15 May 2013. Web. 16 May 2013.

51. ENTRY IN A WIKI. Because wiki content is collectively edited, do not include an author. Treat a wiki as you would a work from a Web site (see model 44). Check with your instructor before using a wiki as a source.

"Fédération Internationale de Football Association." *Wikipedia*.

Wikimedia Foundation, 27 June 2011. Web. 27 June 2011.

52. POSTING TO A DISCUSSION GROUP OR NEWSGROUP. Begin with the author's name and the title of the posting in quotation marks (or the words *Online posting*). Follow with the name of the Web site, the sponsor or publisher of the site (use *N.p.* if there is no sponsor), the date of publication, the medium (*Web*), and the date of access.

Daly, Catherine. "Poetry Slams." *Poetics Discussion List*. SUNY Buffalo,

29 Aug. 2003. Web. 1 Oct. 2005.

53. POSTING TO A SOCIAL NETWORKING SITE. To cite a posting on Facebook or another social networking site, include the writer's name, a description of the posting, the date of the posting, and the medium of delivery. (The MLA does not provide guidelines for citing postings on such sites; this model is based on the MLA's guidelines for citing email.)

Ferguson, Sarah. Status update. 6 Mar. 2013. Facebook posting.

54. EMAIL OR MESSAGE ON A SOCIAL NETWORKING SITE. Include the writer's name; the subject line, in quotation marks (for email); *Message to* (not italicized or in quotation marks) followed by the recipient's name; the date of the message; and the medium of delivery (*E-mail*). (MLA style hyphenates *e-mail*.)

Harris, Jay. "Thoughts on Impromptu Stage Productions." Message to

the author. 16 July 2006. E-mail.

55. TWEET. Include the writer's real name, if known, with the user name (if different) in parentheses. If you don't know the real name, give just the user name. Include the entire tweet, in quotation marks. End with date and time of message and the medium (*Tweet*).

      author   tweet

BedfordBits. "#4C12 'Think of citations as a guide for the engaged

reader.' Writing center tutor quoted by E. Kleinfeld. See

                                     date   time   medium

http://citationproject.net/" 23 Mar. 2012, 4:01 p.m. Tweet.

Visual, audio, multimedia, and live sources

56. FILM, DVD, OR STREAMING VIDEO. If you cite a particular person's work, start with that name. If not, start with the title; then name the director, distributor, and year of release. Other contributors, such as writers or performers, may follow the director. If you cite a DVD instead of a theatrical release, include the original film release date and the label *DVD*.

    title   director   major performer(s)

Black Swan. Dir. Darren Aronofsky. Perf. Natalie Portman.

                     year of

      distributor   release medium

Fox Searchlight, 2010. Film.

Spirited Away. Dir. Hayao Miyazaki. 2001. Walt Disney Video, 2003. DVD.

For material streamed from a Web site, give the name of the site or database, the medium (*Web*), and the access date.

Winner, Michael, dir. *Death Wish*. Perf. Charles Bronson. Paramount, 1974. *Netflix*. Web. 11 Nov. 2012.

57. SHORT ONLINE VIDEO. Cite a short online video as you would a work from a Web site (see model 44).

Weber, Jan. "As We Sow, Part 1: Where Are the Farmers?" *YouTube*. YouTube, 15 Mar. 2008. Web. 27 Sept. 2012.

58. TELEVISION OR RADIO PROGRAM. In general, begin with the title of the program, italicized. Then list important contributors (narrator, writer, director, actors); the network; the local station and city, if any; the broadcast date; and the medium. To cite a particular person's work, begin with that name. To cite a particular episode from a series, begin with the episode title, in quotation marks.

title (program) · major contributor(s)

The American Experience: Buffalo Bill. Writ., dir., prod. Rob Rapley.

network · local station · local city · date of broadcast · medium

PBS. WNET, New York, 25 Feb. 2008. Television.

"For Immediate Release." *Mad Men*. Writ. Matthew Weiner. Dir. Jennifer Getzinger. AMC. 5 May 2013. Television.

Note: For a streaming version online, give the name of the Web site, italicized. Then give the publisher or sponsor, a comma, and the date posted. End with the medium (*Web*) and the access date.

Limbaugh, Rush. *The Rush Limbaugh Show*. RushLimbaugh.com. Premier Radio Networks, 29 Feb. 2012. Web. 2 Apr. 2012.

59. BROADCAST INTERVIEW. List the person interviewed and then the title, if any. If the interview has no title, use the label *Interview* and name the interviewer, if relevant. Then identify the source. To cite a broadcast interview, end with information about the program, the date(s) the interview took place, and the medium.

Revkin, Andrew. Interview with Terry Gross. *Fresh Air*. Natl. Public Radio. WNYC, New York, 14 June 2006. Radio.

Note: If you listened to an archived version online, provide the site's sponsor (if known), the date of the interview, the medium (*Web*), and the access date. For a podcast interview, see model 66.

> Revkin, Andrew. Interview with Terry Gross. *Fresh Air. NPR.org.* NPR, 14 June 2006. Web. 12 Jan. 2013.

60. UNPUBLISHED OR PERSONAL INTERVIEW. List the person interviewed; the label *Telephone interview*, *Personal interview*, or *E-mail interview*; and the date the interview took place.

> Freedman, Sasha. Personal interview. 10 Nov. 2011.

61. SOUND RECORDING. List the name of the person or group you wish to emphasize (such as the composer, conductor, or band); the title of the recording or composition; the artist, if appropriate; the manufacturer; and the year of issue. Give the medium (such as *CD*, *MP3 file*, or *LP*). If you are citing a particular song or selection, include its title, in quotation marks, before the title of the recording.

> Bach, Johann Sebastian. *Bach: Violin Concertos.* Perf. Itzhak Perlman and Pinchas Zukerman. English Chamber Orch. EMI, 2002. CD.
>
> Sonic Youth. "Incinerate." *Rather Ripped.* Geffen, 2006. MP3 file.

Note: If you are citing instrumental music that is identified only by form, number, and key, do not underline, italicize, or enclose it in quotation marks.

> Grieg, Edvard. Concerto in A minor, op. 16. Cond. Eugene Ormandy. Philadelphia Orch. RCA, 1989. LP.

62. MUSICAL COMPOSITION. When you are not citing a specific published version, first give the composer's name, followed by the title.

> Mozart, Wolfgang Amadeus. *Don Giovanni,* K527.
>
> Mozart, Wolfgang Amadeus. Symphony no. 41 in C major, K551.

Note: Cite a published score as you would a book. If you include the date that the composition was written, do so immediately after the title.

> Schoenberg, Arnold. *Chamber Symphony No. 1 for 15 Solo Instruments, Op. 9.* 1906. New York: Dover, 2002. Print.

63. COMPUTER GAME. Include the version after the title, then the city and publisher, date, and medium.

> *Grand Theft Auto: Tales from Liberty City*. PlayStation 3 vers. New
>> York: Rockstar Games, 2009. DVD-ROM.

Cite an online game as you would a work from a Web site (see model 44).

> *The Sims 3*. PC vers. *TheSims.com*. Electronic Arts, 2011. Web. 30 Nov.
>> 2012.

64. LECTURE OR SPEECH. List the speaker; title, in quotation marks; sponsoring institution or group; place; and date. If the speech is untitled, use a label such as *Lecture*.

> Colbert, Stephen. Speech. White House Correspondents' Association
>> Dinner. *YouTube*. YouTube, 29 Apr. 2006. Web. 20 May
>> 2013.
> Eugenides, Jeffrey. Portland Arts and Lectures. Arlene Schnitzer
>> Concert Hall, Portland, OR. 30 Sept. 2003. Lecture.

65. LIVE PERFORMANCE. List the title, appropriate names (such as writer or performer), the place, and the date. To cite a particular person's work, begin the entry with that name.

> *Anything Goes*. By Cole Porter. Perf. Klea Blackhurst. Shubert Theater,
>> New Haven. 7 Oct. 2003. Performance.

66. PODCAST (STREAMING). Include all of the following that are relevant and available: the speaker, the title of the podcast, the title of the program, the host or performers, the title of the site, the site's sponsor, the date of posting, the medium (*Web*), and the access date. (This model is based on MLA guidelines for a short work from a Web site. For a downloaded podcast, see model 67.)

> "Seven Arrested in U.S. Terror Raid." *Morning Report*. Host Krishnan
>> Guru-Murthy. *4 Radio*. Channel 4 News, 23 June 2006. Web.
>> 27 June 2012.

67. DIGITAL FILE. A citation for a file that you can download from the Web — one that exists independently, not only on a Web site — begins with the citation information required for the type of source (a photograph or sound recording, for example). For the medium, indicate the type of file (*MP3 file*, *JPEG file*).

title (photograph)   date of composition

Officer's Winter Quarters, Army of Potomac, Brandy Station. Mar. 1864.

location of photograph   medium: file type

Prints and Photographs Div., Lib. of Cong. TIFF file.

"Return to the Giant Pool of Money." *This American Life.* Narr. Ira

    Glass. NPR, 25 Sept. 2009. MP3 file.

68. WORK OF ART OR PHOTOGRAPH. List the artist or photographer; the work's title, italicized; the date of composition (if unknown, use *n.d.*); and the medium of composition (*Oil on canvas*, *Bronze*). Then cite the name of the museum or other location and the city. To cite a reproduction in a book, add the publication information. To cite artwork found online, omit the medium of composition, and after the location, add the title of the database or Web site, italicized; the medium consulted (*Web*); and the date of access.

Chagall, Marc. *The Poet with the Birds.* 1911. Minneapolis Inst. of

    Arts. *artsmia.org.* Web. 6 Oct. 2013.

General William Palmer in Old Age. 1810. Oil on canvas. National

    Army Museum, London. *White Mughals: Love and Betrayal in*

    Eighteenth-Century India. By William Dalrymple. New York:

    Penguin, 2002. 270. Print.

Kahlo, Frida. *Self-Portrait with Cropped Hair.* 1940. Oil on canvas.

    Museum of Mod. Art, New York.

69. MAP OR CHART. Cite a map or chart as you would a book or a short work within a longer work, and include the word *Map* or *Chart* after the title. Add the medium of publication. For an online source, end with the date of access.

"Australia." Map. *Perry-Castañeda Library Map Collection*. U of Texas,

1999. Web. 4 Nov. 2012.

California. Map. Chicago: Rand, 2002. Print.

70. CARTOON OR COMIC STRIP. List the artist's name; the title (if any) of the cartoon or comic strip, in quotation marks; the label *Cartoon* or *Comic strip*; and the usual publication information for a print periodical (see models 28–31) or a work from a Web site (model 44).

Johnston, Lynn. "For Better or Worse." Comic strip. *FBorFW.com*.

Lynn Johnston Publications, 30 June 2006. Web. 20 July

2006.

Lewis, Eric. "The Unpublished Freud." Cartoon. *New Yorker*

11 Mar. 2002: 80. Print.

71. ADVERTISEMENT. Include the label *Advertisement* after the name of the item or organization being advertised.

Microsoft. Advertisement. *Harper's* Oct. 2003: 2-3. Print.

Microsoft. Advertisement. *New York Times*. New York Times, 11 Nov.

2003. Web. 11 Nov. 2003.

Academic, government, and legal sources (including digital versions)

If an online version is not shown here, you should use the appropriate model for the source and then end with the medium and date of access.

72. REPORT OR PAMPHLET. Follow the guidelines for a print book (models 6–27) or an online book (model 39).

Allen, Katherine, and Lee Rainie. *Parents Online*. Washington: Pew

Internet & Amer. Life Project, 2002. Print.

Environmental Working Group. *Dead in the Water*. Washington:

Environmental Working Group, 2006. Web. 24 Apr. 2011.

73. GOVERNMENT PUBLICATION. Begin with the author, if identified. Otherwise, start with the name of the government, followed by the agency. For congressional documents, cite the number, session, and house of Congress (*S* for Senate, *H* for

House of Representatives); the type (*Report, Resolution, Docu-ment*) in abbreviated form; and the number. End with the pub-lication information. The print publisher is often the Government Printing Office (GPO). For online versions, follow the models for a work from a Web site (model 44) or an entire Web site (model 46).

author ———— title (document)
Gregg, Judd. *Report to Accompany the Genetic Information Act of*

number of   house   place of
Congress   session   type number(s) publication
2003. US 108th Cong., 1st sess. S. Rept. 108-22. Washington:

date
publisher   medium
GPO, 2003. Print.

Kinsella, Kevin, and Victoria Velkoff. *An Aging World: 2001.* US Bureau
of the Census. Washington: GPO, 2001. Print.

United States. Centers for Disease Control and Prevention. "FluView
Interactive." *Centers for Disease Control and Prevention.* Centers
for Disease Control and Prevention, Dec. 2012. Web. 7 Mar. 2013.

74. PUBLISHED PROCEEDINGS OF A CONFERENCE. Cite proceedings as you would a book.

Cleary, John, and Gary Gurtler, eds. *Proceedings of the Boston Area
Colloquium in Ancient Philosophy 2002.* Boston: Brill Academic,
2003. Print.

75. DISSERTATION. Enclose the title in quotation marks. Add the label *Diss.*, the school, and the year the work was accepted.

Paris, Django. "Our Culture: Difference, Division, and Unity in
Multicultural Youth Space." Diss. Stanford U, 2008. Print.

Note: Cite a published dissertation as a book, adding the identifi-cation *Diss.* and the university after the title.

76. DISSERTATION ABSTRACT. Cite as you would an unpublished dissertation (see model 75). For the abstract of a dissertation using *Dissertation Abstracts International* (*DAI*), include the *DAI* vol-ume, year, and page number.

Huang-Tiller, Gillian C. "The Power of the Meta-Genre: Cultural,

Sexual, and Racial Politics of the American Modernist Sonnet."

Diss. U of Notre Dame, 2000. *DAI* 61 (2000): 1401. Print.

77. UNPUBLISHED LETTER. Cite a published letter as a work in an anthology (see model 10). If the letter is unpublished, follow this form, with *MS* (for *manuscript*) as the medium:

Anzaldúa, Gloria. Letter to the author. 10 Sept. 2002. MS.

78. MANUSCRIPT OR OTHER UNPUBLISHED WORK. List the author's name; the title (if any) or a description of the material; the form of the material (such as *TS* for *typescript*) and any identifying numbers; and the name and location of the library or research institution housing the material, if applicable.

Woolf, Virginia. "The Searchlight." N.d. TS. Ser. III, Box 4, Item 184.

Papers of Virginia Woolf, 1902-1956. Smith Coll., Northampton.

79. LEGAL SOURCE. To cite a court case, give the names of the first plaintiff and defendant, the case number, the name of the court, and the date of the decision. To cite an act, give the name of the act followed by its Public Law (*Pub. L.*) number, the date the act was enacted, and its Statutes at Large (*Stat.*) cataloging number.

Eldred v. Ashcroft. No. 01-618. Supreme Ct. of the US. 15 Jan. 2003.

Print.

Museum and Library Services Act of 2003. Pub. L. 108-81. 25 Sept.

2003. Stat. 117.991. Print.

Note: You do not need an entry on the list of works cited when you cite articles of the U.S. Constitution and laws in the U.S. Code.

49e A sample student research project, MLA style

A brief research essay by David Craig appears on the following pages. David followed the MLA guidelines described in this chapter.

1"

David Craig

Professor Turkman

English 219

15 December 2012

Messaging: The Language of Youth Literacy

The English language is under attack. At least, that is what many people seem to believe. From concerned parents to local librarians, everyone seems to have a negative comment on the state of youth literacy today. They fear that the current generation of grade school students will graduate with an extremely low level of literacy, and they point out that although language education hasn't changed, kids are having more trouble reading and writing than in the past. When asked about the cause of this situation, many adults pin the blame on technologies such as texting and instant messaging, arguing that electronic shortcuts create and compound undesirable reading and writing habits and discourage students from learning conventionally correct ways to use language. But although the arguments against messaging are passionate, evidence suggests that they may not hold up.

The disagreements about messaging shortcuts are profound, even among academics. John Briggs, an English professor at the University of California, Riverside, says, "Americans have always been informal, but now the informality of precollege culture is so ubiquitous that many students have no practice in using language in any formal setting at all" (qtd. in McCarroll). Such objections are not new; Sven Birkerts of Mount Holyoke College argued in 1999 that "[students] read more casually. They strip-mine what they read" online and consequently produce "quickly generated, casual prose" (qtd. in Leibowitz A67). However, academics are also among the defenders of texting and instant messaging (IM), with some suggesting that messaging may be a beneficial force in the development of youth literacy because it promotes regular

Craig 2

contact with words and the use of a written medium for
communication.

Texting and instant messaging allow two individuals
who are separated by any distance to engage in real-time,
written communication. Although such communication relies
on the written word, many messagers disregard standard
writing conventions. For example, here is a snippet from an IM
conversation between two teenage girls:[1]

Definition and
example of
messaging

> Teen One: sorry im talkinto like 10 ppl at a time
> Teen Two: u izzyful person
> Teen Two: kwel
> Teen One: hey i g2g

As this brief conversation shows, participants must use words to
communicate via texting and messaging, but their words do not
have to be in standard English.

Writer
considers
argument that
youth literacy
is in decline

The issue of youth literacy does demand attention because
standardized test scores for language assessments, such as the
verbal and writing sections of the College Board's SAT, have
declined in recent years. This trend is illustrated in a chart
distributed by the College Board as part of its 2011 analysis of
aggregate SAT data (see Fig. 1).

Figure
explained
in text and
cited in
parenthetical
reference

The trend lines illustrate a significant pattern that may
lead to the conclusion that youth literacy is on the decline.
These lines display the ten-year paths (from 2001 to 2011) of
reading and writing scores, respectively. Within this period, the
average verbal score dropped a few points—and appears to be
headed toward a further decline in the future.

Discussion of
Figure 1

Based on the preceding statistics, parents and educators
appear to be right about the decline in youth literacy. And
this trend coincides with another phenomenon: digital

Explanatory
note; see 49a.

1. This transcript of an IM conversation was collected on
20 Nov. 2012. The names are concealed to protect privacy.

Craig 3

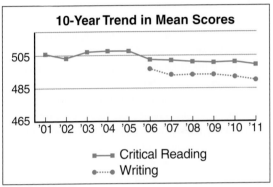

Fig. 1. Ten-year trend in mean SAT reading and writing scores
(2001-2011). Source: College Board, "2011 SAT Trends."

communication is rising among the young. According to the
Pew Internet & American Life Project, 85 percent of those
aged 12-17 at least occasionally write text messages, instant
messages, or comments on social networking sites (Lenhart,
Arafeh, Smith, and Macgill). In 2001, the most conservative
estimate based on Pew numbers showed that American youths
spent, at a minimum, nearly three million hours per day on
messaging services (Lenhart and Lewis 20). These numbers are
now exploding thanks to texting, which was "the dominant
daily mode of communication" for teens in 2012 (Lenhart), and
messaging on popular social networking sites such as Facebook
and Tumblr.

    In the interest of establishing the existence of a
messaging language, I analyzed 11,341 lines of text from
IM conversations between youths in my target demographic:
U.S. residents aged twelve to seventeen. Young messagers
voluntarily sent me chat logs, but they were unaware of the
exact nature of my research. Once all of the logs had been

Figure labeled,
titled, and
credited
to source;
inserted at
appropriate
point in text

Writer
acknowledges
part of critics'
argument;
transition to
next point

Statistical
evidence cited

Writer's field
research
introduced

gathered, I went through them, recording the number of times messaging language was used in place of conventional words and phrases. Then I generated graphs to display how often these replacements were used.

During the course of my study, I identified four types of messaging language: phonetic replacements, acronyms, abbreviations, and inanities. An example of phonetic replacement is using *ur* for *you are*. Another popular type of messaging language is the acronym; for a majority of the people in my study, the most common acronym was *lol*, a construction that means *laughing out loud*. Abbreviations are also common in messaging, but I discovered that typical IM abbreviations, such as *etc.*, are not new to the English language. Finally, I found a class of words that I call "inanities." These words include completely new words or expressions, combinations of several slang categories, or simply nonsensical variations of other words. My favorite from this category is *lolz*, an inanity that translates directly to *lol* yet includes a terminating *z* for no obvious reason.

In the chat transcripts that I analyzed, the best display of typical messaging lingo came from the conversations between two thirteen-year-old Texan girls, who are avid IM users. Figure 2 is a graph showing how often they used certain phonetic replacements and abbreviations. On the *y*-axis, frequency of replacement is plotted, a calculation that compares the number of times a word or phrase is used in messaging language with the total number of times that it is communicated in any form. On the *x*-axis, specific messaging words and phrases are listed.

My research shows that the Texan girls use the first ten phonetic replacements or abbreviations at least 50 percent of the time in their normal messaging writing. For example, every time one of them writes *see*, there is a parallel time when *c* is used in its place. In light of this finding, it

Findings of
field research
presented

Figure
introduced
and explained

Discussion of
findings
presented in
Fig. 2

Craig 5

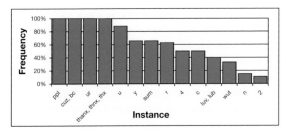

Fig. 2. Usage of phonetic replacements and abbreviations in messaging.

Figure labeled and titled

appears that the popular messaging culture contains at least some elements of its own language. It also seems that much of this language is new: no formal dictionary yet identifies the most common messaging words and phrases. Only in the heyday of the telegraph or on the rolls of a stenographer would you find a similar situation, but these "languages" were never a popular medium of youth communication. Texting and instant messaging, however, are very popular among young people and continue to generate attention and debate in academic circles.

My research shows that messaging is certainly widespread, and it does seem to have its own particular vocabulary, yet these two factors alone do not mean it has a damaging influence on youth literacy. As noted earlier, however, some people claim that the new technology is a threat to the English language.

Writer returns to opposition argument

In an article provocatively titled "Texting Makes U Stupid," historian Niall Ferguson argues, "The good news is that today's teenagers are avid readers and prolific writers. The bad news is that what they are reading and writing are text messages." He goes on to accuse texting of causing the United States to "[fall] behind more-literate societies."

The critics of messaging are numerous. But if we look to the field of linguistics, a central concept—metalinguistics—

Transition to support of thesis and refutation of critics

Craig 6

challenges these criticisms and leads to a more reasonable
conclusion—that messaging has no negative impact on a
student's development of or proficiency with traditional
literacy.

Scholars of metalinguistics offer support for the claim that
messaging is not damaging to those who use it. As noted earlier,
one of the most prominent components of messaging language
is phonetic replacement, in which a word such as *everyone*
becomes *every1*. This type of wordplay has a special importance
in the development of an advanced literacy, and for good reason.
According to David Crystal, an internationally recognized scholar
of linguistics at the University of Wales, as young children
develop and learn how words string together to express ideas,
they go through many phases of language play. The singsong
rhymes and nonsensical chants of preschoolers are vital to their
learning language, and a healthy appetite for such wordplay leads
to a better command of language later in life (182).

Linguistic
authority cited
in support of
thesis

As justification for his view of the connection between
language play and advanced literacy, Crystal presents an
argument for metalinguistic awareness. According to Crystal,
metalinguistics refers to the ability to "step back" and use
words to analyze how language works:

Block format
for a quotation
of more than
four lines

> If we are good at stepping back, at thinking in a
> more abstract way about what we hear and what we
> say, then we are more likely to be good at acquiring
> those skills which depend on just such a stepping
> back in order to be successful—and this means,
> chiefly, reading and writing. . . . [T]he greater our
> ability to play with language, . . . the more advanced
> will be our command of language as a whole.
> (Crystal 181)

Ellipses and
brackets
indicate
omissions and
changes in
quotation

If we accept the findings of linguists such as Crystal
that metalinguistic awareness leads to increased literacy,
then it seems reasonable to argue that the phonetic language

Craig 7

of messaging can also lead to increased metalinguistic awareness and, therefore, increases in overall literacy. As messagers develop proficiency with a variety of phonetic replacements and other types of texting and messaging words, they should increase their subconscious knowledge of metalinguistics.

Metalinguistics also involves our ability to write in a variety of distinct styles and tones. Yet in the debate over messaging and literacy, many critics assume that either messaging or academic literacy will eventually win out in a person and that the two modes cannot exist side by side. This assumption is, however, false. Human beings ordinarily develop a large range of language abilities, from the formal to the relaxed and from the mainstream to the subcultural. Mark Twain, for example, had an understanding of local speech that he employed when writing dialogue for *Huckleberry Finn*. Yet few people would argue that Twain's knowledge of this form of English had a negative impact on his ability to write in standard English.

However, just as Mark Twain used dialects carefully in dialogue, writers must pay careful attention to the kind of language they use in any setting. The owner of the language Web site *The Discouraging Word*, who is an anonymous English literature graduate student at the University of Chicago, backs up this idea in an e-mail to me:

> What is necessary, we feel, is that students learn how to shift between different styles of writing—that, in other words, the abbreviations and shortcuts of messaging should be used online . . . but that they should not be used in an essay submitted to a teacher. . . . Messaging might even be considered . . . a different way of reading and writing, one that requires specific and unique skills shared by certain communities.

Writer links Crystal's views to thesis

Another refutation of critics' assumptions

Example from well-known work of literature used as support

Email correspondence cited in support of claim

Craig 8

Writer
synthesizes
evidence for
claim

The analytical ability that is necessary for writers to
choose an appropriate tone and style in their writing is,
of course, metalinguistic in nature because it involves the
comparison of two or more language systems. Thus, youths
who grasp multiple languages will have a greater natural
understanding of metalinguistics. More specifically, young
people who possess both messaging and traditional skills
stand to be better off than their peers who have been trained
only in traditional or conventional systems. Far from being
hurt by their online pastime, instant messagers can be aided
in standard writing by their experience with messaging
language.

Transition to
final point

Alternate
explanation
for decline in
literacy

The fact remains, however, that youth literacy seems to
be declining. What, if not messaging, is the main cause of this
phenomenon? According to the College Board, which collects
data on several questions from its test takers, course work
in English composition and grammar classes decreased by 14
percent between 1992 and 2002 (Carnahan and Coletti 11). The
possibility of messaging causing a decline in literacy seems
inadequate when statistics on English education for US youths
provide other evidence of the possible causes. Simply put,
schools in the United States are not teaching English as much
as they used to. Rather than blaming texting and messaging
language alone for the decline in literacy and test scores, we
must also look toward our schools' lack of focus on the teaching
of standard English skills.

Transition to
conclusion

My findings indicate that the use of messaging poses
virtually no threat to the development or maintenance of
formal language skills among American youths aged twelve to
seventeen. Diverse language skills tend to increase a person's
metalinguistic awareness and, thereby, his or her ability to
use language effectively to achieve a desired purpose in a
particular situation. The current decline in youth literacy is not

Craig 9

due to the rise of texting and messaging. Rather, fewer young students seem to be receiving an adequate education in the use of conventional English. Unfortunately, it may always be fashionable to blame new tools for old problems, but in the case of messaging, that blame is not warranted. Although messaging may expose literacy problems, it does not create them.

Concluding paragraph sums up argument and reiterates thesis

Craig 10

Heading centered

Report

Graph source

Print book

Email

Article from database

Print newspaper article

Online report

Subsequent lines of each entry indented

Online newspaper article

Works Cited

Carnahan, Kristin, and Chiara Coletti. *Ten-Year Trend in SAT Scores Indicates Increased Emphasis on Math Is Yielding Results: Reading and Writing Are Causes for Concern*. New York: College Board, 2002. Print.

College Board. "2011 SAT Trends." *Collegeboard.org*. College Board, 14 Sept. 2012. Web. 6 Dec. 2012.

Crystal, David. *Language Play*. Chicago: U of Chicago P, 1998. Print.

The Discouraging Word. "Re: Messaging and Literacy." Message to the author. 13 Nov. 2012. E-mail.

Ferguson, Niall. "Texting Makes U Stupid." *Newsweek* 158.12 (2011): 11. *Academic Search Premier*. Web. 7 Dec. 2012.

Leibowitz, Wendy R. "Technology Transforms Writing and the Teaching of Writing." *Chronicle of Higher Education* 26 Nov. 1999: A67-68. Print.

Lenhart, Amanda. *Teens, Smartphones, & Texting*. Pew Research Center's Internet & Amer. Life Project, 19 Mar. 2012. PDF file.

Lenhart, Amanda, Sousan Arafeh, Aaron Smith, and Alexandra Macgill. *Writing, Technology & Teens*. Pew Research Center's Internet & Amer. Life Project, 24 Apr. 2008. PDF file.

Lenhart, Amanda, and Oliver Lewis. *Teenage Life Online: The Rise of the Instant-Message Generation and the Internet's Impact on Friendships and Family Relationships*. Pew Research Center's Internet & Amer. Life Project, 21 June 2001. PDF file.

McCarroll, Christina. "Teens Ready to Prove Text-Messaging Skills Can Score SAT Points." *Christian Science Monitor* 11 Mar. 2005. Web. 10 Dec. 2012.

50 APA Style

Chapter 50 discusses the basic formats prescribed by the American Psychological Association (APA), guidelines that are widely used in the social sciences. For further reference, consult the *Publication Manual of the American Psychological Association*, Sixth Edition (2010).

50a Understand APA citation style.

Why does academic work call for very careful citation practices when writing for the general public may not? The answer is that readers of your academic work will expect source citations for several reasons:

- Source citations demonstrate that you've done your homework on your topic and that you are a part of the conversation surrounding it.

- Source citations show that you understand the need to give credit when you make use of someone else's intellectual property. (See Chapter 15.)

- Source citations give explicit directions to guide readers who want to look for themselves at the works you're using.

The guidelines for APA style tell you exactly what information to include in your citation and how to format that information.

Types of sources. Look at the Directory to APA Style on p. 463 for guidelines on citing various types of sources — print books (or parts of print books), print periodicals (journals, magazines, and newspapers), and digital written-word sources (an online article or a book on an e-reader). A digital version of a source may include updates or corrections that the print version lacks, so it's important to provide the correct information for readers. For sources that consist mainly of material other than written words — such as a film, song, or artwork — consult the "other sources" section of the directory. And if you can't find a model exactly like the source you've selected, see the Checklist on p. 466.

ARTICLES FROM WEB AND DATABASE SOURCES. You need a subscription to look through most databases, so individual researchers almost always gain access to articles in databases through the computer system of a school or public library that pays to subscribe. The easiest way to tell whether a source comes from a database, then, is that its information is *not* generally available for free to anyone with an Internet connection. Many databases are digital collections of articles that originally appeared in edited print periodicals, ensuring that an authority has vouched for the accuracy of the information. Such sources often have more credibility than free material available on the Web.

Parts of citations. APA citations appear in two parts of your text—a brief in-text citation in the body of your written text and a full citation in the list of references, to which the in-text citation directs readers. The most straightforward in-text citations include the author's name, the publication year, and the page number, but many variations on this basic format are discussed in 50c.

MOOD MUSIC   9

References

Baker, F., & Bor, W. (2008). Can music preference indicate
    mental health status in young people? *Australasian
    Psychiatry, 16*(4), 284–288. Retrieved from http://www3
    .interscience.wiley.com/journal/118565538/home

George, D., Stickle, K., Rachid, F., & Wopnford, A. (2007). The
    association between types of music enjoyed and cognitive,
    behavioral, and personality factors of those who listen.

and suicide risk is supported by a meta-analysis done by
Baker and Bor (2008), in which the authors assert that most
studies reject the notion that music is a causal factor and
suggest that music preference is more indicative of emotional
vulnerability. However, it is still unknown whether these genres

    Taiwan. *Issues in Mental Health Nursing, 20,* 229–246.
    doi:10.1080/016128499248637

In the text of her research essay (see 50e and the integrated media), Tawnya Redding includes a paraphrase of material from an online journal that she accessed through the publisher's Web site. She cites the authors' names and the year of publication in a parenthetical reference, pointing readers to the entry for "Baker, F., & Bor, W. (2008)" in her reference list, shown on p. 456.

Content notes. APA style allows you to use content notes, either at the bottom of the page or on a separate page at the end of the text, to expand or supplement your text. Indicate such notes in the text by superscript numerals ([1]). Double-space all entries. Indent the first line of each note five spaces, but begin subsequent lines at the left margin.

SUPERSCRIPT NUMBER IN TEXT

The age of the children involved in the study was an important factor in the selection of items for the questionnaire.[1]

FOOTNOTE

[1]Marjorie Youngston Forman and William Cole of the Child Study Team provided great assistance in identifying appropriate items for the questionnaire.

50b   Follow APA manuscript format.

The following formatting guidelines are adapted from the APA recommendations for preparing manuscripts for publication in journals. However, check with your instructor before preparing the final draft of a print text.

Title page. APA does not provide specific title-page guidelines. Center the title and include your name, the course name and number, the instructor's name, and the date. If your instructor wants you to include a running head, place it flush left on the first line. Write the words *Running head*, a colon, and a short version of the title (fifty characters or fewer, including spaces) using all capital letters. On the same line, flush with the right margin, type the number *1*.

Margins and spacing.   Leave margins of at least one inch at the top and bottom and on both sides of the page. Do not justify the right margin. Double-space the entire text, including headings, set-off quotations (15b), content notes, and the list of references. Indent one-half inch from the left margin for the first line of a paragraph and all lines of a quotation over forty words long.

Short title and page numbers.   Place the running head and the short title in the upper left corner of each page. Place the page number in the upper right corner of each page, in the same position as on the title page.

Long quotations.   For a long, set-off quotation (one having more than forty words), indent it one-half inch from the left margin, and do not use quotation marks. Place the page reference in parentheses one space after the final punctuation.

Abstract.   If your instructor asks for an abstract, the abstract should go immediately after the title page, with the word *Abstract* centered about an inch from the top of the page. Double-space the text of the abstract. In most cases, a one-paragraph abstract of about one hundred words will be sufficient to introduce readers to your topic and provide a brief summary of your major thesis and supporting points.

Headings.   Headings are used within the text of many APA-style projects. In a text with only one or two levels of headings, center the main headings; italicize the subheadings and position them flush with the left margin. Capitalize all major words; however, do not capitalize articles, short prepositions, and coordinating conjunctions unless they are the first word or follow a colon.

Visuals.   Tables should be labeled *Table*, numbered, and captioned. All other visuals (charts, graphs, photographs, and drawings) should be labeled *Figure*, numbered, and captioned with a description and the source information. Remember to refer to each visual in your text, stating how it contributes to the point(s) you are making. Tables and figures should generally appear near the relevant text; check with your instructor for guidelines on placement of visuals.

50c Create APA in-text citations.

An in-text citation in APA style always indicates which source on the reference page the writer is referring to, and it explains in what year the material was published; for quoted material, the in-text citation also indicates where in the source the quotation can be found.

Note that APA style generally calls for using the past tense or present perfect tense for signal verbs: *Baker (2003) showed* or *Baker (2003) has shown*. Use the present tense only to discuss results (*the experiment demonstrates*) or widely accepted information (*researchers agree*).

1. BASIC FORMAT FOR A QUOTATION. Generally, use the author's name in a signal phrase to introduce the cited material, and place the date, in parentheses, immediately after the author's name. The page number, preceded by *p.*, appears in parentheses after the quotation.

> Gitlin (2001) pointed out that "political critics, convinced that the media are rigged against them, are often blind to other substantial reasons why their causes are unpersuasive" (p. 141).

If the author is not named in a signal phrase, place the author's name, the year, and the page number in parentheses following the quotation: (Gitlin, 2001, p. 141). For a long, set-off quotation (more than forty words), place the page reference in parentheses one space after the final quotation.

For quotations from works without page numbers, you may use paragraph numbers, if the source includes them, preceded by the abbreviation *para.*

> Driver (2007) has noticed "an increasing focus on the role of land" in policy debates over the past decade (para. 1).

2. BASIC FORMAT FOR A PARAPHRASE OR SUMMARY. Include the author's last name and the year as in model 1, but omit the page or paragraph number unless the reader will need it to find the material in a long work.

> Gitlin (2001) has argued that critics sometimes overestimate the influence of the media on modern life.

3. TWO AUTHORS. Use both names in all citations. Use *and* in a signal phrase, but use an ampersand (&) in a parentheses.

> Babcock and Laschever (2003) have suggested that many women do not negotiate their salaries and pay raises as vigorously as their male counterparts do.

> A recent study has suggested that many women do not negotiate their salaries and pay raises as vigorously as their male counterparts do (Babcock & Laschever, 2003).

4. THREE TO FIVE AUTHORS. List all the authors' names for the first reference.

> Safer, Voccola, Hurd, and Goodwin (2003) reached somewhat different conclusions by designing a study that was less dependent on subjective judgment than were previous studies.

In subsequent references, use just the first author's name plus *et al.*

> Based on the results, Safer et al. (2003) determined that the apes took significant steps toward self-expression.

5. SIX OR MORE AUTHORS. Use only the first author's name and *et al.* in every citation.

As Soleim et al. (2002) demonstrated, advertising holds the potential for manipulating "free-willed" consumers.

6. CORPORATE OR GROUP AUTHOR. If the name of the organization or corporation is long, spell it out the first time you use it, followed by an abbreviation in brackets. In later references, use the abbreviation only.

FIRST CITATION   (Centers for Disease Control and Prevention [CDC], 2006)

LATER CITATIONS   (CDC, 2006)

7. UNKNOWN AUTHOR. Use the title or its first few words in a signal phrase or in parentheses. A book's title is italicized, as in the following example; an article's title is placed in quotation marks.

The employment profiles for this time period substantiated this trend (*Federal Employment,* 2001).

8. TWO OR MORE AUTHORS WITH THE SAME LAST NAME. Include the authors' initials in each citation.

S. Bartolomeo (2000) conducted the groundbreaking study on teenage childbearing.

9. TWO OR MORE WORKS BY AN AUTHOR IN A SINGLE YEAR. Assign lowercase letters (*a*, *b*, and so on) alphabetically by title, and include the letters after the year.

Gordon (2004b) examined this trend in more detail.

10. TWO OR MORE SOURCES IN ONE PARENTHETICAL REFERENCE. List sources by different authors in alphabetical order by authors' last names, separated by semicolons: (Cardone, 1998; Lai, 2002). List works by the same author in chronological order, separated by commas: (Lai, 2000, 2002).

11. SOURCE REPORTED IN ANOTHER SOURCE. Use the phrase *as cited in* to indicate that you are reporting information from a secondary source. Name the original source in a signal phrase, but list the secondary source in your list of references.

Amartya Sen developed the influential concept that land reform was necessary for "promoting opportunity" among the poor (as cited in Driver, 2007, para. 2).

12. PERSONAL COMMUNICATION. Cite any personal letters, email messages, electronic postings, telephone conversations, or interviews as shown. Do not include personal communications in the reference list.

> R. Tobin (personal communication, November 4, 2006) supported his claims about music therapy with new evidence.

13. ELECTRONIC DOCUMENT. Cite a Web or an electronic document as you would a print source, using the author's name and date.

> Link and Phelan (2005) argued for broader interventions in public health that would be accessible to anyone, regardless of individual wealth.

The APA recommends the following practices for electronic sources without names, dates, or page numbers:

AUTHOR UNKNOWN

Use a shortened form of the title in a signal phrase or in parentheses (see model 7). If an organization is the author, see model 6.

DATE UNKNOWN

Use the abbreviation *n.d.* (for "no date") in place of the year: (*Hopkins, n.d.*).

NO PAGE NUMBERS

Many works found online or in electronic databases lack stable page numbers. (Use the page numbers for an electronic work in a format, such as PDF, that has stable pagination.) If paragraph numbers are included in such a source, use the abbreviation *para.*: (*Giambetti, 2006, para. 7*). If no paragraph numbers are included but the source includes headings, give the heading and identify the paragraph in the section:

> Jacobs and Johnson (2007) have argued that "the South African media is still highly concentrated and not very diverse in terms of race and class" (South African Media after Apartheid, para. 3).

14. TABLE OR FIGURE REPRODUCED IN THE TEXT. Number figures (graphs, charts, illustrations, and photographs) and tables separately.

For a table, place the label (*Table 1*) and an informative heading (*Hartman's Key Personality Traits*) above the table; below, provide information about its source.

Table 1

Hartman's Key Personality Traits

| | Color | | | |
Trait category	Red	Blue	White	Yellow
Motive	Power	Intimacy	Peace	Fun
Strengths	Loyal to tasks	Loyal to people	Tolerant	Positive
Limitations	Arrogant	Self-righteous	Timid	Uncommitted

Note: Adapted from The Hartman Personality Profile, by N. Hayden. Retrieved February 24, 2009, from http://students.cs.byu.edu/~nhayden /Code/index.php

For a figure, place the label (*Figure 3*) and a caption indicating the source below the image. If you do not cite the source of the table or figure elsewhere in your text, you do not need to include the source on your list of references.

50d Create an APA list of references.

The alphabetical list of the sources cited in your document is called *References*. If your instructor asks that you list everything you have read—not just the sources you cite—call the list *Bibliography*.

All the entries in this section of the book use hanging indent format, in which the first line aligns on the left and the subsequent lines indent one-half inch, or five spaces. This is the customary APA format.

CHECKLIST

Formatting a List of References

✔ Start your list on a new page after the text of your document but before appendices or notes. Continue consecutive page numbers.

✔ Center the heading *References* one inch from the top of the page.

✔ Begin each entry flush with the left margin, but indent subsequent lines one-half inch or five spaces. Double-space the entire list.

✔ List sources alphabetically by author's last name. If no author is given, alphabetize the source by the first word of the title other than *A*, *An*, or *The*. If the list includes two or more works by the same author, list them in chronological order.

✔ Italicize titles and subtitles of books and periodicals. Do not italicize titles of articles, and do not enclose them in quotation marks.

✔ For titles of books and articles, capitalize only the first word of the title and the subtitle and any proper nouns or proper adjectives.

✔ For titles of periodicals, capitalize all major words.

Guidelines for author listings

List authors' last names first, and use only initials for first and middle names. The in-text citations in your text point readers toward particular sources in your list of references (see 50c).

NAME CITED IN SIGNAL PHRASE IN TEXT

Driver (2007) has noted . . .

NAME IN PARENTHETICAL CITATION IN TEXT

. . . (Driver, 2007).

BEGINNING OF ENTRY IN LIST OF REFERENCES

Driver, T. (2007).

Models 1–5 on pp. 466–67 explain how to arrange author names. The information that follows the name of the author depends on the type of work you are citing—a book (models 6–15), a print periodical (models 16–23), a digital written-word source (models 24–34), or another kind of source (models 35–48).

1. **ONE AUTHOR.** Give the last name, a comma, the initial(s), and the date in parentheses.

Zimbardo, P. G. (2009).

2. **MULTIPLE AUTHORS.** List up to seven authors, last name first, with commas separating authors' names and an ampersand (&) before the last author's name.

Walsh, M. E., & Murphy, J. A. (2003).

Note: For a work with more than seven authors, list the first six, then an ellipsis (. . .), and then the final author's name.

3. **CORPORATE OR GROUP AUTHOR**

Resources for Rehabilitation. (2003).

4. **UNKNOWN AUTHOR.** Begin with the work's title. Italicize book titles, but do not italicize article titles or enclose them in quotation

marks. Capitalize only the first word of the title and subtitle (if any) and proper nouns and proper adjectives.

Safe youth, safe schools. (2009).

5. TWO OR MORE WORKS BY THE SAME AUTHOR. List works by the same author in chronological order. Repeat the author's name in each entry.

Goodall, J. (1999).

Goodall, J. (2002).

If the works appeared in the same year, list them alphabetically by title, and assign lowercase letters (*a*, *b*, etc.) after the dates.

Shermer, M. (2002a). On estimating the lifetime of civilizations. *Scientific American, 287*(2), 33.

Shermer, M. (2002b). Readers who question evolution. *Scientific American, 287*(1), 37.

Print books

6. BASIC FORMAT FOR A BOOK. Begin with the author name(s). (See models 1–5.) Then include the publication year, title and subtitle, city of publication, country or state abbreviation, and publisher. The source map on pp. 468–69 shows where to find this information in a typical book.

author: last
name + initial(s)   year   title and subtitle (book)

Levick, S. E. (2003). *Clone being: Exploring the psychological and*

place of
publication   publisher

social dimensions. Lanham, MD: Rowman & Littlefield.

7. EDITOR. For a book with an editor but no author, list the source under the editor's name.

editor: last
name + initial(s)   year   title and subtitle (book)

Dickens, J. (Ed.). (1995). *Family outing: A guide for parents of*

place of
publication   publisher

gays, lesbians and bisexuals. London, England: Peter Owen.

APA SOURCE MAP: Books

Take information from the book's title page and copyright page (on the reverse side of the title page), not from the book's cover or a library catalog.

1 **Author.** List all authors' last names first, and use only initials for first and middle names. For more about citing authors, see models 1–5.

2 **Publication year.** Enclose the year of publication in parentheses.

3 **Title.** Italicize the title and any subtitle. Capitalize only the first word of the title and the subtitle and any proper nouns or proper adjectives.

4 **City and state of publication, and publisher.** List the city of publication and the country or state abbreviation, a colon, and the publisher's name, dropping any *Inc.*, *Co.*, or *Publishers*.

A citation for the book on p. 469 would look like this:

A citation for the book on p. 469 would look like this:

   1   2   3

Tsutsui, W. (2004). *Godzilla on my mind: Fifty years of the king of monsters.*

              4

New York, NY: Palgrave Macmillan.

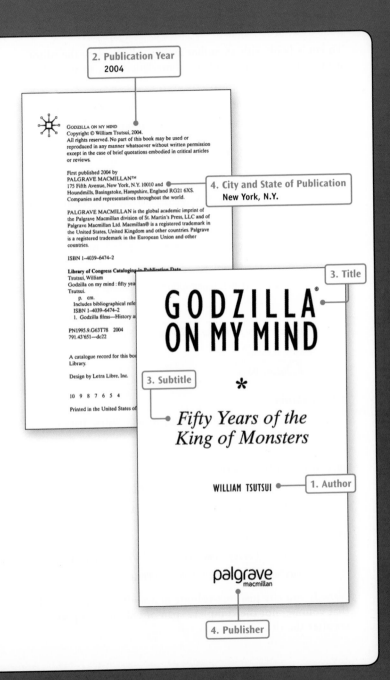

2. Publication Year
2004

GODZILLA ON MY MIND.
Copyright © William Tsutsui, 2004.
All rights reserved. No part of this book may be used or
reproduced in any manner whatsoever without written permission
except in the case of brief quotations embodied in critical articles
or reviews.

First published 2004 by
PALGRAVE MACMILLAN™
175 Fifth Avenue, New York, N.Y. 10010 and
Houndmills, Basingstoke, Hampshire, England RG21 6XS.
Companies and representatives throughout the world.

4. City and State of Publication
New York, N.Y.

PALGRAVE MACMILLAN is the global academic imprint of
the Palgrave Macmillan division of St. Martin's Press, LLC and of
Palgrave Macmillan Ltd. Macmillan® is a registered trademark in
the United States, United Kingdom and other countries. Palgrave
is a registered trademark in the European Union and other
countries.

ISBN 1–4039–6474–2

Library of Congress Cataloging-in-Publication Data
Tsutsui, William
Godzilla on my mind : fifty yea
Tsutsui.
    p. cm.
    Includes bibliographical refe
    ISBN 1–4039–6474–2
    1. Godzilla films—History a

PN1995.9.G63T78   2004
791.43'651—dc22

A catalogue record for this boo
Library.

Design by Letra Libre, Inc.

10 9 8 7 6 5 4

Printed in the United States of

3. Title

GODZILLA®
ON MY MIND

3. Subtitle

*

*Fifty Years of the
King of Monsters*

WILLIAM TSUTSUI   **1. Author**

palgrave
macmillan

4. Publisher

469

To cite a book with an author and an editor, place the editor's name, with a comma and the abbreviation *Ed.*, in parentheses after the title.

> Austin, J. (1995). *The province of jurisprudence determined.* (W. E. Rumble, Ed.). Cambridge, England: Cambridge University Press.

8. SELECTION IN A BOOK WITH AN EDITOR

author(s) of selection:
last name + initial(s)   year   title (selection)

Burke, W. W., & Nourmair, D. A. (2001). The role of personality

book editor(s):
initial(s) + last name

assessment in organization development. In J. Waclawski &

title (book)

A. H. Church (Eds.), *Organization development: A data-driven*

page(s) of selection   place of publication

approach to organizational change (pp. 55–77). San Francisco,

publisher

CA: Jossey-Bass.

9. TRANSLATION

> Al-Farabi, A. N. (1998). *On the perfect state* (R. Walzer, Trans.). Chicago, IL: Kazi.

10. EDITION OTHER THAN THE FIRST

> Moore, G. S. (2002). *Living with the earth: Concepts in environmental health science* (2nd ed.). New York, NY: Lewis.

11. MULTIVOLUME WORK WITH AN EDITOR

> Barnes, J. (Ed.). (1995). *Complete works of Aristotle* (Vols. 1–2). Princeton, NJ: Princeton University Press.

Note: If you cite just one volume of a multivolume work, list that volume, not the complete span of volumes, in parentheses after the title.

12. ARTICLE IN A REFERENCE WORK

> Dean, C. (1994). Jaws and teeth. In *The Cambridge encyclopedia of human evolution* (pp. 56–59). Cambridge, England: Cambridge University Press.

If no author is listed, begin with the title.

13. REPUBLISHED BOOK

> Piaget, J. (1952). *The language and thought of the child*. London, England: Routledge & Kegan Paul. (Original work published 1932)

14. INTRODUCTION, PREFACE, FOREWORD, OR AFTERWORD

> Klosterman, C. (2007). Introduction. In P. Shirley, *Can I keep my jersey? 11 teams, 5 countries, and 4 years in my life as a basketball vagabond* (pp. v–vii). New York, NY: Villard-Random House.

15. BOOK WITH A TITLE WITHIN THE TITLE. Do not italicize or enclose in quotation marks a title within a book title.

> Klarman, M. J. (2007). Brown v. Board of Education *and the civil rights movement*. New York, NY: Oxford University Press.

Print periodicals

Begin with the author name(s). (See models 1–5.) Then include the publication date (year only for journals, and year, month, and day for other periodicals); the article title; the periodical title; the volume number and issue number, if any; and the page numbers. The source map on pp. 472–73 shows where to find this information in a sample periodical.

16. ARTICLE IN A JOURNAL PAGINATED BY VOLUME

author(s)	year	title and subtitle (article)

O'Connell, D. C., & Kowal, S. (2003). Psycholinguistics: A half century of

	title (journal)	volume	page(s)

monologism. *The American Journal of Psychology, 116,* 191–212.

APA SOURCE MAP: Articles from Print Periodicals

1 **Author.** List all authors' last names first, and use only initials for first and middle names. For more about citing authors, see models 1–5.

2 **Publication date.** Enclose the date in parentheses. For journals, use only the year. For magazines and newspapers, use the year, a comma, the month (spelled out), and the day, if given.

3 **Article title.** Do not italicize or enclose article titles in quotation marks. Capitalize only the first word of the article title and subtitle and any proper nouns or proper adjectives.

4 **Periodical title.** Italicize the periodical title (and subtitle, if any), and capitalize all major words. Follow the periodical title with a comma.

5 **Volume and issue numbers.** Give the volume number (italicized) and, without a space in between, the issue number (if given) in parentheses. Follow with a comma.

6 **Page numbers.** Give the inclusive page numbers of the article. For newspapers only, include the abbreviation *p.* ("page") or *pp.* ("pages") before the page numbers. End the citation with a period.

A citation for the periodical article on p. 473 would look like this:

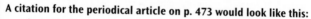

Etzioni, A. (2006). Leaving race behind: Our growing Hispanic population

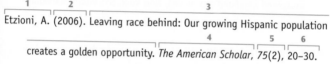

creates a golden opportunity. *The American Scholar, 75*(2), 20–30.

The AMERICAN
SCHOLAR

4. Periodical Title

Spring 2006 | Vol. 75, No. 2

5. Volume and Issue Numbers

2. Publication Date

ROBERT WILSON
Editor

JEAN STIPICEVIC
Managing Editor

The AMERICAN
SCHOLAR

3. Article Title

Leaving Race Behind

Our growing Hispanic population creates a golden opportunity

AMITAI ETZIONI

1. Author

Some years ago the United States government asked me what my race was. I was reluctant to respond because my 50 years of practicing sociology—and some powerful personal experiences—have underscored for me what we all know to one degree or another, that racial divisions bedevil America, just as they do many other societies across the world. Not wanting to encourage these divisions, I refused to check off one of the specific racial options on the U.S. Census form and instead marked a box labeled "Other." I later found out that the federal government did not accept such an attempt to de-emphasize race, by me or by some 6.75 million other Americans who tried it. Instead the government assigned me to a racial category, one it chose for me. Learning this made me conjure up what I admit is a far-fetched association. I was in this place once before. When I was a Jewish child in Nazi Germany in the early 1930s, many Jews who saw themselves as good Germans wanted to "pass" as Aryans. But the Nazi regime would have none of it. Never mind, they told these Jews, *we determine* who is Jewish and who is not. A similar practice prevailed in the Old South, where if you had one drop of African blood you were a Negro, disregarding all other facts and considerations, including how you saw yourself.

You might suppose that in the years since my little Census-form protest

Amitai Etzioni is University Professor at George Washington University and the author of *The Monochrome Society*.

6. Page Numbers

For a sub
$48 two
internati
Newsstan
advertisi
THE AME
Phi Beta
scholarsh
AMERICA
Periodica
P.O. Box
additiona
deleted s

17. ARTICLE IN A JOURNAL PAGINATED BY ISSUE. If each issue begins with page 1, include the issue number (in parentheses and not italicized) after the volume number (italicized).

author   year   title (article)

Hall, R. E. (2000). Marriage as vehicle of racism among women of

title (journal)   volume + issue   page(s)

color. *Psychology: A Journal of Human Behavior, 37*(2), 29–40.

18. ARTICLE IN A MAGAZINE. Include the month (and day, if given).

Ricciardi, S. (2003, August 5). Enabling the mobile work force. *PC Magazine, 22,* 46.

19. ARTICLE IN A NEWSPAPER. Use *p.* or *pp.* for the page number(s) of a newspaper article.

author   year, month + day   title (article)

Reynolds Lewis, K. (2011, December 22). Why some business owners

title (newspaper)   page(s)

think now is the time to sell. *The New York Times,* p. B5.

20. EDITORIAL OR LETTER TO THE EDITOR. Include an identifying label.

Zelneck, B. (2003, July 18). Serving the public at public universities [Letter to the editor]. *The Chronicle Review,* p. B18.

21. UNSIGNED ARTICLE

Annual meeting announcement. (2003, March). *Cognitive Psychology, 46,* 227.

22. REVIEW. Identify the work reviewed.

Ringel, S. (2003). [Review of the book *Multiculturalism and the therapeutic process*]. *Clinical Social Work Journal, 31,* 212–213.

23. PUBLISHED INTERVIEW. Identify the person interviewed.

Smith, H. (2002, October). [Interview with A. Thompson]. *The Sun,* pp. 4–7.

Digital written-word sources

Updated guidelines for citing digital resources are maintained at the APA's Web site (www.apa.org).

24. ARTICLE FROM AN ONLINE PERIODICAL. Give the author, date, title, and publication information as you would for a print document. Include both the volume and issue numbers for all journal articles. If the article has a digital object identifier (DOI), include it. If there is no DOI, write *Retrieved from* and the URL for the periodical's home page or for the article (if the article is difficult to find from the home page). For newspaper articles accessible from a searchable Web site, give the site URL only.

author · date of publication · title (article)

Barringer, F. (2008, February 7). In many communities, it's not

title (periodical)

easy going green. *The New York Times.* Retrieved from

URL (home page)

http://www.nytimes.com

Cleary, J. M., & Crafti, N. (2007). Basic need satisfaction, emotional

eating, and dietary restraint as risk factors for recurrent

overeating in a community sample. *E-Journal of Applied*

Psychology, 2(3), 27–39. Retrieved from http://ojs.lib.swin.edu

.au/index.php/ejap/article/view/90/116

25. ARTICLE FROM A DATABASE. Give the author, date, title, and publication information as you would for a print document. Include both the volume and issue numbers for all journal articles. If the article has a DOI, include it. If there is no DOI, write *Retrieved from* and the URL of the journal's home page (not the URL of the database). The source map on pp. 476–77 shows where to find this information for a typical article from a database.

author · date of publication · title and subtitle (article)

Hazleden, R. (2003, December). Love yourself: The relationship of

title (journal)

the self with itself in popular self-help texts. *Journal of Sociology,*

volume
+ issue · page(s) · URL (home page)

39(4), 413–428. Retrieved from http://jos.sagepub.com

APA SOURCE MAP: Articles from Databases

1 **Author.** Include the author's name as you would for a print source. List all authors' last names first, and use initials for first and middle names. For more about citing authors, see models 1–5.

2 **Publication date.** Enclose the date in parentheses. For journals, use only the year. For magazines and newspapers, use the year, a comma, the month, and the day if given.

3 **Article title.** Capitalize only the first word of the article title and the subtitle and any proper nouns or proper adjectives.

4 **Periodical title.** Italicize the periodical title.

5 **Volume and issue numbers.** For journals and magazines, give the volume number (italicized) and the issue number (in parentheses).

6 **Page numbers.** For journals only, give inclusive page numbers.

7 **Retrieval information.** If the article has a DOI (digital object identifier), include that number after the publication information; do not include the name of the database. If there is no DOI, write *Retrieved from* followed by the URL of the journal's home page (not the database URL).

A citation for the article on p. 477 would look like this:

Knobloch-Westerwick, S., & Crane, J. (2012). A losing battle: Effects

of prolonged exposure to thin-ideal images on dieting and

body satisfaction. *Communication Research, 39*(1), 79–102.

doi:10.1177/0093650211400596

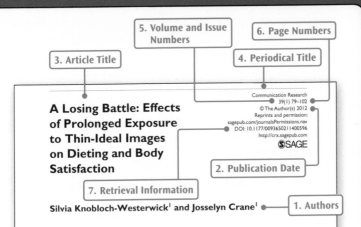

5. Volume and Issue Numbers

6. Page Numbers

3. Article Title

4. Periodical Title

Communication Research
39(1) 79–102
© The Author(s) 2012
Reprints and permission:
sagepub.com/journalsPermissions.nav
DOI: 10.1177/0093650211400596
http://crx.sagepub.com
⑤SAGE

A Losing Battle: Effects of Prolonged Exposure to Thin-Ideal Images on Dieting and Body Satisfaction

2. Publication Date

7. Retrieval Information

Silvia Knobloch-Westerwick[1] and Josselyn Crane[1]

1. Authors

Abstract

The present study examined prolonged exposure effects of thin-ideal media messages. College-aged females participated in seven online sessions over 10 days including a baseline measures session, five daily measures, and a posttest. Two experimental groups viewed magazine pages with thin-ideal imagery. One of those groups was induced to engage in social comparisons with the thin-ideal models. The control group viewed messages with body-neutral images of women. Prolonged exposure to thin-ideal messages led to greater body satisfaction. This finding was attributed to the fact that the experimental groups reported more dieting behaviors. A mediation analysis showed that the impact of thin-ideal message exposure on body satisfaction was mediated by dieting.

Keywords

body dissatisfaction, body image, dieting, prolonged exposure, social comparison

Idealized body images in the media have been linked to unrealistic body shape aspirations and body dissatisfaction (see meta-analysis by Grabe, Ward, & Hyde, 2008), which, in turn, have been linked to numerous pathological problems, including depression, obesity, dieting, and eating disorders (e.g., Johnson & Wardle, 2005; Neumark-Sztainer, Paxton, Hannan, Haines, & Story, 2006; Ricciardelli & McCabe, 2001). However, another meta-analysis by Holmstrom (2004) found that the longer the media exposure, the *better* the individuals felt about their body. This inconsistency indicates that the factors and processes at work have not yet been fully understood and captured by the research at hand and deserve further investigation. Social comparison theory is the theoretical framework that has guided much

[1]The Ohio State University

Corresponding Author:
Silvia Knobloch-Westerwick, The Ohio State University, 154 N Oval Mall, Columbus, OH 43210
Email: knobloch-westerwick.1@osu.edu

CHECKLIST

Citing Digital Sources

When citing sources accessed online or from an electronic database, include as many of the following elements as you can find:

✔ **Author.** Give the author's name, if available.

✔ **Publication date.** Include the date of electronic publication or of the latest update, if available. When no publication date is available, use *n.d.* ("no date").

✔ **Title.** If the source is not part of a larger whole, italicize the title.

✔ **Print publication information.** For articles from online journals, magazines, or reference databases, give the publication title and other publishing information as you would for a print periodical (see models 16–23).

✔ **Retrieval information.** For a work from a database, do the following: if the article has a DOI (digital object identifier), include that number after the publication information; do not include the name of the database. If there is no DOI, write *Retrieved from* followed by the URL for the journal's home page (not the database URL). For a work found on a Web site, write *Retrieved from* and include the URL. If the work seems likely to be updated, include the retrieval date. If the URL is longer than one line, break it only before a punctuation mark; do not break *http://*.

Morley, N. J., Ball, L. J., & Ormerod, T. C. (2006). How the detection of insurance fraud succeeds and fails. *Psychology, Crime, & Law, 12*(2), 163–180. doi:10.1080/10683160512331316325

26. **ABSTRACT FOR AN ONLINE ARTICLE.** Include a label.

Gudjonsson, G. H., & Young, S. (2010). Does confabulation in memory predict suggestibility beyond IQ and memory? [Abstract]. *Personality & Individual Differences, 49*(1), 65–67. doi:10.1016/j.paid.2010.03.014

27. **REPORT OR LONG DOCUMENT FROM A WEB SITE.** Include all of the following information that you can find: the author's name; the publication date (or *n.d.* if no date is available); the title of the document,

italicized; and *Retrieved from* and the URL. Provide your date of access only if an update seems likely. The source map on pp. 480–81 shows where to find this information for a report from a Web site.

author(s)   date   title (document)

Nice, M. L., & Katzev, R. (n.d.). *Internet romances: The frequency*

and nature of romantic on-line relationships. Retrieved from
                            URL

http://www.publicpolicyresearch.net/papers.html

28. CHAPTER OR SECTION OF A WEB DOCUMENT. Follow model 27. After the chapter or section title, type *In* and give the document title, with identifying information, if any, in parentheses. End with the date of access (if needed) and the URL.

Salamon, Andrew. (n.d.). War in Europe. In *Childhood in times of war*

(chap. 2). Retrieved April 11, 2008, from http://remember.org

/jean

29. SHORT WORK FROM A WEB SITE. Include the name of the work (with no italics) and the name of the site, italicized.

author   year   title (work)   title (site)

Zimbardo, P. G. (2013). Constructing the experiment. *Stanford*
                                    URL

Prison Experiment. Retrieved from http://www.prisonexp.org

/psychology/5

APA SOURCE MAP: Reports and Long Works from Web Sites

1 **Author.** If one is given, include the author's name (see models 1–5). List last names first, and use only initials for first names. The site's sponsor may be the author. If no author is identified, begin the citation with the title of the document.

2 **Publication date.** Enclose the date of publication or latest update in parentheses. Use *n.d.* ("no date") when no publication date is available.

3 **Title of work.** Italicize the title. Capitalize only the first word of the title and subtitle and any proper nouns or proper adjectives.

4 **Retrieval information.** Write *Retrieved from* and include the URL. For a report from an organization's Web site, identify the organization in the retrieval statement. If the work seems likely to be updated, include the retrieval date.

A citation for the Web document on p. 481 would look like this:

Parker, K., & Wang, W. (2013, March 14). *Modern parenthood: Roles*

of moms and dads converge as they balance work and family.

Retrieved from the Pew Research Center Web site: http://www

.pewsocialtrends.org/2013/03/14/modern-parenthood-roles

-of-moms-and-dads-converge-as-they-balance-work-and-family/

3. Title of Work

4. Retrieval Information

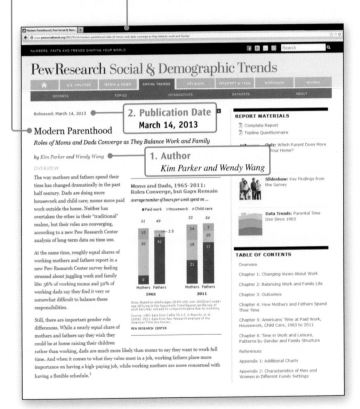

NUMBERS, FACTS AND TRENDS SHAPING YOUR WORLD   Search

PewResearch Social & Demographic Trends

| HOME | U.S. POLITICS | MEDIA & NEWS | SOCIAL TRENDS | RELIGION | INTERNET & TECH | HISPANICS | GLOBAL |

| REPORTS | TOPICS | INTERACTIVES | DATASETS | ABOUT |

Released: March 14, 2013

2. Publication Date
March 14, 2013

Modern Parenthood
Roles of Moms and Dads Converge as They Balance Work and Family

by Kim Parker and Wendy Wang

1. Author
Kim Parker and Wendy Wang

OVERVIEW

The way mothers and fathers spend their time has changed dramatically in the past half century. Dads are doing more housework and child care; moms more paid work outside the home. Neither has overtaken the other in their "traditional" realms, but their roles are converging, according to a new Pew Research Center analysis of long-term data on time use.

At the same time, roughly equal shares of working mothers and fathers report in a new Pew Research Center survey feeling stressed about juggling work and family life: 56% of working moms and 50% of working dads say they find it very or somewhat difficult to balance these responsibilities.

Still, there are important gender role differences. While a nearly equal share of mothers and fathers say they wish they could be at home raising their children rather than working, dads are much more likely than moms to say they want to work full time. And when it comes to what they value most in a job, working fathers place more importance on having a high-paying job, while working mothers are more concerned with having a flexible schedule.[1]

Moms and Dads, 1965-2011: Roles Converge, but Gaps Remain
Average number of hours per week spent on ...

■ Paid work ■ Housework ■ Child care

	1965		2011	
	Mothers	Fathers	Mothers	Fathers

Note: Based on adults ages 18-64 with own child(ren) under age 18 living in the household. Total figures (at the top of each bar) may not add to component parts due to rounding.
Source: 1965 data from Table 5A.1-2 in Bianchi, et al. (2006). 2011 data from Pew Research analysis of the American Time Use Survey.

PEW RESEARCH CENTER

REPORT MATERIALS

📄 Complete Report
📄 Topline Questionnaire

Infographic · Quiz: Which Parent Does More in Your Home?

Slideshow: Key Findings from the Survey

Data Trends: Parental Time Use Since 1965

TABLE OF CONTENTS

30. ONLINE BOOK. Give the original print publication date, if different, in parentheses at the end of the entry.

> Russell, B. (2008). *The analysis of mind*. Retrieved from
>
> http://onlinebooks.library.upenn.edu/webbin/gutbook
>
> /lookup?num=2529 (Original work published 1921)

31. EMAIL MESSAGE OR REAL-TIME COMMUNICATION. Because the APA stresses that any sources cited in your list of references be retrievable by your readers, you should not include entries for email messages, real-time communications (such as IMs), or any other postings that are not archived. Instead, cite these sources in your text as forms of personal communication (see p. 462).

32. ONLINE POSTING. List an online posting in the reference list only if you are able to retrieve the message from an archive. Provide the author's name, the date of posting, and the subject line. Include other identifying information in square brackets. End with the retrieval statement and the URL of the archived message.

> Troike, R. C. (2001, June 21). Buttercups and primroses [Electronic
>
> mailing list message]. Retrieved from http://listserv.linguistlist
>
> .org/archives/ads-l.html
>
> Wittenberg, E. (2001, July 11). Gender and the Internet [Newsgroup
>
> message]. Retrieved from news://comp.edu.composition

33. BLOG (WEB LOG) POST

> Spaulding, P. (2010, April 27). Who believes in a real America? [Web log
>
> post]. Retrieved from http://pandagon.net/index.php/site/2010/04

34. WIKI ENTRY. Use the date of posting, if there is one, or *n.d.* for "no date" if there is none. Include the retrieval date because wiki content can change frequently.

> Happiness. (2007, June 14). Retrieved March 24, 2008, from
>
> PsychWiki: http://www.psychwiki.com/wiki/Happiness

Other sources (including online versions)

35. GOVERNMENT PUBLICATION

> Office of the Federal Register. (2003). *The United States government*
>
> *manual 2003/2004*. Washington, DC: U.S. Government Printing
>
> Office.

Cite an online government document as you would a printed government work, adding the URL at the end. If there is no date, use *n.d.*

> U.S. Public Health Service. (1999). *The surgeon general's call to action to prevent suicide.* Retrieved from http://www .mentalhealth.org/suicideprevention/calltoaction.asp

36. DATA SET

> U.S. Department of Education, Institute of Education Sciences. (2009). *NAEP state comparisons* [Data set]. Retrieved from http://nces.ed.gov/nationsreportcard/statecomparisons/

37. DISSERTATION. If you retrieved the dissertation from a database, give the database name and the accession number, if one is assigned.

> Lengel, L. L. (1968). *The righteous cause: Some religious aspects of Kansas populism.* Retrieved from ProQuest Digital Dissertations. (6900033)

If you retrieve a dissertation from a Web site, give the type of dissertation and the institution after the title, and provide a retrieval statement.

> Meeks, M. G. (2006). *Between abolition and reform: First-year writing programs, e-literacies, and institutional change* (Doctoral dissertation, University of North Carolina). Retrieved from http://dc.lib.unc.edu/etd/

38. TECHNICAL OR RESEARCH REPORT. Give the report number, if available, in parentheses after the title.

> McCool, R., Fikes, R., & McGuinness, D. (2003). *Semantic Web tools for enhanced authoring* (Report No. KSL-03-07). Retrieved from www.ksl.stanford.edu/KSL_Abstracts/KSL-03-07.html

39. CONFERENCE PROCEEDINGS

> Robertson, S. P., Vatrapu, R. K., & Medina, R. (2009). YouTube and Facebook: Online video "friends" social networking. In *Conference proceedings: YouTube and the 2008 election cycle*

(pp. 159–176). Amherst, MA: University of Massachusetts.

Retrieved from http://scholarworks.umass.edu/jitpc2009

40. PAPER PRESENTED AT A MEETING OR SYMPOSIUM, UNPUBLISHED.
Cite the month of the meeting if it is available.

Jones, J. G. (1999, February). *Mental health intervention in
mass casualty disasters.* Paper presented at the Rocky
Mountain Region Disaster Mental Health Conference,
Laramie, WY.

41. POSTER SESSION

Barnes Young, L. L. (2003, August). *Cognition, aging, and dementia.*
Poster session presented at the 2003 Division 40 APA
Convention, Toronto, Ontario, Canada.

42. PRESENTATION SLIDES

Mader, S. (2007, March 2007). *The Zen aesthetic* [Presentation
slides]. Retrieved from http://www.slideshare.net/slmader
/the-zen-aesthetic

43. FILM, VIDEO, DVD, OR BLU-RAY. Begin with the director, the producer, and other relevant contributors.

major
contributor(s)

Bigelow, K. (Director, Producer), Boal, M. (Producer), & Ellison, M.

year · title · medium · country

(Producer). (2012). *Zero dark thirty* [Motion picture]. United

studio

States: Annapurna.

If you watched the film in another medium, such as on a DVD
or Blu-ray disc, indicate the medium in brackets. If the DVD or
Blu-ray and the film were not released in the same year, put
Original release and the year in parentheses at the end of the
entry.

Hitchcock, A. (Director, Producer). (2010). *Psycho* [Blu-ray]. United

States: Universal. (Original release 1960).

44. ONLINE (STREAMING) AUDIO OR VIDEO FILE

author   date   title

Klusman, P. (2008, February 13). An engineer's guide to cats

descriptive
label   URL

[Video file]. Retrieved from http://www.youtube.com

/watch?v=mHXBL6bzAR4

Koenig, S. (2013, January 25). Petticoats in a twist [Audio file].

Retrieved from http://www.thisamericanlife.org/radio-archives

/episode/485/surrogates

45. TELEVISION PROGRAM, SINGLE EPISODE

Imperioli, M. (Writer), & Buscemi, S. (Director). (2002). Everybody

hurts [Television series episode]. In D. Chase (Executive

Producer), *The Sopranos*. New York, NY: Home Box Office.

46. TELEVISION SERIES

Abrams, J. J., Lieber, J., & Lindelof, D. (2004). *Lost.* [Television

series]. New York, NY: WABC.

47. PODCAST (DOWNLOADED AUDIO FILE)

author   date of posting   title (podcast)

Noguchi, Yugi. (2010, 24 May). BP hard to pin down on oil spill

descriptive label   title (series)

claims. [Audio podcast]. *NPR morning edition.* Retrieved from

URL

http://www.npr.org

48. RECORDING

The Avalanches. (2001). Frontier psychiatrist. On *Since I left you*

[CD]. Los Angeles, CA: Elektra/Asylum Records.

50e A sample student writing project, APA style

Following are excerpts from a paper by Tawnya Redding that conforms to the APA guidelines described in this chapter. Note that this essay has been reproduced in a narrow format to allow for annotation.

1

STUDENT
WRITING

Running
head (fifty
characters
or fewer)
appears flush
left on first line
of title page

Page number
appears flush
right on first
line of every
page

Mood Music: Music Preference and the Risk for Depression

and Suicide in Adolescents

Tawnya Redding

Psychology 480

Professor Ede

February 23, 2013

Title, name,
and affiliation
centered and
double-spaced

Annotations indicate effective choices or APA-style formatting.

STUDENT
WRITING

MOOD MUSIC   2

Heading
centered

No indentation

Use of
passive voice
appropriate
for social
sciences

Clear, straight-
forward
description
of literature
under review

Conclusions
indicated

Double-
spaced text

                                    Abstract

There has long been concern for the effects that certain genres
of music (such as heavy metal and country) have on youth.
While a correlational link between these genres and increased
risk for depression and suicide in adolescents has been
established, researchers have been unable to pinpoint what is
responsible for this link, and a causal relationship has not been
determined. This paper will begin by discussing correlational
literature concerning music preference and increased risk for
depression and suicide, as well as the possible reasons for this
link. Finally, studies concerning the effects of music on mood
will be discussed. This examination of the literature on music
and increased risk for depression and suicide points out the
limitations of previous research and suggests the need for new
research establishing a causal relationship for this link as well
as research into the specific factors that may contribute to an
increased risk for depression and suicide in adolescents.

STUDENT WRITING

Mood Music: Music Preference and the Risk for Depression and
Suicide in Adolescents

Music is a significant part of American culture. Since
the explosion of rock and roll in the 1950s, there has been
a concern for the effects that music may have on listeners,
and especially on young people. The genres most likely to
come under suspicion in recent decades have included heavy
metal, country, and blues. These genres have been suspected
of having adverse effects on the mood and behavior of young
listeners. But can music really alter the disposition and create
self-destructive behaviors in listeners? And if so, which genres
and aspects of those genres are responsible? The following
review of the literature will establish the correlation between
potentially problematic genres of music such as heavy metal
and country and depression and suicide risk. First, correlational
studies concerning music preference and suicide risk will be
discussed, followed by a discussion of the literature concerning
the possible reasons for this link. Finally, studies concerning
the effects of music on mood will be discussed. Despite the link
between genres such as heavy metal and country and suicide
risk, previous research has been unable to establish the causal
nature of this link.

The Correlation between Music and Depression and Suicide Risk

Studies over the past two decades have set out to answer
this question by examining the correlation between youth
music preference and risk for depression and suicide. A large
portion of these studies have focused on heavy metal and
country music as the main genre culprits associated with youth
suicidality and depression (Lacourse, Claes, & Villeneuve, 2001;
Scheel & Westefeld, 1999; Stack & Gundlach, 1992). Stack and
Gundlach (1992) examined the radio airtime devoted to country
music in 49 metropolitan areas and found that the higher the
percentages of country music airtime, the higher the incidence

Full title
centered

Paragraphs
indented

Background
information
about review
supplied

Questions
focus reader's
attention

Boldface
headings
help organize
review

Parenthetical
references
follow APA
style

MOOD MUSIC   4

of suicides among whites. The researchers hypothesized that themes in country music (such as alcohol abuse) promoted audience identification and reinforced a preexisting suicidal mood, and that the themes associated with country music were responsible for elevated suicide rates. Similarly, Scheel and Westefeld (1999) found a correlation between heavy metal music listeners and an increased risk for suicide, as did Lacourse et al. (2001).

Reasons for the Link: Characteristics of Those Who Listen to Problematic Music

Discussion of correlation vs. causation points out limitations of previous studies

Unfortunately, previous studies concerning music preference and suicide risk have been unable to determine a causal relationship and have focused mainly on establishing a correlation between suicide risk and music preference. This leaves the question open as to whether an individual at risk for depression and suicide is attracted to certain genres of music or whether the music helps induce the mood—or both. Some studies have suggested that music preference may simply be a reflection of other underlying problems associated with increased risk for suicide (Lacourse et al., 2001; Scheel & Westefeld, 1999). For example, in research done by Scheel and Westefeld (1999), adolescents who listened to heavy metal were found to have lower scores on the Reason for Living Inventory, a self-report measure designed to assess potential reasons for not committing suicide. These adolescents were also found to have lower scores on several subscales of the Reason for Living Inventory, including responsibility to family along with survival and coping beliefs.

Alternative explanations considered

Other risk factors associated with suicide and suicidal behaviors include poor family relationships, depression, alienation, anomie, and drug and alcohol abuse (Lacourse et al., 2001). Lacourse et al. (2001) examined 275 adolescents in the Montreal region with a preference for heavy metal and found that this preference was not significantly related to suicide risk when other risk factors were controlled for. This was also the conclusion of Scheel and

Westefeld (1999), in which music preference for heavy metal was thought to be a red flag for suicide vulnerability, suggesting that the source of the problem may lie more in personal and familial characteristics.

George, Stickle, Rachid, and Wopnford (2007) further explored the correlation between suicide risk and music preference by attempting to identify the personality characteristics of those with a preference for different genres of music. A sample of 358 individuals was assessed for preference of 30 different styles of music along with a number of personality characteristics, including self-esteem, intelligence, spirituality, social skills, locus of control, openness, conscientiousness, extraversion, agreeableness, emotional stability, hostility, and depression (George et al., 2007). The 30 styles of music were then categorized into 8 factors: rebellious (for example, punk and heavy metal), classical, rhythmic and intense (including hip-hop, rap, and pop), easy listening, fringe (for example, techno), contemporary Christian, jazz and blues, and traditional Christian. The results revealed an almost comprehensively negative personality profile for those who preferred to listen to the rebellious and rhythmic and intense categories, while those who preferred classical music tended to have a comprehensively positive profile. Like Scheel and Westefeld (1999) and Lacourse et al. (2001), this study also supports the theory that youth are drawn to certain genres of music based on already existing factors, whether they be related to personality or situational variables.

Reasons for the Link: Characteristics of Problematic Music

Another possible explanation is that the lyrics and themes of the music have an effect on listeners. In this scenario, music is thought to exacerbate an already depressed mood and hence contribute to an increased risk for suicide. This was the proposed reasoning behind higher suicide rates in whites in Stack and Gundlach's (1992) study linking country

Transition links paragraphs

MOOD MUSIC   6

music to suicide risk. In this case, the themes associated with country music were thought to promote audience identification and reinforce preexisting self-destructive behaviors (such as excessive alcohol consumption). Stack (2000) also studied individuals with a musical preference for blues to determine whether the genre's themes could increase the level of suicide acceptability. The results demonstrated that blues fans were no more accepting of suicide than nonfans, but that blues listeners were found to have low religiosity levels, an important factor for suicide acceptability (Stack, 2000). Despite this link between possible suicidal behavior and a preference for blues music, the actual suicide behavior of blues fans has not been explored, and thus no concrete associations can be made.

The Effect of Music on Mood

While studies examining the relationship between music genres such as heavy metal, country, and blues have been able to establish a correlation between music preference and suicide risk, it is still unclear from these studies what effect music has on the mood of the listener. Previous research has suggested that some forms of music can both improve and depress mood (Lai, 1999; Siedliecki & Good, 2006; Smith & Noon, 1998). Lai (1999) found that changes in mood were more likely to be found in an experimental group of depressed women versus a control group. It was also found that both the experimental and control groups showed significant increases in the tranquil mood state, but the amount of change was not significant between the groups (Lai, 1999). This study suggests that music can have a positive effect on depressed individuals when they are allowed to choose the music they are listening to. In a similar study, Siedliecki and Good (2006) found that music can increase a listener's sense of power and decrease depression, pain, and disability. Researchers randomly assigned 60 African American and Caucasian participants with chronic nonmalignant pain to a standard music group

Need for more research indicated

Discussion of previous research

(offering them a choice of instrumental music types—piano, jazz, orchestra, harp, and synthesizer), a patterning music group (asking them to choose music to ease muscle tension, to facilitate sleep, or to decrease anxiety), or a control group. There were no statistically significant differences between the two music groups. However, the music groups had significantly less pain, depression, and disability than the control group (Siedliecki & Good, 2006). On the other hand, Martin, Clark, and Pearce (1993) identified a subgroup of heavy metal fans who reported feeling worse after listening to their music of choice. Although this subgroup did exist, there was also evidence that listening to heavy metal results in more positive affect, and it was hypothesized that those who experience negative effects after listening to their preferred genre of heavy metal may be most at risk for suicidal behaviors (Martin et al., 1993).

Smith and Noon (1998) also determined that music can have a negative effect on mood. Six songs were selected for the particular theme they embodied: (1) vigorous, (2) fatigued, (3) angry, (4) depressed, (5) tense, and (6) all moods. The results indicated that selections 3–6 had significant effects on the mood of participants, with selection 6 (all moods) resulting in the greatest positive change in the mood and selection 5 (tense) resulting in the greatest negative change in mood. Selection 4 (depressed) was found to sap the vigor and increase anger / hostility in participants, while selection 5 (tense) significantly depressed participants and made them more anxious. Although this study did not specifically comment on the effects of different genres on mood, the results do indicate that certain themes can indeed depress mood. The participants for this study were undergraduate students who were not depressed, and thus it seems that certain types of music can have a negative effect on the mood of healthy individuals.

MOOD MUSIC   8

Is There Evidence for a Causal Relationship?

Conclusion
indicates need
for further
research

Despite the correlation between certain music genres (especially heavy metal) and increased risk for depression and suicidal behaviors in adolescents, it remains unclear whether these types of music can alter the mood of at-risk youth in a negative way. This view of the correlation between music and suicide risk is supported by a meta-analysis done by Baker and Bor (2008), in which the authors assert that most studies reject the notion that music is a causal factor and suggest that music preference is more indicative of emotional vulnerability. However, it is still unknown whether these genres can negatively alter mood at all, and if they can, whether the themes and lyrics associated with the music are responsible. Clearly, more research is needed to further examine this correlation, as a causal link between these genres of music and adolescent suicide risk has yet to be shown. However, even if the theory put forth by Baker and Bor and other researchers is true, it is still important to investigate the effects that music can have on those who may be at risk for suicide and depression. Even if music genres are not the ultimate cause of suicidal behavior, they may act as a catalyst that further pushes adolescents into a state of depression and increased risk for suicidal behavior.

References

Baker, F., & Bor, W. (2008). Can music preference indicate mental health status in young people? *Australasian Psychiatry, 16*(4), 284–288. Retrieved from http://www3.interscience.wiley.com/journal/118565538/home

George, D., Stickle, K., Rachid, F., & Wopnford, A. (2007). The association between types of music enjoyed and cognitive, behavioral, and personality factors of those who listen. *Psychomusicology, 19*(2), 32–56.

Lacourse, E., Claes, M., & Villeneuve, M. (2001). Heavy metal music and adolescent suicidal risk. *Journal of Youth and Adolescence, 30*(3), 321–332.

Lai, Y. (1999). Effects of music listening on depressed women in Taiwan. *Issues in Mental Health Nursing, 20,* 229–246. doi:10.1080/016128499248637

Martin, G., Clark, M., & Pearce, C. (1993). Adolescent suicide: Music preference as an indicator of vulnerability. *Journal of the American Academy of Child and Adolescent Psychiatry, 32,* 530–535.

Scheel, K., & Westefeld, J. (1999). Heavy metal music and adolescent suicidality: An empirical investigation. *Adolescence, 34*(134), 253–273.

Siedliecki, S., & Good, M. (2006). Effect of music on power, pain, depression and disability. *Journal of Advanced Nursing, 54*(5), 553–562. doi:10.1111/j.1365-2648.2006.03860.x

Smith, J. L., & Noon, J. (1998). Objective measurement of mood change induced by contemporary music. *Journal of Psychiatric & Mental Health Nursing, 5,* 403–408.

Stack, S. (2000). Blues fans and suicide acceptability. *Death Studies, 24,* 223–231.

Stack, S., & Gundlach, J. (1992). The effect of country music on suicide. *Social Forces, 71*(1), 211–218. Retrieved from http://socialforces.unc.edu/

STUDENT
WRITING

References
begin on new
page

Journal
article from a
database, no
DOI

Print journal
article

Journal
article from a
database with
DOI

51 *Chicago* Style

The style guide of the University of Chicago Press has long been used in history as well as in other areas of the arts and humanities. The Sixteenth Edition of *The Chicago Manual of Style* (2010) provides a complete guide to *Chicago* style, including two systems for citing sources. This chapter presents the notes and bibliography system.

51a Understand *Chicago* citation style.

Why does academic work call for very careful citation practices when writing for the general public may not? The answer is that readers of your academic work will expect source citations for several reasons:

- Source citations demonstrate that you've done your homework on your topic and that you are a part of the conversation surrounding it.

- Source citations show that you understand the need to give credit when you make use of someone else's intellectual property. (See Chapter 15.)

- Source citations give explicit directions to guide readers who want to look for themselves at the works you're using.

Guidelines from *The Chicago Manual of Style* will tell you exactly what information to include in your citation and how to format that information.

Types of sources. Look at the Directory to *Chicago* Style on p. 500. You will need to be careful to tell your readers whether you read a print version or a digital version of a source that consists mainly of written words. Digital magazine and newspaper articles may include updates or corrections that the print version lacks; digital books may not number pages or screens the same way that a print book does. If you are citing a source that has media elements—such as a film, a song, or artwork—consult the "other sources" section of the directory. And if you can't find a model exactly like the source you've selected, see the Checklist on p. 506.

ARTICLES FROM WEB AND DATABASE SOURCES. You need a subscription to look through most databases, so individual researchers almost always gain access to articles in databases through the computer system of a school or public library that pays to subscribe. The easiest way to tell that a source comes from a database, then, is if its information is *not* generally available free to anyone with an Internet connection. Many databases are digital collections of articles that originally appeared in edited print periodicals, ensuring that an authority has vouched for the accuracy of the information. Such sources may have more credibility than free material available on the Web.

Parts of citations. Citations in *Chicago* style appear in three places in your text—a note number in the text marks the material from the source, a footnote or an endnote includes information to identify the source (or information about supplemental material), and the bibliography provides the full citation.

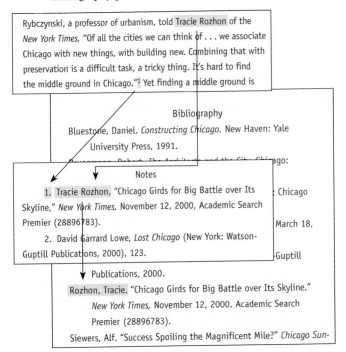

Rybczynski, a professor of urbanism, told Tracie Rozhon of the *New York Times,* "Of all the cities we can think of . . . we associate Chicago with new things, with building new. Combining that with preservation is a difficult task, a tricky thing. It's hard to find the middle ground in Chicago."1 Yet finding a middle ground is

Bibliography

Bluestone, Daniel. *Constructing Chicago.* New Haven: Yale University Press, 1991.

Notes

1. Tracie Rozhon, "Chicago Girds for Big Battle over Its Skyline," *New York Times,* November 12, 2000, Academic Search Premier (28896783).

2. David Garrard Lowe, *Lost Chicago* (New York: Watson-Guptill Publications, 2000), 123.

Publications, 2000.

Rozhon, Tracie. "Chicago Girds for Big Battle over Its Skyline." *New York Times,* November 12, 2000. Academic Search Premier (28896783).

Siewers, Alf. "Success Spoiling the Magnificent Mile?" *Chicago Sun-*

51b Follow *Chicago* manuscript format.

Title page. About halfway down the title page, center the full title of your project and your name. Unless otherwise instructed, at the bottom of the page also list the course name, the instructor's name, and the date submitted. Do not type a number on this page. Check your instructor's preference on whether to count the title page as part of the text (if so, the first text page will be page 2) or as part of the frontmatter (if so, the first text page will be page 1).

Margins and spacing. Leave one-inch margins at the top, bottom, and sides of your pages. Double-space the entire text, including block quotations, notes, and bibliography.

Page numbers. Number all pages (except the title page) in the upper right-hand corner. Also use a short title or your name before page numbers.

Long quotations. For a long quotation, indent one-half inch (or five spaces) from the left margin, and do not use quotation marks. *Chicago* defines a long quotation as one hundred words or eight lines, though you may set off shorter quotes for emphasis (39a).

Headings. *Chicago* style allows, but does not require, headings. Many students and instructors find them helpful.

Visuals. Visuals (such as photographs, drawings, charts, graphs, and tables) should be placed as near as possible to the relevant text. (See 15c for guidelines on incorporating visuals into your text.) Tables should be labeled *Table*, numbered, and captioned. All other visuals should be labeled *Figure* (abbreviated *Fig.*), numbered, and captioned. Remember to refer to each visual in your text, pointing out how it contributes to the point(s) that you are making.

Notes. Notes can be footnotes (each one appearing at the bottom of the page on which its citation appears) or endnotes (in a list on a separate page at the end of the text). (Check your instructor's preference.) Indent the first line of each note one-half inch and begin with a number, a period, and one space before the first word. All remaining lines of the entry are flush with the left margin. Single-space footnotes and endnotes, with a double space between each entry.

Use superscript numbers (¹) to mark citations in the text. Place the superscript number for each note just after the relevant quotation, sentence, clause, or phrase. Type the number after any punctuation mark except the dash; do not leave a space before the superscript. Number citations sequentially throughout the text. When you use signal phrases to introduce source material, note that *Chicago* style requires you to use the present tense (*citing Bebout's studies, Meier points out . . .*).

IN THE TEXT

> Sweig argues that Castro and Che Guevara were not the only key players in the Cuban Revolution of the late 1950s.[19]

IN THE FIRST NOTE REFERRING TO THE SOURCE

> 19. Julia Sweig, *Inside the Cuban Revolution* (Cambridge, MA: Harvard University Press, 2002), 9.

After giving complete information the first time you cite a work, shorten additional references to that work: list only the author's last name, a comma, a short version of the title, a comma, and the page number. If you refer to the same source cited in the previous note, you can use the Latin abbreviation *Ibid.* ("in the same place") instead of the name and title.

IN FIRST AND SUBSEQUENT NOTES

> 19. Julia Sweig, *Inside the Cuban Revolution* (Cambridge, MA: Harvard University Press, 2002), 9.
>
> 20. Ibid., 13.
>
> 21. Ferguson, "Comfort of Being Sad," 63.
>
> 22. Sweig, *Cuban Revolution*, 21.

Bibliography. Begin the list of sources on a separate page after the main text and any endnotes. Continue numbering the pages consecutively. Center the title *Bibliography* (without underlining, italics, or quotation marks) one inch below the top of the page. Double-space, and then begin each entry at the left margin. Indent the second and subsequent lines of each entry one-half inch, or five spaces.

List sources alphabetically by authors' last names or by the first major word in the title if the author is unknown. See p. 522 for an example of a *Chicago*-style bibliography.

In the bibliographic entry, include the same information as in the first note for that source, but omit the page reference. Give the

DIRECTORY TO *CHICAGO* STYLE

Chicago style for notes and bibliographic entries

first author's last name first, followed by a comma and the first name; separate the main elements of the entry with periods rather than commas; and do not enclose the publication information for books in parentheses.

IN THE BIBLIOGRAPHY

> Sweig, Julia. *Inside the Cuban Revolution*. Cambridge, MA: Harvard University Press, 2002.

51c Create *Chicago* notes and bibliographic entries.

The following examples demonstrate how to format both notes and bibliographic entries according to *Chicago* style. The note, which is numbered, appears first; the bibliographic entry, which is not numbered, follows the note.

Print and digital books

For the basic format for citing a print book, see the source map on pp. 504–5. The note for a book typically includes five elements: author's name, title and subtitle, city of publication and publisher, year, and page number(s) or electronic locator information for the information in the note. The bibliographic entry usually includes all but the page number (and does include a URL or other locator if the book is digitally published), but it is styled differently: commas separate major elements of a note, but a bibliographic entry uses periods.

1. ONE AUTHOR

author:
first name first title city of publication

1. Nell Irvin Painter, *The History of White People* (New York:

publisher year page(s)

W. W. Norton, 2010), 119.

> Painter, Nell Irvin. *The History of White People*. New York: W. W. Norton, 2010.

2. MULTIPLE AUTHORS

author(s) — title + subtitle

2. Margaret Macmillan and Richard Holbrooke, *Paris 1919:*

city of publication — publisher

Six Months That Changed the World (New York: Random House,

year — page(s)

2003), 384.

Macmillan, Margaret, and Richard Holbrooke. *Paris 1919: Six Months That Changed the World.* New York: Random House, 2003.

With more than three authors, you may give the first-listed author followed by *et al.* in the note. In the bibliography, list all of the authors' names.

2. Stephen J. Blank et al., *Conflict, Culture, and History: Regional Dimensions* (Miami: University Press of the Pacific, 2002), 276.

Blank, Stephen J., Lawrence E. Grinter, Karl P. Magyar, Lewis B. Ware, and Bynum E. Weathers. *Conflict, Culture, and History: Regional Dimensions.* Miami: University Press of the Pacific, 2002.

3. ORGANIZATION AS AUTHOR

organization — title

3. World Intellectual Property Organization, *Intellectual Property*

place of publication — publisher

Profile of the Least Developed Countries (Geneva: World Intellectual

year — page(s)

Property Organization, 2002), 43.

World Intellectual Property Organization. *Intellectual Property Profile of the Least Developed Countries.* Geneva: World Intellectual Property Organization, 2002.

4. UNKNOWN AUTHOR

4. *Broad Stripes and Bright Stars* (Kansas City, MO: Andrews McMeel, 2002), 10.

Broad Stripes and Bright Stars. Kansas City, MO: Andrews McMeel, 2002.

5. ONLINE BOOK

5. Dorothy Richardson, *Long Day: The Story of a New York Working Girl, as Told by Herself* (1906; UMDL Texts, 2010), 159, http://quod.lib .umich.edu/cgi/t/text/text-idx?c=moa;idno=AFS7156.0001.001.

Richardson, Dorothy. *Long Day: The Story of a New York Working Girl, as Told by Herself.* 1906. UMDL Texts, 2010. http://quod.lib .umich.edu/cgi/t/text/text-idx?c=moa;idno=AFS7156.0001.001.

6. ELECTRONIC BOOK (E-BOOK)

6. Manal M. Omar, *Barefoot in Baghdad* (Naperville, IL: Sourcebooks, 2010), Kindle edition, ch. 4.

Omar, Manal M. *Barefoot in Baghdad.* Naperville, IL: Sourcebooks, 2010. Kindle edition.

7. EDITED BOOK WITH NO AUTHOR

7. James H. Fetzer, ed., *The Great Zapruder Film Hoax: Deceit and Deception in the Death of JFK* (Chicago: Open Court, 2003), 56.

Fetzer, James H., ed. *The Great Zapruder Film Hoax: Deceit and Deception in the Death of JFK.* Chicago: Open Court, 2003.

8. EDITED BOOK WITH AUTHOR

8. Leopold von Ranke, *The Theory and Practice of History*, ed. Georg G. Iggers (New York: Routledge, 2010), 135.

von Ranke, Leopold. *The Theory and Practice of History.* Edited by Georg G. Iggers. New York: Routledge, 2010.

9. SELECTION IN AN ANTHOLOGY OR CHAPTER IN A BOOK WITH AN EDITOR

    author title (selection)   title (anthology)

9. Denise Little, "Born in Blood," in *Alternate Gettysburgs,* ed.

            place of
    editor(s)   publication publisher

Brian Thomsen and Martin H. Greenberg (New York: Berkley

      year page(s)

Publishing Group, 2002), 245.

Give the inclusive page numbers of the selection or chapter in the bibliographic entry.

Little, Denise. "Born in Blood." In *Alternate Gettysburgs.* Edited by Brian Thomsen and Martin H. Greenberg, 242–55. New York: Berkley Publishing Group, 2002.

CHICAGO SOURCE MAP: Books

Take information from the book's title page and copyright page (on the reverse side of the title page), not from the book's cover or a library catalog. Look carefully at the differences in punctuation between the note and the bibliographic entry.

1 **Author.** In a note, list the author(s) first name first. In a bibliographic entry, list the first author last name first. List other authors first name first.

2 **Title.** Italicize the title and subtitle and capitalize all major words.

3 **City of publication and publisher.** List the city (and country or state abbreviation for an unfamiliar city) followed by a colon. In a note only, city, publisher, and year appear in parentheses. Drop *Inc.*, *Co.*, *Publishing*, or *Publishers*. Follow with a comma.

4 **Publication year.** In a bibliographic entry only, end with a period.

5 **Page number.** In a note only, end with the page number and a period.

Citations for the book on p. 505 would look like this:

ENDNOTE

1. Alex von Tunzelmann, *Red Heat: Conspiracy, Murder, and the Cold War in the Caribbean* (New York: Picador, 2011), 178.

BIBLIOGRAPHIC ENTRY

von Tunzelmann, Alex. *Red Heat: Conspiracy, Murder, and the Cold War in the Caribbean*. New York: Picador, 2011.

4. Publication Year
2011

RED HEAT

2. Title

CONSPIRACY, MURDER, AND THE COLD WAR IN THE CARIBBEAN

ALEX VON TUNZELMANN

1. Author

PICADOR
HENRY HOLT AND COMPANY
NEW YORK

**3. Publisher and
City of Publication**

10. INTRODUCTION, PREFACE, FOREWORD, OR AFTERWORD

10. Robert B. Reich, introduction to *Making Work Pay: America after Welfare,* ed. Robert Kuttner (New York: New Press, 2002), xvi.

Reich, Robert B. Introduction to *Making Work Pay: America after Welfare,* vii–xvii. Edited by Robert Kuttner. New York: New Press, 2002.

11. TRANSLATION

11. Suetonius, *The Twelve Caesars,* trans. Robert Graves (London: Penguin Classics, 1989), 202.

Suetonius. *The Twelve Caesars.* Translated by Robert Graves. London: Penguin Classics, 1989.

12. EDITION OTHER THAN THE FIRST

12. Dee Brown, *Bury My Heart at Wounded Knee: An Indian History of the American West,* 4th ed. (New York: Owl Books, 2007), 12.

Brown, Dee. *Bury My Heart at Wounded Knee: An Indian History of the American West,* 4th ed. New York: Owl Books, 2007.

13. MULTIVOLUME WORK

13. John Watson, *Annals of Philadelphia and Pennsylvania in the Olden Time,* vol. 2 (Washington, DC: Ross & Perry, 2003), 514.

Watson, John. *Annals of Philadelphia and Pennsylvania in the Olden Time.* Vol. 2. Washington, DC: Ross & Perry, 2003.

CHECKLIST

Citing Sources without Models in *Chicago* Style

To cite a source for which you cannot find a model, collect as much information as you can find—about the creator, title, date of creation or update, and location of the source— with the goal of helping your readers find the source for themselves, if possible. Then look at the models in this section to see which one most closely matches the type of source you are using.

In an academic writing project, before citing an electronic source for which you have no model, also be sure to ask your instructor's advice.

14. REFERENCE WORK. In a note, use *s.v.*, the abbreviation for the Latin *sub verbo* ("under the word"), to help your reader find the entry. Do not list reference works such as encyclopedias or dictionaries in your bibliography.

> 14. *Encyclopedia Britannica,* s.v. "carpetbagger."

15. WORK WITH A TITLE WITHIN THE TITLE. Use quotation marks around any title within a book title.

> 15. John A. Alford, *A Companion to "Piers Plowman"* (Berkeley: University of California Press, 1988), 195.

> Alford, John A. *A Companion to "Piers Plowman."* Berkeley: University of California Press, 1988.

16. SACRED TEXT. Do not include sacred texts in the bibliography.

> 16. Luke 18:24–25 (New International Version)

> 16. Qur'an 7:40–41

17. SOURCE QUOTED IN ANOTHER SOURCE. Identify both the original and the secondary source.

> 17. Frank D. Millet, "The Filipino Leaders," *Harper's Weekly,* March 11, 1899, quoted in Richard Slotkin, *Gunfighter Nation: The Myth of the Frontier in Twentieth-Century America* (New York: HarperCollins, 1992), 110.

> Millet, Frank D. "The Filipino Leaders." *Harper's Weekly,* March 11, 1899. Quoted in Richard Slotkin, *Gunfighter Nation: The Myth of the Frontier in Twentieth-Century America* (New York: HarperCollins, 1992), 110.

Print and digital periodicals

The note for an article in a periodical typically includes the author's name, the article title, and the periodical title. The format for other information, including the volume and issue numbers (if any), the date of publication, and the page number(s) to which the note refers, varies according to the type of periodical and whether you consulted it in print, on the Web, or in a database. In a bibliographic entry for a journal or magazine article from a database or a print periodical, also give the inclusive page numbers.

18. ARTICLE IN A PRINT JOURNAL

author — title (article)

18. Karin Lützen, "The Female World: Viewed from Denmark,"

title (journal) — volume + issue — year — page(s)

Journal of Women's History 12, no. 3 (2000): 36.

Lützen, Karin. "The Female World: Viewed from Denmark." *Journal of Women's History* 12, no. 3 (2000): 34–38.

19. ARTICLE IN AN ONLINE JOURNAL. Give the DOI (digital object identifier) if there is one. If not, include the article URL. If page numbers are provided, include them as well.

author — title (article)

19. Jeffrey J. Schott, "America, Europe, and the New Trade Order,"

title (journal) — volume + issue — year — DOI

Business and Politics 11, no. 3 (2009), doi:10.2202/1469-3569.1263.

Schott, Jeffrey J. "America, Europe, and the New Trade Order." *Business and Politics* 11, no. 3 (2009). doi:10.2202/1469-3569.1263.

20. JOURNAL ARTICLE FROM A DATABASE. For basic information on citing a periodical article from a database in *Chicago* style, see the source map on pp. 510–11.

author(s) — title (article)

20. W. Trent Foley and Nicholas J. Higham, "Bede on

title (journal) — volume + issue — year — page(s)

the Britons," *Early Medieval Europe* 17, no. 2 (2009), 157,

DOI

doi:10.1111/j.1468-0254.2009.00258.x.

Foley, W. Trent, and Nicholas J. Higham. "Bede on the Britons." *Early Medieval Europe* 17, no. 2 (2009). 154–85. doi:10.1111/j.1468-0254.2009.00258.x.

21. ARTICLE IN A PRINT MAGAZINE

author — title (article)

21. Terry McDermott, "The Mastermind: Khalid Sheikh Mohammed

title (magazine) — date: month + day + year — page(s)

and the Making of 9/11," *New Yorker,* September 13, 2010, 42.

McDermott, Terry. "The Mastermind: Khalid Sheikh Mohammed and the Making of 9/11." *New Yorker,* September 13, 2010, 38–51.

22. ARTICLE IN AN ONLINE MAGAZINE

22. Tracy Clark-Flory, "Educating Women Saves Kids' Lives," *Salon,* September 17, 2010, http://www.salon.com/life /broadsheet/2010/09/17/education_women/index.html.

Clark-Flory, Tracy. "Educating Women Saves Kids' Lives." *Salon,* September 17, 2010. http://www.salon.com/life /broadsheet/2010/09/17/education_women/index.html.

23. MAGAZINE ARTICLE FROM A DATABASE

23. Sami Yousafzai and Ron Moreau, "Twisting Arms in Afghanistan," *Newsweek,* November 9, 2009, 8, Academic Search Premier (44962900).

[labels above entry: author(s), title (article), title (magazine), date, page(s), database, access number]

Yousafzai, Sami, and Ron Moreau. "Twisting Arms in Afghanistan." *Newsweek,* November 9, 2009, 8. Academic Search Premier (44962900).

24. ARTICLE IN A NEWSPAPER. Do not include page numbers for a newspaper article, but you may include the section, if any.

24. Caroline E. Mayer, "Wireless Industry to Adopt Voluntary Standards," *Washington Post,* September 9, 2003, sec. E.

Mayer, Caroline E. "Wireless Industry to Adopt Voluntary Standards." *Washington Post,* September 9, 2003, sec. E.

If you provide complete documentation of a newspaper article in a note, you may not need to include it in the bibliography. Check your instructor's preference.

25. ARTICLE IN AN ONLINE NEWSPAPER. If the URL for the article is very long, use the URL for the newspaper's home page.

25. Andrew C. Revkin, "Arctic Melt Unnerves the Experts," *New York Times,* October 2, 2007, http://www.nytimes.com.

[labels above entry: author, title (article), title (newspaper), date: month + day + year, URL (home page)]

Revkin, Andrew C. "Arctic Melt Unnerves the Experts." *New York Times,* October 2, 2007. http://www.nytimes.com.

CHICAGO SOURCE MAP: Articles from Databases

1 **Author.** In a note, list the author(s) first name first. In the bibliographic entry, list the first author last name first, comma, first name; list other authors first name first.

2 **Article title.** Enclose the title and subtitle (if any) in quotation marks, and capitalize major words. In the notes section, put a comma before and after the title. In the bibliography, put a period before and after.

3 **Periodical title.** Italicize the title and subtitle, and capitalize all major words. For a magazine or newspaper, follow with a comma.

4 **Volume and issue numbers (for journals) and date.** For journals, follow the title with the volume number, a comma, the abbreviation *no.*, and the issue number; enclose the publication year in parentheses and follow with a comma (in a note) or with a period (in a bibliography). For other periodicals, give the month and year or month, day, and year, not in parentheses, followed by a comma.

5 **Page numbers.** In a note, give the page where the information is found. In the bibliographic entry, give the page range.

6 **Retrieval information.** Provide the article's DOI, if one is given; the name of the database and an accession number; or a "stable or persistent" URL for the article in the database. Because you provide stable retrieval information, you do not need to identify the electronic format of the work (for example, a PDF, as in the following model). End with a period.

Citations for the journal article on p. 511 would look like this:

ENDNOTE

1. Daniel Herda, "How Many Immigrants? Foreign-Born Population Innumeracy in Europe," *Public Opinion Quarterly* 74, no. 4 (2010), 677, doi:10.1093/poq/nfq013.

BIBLIOGRAPHIC ENTRY

Herda, Daniel. "How Many Immigrants? Foreign-Born Population Innumeracy in Europe." *Public Opinion Quarterly* 74, no. 4 (2010). 674–95. doi:10.1093/poq/nfq013.

3. Periodical Title

4. Volume and Issue Numbers and Date

Public Opinion Quarterly, Vol. 74, No. 4, Winter 2010, pp. 674–695

5. Page Numbers

2. Article Title

HOW MANY IMMIGRANTS?
FOREIGN-BORN POPULATION INNUMERACY IN EUROPE

DANIEL HERDA*   **1. Author**

Abstract   Individuals frequently perceive immigrant and minority population sizes to be much larger than they are in reality. To date, little is understood about the extent or causes of this phenomenon, known as innumeracy, which may have consequences for inter-group relations. However, before the literature can assess these consequences, a better understanding of the development of these misperceptions is needed. The extant literature focuses only on the United States and lacks a clear understanding of how innumeracy arises. Drawing from the 2002 European Social Survey (ESS), this study attempts to make sense of this phenomenon by proposing and testing a framework that views innumeracy among majority group members as developing in two ways: as cognitive mistakes and emotional responses. I establish the existence and extent of the phenomenon across 21 European nations, test new key predictors such as media exposure and socio-economic status, and find independent associations with cognitive and emotional factors using multi-level regression analyses.

When asked to estimate the size of minority populations, survey respondents frequently over-estimate. Research on this curious phenomenon, dubbed innumeracy,[1] indicates that a substantial proportion of majority group members perceive minority populations as much larger than they are in reality (Paulos

DANIEL HERDA is a Ph.D. candidate in the Department of Sociology, University of California–Davis, Davis, CA, USA. The author would like to thank Mary Jackman, Dina Okamoto, Diane Felmlee, Brad Jones, Xiaoling Shu, Golnaz Komaie, Danielle Presti, the editors and anonymous reviewers for their helpful advice on this research. The data used in this study were provided by Norwegian Social Sciences Data Service and are available for download at http://ess.nsd.uib.no/. An earlier version of this research was presented at the 2009 annual meeting of the Pacific Sociological Association in San Diego, CA, USA. *Address correspondence to Daniel Herda, University of California–Davis, One Shields Avenue, Davis, CA 95616-8701, USA; e-mail: deherda@ucdavis.edu.

1. While the term innumeracy is very general, I use it to specifically refer to the over-estimation of the immigrant population size.

doi: 10.1093/poq/nfq013

Advance Access published on March 29, 2010

6. Retrieval Information

26. NEWSPAPER ARTICLE FROM A DATABASE

26. Demetria Irwin, "A Hatchet, Not a Scalpel, for NYC Budget Cuts," *New York Amsterdam News,* November 13, 2008, Academic Search Premier (35778153).

Irwin, Demetria. "A Hatchet, Not a Scalpel, for NYC Budget Cuts." *New York Amsterdam News,* November 13, 2008. Academic Search Premier (35778153).

27. BOOK REVIEW. After the information about the book under review, give publication information for the appropriate kind of source (see models 18–26).

27. Arnold Relman, "Health Care: The Disquieting Truth," review of *Tracking Medicine: A Researcher's Quest to Understand Health Care,* by John E. Wennberg, *New York Review of Books* 57, no. 14 (2010), 45.

Relman, Arnold. "Health Care: The Disquieting Truth." Review of *Tracking Medicine: A Researcher's Quest to Understand Health Care,* by John E. Wennberg. *New York Review of Books* 57, no. 14 (2010), 45–48.

Online sources

In general, include the author (if given); the title of a work from a Web site (in quotation marks); the name of the site (in italics, if the site is an online publication, but otherwise neither italicized nor in quotation marks); the sponsor of the site, if different from the name of the site or name of the author; the date of publication or most recent update; and a URL. If the online source does not indicate when it was published or last modified, or if your instructor requests an access date, place it before the URL.

For basic information on citing works from Web sites in *Chicago* style, see the source map on pp. 514–15.

28. WEB SITE

author — title (site)
28. Rutgers School of Arts and Sciences, *The Rutgers Oral History*

date of publication — URL
Archive, 2010, http://oralhistory.rutgers.edu/.

Rutgers School of Arts and Sciences. *The Rutgers Oral History Archive.* 2010. http://oralhistory.rutgers.edu/.

29. WORK FROM A WEB SITE

author   title (work)   title (site)

29. Rose Cohen, "My First Job," *The Triangle Factory Fire,*

sponsor   date of publication

Cornell University School of Industrial and Labor Relations, 2005,

URL

http://www.ilr.cornell.edu/trianglefire/texts/.

Cohen, Rose. "My First Job." *The Triangle Factory Fire.* Cornell University School of Industrial and Labor Relations. 2005. http://www.ilr.cornell.edu/trianglefire/texts/.

30. BLOG (WEB LOG) POST. Treat a blog post as a short work from a Web site (see model 29).

30. Jai Arjun Singh, "On the Road in the USSR," *Jabberwock* (blog), November 29, 2007, http://jaiarjun.blogspot.com/2007/11/on-road-in-ussr.html.

Chicago recommends that blog posts appear in the notes section only, not in the bibliography, unless the blog is cited frequently. Check your instructor's preference. A bibliography reference to an entire blog would look like this:

Singh, Jai Arjun. *Jabberwock* (blog). http://jaiarjun.blogspot.com/.

31. EMAIL AND OTHER PERSONAL COMMUNICATIONS. Cite email messages and other personal communications, such as letters and telephone calls, in the text or in a note only, not in the bibliography. (*Chicago* style recommends hyphenating *e-mail.*)

31. Kareem Adas, e-mail message to author, February 11, 2010.

32. PODCAST. Treat a podcast as a short work from a Web site (see model 29), and give as much of the following information as you can find: the author or speaker, the title or a description of the podcast, the title of the site, the site sponsor (if different from the

CHICAGO SOURCE MAP: Works from Web Sites

1 **Author.** In a note, list the author(s) first name first. In a bibliographic entry, list the first author last name first, comma, first name; list additional authors first name first. Note that the host may serve as the author.

2 **Document title.** Enclose the title in quotation marks, and capitalize all major words. In a note, put a comma before and after the title. In the bibliography, put a period before and after.

3 **Title of Web site.** Capitalize all major words. If the site's title is analogous to a book or periodical title, italicize it. In the notes section, put a comma after the title. In the bibliography, put a period after the title.

4 **Sponsor of site.** If the sponsor is the same as the author or site title, you may omit it. End with a comma (in the note) or a period (in the bibliographic entry).

5 **Date of publication or last modification.** If no date is available, or if your instructor requests it, include your date of access (with the word *accessed*).

6 **Retrieval information.** Give the URL for the Web site. If you are required to include a date of access, put the word *accessed* and the date in parentheses after the URL. End with a period.

Citations for the Web site on p. 515 would look like this:

ENDNOTE

              1   2   3

1. Rebecca Edwards, "The Populist Party," *1896: The Presidential*

                                  4   5   6

Campaign: Cartoons & Commentary, Vassar College, 2000, http://projects

.vassar.edu/1896/populists.html.

BIBLIOGRAPHIC ENTRY

          1   2   3

Edwards, Rebecca. "The Populist Party." *1896: The Presidential*

                                4   5

    Campaign: Cartoons & Commentary. Vassar College. 2000.

                      6

    http://projects.vassar.edu/1896/populists.html.

← → projects.**vassar.edu**/1896/populists.html

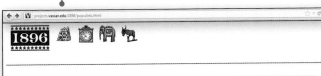

The Populist Party ← 2. Document Title

The Rise of Populism

The People's Party (or Populist Party, as it was widely known) was much younger than the Democratic and Republican Parties, which had been founded before the Civil War. Agricultural areas in the West and South had been hit by economic depression years before industrial areas. In the 1880s, as drought hit the wheat-growing areas of the Great Plains and prices for Southern cotton sunk to new lows, many tenant farmers fell into deep debt. This exacerbated long-held grievances against railroads, lenders, grain-elevator owners, and others with whom farmers did business. By the early 1890s, as the depression worsened, some industrial workers shared these farm families' views on labor and the trusts.

In 1890 Populists won control of the Kansas state legislature, and Kansan **William Peffer** became the party's first U.S. Senator. Peffer, with his long white beard, was a humorous figure to many Eastern journalists and politicians, who saw little evidence of Populism in their states and often treated the party as a joke. Nonetheless, Western and Southern Populists gained support rapidly. In 1892 the national party was officially founded through a merger of the Farmers' Alliance and the Knights of Labor. In that year the Populist presidential candidate, James B. Weaver, won over one million votes. Between 1892 and 1896, however, the party failed to make further gains, in part because of fraud, intimidation, and violence by Southern Democrats.

By 1896 the Populist organization was in even more turmoil than that of Democrats. Two main factions had appeared. One, the fusion Populists, sought to merge with the Democrats, using the threat of independent organization t

"fused"--over

third party co

Homepage ← 3. Title of Web Site

© 2000, Rebecca Edwards, Vassar College

5. Date of Publication   4. Sponsor of Site

1. Author

515

author or site name), the type of podcast or file format, the date of posting or access, and the URL.

> 32. Barack Obama, "Weekly Address: A Solar Recovery," *The White House,* podcast video, July 3, 2010, http://www.whitehouse.gov/photos-and-video/video/weekly-address-a-solar-recovery.

> Obama, Barack. "Weekly Address: A Solar Recovery." *The White House.* Podcast video. July 3, 2010. http://www.whitehouse.gov/photos-and-video/video/weekly-address-a-solar-recovery.

33. ONLINE AUDIO OR VIDEO. Treat an online audio or video source as a short work from a Web site (see model 29). If the source is downloadable, give the medium or file format before the URL (see model 32).

```
                author                        title (work)
```
> 33. Alyssa Katz, "Did the Mortgage Crisis Kill the American
```
          medium    duration           user name   date of posting
```
> Dream?" YouTube video, 4:32, posted by NYCRadio, June 24, 2009,
```
                         URL
```
> http://www.youtube.com/watch?v=uivtwjwd_Qw.

> Katz, Alyssa. "Did the Mortgage Crisis Kill the American Dream?" YouTube video, 4:32. Posted by NYCRadio. June 24, 2009. http://www.youtube.com/watch?v=uivtwjwd_Qw.

Other sources

34. PUBLISHED OR BROADCAST INTERVIEW

> 34. Nina Totenberg, interview by Charlie Rose, *The Charlie Rose Show,* PBS, June 29, 2010.

> Totenberg, Nina. Interview by Charlie Rose. *The Charlie Rose Show.* PBS, June 29, 2010.

Interviews you conduct are considered personal communications (see model 31).

35. VIDEO OR DVD

> 35. Edward Norton and Edward Furlong, *American History X,* directed by Tony Kaye (1998; Los Angeles: New Line Studios, 2002), DVD.

Norton, Edward, and Edward Furlong. *American History X.* Directed
by Tony Kaye, 1998. Los Angeles: New Line Studios, 2002.
DVD.

36. SOUND RECORDING

36. Paul Robeson, *The Collector's Paul Robeson,* recorded 1959,
Monitor MCD-61580, 1989, compact disc.

Robeson, Paul. *The Collector's Paul Robeson.* Recorded 1959. Monitor
MCD-61580, 1989, compact disc.

37. WORK OF ART. Begin with the artist's name and the title of the
work. If you viewed the work in person, give the medium, the
date, and the name of the place where you saw it.

37. Mary Cassatt, *The Child's Bath,* oil on canvas, 1893, The Art
Institute of Chicago, Chicago, IL.

Cassatt, Mary. *The Child's Bath.* Oil on canvas, 1893. The Art Institute
of Chicago, Chicago, IL.

If you refer to a reproduction, give the publication information.

37. Mary Cassatt, *The Child's Bath,* oil on canvas, 1893,
on *Art Access*, The Art Institute of Chicago, August 2004,
http://www.artic.edu/artaccess/AA_Impressionist/pages/IMP
_6.shtml#.

Cassatt, Mary. *The Child's Bath.* Oil on canvas, 1893. On *Art Access*,
The Art Institute of Chicago. August 2004. http://www.artic
.edu/artaccess/AA_Impressionist/pages/IMP_6.shtml#.

38. PAMPHLET, REPORT, OR BROCHURE. Information about the author
or publisher may not be readily available, but give enough information to identify your source.

38. Jamie McCarthy, *Who Is David Irving?* (San Antonio, TX:
Holocaust History Project, 1998).

McCarthy, Jamie. *Who Is David Irving?* San Antonio, TX: Holocaust
History Project, 1998.

39. GOVERNMENT DOCUMENT

39. U.S. House Committee on Ways and Means, *Report on Trade
Mission to Sub-Saharan Africa,* 108th Cong., 1st sess. (Washington,
DC: Government Printing Office, 2003), 28.

U.S. House Committee on Ways and Means. *Report on Trade Mission to Sub-Saharan Africa*. 108th Cong., 1st sess. Washington, DC: Government Printing Office, 2003.

51d A sample student research essay, *Chicago* style

Following are excerpts from an essay by Amanda Rinder that conforms to the *Chicago* guidelines described in this chapter.

STUDENT
WRITING

Sweet Home Chicago: Preserving the Past,
Protecting the Future of the Windy City

Title
announces
topic clearly
and succinctly

Amanda Rinder

Title and
writer's name
centered

Course title,
instructor's
name, and
date centered
at bottom of
title page

Twentieth-Century U.S. History
Professor Goldberg
November 27, 2006

Annotations indicate effective choices or *Chicago*-style formatting.

Rinder 2

First page
of body text
is p. 2

Refers to
each figure
by number

Thesis
introduced

Double-
spaced text

Source
cited using
superscript
numeral

Figure caption
includes
number, short
title, and
source

     Only one city has the "Big Shoulders" described by Carl Sandburg: Chicago (fig. 1). So renowned are its skyscrapers and celebrated building style that an entire school of architecture is named for Chicago. Presently, however, the place that Frank Sinatra called "my kind of town" is beginning to lose sight of exactly what kind of town it is. Many of the buildings that give Chicago its distinctive character are being torn down in order to make room for new growth. Both preserving the classics and encouraging new creation are important; the combination of these elements gives Chicago architecture its unique flavor. Witold Rybczynski, a professor of urbanism, told Tracie Rozhon of the *New York Times,* "Of all the cities we can think of . . . we associate Chicago with new things, with building new. Combining that with preservation is a difficult task, a tricky thing. It's hard to find the middle ground in Chicago."[1] Yet finding a middle ground is essential if the city is to retain the original character that sets it apart from the rest. In order to maintain Chicago's distinctive identity and its delicate balance between the old and the new,

Fig. 1. Chicago skyline, circa 1940s. (Postcard courtesy of Minnie Dangburg.)

Notes

1. Tracie Rozhon, "Chicago Girds for Big Battle over Its Skyline," *New York Times,* November 12, 2000, Academic Search Premier (28896783).

Newspaper article in database

2. David Garrard Lowe, *Lost Chicago* (New York: Watson-Guptill Publications, 2000), 123.

Print book

3. *Columbia Encyclopedia,* Sixth Ed., s.v. "Louis Sullivan."

4. Daniel Bluestone, *Constructing Chicago* (New Haven: Yale University Press, 1991), 105.

5. Alan J. Shannon, "When Will It End?" *Chicago Tribune,* September 11, 1987, quoted in Karen J. Dilibert, *From Landmark to Landfill* (Chicago: Chicago Architectural Foundation, 2000), 11.

Indirect source

6. Steve Kerch, "Landmark Decisions," *Chicago Tribune,* March 18, 1990, sec. 16.

7. John W. Stamper, *Chicago's North Michigan Avenue* (Chicago: University of Chicago Press, 1991), 215.

8. Alf Siewers, "Success Spoiling the Magnificent Mile?" *Chicago Sun-Times,* April 9, 1995, http://www.sun-times.com/.

Newspaper article online

9. Paul Gapp, "McCarthy Building Puts Landmark Law on a Collision Course with Developers," *Chicago Tribune,* April 20, 1986, quoted in Karen J. Dilibert, *From Landmark to Landfill* (Chicago: Chicago Architectural Foundation, 2000), 4.

10. Ibid.

Reference to previous source

11. Rozhon, "Chicago Girds for Big Battle."

12. Kerch, "Landmark Decisions."

Second reference to source

13. Robert Bruegmann, *The Architects and the City* (Chicago: University of Chicago Press, 1997), 443.

STUDENT
WRITING

Bibliography
starts on new
page

Bibliography

Bluestone, Daniel. *Constructing Chicago*. New Haven: Yale
    University Press, 1991.

Print book
Bruegmann, Robert. *The Architects and the City*. Chicago:
    University of Chicago Press, 1997.

Pamphlet
Dilibert, Karen J. *From Landmark to Landfill*. Chicago: Chicago
    Architectural Foundation, 2000.

Newspaper
article
Kerch, Steve. "Landmark Decisions." *Chicago Tribune,* March 18,
    1990, sec. 16.

Lowe, David Garrard. *Lost Chicago*. New York: Watson-Guptill
    Publications, 2000.

Article from
database
Rozhon, Tracie. "Chicago Girds for Big Battle over Its Skyline."
    New York Times, November 12, 2000. Academic Search
    Premier (28896783).

Bibliography
entries use
hanging indent
and are not
numbered
Siewers, Alf. "Success Spoiling the Magnificent Mile?" *Chicago Sun-*
    Times, April 9, 1995. http://www.sun-times.com/.

Stamper, John W. *Chicago's North Michigan Avenue*. Chicago:
    University of Chicago Press, 1991.

52 CSE Style

Writers in the physical sciences, the life sciences, and mathematics often use the documentation style set forth by the Council of Science Editors (CSE). Guidelines for citing print sources can be found in *Scientific Style and Format: The CSE Manual for Authors, Editors, and Publishers*, Seventh Edition (2006).

52a Follow CSE manuscript format.

Title page.   Center the title of your paper. Beneath it, center your name. Include other relevant information, such as the course name and number, the instructor's name, and the date submitted.

Margins and spacing.   Leave standard margins at the top and bottom and on both sides of each page. Double-space the text and the reference list.

Page numbers.   Type a short version of the paper's title and the page number in the upper right-hand corner of each page.

Abstract.   CSE style often calls for a one-paragraph abstract (about one hundred words). The abstract should be on a separate page, right after the title page, with the title *Abstract* centered one inch from the top of the page.

Headings.   CSE style does not require headings, but it notes that they can help readers quickly find the contents of a section of the paper.

Tables and figures.   Tables and figures must be labeled *Table* or *Figure* and numbered separately, one sequence for tables and one for figures. Give each table and figure a short, informative title. Be sure to introduce each table and figure in your text, and comment on its significance.

List of references.   Start the list of references on a new page at the end of the essay, and continue to number the pages consecutively. Center the title *References* one inch from the top of the page, and double-space before beginning the first entry. See p. 540 for an example of a CSE-style list of references.

See p. 540

52b Create CSE in-text citations.

In CSE style, the citations within an essay follow one of three formats.

- The *citation-sequence format* calls for a superscript number or a number in parentheses after any mention of a source. The sources are numbered in the order they appear. Each number refers to the same source every time it is used. The first source mentioned in the paper is numbered *1*, the second source is numbered *2*, and so on.

- The *citation-name format* also calls for a superscript number or a number in parentheses after any mention of a source. The numbers are added after the list of references is completed and alphabetized, so that the source numbered *1* is alphabetically first in the list of references, *2* is alphabetically second, and so on.

- The *name-year format* calls for the last name of the author and the year of publication in parentheses after any mention of a source. If the last name appears in a signal phrase, the name-year format allows for giving only the year of publication in parentheses.

Before deciding which system to use for your essay, ask your instructor's preference.

1. IN-TEXT CITATION USING CITATION-SEQUENCE OR CITATION-NAME FORMAT

VonBergen[12] provides the most complete discussion of this phenomenon.

For the citation-sequence and citation-name formats, you would use the same superscript ([12]) for each subsequent citation of this work by VonBergen.

2. IN-TEXT CITATION USING NAME-YEAR FORMAT

VonBergen (2003) provides the most complete discussion of this phenomenon.

Hussar's two earlier studies of juvenile obesity (1995, 1999) examined only children with diabetes.

The classic examples of such investigations (Morrow 1968; Bridger et al. 1971; Franklin and Wayson 1972) still shape the assumptions of current studies.

52c   Create a CSE list of references.

The citations in the text of an essay correspond to items on a list titled *References*, which starts on a new page at the end of the essay. Continue to number the pages consecutively, center the title *References* one inch from the top of the page, and double-space before beginning the first entry.

The order of the entries depends on which format you follow:

- **Citation-sequence format:** number and list the references in the order the references are first cited in the text.
- **Citation-name format:** list and number the references in alphabetical order.
- **Name-year format:** list the references, unnumbered, in alphabetical order.

In the following examples, you will notice that the citation-sequence and citation-name formats call for listing the date after the publisher's name in references for books and after the periodical name in references for articles. The name-year format calls for listing the date immediately after the author's name in any kind of reference.

CSE style also specifies the treatment and placement of the following basic elements in the list of references:

- **Author.** List all authors last name first, and use only initials for first and middle names. Do not place a comma after the author's last name, and do not place periods after or spaces between the initials. Use a period after the last initial of the last author listed.
- **Title.** Do not italicize titles and subtitles of books and titles of periodicals. Do not enclose titles of articles in quotation marks. For books and articles, capitalize only the first word

of the title and any proper nouns or proper adjectives. Abbreviate and capitalize all major words in a periodical title.

As you refer to these examples, pay attention to how publication information (publishers for books, details about periodicals for articles) and other specific elements are styled and punctuated.

Books

For the basic format for citing a print book, see the source map on pp. 528–29.

1. ONE AUTHOR

CITATION-SEQUENCE AND CITATION-NAME

author: last name
+ first initial   title + subtitle

1. Buchanan M. Nexus: small worlds and the groundbreaking theory

place of
publication   publisher   year

of networks. New York: Norton; 2003.

DIRECTORY TO CSE STYLE

CSE style for a list of references

NAME-YEAR

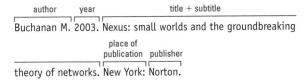

Buchanan M. 2003. Nexus: small worlds and the groundbreaking

theory of networks. New York: Norton.

2. TWO OR MORE AUTHORS

CITATION-SEQUENCE AND CITATION-NAME

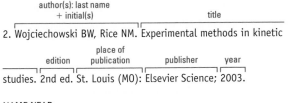

2. Wojciechowski BW, Rice NM. Experimental methods in kinetic

studies. 2nd ed. St. Louis (MO): Elsevier Science; 2003.

NAME-YEAR

author(s)   year   title

Wojciechowski BW, Rice NM. 2003. Experimental methods in kinetic

studies. 2nd ed. St. Louis (MO): Elsevier Science.

3. ORGANIZATION AS AUTHOR

CITATION-SEQUENCE AND CITATION-NAME

3. World Health Organization. The world health report 2002: reducing

risks, promoting healthy life. Geneva (Switzerland): The Organization;

2002.

Provide the organization's abbreviation at the beginning of the
name-year entry, and use the abbreviation in the corresponding
in-text citation. Alphabetize the entry by the first word of the full
name, not by the abbreviation.

NAME-YEAR

[WHO] World Health Organization. 2002. The world health report

2002: reducing risks, promoting healthy life. Geneva (Switzerland):

The Organization.

Note that depending on whether you are using the citation-sequence or citation-name format or the name-year format, the date placement will vary.

1 Author. List author(s) last name first, and use initials for first and middle names, with no periods or spaces. Use a period only after the last initial of the last author.

2, 5 Publication year. In name-year format, put the year of publication immediately after the author name(s). In citation-sequence or citation-name format, put the year of publication after the publisher's name.

3 Title. Do not italicize or put quotation marks around titles and subtitles of books. Capitalize only the first word of the title and any proper nouns or proper adjectives. If an edition number is given, list it after the title.

4 City of publication and publisher. List the city of publication (and the country or state abbreviation for unfamiliar cities) followed by a colon. Give the publisher's name. In citation-sequence or citation-name format, follow with a semicolon. In name-year format, follow with a period.

A citation for the book on p. 529 would look like this:

CITATION-SEQUENCE OR CITATION-NAME FORMAT

    1   **3**

1. Creighton TE. Proteins: structures and molecular properties. 2nd ed.

    4   **5**

New York: WH Freeman; 1993.

NAME-YEAR FORMAT

    1   **2**   **3**

Creighton TE. 1993. Proteins: structures and molecular properties. 2nd ed.

    4

New York: WH Freeman.

PROTEINS

Structures and Molecular Properties

Second Edition

[3. Title]

[1. Author]

Thomas E. Creighton

European Molecular Biology Laboratory
Heidelberg, Germany

Cover image provid

Library of Congres
Creighton, Thomas
   Proteins : struct
Creighton.—2nd e
   p.   cm.
   Includes bibliog
   ISBN-13: 978-0
   ISBN-10: 0-716
   1. Proteins—Str
QP551.C737   199
574.19'245—dc20

[4. Publisher and City of Publication]

W. H. Freeman and Company • New York

CIP

[2, 5. Publication Year]

Printed in the United States of America

Eighth printing

W. H. Freeman and Company
41 Madison Avenue
New York, NY 10010

www.whfreeman.com

4. BOOK PREPARED BY EDITOR(S)

CITATION-SEQUENCE AND CITATION-NAME

4. Torrence ME, Isaacson RE, editors. Microbial food safety in animal agriculture: current topics. Ames: Iowa State University Press; 2003.

NAME-YEAR

Torrence ME, Isaacson RE, editors. 2003. Microbial safety in animal agriculture: current topics. Ames: Iowa State University Press.

5. SECTION OF A BOOK WITH AN EDITOR

CITATION-SEQUENCE AND CITATION-NAME

5. Kawamura A. Plankton. In: Perrin MF, Wursig B, Thewissen JGM, editors. Encyclopedia of marine mammals. San Diego: Academic Press; 2002. p. 939–942.

NAME-YEAR

Kawamura A. 2002. Plankton. In: Perrin MF, Wursig B, Thewissen JGM, editors. Encyclopedia of marine mammals. San Diego: Academic Press. p. 939–942.

6. CHAPTER OF A BOOK

CITATION-SEQUENCE AND CITATION-NAME

6. Honigsbaum M. The fever trail: in search of the cure for malaria. New York: Picador; 2003. Chapter 2, The cure; p. 19–38.

NAME-YEAR

Honigsbaum M. 2003. The fever trail: in search of the cure for malaria. New York: Picador. Chapter 2, The cure; p. 19–38.

7. PAPER OR ABSTRACT IN CONFERENCE PROCEEDINGS

CITATION-SEQUENCE AND CITATION-NAME

7. Gutierrez AP. Integrating biological and environmental factors in crop system models [abstract]. In: Integrated Biological Systems Conference;

2003 Apr 14–16; San Antonio, TX. Beaumont (TX): Agroeconomics Research Group; 2003. p. 14–15.

NAME-YEAR

Gutierrez AP. 2003. Integrating biological and environmental factors in crop system models [abstract]. In: Integrated Biological Systems Conference; 2003 Apr 14–16; San Antonio, TX. Beaumont (TX): Agroeconomics Research Group. p. 14–15.

Periodicals

Provide volume and issue numbers for journals. For newspaper and magazine articles, include the section designation and column number, if any, and the date. For all periodicals, give inclusive page numbers. For rules on abbreviating journal titles, consult the CSE manual, or ask your instructor to suggest other examples.

8. ARTICLE IN A JOURNAL

CITATION-SEQUENCE AND CITATION-NAME

      author(s)   title (article)

8. Mahmud K, Vance ML. Human growth hormone and aging.

                volume +
  title (journal)   year   issue   page(s)

New Engl J Med. 2003;348(2):2256–2257.

NAME-YEAR

Mahmud K, Vance ML. 2003. Human growth hormone and aging. New Engl J Med. 348(2):2256–2257.

9. ARTICLE IN A WEEKLY JOURNAL

CITATION-SEQUENCE AND CITATION-NAME

9. Holden C. Future brightening for depression treatments. Science. 2003 Oct 31:810–813.

NAME-YEAR

Holden C. 2003. Future brightening for depression treatments. Science. Oct 31:810–813.

10. ARTICLE IN A MAGAZINE

CITATION-SEQUENCE AND CITATION-NAME

author   title (article)

10. Livio M. Moving right along: the accelerating universe holds

secrets to dark energy, the Big Bang, and the ultimate beauty of

title date: year
(magazine) + month page(s)

nature. Astronomy. 2002 Jul:34–39.

NAME-YEAR

Livio M. 2002 Jul. Moving right along: the accelerating universe holds secrets to dark energy, the Big Bang, and the ultimate beauty of nature. Astronomy. 34–39.

11. ARTICLE IN A NEWSPAPER

CITATION-SEQUENCE AND CITATION-NAME

11. Kolata G. Bone diagnosis gives new data but no answers. New York Times (National Ed.). 2003 Sep 28;Sect. 1:1 (col. 1).

NAME-YEAR

Kolata G. 2003 Sep 28. Bone diagnosis gives new data but no answers. New York Times (National Ed.). Sect. 1:1 (col. 1).

Digital sources

These examples use the citation-sequence or citation-name system. To adapt them to the name-year system, delete the note number and place the revision date immediately after the author's name.

The basic entry for most sources accessed through the Internet should include the following elements:

- **Author.** Give the author's name, if available, last name first, followed by the initial(s) and a period.
- **Title.** For book, journal, and article titles, follow the style for print materials. For all other types of electronic material, reproduce the title that appears on the screen.
- **Medium.** Indicate, in brackets, that the source is not in print format by using a designation such as *[Internet]*.
- **Place of publication.** The city usually should be followed by the two-letter abbreviation for the state. No state abbreviation

is necessary for well-known cities such as New York, Chicago, Boston, and London or for a publisher whose location is part of its name (for example, University of Oklahoma Press). If the city is implied, put the city and state in brackets. If the city cannot be inferred, use the words *place unknown* in brackets.

- **Publisher.** For material other than journal articles from Web sites and online databases, include the individual or organization that produces or sponsors the site. If no publisher can be determined, use the words *publisher unknown* in brackets.

- **Dates.** Cite three important dates if possible: the date the publication was placed on the Internet or the copyright date; the latest date of any update or revision; and the date the publication was accessed by you.

- **Page, document, volume, and issue numbers.** When citing a portion of a larger work or site, list the inclusive page numbers or document numbers of the specific item being cited. For journals or journal articles, include volume and issue numbers. If exact page numbers are not available, include in brackets the approximate length in computer screens, paragraphs, or bytes: [2 screens], [10 paragraphs], [332K bytes].

- **Address.** Include the URL or other electronic address; use the phrase *Available from:* to introduce the address. Only URLs that end with a slash are followed by a period.

12. MATERIAL FROM AN ONLINE DATABASE

For the basic format for citing an article from a database, see the source map on pp. 534–35. (Because CSE does not provide guidelines for citing an article from an online database, this model has been adapted from CSE guidelines for citing an online journal article.)

author — title (article) — title (magazine) — medium — date of publication

12. Shilts E. Water wanderers. Can Geographic [Internet]. 2002

date of access — volume + issue — page(s) — database

[cited 2010 Jan 27];122(3):72–77. Academic Search Premier.

place of publication (database) — publisher (database) — URL

Ipswich (MA): EBSCO. Available from: http://www.ebscohost.com/.

document number

Document No.: 6626534.

CSE SOURCE MAP: Articles from Databases

Note that date placement will vary depending on whether you are using the citation-sequence or citation-name format or the name-year format.

1 Author. List author(s) last name first, and use only initials for first and middle names.

2, 5 Publication date. For name-year format, put publication date after author name(s). In citation-sequence or citation-name format, put it after periodical title. Use year only (for journals) or year, month, and day (for other periodicals).

3 Article title. Capitalize first word and proper nouns/adjectives.

4 Periodical title. Capitalize major words. Abbreviate journal titles. Follow with *[Internet]* and a period.

6 Date of access. In brackets, write *cited* and year, month, and day. End with a semicolon.

7 Publication information for article. Give volume number, issue number (in parentheses), and a colon.

8 Page numbers. Give the page range. End with a period.

9 Name of database. End with a period.

10 Publication information for database. Include the city, the state abbreviation in parentheses, a colon, the publisher's name, and a period.

11 Web address and document number. Write *Available from:* and the brief URL, then *Document No.* and the identifying number.

A citation for the article on p. 535 would look like this:

CITATION-SEQUENCE OR CITATION-NAME FORMAT

1. Miller AL. Epidemiology, etiology, and natural treatment of seasonal affective disorder. Altern Med Rev [Internet]. 2005 [cited 2010 May 25]; 10(1):5–13. Academic Search Premier. Ipswich (MA): EBSCO. Available from: http://www.ebscohost.com/. Document No.: 16514813.

NAME-YEAR FORMAT

Miller AL. 2005. Epidemiology, etiology, and natural treatment of seasonal affective disorder. Altern Med Rev [Internet]. [cited 2010 May 25];10(1):5–13. Academic Search Premier. Ipswich (MA): EBSCO. Available from: http://www.ebscohost.com/. Document No.: 16514813.

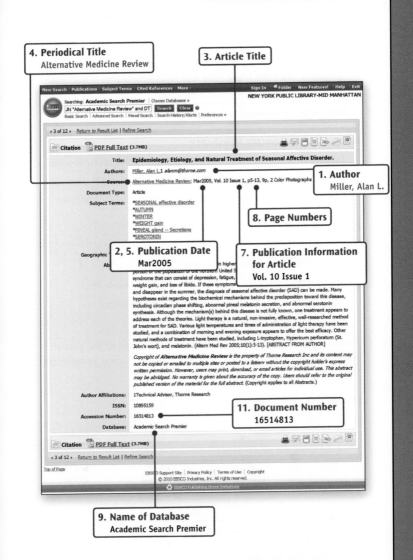

4. Periodical Title
Alternative Medicine Review

3. Article Title

New Search | Publications | Subject Terms | Cited References | More ·

Sign In | 🗀 Folder | New Features! | Help | Exit

NEW YORK PUBLIC LIBRARY-MID MANHATTAN

Searching: **Academic Search Premier** | Choose Databases »
JN "Alternative Medicine Review" and DT | Search | Clear | 🟢
Basic Search | Advanced Search | Visual Search | Search History/Alerts | Preferences »

‹ 3 of 12 › | Return to Result List | Refine Search

📄 Citation | 📄 PDF Full Text (3.7MB)

Title:	**Epidemiology, Etiology, and Natural Treatment of Seasonal Affective Disorder.**
Authors:	Miller, Alan L,1 *alanm@thorne.com*
Source:	Alternative Medicine Review; Mar2005, Vol. 10 Issue 1, p5-13, 9p, 2 Color Photographs
Document Type:	Article
Subject Terms:	*SEASONAL affective disorder
	*AUTUMN
	*WINTER
	*WEIGHT gain
	*PINEAL gland -- Secretions
	*SEROTONIN

1. Author
Miller, Alan L.

8. Page Numbers

Geographic T...
Ab...

2, 5. Publication Date
Mar2005

7. Publication Information for Article
Vol. 10 Issue 1

...in higher portion of the population of the northern United S... syndrome that can consist of depression, fatigue, weight gain, and loss of libido. If these symptoms and disappear in the summer, the diagnosis of seasonal affective disorder (SAD) can be made. Many hypotheses exist regarding the biochemical mechanisms behind the predisposition toward this disease, including circadian phase shifting, abnormal pineal melatonin secretion, and abnormal serotonin synthesis. Although the mechanism(s) behind this disease is not fully known, one treatment appears to address each of the theories. Light therapy is a natural, non-invasive, effective, well-researched method of treatment for SAD. Various light temperatures and times of administration of light therapy have been studied, and a combination of morning and evening exposure appears to offer the best efficacy. Other natural methods of treatment have been studied, including L-tryptophan, Hypericum perforatum (St. John's wort), and melatonin. (Altern Med Rev 2005;10(1):5-13). [ABSTRACT FROM AUTHOR]

Copyright of **Alternative Medicine Review** is the property of Thorne Research Inc and its content may not be copied or emailed to multiple sites or posted to a listserv without the copyright holder's express written permission. However, users may print, download, or email articles for individual use. This abstract may be abridged. No warranty is given about the accuracy of the copy. Users should refer to the original published version of the material for the full abstract. (Copyright applies to all Abstracts.)

Author Affiliations:	1Technical Advisor, Thorne Research
ISSN:	10895159
Accession Number:	16514813
Database:	Academic Search Premier

11. Document Number
16514813

📄 Citation | 📄 PDF Full Text (3.7MB)

‹ 3 of 12 › | Return to Result List | Refine Search

Top of Page

EBSCO Support Site | Privacy Policy | Terms of Use | Copyright
© 2010 EBSCO Industries, Inc. All rights reserved.
🌿 EBSCO Publishing Green Initiatives

9. Name of Database
Academic Search Premier

13. ARTICLE IN AN ONLINE JOURNAL

author(s)   title (article)   title (journal)

13. Perez P, Calonge TM. Yeast protein kinase C. J Biochem

           date of   volume +
medium   publication   date of access   issue   page(s)

[Internet]. 2002 Oct [cited 2008 Nov 3];132(4):513–517. Available

URL

from: http://edpex104.bcasj.or.jp/jb-pdf/132-4/jb132-4-513.pdf

14. ARTICLE IN AN ONLINE NEWSPAPER

14. Brody JE. Reasons, and remedies, for morning sickness. New York
Times Online [Internet]. 2004 Apr 27 [cited 2009 Apr 30]. Available
from: http://www.nytimes.com/2009/04/27/health/27BROD.html

15. ONLINE BOOK

15. Patrick TS, Allison JR, Krakow GA. Protected plants of
Georgia [Internet]. Social Circle (GA): Georgia Department of
Natural Resources; c1995 [cited 2010 Dec 3]. Available from:
http://www.georgiawildlife.com/content/displaycontent
.asp?txtDocument=89&txtPage=9

To cite a portion of an online book, give the name of the part after
the publication information: *Chapter 6, Encouraging germination.*
See model 6.

16. WEB SITE

                                  place of
title (site)   medium   publication   sponsor

16. Geology and public policy [Internet]. Boulder (CO): Geological

           date of   date of   date of
           publication   last update   access

Society of America; c2010 [updated 2010 Jun 3; cited 2010 Sep 19].

URL

Available from: http://www.geosociety.org/geopolicy.htm

17. GOVERNMENT WEB SITE

17. Health disparities: reducing health disparities in cancer
[Internet]. Atlanta (GA): Centers for Disease Control and Prevention
(US); 2010 [updated 2010 Apr 5; cited 2010 May 1]. Available

52d A sample student writing project, CSE style

The following excerpt from a literature review by Joanna Hays conforms to the name-year format in the CSE guidelines described in this chapter.

Specific and
informative
title

Niemann-Pick Disease
A Synopsis of the Genetic Variation among Various Types

Information
centered on
title page

Joanna Hays

Prof. John Hnida
Peru State College
April 19, 2006

Annotations indicate effective choices or CSE-style formatting.

STUDENT
WRITING

Overview

Niemann-Pick Disease (NP) occurs in patients with deficient acid sphingomyelinase (ASM) activity as well as with the lysosomal accumulation of sphingomyelin. It is an autosomal recessive disorder (Levran et al. 1991). As recently as 1991, researchers had classified two major phenotypes: Type A and Type B (Levran et al. 1991). In more recent studies several more phenotypes have been identified, including Types C and D. Each type of NP has distinct characteristics and effects on the patient. NP is distributed worldwide, but is closely associated with Ashkenazi Jewish descendants. Niemann-Pick Disease is relevant to the molecular world today because of advances being made in the ability to identify mutations, to trace ancestry where the mutation may have originated, and to counsel patients with a high potential of carrying the disease. Genetic counseling primarily consists of confirmation of the particular disease and calculation of the possible future reappearance in the same gene line (Brock 1974). The following discussion will summarize the identification of mutations causing the various forms of NP, the distribution of NP, as well as new genotypes and phenotypes that are correlated with NP.

Mutations Causing NP

Levran et al. (1991) inform readers of the frequent identification of missense mutations in the gene associated with Ashkenazi Jewish persons afflicted by Type A and Type B NP. This paper identifies the mutations associated with NP and the beginning of many molecular techniques to develop diagnoses. Greer et al. (1998) identify a new mutation that is specifically identified to be the cause of Type D. NP in various forms is closely associated with the founder effect caused by a couple married in the early 1700s in what is now Nova Scotia. Simonaro et al. (2002) discusses the distribution of Type B NP as well as new phenotypes and genotypes. All three of these papers

Running head
has short title,
page number

Headings
organize
project

Niemann-Pick Disease 9

References

Alphabetical by name

Brock DJH. 1974. Prenatal diagnosis and genetic counseling. J Clin Pathol Suppl. (R Coll Path.) 8:150–155.

Greer WL, Ridell DC, Gillan TL, Girouard GS, Sparrow SM, Byers DM, Dobson MJ, Neumann PE. 1998. The Nova Scotia (type D) form of Niemann-Pick Disease is caused by a $G_{3097} \rightarrow T$ transversion in NPC1. Am J Hum Genet. 63:52–54.

Levran O, Desnick RJ, Schuchman EH. 1991. Niemann-Pick disease: a frequent missense mutation in the acid sphingomyelinase gene of Ashkenazi Jewish type A and B patients. P Natl Acad Sci USA. 88:3748–3752.

Simonaro CM, Desnick RJ, McGovern MM, Wasserstein MP, Schuchman EH. 2002. The demographics and distribution of type B Niemann-Pick disease: novel mutations lead to new genotype/phenotype correlations. Am J Hum Genet. 71:1413–1419.

Acknowledgments

by Henry Holt and Company, LLC. Reprinted by permission of Henry Holt and Company, LLC.

p. 511, Daniel Herda, "How Many Immigrants? Foreign-Born Population Innumeracy in Europe." *Public Opinion Quarterly*, Vol. 74 (4): 674–95 (2010), p. 674, by permission of Oxford University Press.

p. 515, Rebecca Edwards

p. 529, From *Proteins: Structures and Molecular Properties*, Second Edition, by Thomas E. Creighton. Copyright © 1993 by W. H. Freeman and Company. Used with permission.

p. 535, EBSCOhost

INTEGRATED MEDIA

Chicago-style project, Amanda Rinder

p. 5, Courtesy College of Architecture and the Arts, University of Illinois at Chicago

Critical analysis, Shuqiao Song

p. 2, Digital Image © 2013 Museum Associates/LACMA. Licensed by Art Resource, NY. © 2013. C. Herscovici, London/Artists Rights Society (ARS), New York, LLC.

pp. 3, 5, 6, From *Fun Home: A Family Tragicomic* by Alison Bechdel. Copyright © 2006 by Alison Bechdel. Reprinted by permission of Houghton Mifflin Harcourt Publishing Company. All rights reserved.

Index

with Glossary of Terms

Words in **green** are followed by a definition. **Boldface** terms in definitions are themselves defined elsewhere in this index.

fragment, 11, 312–16 A group
of words that is not a complete
sentence but is punctuated as
one. Usually a fragment lacks a
subject, a **verb**, or both, or it is a
dependent clause.

**fused (run-on) sentences, 9,
308–12** Sometimes called a
"run-on," a sentence in which
two **independent clauses** are run
together without a **conjunction** or
punctuation between them (*My
dog barked he woke me up*).

future tense, 279–80 The **tense** of
a **verb** that indicates an action or
condition has not yet happened:
They <u>will arrive</u> next week.

G

possessive form The form of
a **noun** or **pronoun** that shows
possession. Personal pronouns
in the possessive case don't
use apostrophes (*ours, hers*),
but possessive nouns and
indefinite pronouns do (*Harold's,
everyone's*).

predicate, 250–51, 264–66
The **verb** and related words in a
clause or sentence. The predicate
expresses what the subject does,
experiences, or is. The simple
predicate is the verb or **verb
phrase**: *We have been living in
the Atlanta area.* The complete
predicate includes the simple
predicate and its **modifiers**,
objects, and complements: *We
have been living in the Atlanta
area.*

preposition, 258–59 A word
or word group that indicates
the relationship of a **noun** or
pronoun to another part of
the sentence: *From the top of
the ladder we looked over the
rooftops.*

restrictive element, 6, 341–43, 348 A word, **phrase**, or **clause** that changes the essential meaning of a sentence. A restrictive element is not set off from the rest of the sentence with commas or other punctuation: *The tree that I hit was an oak.*

rhetorical situation, 30–39 The whole context for a piece of writing, including the person communicating, the topic and the person's attitude toward it, and the intended audience.

S

subject, 250, 262–63 The **noun** or **pronoun** and related words that indicate who or what a sentence is about. The simple subject is the noun or pronoun: *The timid gray <u>mouse</u> ran away.* The complete subject is the simple subject and its modifiers: <u>*The timid gray mouse*</u> *ran away. See also* topic.

transition A word or **phrase** that signals a progression from one sentence or part of a sentence to another.

transitive verb, 265, 384 A **verb** that acts on an **object**: *I posted my review online.*

voice, 282–83, 328, 333 The
form of a **verb** that indicates
whether the subject is acting
or being acted on. In the **active
voice**, the subject performs
the action: *Parker <u>played</u> the
saxophone.* In the **passive voice**,
the subject receives the action:
*The saxophone <u>was played</u> by
Parker.*

W

warrant, 116 An assumption,
sometimes unstated, that
connects an argument's **claim**
to the reasons for making the
claim.

Notes

Notes

Notes

Notes

Directories

Directory of Student Writing

For Multilingual Writers

Considering Disabilities

Revision Symbols

Numbers in bold refer to sections of this book.

abbr	abbreviation **42a**		pass	inappropriate passive **23e, 34b**
ad	adjective/adverb **25**		ref	unclear pronoun reference **27c**
agr	agreement **24, 27b**		run-on	run-on (fused) sentence **28**
awk	awkward			
cap	capitalization **41**		sexist	sexist language **18b, 27b**
case	case **27a**		shift	shift **34**
cliché	cliché **20d**		slang	slang **20a**
com	incomplete comparison **30d**		sp	spelling **20e–f**
concl	weak conclusion **6b, 16b**		sum	summarize **15a**
cs	comma splice **28**		trans	transition
def	define		verb	verb form **23**
dm	dangling modifier **26c**		vs	verb sequence **23d**
doc	documentation **49–52**		vt	verb tense **23c–d**
emph	emphasis unclear		wc	word choice **20**
ex	example needed		wrdy	wordy **32**
frag	sentence fragment **29**		wv	weak verb **32d**
fs	fused sentence **28**		ww	wrong word **20b**
hyph	hyphen **44**		.?!	period, question mark, exclamation point **37**
inc	incomplete construction **30**		,	comma **35**
it	italics **43**		;	semicolon **36**
jarg	jargon **20a**		,	apostrophe **38**
lc	lower case **41**		" "	quotation marks **39**
lv	language variety **19**		( ) [ ] —	parentheses, brackets, dash **40**
mix	mixed construction **30, 34**		: / …	colon, slash, ellipses **40**
mm	misplaced modifier **26a**		^	insert
ms	manuscript form **49b, 50b, 51b, 52a**		∼	transpose
no ,	no comma **35i**		⌒	close up
num	number **42b**		X	delete
¶	paragraph			
//	faulty parallelism **33**			
para	paraphrase **15a**			

Contents

ⓒ◙✓ Icons indicate additional integrated media resources available at
bedfordstmartins.com/wia.